America I

To the memory of my parents
John and Mary Hanahoe

Acknowledgements

To all who collaborated with, and encouraged, me during the book's seven-year gestation period, I extend heartfelt thanks. I am especially grateful to Clodagh Burke for her editorial advice, to Joe Murray of the Irish peace and justice group Afri, to my sister Máire – who read, and critiqued, the first draft text – to my nephews Ronan and Vincent Cunniffe for their help in overcoming so many computer-related glitches, and to the library staff of University College Dublin for their assistance in research. Finally, my thanks to all at Brandon.

TOM HANAHOE

AMERICA RULES

US Foreign Policy, Globalization and Corporate USA

A Brandon Original Paperback

First published in 2003 by
Brandon
an imprint of Mount Eagle Publications
Dingle, Co. Kerry, Ireland

10 9 8 7 6 5 4 3 2 1

Copyright © Tom Hanahoe 2003

The author has asserted his moral rights.

ISBN 0 86322 309 5

Cover design: Anú Design
Typesetting by Red Barn Publishing, Skeagh, Skibbereen
Printed by the Woodprintcraft Group Ltd, Dublin

Contents

Introduction

The Hyperpower

The Minsk Treaty of December 1991 was an event of immense significance. Formally dissolving the Soviet Union, it heralded the dawning of a new global era. The Cold War was over. With the domino-like downfall of communist and socialist governments in the Soviet Union and in eastern and central Europe, the previously bipolar world became unipolar. The US attained an unimaginable level of global economic and military dominance, becoming the world's sole superpower.

This post-Cold War power imbalance disturbed even US allies. In 1991 French Foreign Minister Roland Dumas expressed his unease at how, with the recent collapse of Soviet power, "American might reigns. . . without balancing weight".[1] In November 1999, another French foreign minister, Hubert Vedrine, outlined the disparity that had evolved between the power of the United States and that of other countries. The term "superpower", he held, no longer accurately described the global role of the US. "The term has a Cold War connotation, and is too exclusively military, whereas US supremacy today extends to the economy, currency, technology, military areas, lifestyle, language and the products of mass culture that inundate the world, forming thought and fascinating even the enemies of the United States." He suggested that the term "hyperpower" was a more apt label for the United States.[2]

During the Cold War decades after the Second World War, Washington had defined its global role in terms of East-West confrontation. The latter war had reconfigured the global balance of power, with the US emerging as the world's superpower, dominating the world politically, economically and militarily. Securing and extending this dominance became the primary objective of successive Washington administrations. Interventionism became a favoured strategy. Between the end of this war and the start of Washington's war in Afghanistan, the US attempted to depose over forty governments around the world and to crush over thirty populist movements opposing oppressive rulers.[3]

The Cold War power struggle with its rival superpower, the Soviet Union, transformed the United States into a national security state with two to three million armed forces personnel, a vast global and national intelligence network and an avaricious military-industrial complex that consumed billions of taxpayers' dollars annually. The US Department of Defense became the world's largest single organization.[4]

The Cold War decades were marked by a suspension of rational political and ideological debate in the United States. A climate of anti-communism and militarism was fostered. War and intervention came to be regarded in Washington, and among the American people, as normal and acceptable forms of behaviour towards other countries. Under the guise of combating communist totalitarianism, interventionist strategies were employed by Washington's foreign policy planners, encompassing: direct military aggression; the assassination of political leaders; overthrowing constitutional governments; the manipulation of national elections; the exclusion of countries from loans; trade embargoes; sabotage of industrial and agricultural plants; CIA-staged civil disorder; funding opposition parties; creating, training, financing and arming terrorist groups; installing and maintaining undemocratic regimes in power.

With the collapse of the Soviet Union and its satellite countries[5] and the concomitant diminution of the communist threat, the US hyperpower might reasonably be expected to reduce its military commitments and interventions abroad. Instead, within a decade of the signing of the Minsk Treaty, the 11 September 2001 attacks on the World Trade Center and the Pentagon provided the United States with a new rationale for intervening militarily in the affairs of other countries. The Cold War against communism was replaced by a global "crusade" to destroy terrorist organizations.

This war against terrorists, President George W. Bush warned, would be a lengthy affair. "It will not end until every terrorist group of global reach has been found, stopped and defeated," he stated.[6] As the president expanded his war operations, the world witnessed one of the most far-reaching developments of the post-Second World War era. A world that had previously comprised opposing capitalist and communist blocs was now experiencing the global military power of the world's sole superpower in a unipolar world. Appropriating to itself, professedly to fight terrorism, the right to wage war wherever and whenever it wished, the US intended to intervene militarily in the affairs of countries that had no direct link to the 11 September attacks.

It was an uncompromising assertion of US superiority in the post-Cold War world and of its determination to protect US interests, even to the extent of not consulting, and disregarding the views of, the international community of nations. The US was artificially dividing the world into two camps, of good guys and bad guys. Decisions to wage war against US-designated "baddies" would be taken in Washington, not in the United Nations or in other capitals. In opting to wage wars around the world, the Bush administration was continuing a time-honoured American tradition. War has always been at the very heart of US foreign policy.

Statesmen and Terrorists

The quintessence of foreign policy is the promotion of national interests. In furthering their own interests, wealthy developed nations relate to, and negotiate with, poorer nations – those with weak economies, scant resources and underdeveloped industrial sectors – from a position of strength. Coercive foreign policy mechanisms, both economic and political, have been routinely employed by developed nations to oblige weaker nations to comply with their demands. Uniquely among the world's nations, the United States is accustomed to relying enormously on another form of coercion. What sets it apart is its predilection for employing military force and the threat of aggression ("gunboat diplomacy") to accomplish its foreign policy goals.

In 1991, former CIA official John Stockwell succinctly outlined how the history of the United States has, contrary to the prevailing perception, been one of near-incessant US-waged wars and interventions. "Although the United States promotes itself as a 'peace-loving nation', the United States in fact has a history of constant wars," he wrote. "In our 200-plus-year history, we have fought 15 wars. We have put our military into other countries to force them to bend to our will about 200 times, or about once a year."[7]

Harold Pinter, widely regarded as Britain's foremost post-Second World War playwright, has argued that the United States was "responsible for more infringements of international law than anyone else. The United States has performed so many criminal acts, constantly, consistently, remorselessly, ruthlessly, indifferently, brutally for years and years. But nobody ever talks about it. It is as if it never happened. Even while it was happening, it wasn't happening. Because it wasn't reported."[8]

Paradoxically, whenever Washington intervened brutally in the affairs of other countries, it was termed foreign policy; but when countries deemed to be a threat to US interests did likewise, it was called terrorism. The difference between "terrorists" and US statesmen, it seemed to targeted populations, was that terrorists waged small wars and killed few people while American statesmen conducted large wars and killed huge numbers.

Foreign policies implemented by US statesmen were the very antithesis of the country's professed lofty objectives. Instead of serving as the global protector of freedom, democracy and human rights, the United States showed contempt for these ideals. Principles of civilized behaviour were upheld and enforced when they converged with Washington's interests, but discarded and abused when they diverged. The law of force supplanted the force of law.

The effects of this inversion of the norms of international behaviour on the part of the United States were written in blood around the globe. However, an image of the United States as a global tyrant rests uncomfortably with Americans and their statesmen who, averse to admitting that they have blood on their hands, prefer that Washington's interventionist guardianship of their country's foreign interests be cloaked in a mantle of moral idealism. Camouflaging US foreign policy goals behind a smokescreen of vacuous platitudes and pious aspirations and pledges, successive administrations fostered an image of a chivalric United States eager to respect and to live in peace and harmony with other nations, yet willing to make enormous sacrifices to defend entire populations against unjust and repressive rulers and ideologies. The reality was very different.

During the Cold War, millions of non-combatant civilians – the very people US foreign policy operations were purportedly intended to help – were killed. Estimates of the numbers killed in US-waged wars, in US military and covert interventions, in US-abetted terrorist campaigns and by US-installed and US-backed despotic regimes in the course of the Cold War can only offer a vague inkling of the torment endured in many countries because of Washington's foreign policy decisions and alliances: over one million Angolans killed; 800,000 Indonesians; 600,000 Cambodians; 350,000 Laotians; 200,000 East Timorese; 150,000 Guatemalans; 80,000 Nicaraguans[9]; 75,000 Salvadorans; and tens of thousands killed by US-approved military rulers in Brazil, Chile, Paraguay and elsewhere. In Argentina at least 30,000 civilians were killed by the country's US-backed military between 1976 and 1983.

Around three million Vietnamese men, women and children died in the course of the US-directed Vietnam War. If the United States had sustained a similar level of fatalities, instead of the 58,000 Americans who died in the conflict around 15 million would have been killed. Millions of others would have been horrifically mutilated or wounded. Altogether, the Cold War claimed the lives of almost 100,000 Americans and cost the country's taxpayers the equivalent of $13 trillion.[10]

A New World Order

Towards the start of the Cold War era, Washington established manipulable international institutional structures, including the

International Monetary Fund, the World Bank, the United Nations and GATT (General Agreement on Tariffs and Trade). America's power and influence permeated the top echelons of these and other important international and regional organizations and also the loci of political and economic control in most of the world's nations. Its power and influence in the most important organizations was so overwhelming that, as a rule, it could determine the outcome of their deliberations on issues deemed of vital importance to the United States. It could usually impose its own favoured candidates on these forums, and it could often remove those whom it regarded with displeasure, particularly leaders who responded negatively to US pressures and intimidation.

This US control, together with Washington's penchant for military interventions, aided the country's rise to a position of almost unchallengeable post-Cold War dominance. The attainment of this dominance was paralleled by the emergence of a new world order, called globalization. In its broadest sense the word globalization denotes the increasing multidimensional linkage and interdependence of nations on a worldwide scale, encompassing the economic, industrial, political, security, cultural, environmental and other spheres. In a narrower sense, it has come to signify a post-Cold War US and corporate-dominated global economic model, or economic globalization.

The most important aspect of economic globalization is the concept of free trade – the right to move capital, goods, plants, profits and technology across national boundaries without hindrance from nation states, thus opening up markets around the world to international competition. The breaking down of barriers to trade and investment enabled America and its corporations[11] to dominate the economies of most nations. A conspicuous feature of the new order was the degree to which it concentrated control over much of the planet's trade, wealth and resources in the boardrooms of the world's largest transnational corporations, enabling corporate giants to wield more economic power in the global arena than many national governments.

As more and more economic power was acquired by the corporate sector, governments were divested of the power to control their countries' destinies. This ascendancy of the corporate sector was marked by the transfer of economic power from elected governments to unaccountable corporate elites, transforming megacorporations, collectively, into one of the world's most powerful hegemons. Increasingly, monopoly capitalism displaced democratic capitalism, and the rights of corporate giants supplanted the rights of the world's peoples.

The inequitable corporate-friendly world order of globalization is not the product of an accidental evolutionary aberration. It owes its existence, above all, to pro-corporate policies deliberately formulated by Washington. America's attainment of its hyperpower status and the emergence of the new world order of globalization were the climactic events of almost two centuries of US military interventions abroad, which were usually conducted to defend or expand US trade.

Trade considerations have always been a determinant of the general direction of US foreign policy. War and military interventions became instrumentalities of US commerce. Such intervention in, and control over, the affairs of other countries is normally called imperialism.

"Yankee imperialism" has long been an emotive catchphrase in Third World countries, providing nationalistic movements with a potent focus and a rallying stimulus against US domination of their countries and exploitation of their resources. Predictably, Washington's foreign policy strategists endeavour to counter and repudiate inferences of US imperialism, a phrase which – with its connotations of subjugation, coercion and exploitation – calls into question the country's self-professed role as the world's bulwark of freedom and democracy.

Master and Subject Classes

With less than 5 per cent of the world's population, the US usually accounts for over one-third of global defence expenditure.[12] This disproportionate allocation of tax dollars for military affairs inevitably drains money from people-centred programmes in the United States. However, the American electorate has rarely seriously questioned the necessity for such enormous defence budgets, their country's pursuit of global hegemony or the motivation for coercive foreign policies which – culminating in the imposition of globalization and President George W. Bush's post-11 September war – inflicted suffering and injustices on entire populations, particularly on Third World peasant societies, most recently on Muslim societies.

Among those to propound an explanation for the pernicious nature of America's "defence"-related foreign policies was Eugene V. Debs, a socialist labour leader and a candidate for the presidency of the United States on several occasions in the early years of the twentieth century. In June 1918, a year after the US entered the First World War, Debs condemned the war at a meeting in Canton, Ohio, arguing that without any public approval or consultation the American people were being embroiled in wars and military confrontations by a self-serving capitalist elite. "They tell us that we live in a great free republic; that our institutions are democratic; that we are a free and self-governing people. That is too much, even for a joke," he stated. "Wars throughout history have been waged for conquest and plunder. . . The master class has always declared the wars; the subject class has always fought the battles. The master class has had all to gain and nothing to lose, while the subject class has had nothing to gain and all to lose – especially their lives."[13]

Holding that Debs' anti-war discourse violated the Espionage Act of 1917, a court sentenced him to a ten-year term in prison. The Espionage Act and the Sedition Act of 1918 were drafted by Washington to stifle dissent at the nation's entry into the war, through making public condemnation of the government's war effort illegal.

The essence of Debs' thesis is that American society is neither monolithic nor egalitarian but rather is stratified into a large but essentially impotent subject class and a small affluent "master class"; that the latter controls or exerts an inordinate influence over the governmental process, converting the government of the United States into a pliable surrogate of the "master class"; and that it is at the behest, and in the interests, of this elite class that US foreign policy is formulated, that US-waged wars and interventions are conducted and US hegemony is pursued.

If this thesis is valid, then we are left with an inescapable and repellent conclusion. It is that the millions of people, including Americans, killed in the course of US wars and interventions, were sacrificed by the highest strata of US foreign policy decision-makers – headed by the president of the United States – not for the benefit of the people in the targeted countries nor of the broad mass of the American people, but rather to insulate the interests of a US "master" ruling class from the risks and threats posed by foreign governments and movements. This book analyses Debs' thesis, in an historical context.

Essentially, this book is the story of the American-coordinated and war-accompanied march to globalization, a journey that began two centuries ago with a trade-driven war against Barbary pirates. It is the story of the rise of the United States and the world's largest corporations to a position of near-global joint hegemony. Above all, it is the story of how the lives of all Americans and the affairs, both domestic and foreign, of their country are controlled by a small elite ruling class, whose members are drawn from, or linked to, the corporate sector. It is a validation of Eugene V. Debs' thesis of an American "master class".

It is also the story of how, in shaping the nation's foreign policy and in intervening militarily, politically and economically in so many of the world's other nations – through the Cold War, the United Nations, NATO, the International Monetary Fund, the World Bank, GATT, the World Trade Organization and, ultimately, through globalization and President George W. Bush's war against terrorists – Washington's corporate-dominated rulers have been complicit in subordinating the rights, the needs and the lives of many of the world's people to US corporate needs and demands.

US wars and interventions, it will be shown, are conducted to make the world a safer and more profitable place for Corporate USA. A primary consideration in these wars and US military, political and economic interventions is the attainment of control by Corporate USA over much of the world's trade and resources, especially oil.

One of America's "master class" families was singled out by Debs in his Canton speech – the Rockefellers, heirs to a vast oil-derived fortune. It is a name that turns up, time after time, in the following pages.

Notes

1. "US Must not Try to Rule the World Warn the French", *Irish Press*, 3 September 1991.
2. Lara Marlowe, "French Minister Urges Greater UN Role to Counter US Hyperpower", *The Irish Times*, 4 November 1999.
3. William Blum, *Rogue State: A Guide to the World's Only Superpower* (London: Zed Books, 2001), p. 2.
4. William H. Chafe and Harvard Sitkoff, eds, *A History of Our Time: Readings on Postwar America* (New York: Oxford University Press, 1999), p. 295.
5. The terms country, nation, nation state and state are used interchangeably, although some of these could more accurately be described as territories or dependencies.
6. President Bush's address to a joint session of Congress, 20 September 2001.
7. John Stockwell, *The Praetorian Guard: The US Role in the New World Order* (Boston: South End Press, 1991), p. 86.
8. Ciaran Carty, "This Empty Room", *The Sunday Tribune* (Ireland), 23 March 1997.
9. The 80,000 deaths in Nicaragua include people killed by the forces of the US-supported Somoza dictatorship up to 1979 and subsequently during the US-backed Contra war.
10. The $13 trillion figure is cited by US Deputy Secretary of State Strobe Talbott in "After the Madrid Summit", *Time*, 14 July 1997.
11. The words corporation and corporate are used throughout the book as synonyms for big business, both financial (banks, investment houses etc.) and non-financial (manufacturers etc.).
12. *Human Development Report 1996* (New York: published for the UN Development Programme by Oxford University Press, 1996), pp. 174, 201.
13. Ray Ginger, *Eugene V. Debs: The Making of an American Radical* (New York: Collier Books, 1949), pp. 376–77. See also Ray Ginger, *The Bending Crisis: A Biography of Eugene Victor Debs* (New Brunswick: Rutgers University Press, 1969). See also De Paul University, Chicago, website, http://www.depaul.edu/~clio/Edebs2.html

Chapter 1

The Age of Globalization

Social Engineering

Globalization constitutes a new world order. The most far-reaching process of social engineering in modern history, it established new internationally binding rules and structures that placed the rights of multinational corporations above the rights of entire populations and outside the compass of democratic control and accountability.

By 1999, corporate power had reached such a dizzying level that fifty-one of the world's 100 biggest "economies" comprised transnationals rather than sovereign countries.[1] The aggregate sales of the world's 200 richest companies exceeded the combined gross domestic product of all but ten of the world's nations.[2] Corporate leaders, in tandem with Washington's leaders, were becoming the helmsmen of the world's destiny.

As corporate power, influence and profits soared, so also did the power, influence and wealth of the sector's largest shareholders. Extraordinarily, by 1997 the assets of the world's three richest people exceeded the combined GNP of the poorest 48 countries and their 600 million people. The assets of the 200 richest – who, with few exceptions, had close corporate connections – exceeded the combined income of over 40 per cent of mankind. An annual contribution of just 1 per cent of the wealth of these 200 people could provide universal access to primary education for all the world's people.[3]

In this world of wealth and abundance, almost a half of all mankind was subsisting on $2 or less a day, and of these an estimated 1.3 billion lived on less than $1 a day. The world's richest 1 per cent received as much income as the poorest 57 per cent. The fifth of the world's people living in the highest-income countries accounted for 86 per cent of all private consumption, the bottom fifth just 1.3 per cent. America's share of the world's gross national product exceeded the combined GNPs of all Third World countries, encompassing over three-quarters of mankind.[4]

Today, around 60 per cent of the 4.4 billion people in the Third World lack basic sanitation, a quarter of them do not have access to clean water, 800 million are chronically malnourished, two billion lack food security, one billion lack adequate shelter, 880 million have no access to health services and 90–95 per cent of Third World sewage and 70 per cent of its industrial wastes are dumped untreated into surface waters, polluting drinking water sources.[5] Around 246 million children, boys and girls, are engaged in child labour, many in hazardous occupations such as mining or construction. At least eight million of these are used as slaves, prostitutes and child soldiers in armed conflicts.[6] At least 700,000 people, mostly women and children, are trafficked worldwide annually in a modern-day form of slavery.[7] Over a half of the world's people live in countries which are in virtual receivership. Controlled by the International Monetary Fund, the World Bank and other multilateral institutions, the countries lack even theoretical control over national economic policies and sovereignty.

Globalization has fostered many of these inequalities. Globalization is a US-born global culture that almost sanctifies corporate monopoly capitalism and free-trade economics. Within such a culture, which has as its principal motivating goal the amassment of wealth, traditional human values of justice, compassion and love are being discarded and lost. Single-mindedly pursuing more growth and profit, corporations increasingly eschew the notions of ethical behaviour and social concern and obligations. Opponents of globalization are condemned and derided, likened to members of the flat earth society.

Minimalist States

A plethora of words and phrases have been coined or resurrected to describe the new economic order – globalization, neoliberalism, trade liberalization, free-market economics, laissez-faire capitalism. All espouse a similar ideology of freedom to pursue economic activities without governmental interference or impediments. The ultimate goal is to metamorphose all nations into a one-world, borderless, free-trade zone. This translates into giving transnational corporations and international investors and banks freer rein to move capital, goods, plants, profits and technology across national boundaries without hindrance from nation states, thus opening up markets around the world to international competition.

In such a deregulated environment, the strong are free to exploit the weak. With few international laws or regulations to curb their operations, controlling vast resources, technological expertise and patents, benefiting from economies of scale and underpinned by Washington's pro-corporate political, economic and military agendas, corporate giants came to dominate the economic affairs of most countries.

Under Washington's aegis, as economic activities became globalized, free trade rather than governmental controls took precedence in the new economic order. In this new order, nation states, particularly those in the Third World, were assigned a minimal role. The governments of these "minimalist" states had little real power – no longer able to act as guarantors of democracy and national sovereignty; divested of the wherewithal to provide adequate safety nets to protect the most disadvantaged in their societies; their freedom to pursue national employment-creating programmes severely curtailed.

The attainment of globalization and corporate hegemony was conditional on achieving a state of "small" government worldwide. That is, it required that national governments relinquish mechanisms of economic development and self-defence – that they withdraw from direct and indirect ownership of business enterprises, cease sheltering domestic companies and markets from international competition and that they surrender their right to control the movement of wealth-creating assets (capital, goods and manufacturing plants) across their borders.

The relinquishment of these traditional mechanisms of economic development curbed the role of national governments in the economic sphere to such an extent that governments were becoming almost obsolete, their responsibilities in the economic sphere being confined to little more than balancing national budgets, reducing indebtedness and restricting inflation. This represented a removal of democratic checks on corporate practices and the cession by elected governments of economic power and influence to those that already controlled an enormous amount of the world's wealth and of its wealth-generating resources, especially transnational manufacturing giants, banking magnates and financial speculators and investors.

Third World countries were left virtually powerless to determine their own future. Dr David C. Korten, a former senior advisor to the US Agency for International Development (USAID), has written about the tyranny of the new order: "Corporations have emerged as the dominant governance institutions on the planet, with the largest among them reaching into virtually every country of the world and exceeding most governments in size and power. Increasingly, it is the corporate interest more than the human interest that defines the policy agendas of states and international bodies, although this reality and its implications have gone largely unnoticed and unaddressed."[8]

The implications are immense. Today, any country whose government seeks to prioritize the welfare of its citizens through taking control of the direction of its economic affairs is deemed by America's leading "statesmen" to be a threat to globalization and to US hegemony. Instead, through the collaboration of Washington's policy-making community, in country after country the world's megacorporations are assuming powers and functions that have been traditionally the sole preserve of governments. They have become a new collective superpower.

Modern-Day Robber Barons

The story of globalization is a story of capitalism gone appallingly awry. Through removing barriers to trade and investment, it transmuted the world's largest industrial corporations and the largest banks and other giant financial institutions into modern-day robber barons – industrial and economic colonizers that can displace, wipe out or buy out local competitors in poor countries which, until the advent of globalization, could avail of protectionist barriers for survival.

Protectionist barriers created environments within which Third World and other governments could initiate programmes for economic and industrial development. Import substitution industrialization (ISI) was, almost invariably, a crucial component of such programmes. Based on direct state support, ISI entailed nurturing domestic industries to produce goods that would otherwise have to be imported. In general, such industries could only survive and thrive if protected by tariff and trade barriers from competition from larger and more powerful foreign rivals. The removal of protectionist barriers stripped these small producers of whatever little protection they had. Unable to compete with their foreign rivals, countless manufacturers closed or were bought by foreign competitors. With investment restrictions removed and using their vast financial resources, transnational manufacturers and the world's largest banks could now buy up or close down almost anything they wished in the Third World.

The deregulation of cross-border trade and capital flows opened Third World countries to transnational manufacturers, foreign retailing and wholesaling giants, international banks, financiers and speculators whose resources could overwhelm governments and their nations' economic sectors, including their industrial and banking sectors. Under such circumstances, the principle of domestic jurisdiction, whereby a state rules supreme within its own territorial boundaries, became almost irrelevant. Unable to protect their domestic sectors, governments became dependent on foreign direct investment (FDI) by global financial and nonfinancial corporations for the creation of employment.

However, the vast bulk of FDI went to the industrialized regions of North America, western Europe and Japan. In 1997, around 68 per cent of FDI went to regions comprising the world's richest 20 per cent, only 32 per cent to areas comprising the remaining 80 per cent of mankind.[9] Huge areas of the Third World received almost no FDI or other forms of direct or indirect international capital flows, such as international bank loans and export credits, condemning them to a future of underdevelopment and poverty. At times, FDI in the Third World involved no more than acquiring control over an enterprise and then closing it down to eliminate local competition. The privileges and control attained in the Third World by corporate investors through FDI, a former World Bank chief economist and senior vice president admitted, were often "the result of corruption, the bribery of government officials".[10]

Rivalry among nation states for the location of transnational-owned manufacturing plants and for the awarding of assembling and manufacturing contracts to local companies enabled transnationals to engage in a form of investment and job auctioneering, playing one nation off against another to extort the most favourable terms from governments as regards exemption from taxes, the provision of grants, infrastructure, employee training schemes and other incentives such as low wage rates, flexible work practices, the absence of trade unions, lax employee health and safety regulations and minimal environmental controls. If their demands were refused, financiers and corporations could invest elsewhere, locating their manufacturing or subcontracted operations in countries where the authorities were more obeisant. In such circumstances, it became difficult for governments to adequately tax multinationals or to regulate their activities.

Deregulation under globalization removed almost all possibilities Third World countries had of developing economic policies based on their own realities and needs. It was a formula for promoting the strong and oppressing the weak, for augmenting corporate power while shrinking the power of governments and electorates.

The Uruguay Round

Globalization restructured the world order, concentrating economic power around corporations. The General Agreement on Tariffs and Trade (GATT) was a pivotal facilitator in this global economic power realignment. Both an organization and a series of trade agreements, GATT's forty-seven-year existence – in January 1995 it was replaced by the World Trade Organization – was marked by a stunning progression towards the fulfilment of Washington's post-war ambition to create a corporate-friendly global free-trade system. This progress was achieved through a series of eight GATT-hosted multilateral trade-negotiating rounds, each of which was followed by a new agreement that further reduced restrictions on cross-border trade.

The eighth, and final, round of negotiations, in which over 120 countries participated, was completed in April 1994 after seven and a half years of fractious talks. Called the Uruguay Round, the agreement was by far the most complex and comprehensive trade accord ever negotiated. Its unprecedented compass was later described by the World Trade Organization as covering "almost all trade, from tooth-brushes to pleasure boats, from banking to telecommunications, from the genes of wild rice to AIDS treatments. It was quite simply the largest trade negotiation ever, and most probably the largest negotiation of any kind in history."[11]

The significance of the Uruguay Round was commented on by GATT's Director General Peter Sutherland, who brokered the agreement. It was, he wrote, "central to the efforts to create a new world order able to cope with the geopolitical realities of the next decades".[12] Renato Ruggiero, director general of the World Trade Organization, outlined the enormous compass of the proposed agenda. "We are no longer writing the rules of interaction among separate national economies. We are writing the constitution of a single global economy," he stated in 1996.[13]

The Uruguay Round agreement was the single most influential factor in the upsurge of corporate power and in the advancement of globalization towards the end of the twentieth century. Comprising over 20,000 pages, the agreement was mind-numbing in its complexity, scope and ramifications. Its repercussions impacted everywhere, in all spheres of life – economic, social, political, cultural, technological and legal.

Holding that decreased protectionism and increased free trade would mean more investment, more jobs and an increase of over $200 billion in the annual global economy, the agreement's advocates forecast that the rising tide of economic prosperity would lift the boats of all nations. The Ministerial Declaration, made at the conclusion of the round in April 1994, promised that it would "strengthen the world economy and lead to more trade, investment, employment and income growth throughout the world".[14] Peter Sutherland argued that no nation "would come out as an overall loser".[15] Many did, and disastrously so.

Under the terms of the agreement, participating nations agreed to slash tariffs on average by almost 40 per cent, to reduce protectionist measures in the agricultural and textile sectors, to axe or curtail subsidies and to conform with new rules and regulations encompassing services, investment, quotas and intellectual property rights. Signatory nations also agreed to the formation of a new body to replace GATT, the World Trade Organization.

The objective of the Uruguay Round was to remove barriers to the free flow of goods, capital and profits. In prising open national borders to accommodate this free flow, the agreement severely restricted sovereign nations in choosing the kind of economic, political and social orders they wanted or needed; destabilized the existing orders;

compelled national governments to relinquish mechanisms of economic self-defense, stripping the governments of the capacity to protect domestic industries and markets; forced governments to discard policies of social justice; created a greater inequality between nations; fostered a new dependency in the Third World on foreign capital; and denied future governments the prerogative of imposing new restrictions on the movement of goods, profits and capital. The round's impact was astounding. Its effect was to reshape, on a global scale, the architecture of the existing political and economic orders.

NAFTA

In parallel with the Uruguay Round negotiations, the Clinton administration was pursuing other market-opening deals. On 1 January 1994, the North American Free Trade Agreement (NAFTA) came on stream. A mini-GATT accord between the United States, Canada and Mexico, its objective was to dismantle barriers to trade and investment within the new three-nation bloc.

Like the Uruguay Round's advocates, NAFTA's political sponsors depicted their project as one that would benefit the populations in the three participating countries, with the gains gradually trickling down to the most disadvantaged sectors of society. For Mexicans the agreement was a disaster.

Market reforms implemented in Mexico in accordance with the terms of the accord were supposed to promote export-led economic growth, vaulting the country into the First World. Instead, within a year of the agreement coming into effect, Mexico had almost been bankrupted, had accumulated a staggering trade deficit with the United States, and Mexican manufacturers and farmers were being battered by competition from US megacorporations and low-cost US grain. Unable to compete, hundreds of Mexican factories closed. Hundreds of thousands of workers and small farmers joined Mexico's mass of unemployed.

By January 1995, just one year after NAFTA's launch, the Mexican government was begging Washington to bail out its troubled economy. In response to the crisis, US Treasury Secretary Robert Rubin and Michel Camdessus, head of the International Monetary Fund, arranged the largest emergency loan ever made to one country, over $50 billion.

The terms of the US-IMF rescue package were draconian, requiring that Mexico's oil export revenues be deposited in the United States as collateral for the loans. A report submitted by Treasury Secretary Rubin to Congress outlined these terms, noting how the loan agreement was "backed by proceeds from Mexico's crude oil, oil products and petrochemical product exports. Payments for these exports flow through a special account at the Federal Reserve Bank of New York"[16] – a loan condition which many Mexicans regarded as tantamount to mortgaging their country's national sovereignty to Washington and to US banks. Economist Carlos Heredia outlined the predicament faced by his country as a consequence of its NAFTA-induced difficulties. Mexico's economy, he stated, was now "being run by New York investment bankers, the US Treasury and the US Federal Reserve".[17]

Mexico's financial sector soon experienced the realities of life in a deregulated competitive environment. In May 2001, America's giant Citigroup conglomerate announced its takeover of Mexico's largest commercial bank, Banamex, thus completing the acquisition of the country's leading banks by outside interests. Its banking sector was now being controlled from the boardrooms of foreign financial corporations. Among those to join Banamex's board was Citigroup's Robert Rubin, the former US treasury secretary. By then up to 40 per cent of the country's 90 million-plus population was surviving on less than $2 per person per day.[18]

The effects of deregulation, under the terms of the Uruguay Round and NAFTA accords, served to undermine both democracy and national sovereignty – which may be defined as the right of nations to independently choose what course they follow, free from outside interference or control. Other agreements were also being planned to accelerate this process. In December 1994, a Summit of the Americas was hosted by President Clinton in Miami, which was attended by thirty-four presidents and prime ministers representing every nation in the hemisphere with the sole exception of Cuba. The largest ever meeting of hemispheric leaders, its participants set a target for the formation of a Free Trade Area of the Americas (FTAA) by the year 2005, to link together over 800 million consumers and the economies of all the countries in the hemisphere, Cuba alone being excluded.

Earlier, President Clinton had backed an even more ambitious free-trade agreement. Shortly before the Miami meeting, he visited Indonesia for a summit of the Asia-Pacific Economic Cooperation (APEC) forum, at which Asia-Pacific leaders committed their nations to the creation of the world's largest ever regional free-trade zone, encompassing over a third of all the world's consumers, by the year 2020.

In January 1994, in his State of the Union address, President Clinton trumpeted his free-trade successes: "In one year, with NAFTA, with GATT, with our efforts in Asia and the national export strategy, we did more to open world markets to American products than at any time in the last two generations."[19]

GATT's Uruguay Round and hemispheric and regional trade agreements such as NAFTA, the FTAA and APEC signed or progressed by the Clinton administration provided a super-charged impetus for economic globalization; that is, for the intensified global integration of goods, services and capital markets. They were giant steps towards a virtually borderless world in which democratic capitalism was being jettisoned and national economies were being compelled to integrate into a global economic order shaped by the United States and dominated by transnational corporations and their political patrons.

The WTO

GATT's successor, the World Trade Organization, is a pillar of the new economic order. The WTO, the IMF and the World Bank together constitute a trinity of organizations that supervises and enforces a system of near-global economic governance, slowly stifling the democratic autonomy of nation states.

Critics denounce the three institutions as handmaidens of global corporations and global capitalism. A former director of the UN African Institute for Planning described the WTO as "an organization entirely subservient to the transnationals. . . it is the most opaque institution imaginable".[20] Another critic described the WTO as "an unaccountable international body [which] is empowered to force changes in broad swathes of national health, safety, environmental and economic development programmes and laws".[21] Within the WTO, a UN report noted, "developing countries are, de facto, kept away from decision-making mechanisms and from policy-making. . . forever condemned to a marginal negotiating position within the WTO framework". The WTO's rules, it added, "reflect an agenda that serves only to promote dominant corporatist interests that already monopolize the arena of international trade".[22]

The power of the WTO is astonishing. A virtual international ministry of trade, its primary goal is to make all national frontiers more porous for cross-border trade. In pursuing this goal, the organization can infringe upon the sovereignty of member states, overrule decisions of national legislatures and curb the freedom of governments to manage their countries' economic affairs. By September 1997, thirty-two months after its formation, the WTO had 132 member nations. Around 100 of these were Third World countries, each of which had ceded part-control of their national sovereignty to the corporate-friendly international body.

According to the WTO, it is "the only international body dealing with the rules of trade between nations. At its heart are the WTO agreements, negotiated and signed by the bulk of the world's trading nations. These documents provide the legal ground-rules for international commerce. They are essentially contracts, binding governments to keep their trade policies within agreed limits. Although negotiated and signed by governments, the goal is to help producers of goods and services, exporters, and importers conduct their business."[23]

This description by the WTO of its trade policies is important. While the WTO's contracting parties are member governments, the organization's objective is not so much to help the governments and their citizens, but rather to assist the international operations of manufacturers, service providers, exporters and importers – primarily transnational corporations that are not signatories of the WTO agreements.

Inevitably, the trade rules and trade relationships encompassed by WTO agreements give rise to conflicting interests, and consequently to disputes, between member states. In the first thirty-two months after its inception, 100 disputes were referred to the WTO. The complainant on thirty-one occasions was the United States, and on a further three occasions the US complained jointly with from three to five other member states.

The settlement of these disputes is the responsibility of the WTO's Dispute Settlement Body, which "has the power to authorize retaliation when a country does not comply with a ruling". The rulings of its dispute settlement system, the WTO points out, "cannot be blocked".[24]

"Few Countries Ever Retaliate against the United States"

The United Nations Research Institute for Social Development, commenting in 1995 on the freedom and power of transnational corporations vis-à-vis national governments, noted how in recent years "governments have been unable to protect their people from disturbing trends in the international economic environment. Among the most powerful of these external forces are transnational corporations (TNCs) – whose investments, activities and products have been penetrating national frontiers virtually at will. Despite their massive influence and reach, TNCs remain largely untouched by any form of international regulation. . . Even the most far-reaching piece of international regulation, the GATT, which primarily benefits TNCs, manages to do so without mentioning them at all in its documentation."[25]

While national legislatures can be compelled by the WTO to repeal laws deemed to breach the organisation's free-trade rules and agreements, multinational corporations are permitted to pursue their activities in the international arena almost totally free of any restrictions or social and ethical obligations. This imbalance between the obligations imposed on governments and the freedom granted to corporations owes much to the influence of Washington's foreign policy strategists on the outcome of the Uruguay Round agreement.

Within the post-Uruguay Round global order, the United States is the sole hyperpower, capable of doing virtually as it wants – free to dominate international organizations such as the WTO and to intimidate countries that oppose Washington's sway or that seek to protect national resources, industries and financial institutions from Corporate USA. While the rules of the WTO require that the legislatures of member states subordinate themselves to the authority of the WTO in matters of trade, the legislature of the United States can circumvent the rules.

A 1994 book published by an influential American pro-Uruguay Round think-tank, the Institute for International Economics, commented on this anomalous position. When the United States fails to comply with its WTO obligations, the authors state, "there is little risk that economic pressure will be brought to bear on the United States to conform to WTO rulings if the Congress does not believe it to be in the US interest to do so. Few countries ever retaliate against the United States, because such action imposes costs on their own producers and consumers and sours relations with the world's largest trading nation."[26]

Almost immune from retaliation, except occasionally from the European Union and Japan, the world's largest trading nation can thumb its nose at other nations, demanding virtually unrestricted access to the world's markets while denying or limiting the access of other countries to the US market. Globalization enables American and other multinational corporations to exploit the cheap labour and the mineral, oil and other resources of Third World countries. However, when these countries seek even a token quid pro quo, such as access for their agricultural products to the US market, the door is often slammed shut in their faces.

Washington's superficial commitment to free trade and open markets is, perhaps, best exemplified by the attitude of President George W. Bush. Although publicly elevating free trade to the status of a "moral imperative"[27], he nevertheless chose to impose anti-free-trade protectionist measures such as heavy tariffs on steel imports, effectively barring foreign producers from the US market in order to safeguard US steel manufacturers from more efficient foreign competitors.

Corporate Influence

Represented by its devotees as being about "free trade", in reality the Uruguay Round accord concentrated control over global trade and resources. Its rules, rigged by the US and other rich countries, facilitated a form of colonization by unaccountable transnational oligopolies, transforming them into a collective global superpower in a new supranational economic system. "Free trade" would not mean fair trade.

While the world's underdeveloped countries were consigned to the periphery of the negotiations, America's largest corporations, representing only themselves and their shareholders, were granted important roles in determining the outcome of the Uruguay Round negotiations. The Intellectual Property Committee (IPC), a coalition of US corporations, boasted of how its "close association with the US Trade Representative and Commerce [Department] has permitted the IPC to shape the US proposals and negotiating positions during the course of the [GATT] negotiations".[28] When US government trade representatives attended the negotiating sessions, they were accompanied by, and consulted with, dozens of advisers from the US corporate sector, who provided staff to help the US delegation. This corporate influence helped achieve a further cession of control over the global economy and the planet's resources to the world's largest transnational corporations.

By the late 1990s, three US and two European corporations had a stranglehold over the world's grain trade, controlling around three-quarters of the total trade. These were able to bring considerable pressure to bear during the Uruguay Round grain negotiations. Representatives of hundreds of millions of Third World people, for whom grain is a basic staple, were forced to accept the grain agreements as a fait accompli.

What the United States accomplished through the Uruguay Round went far beyond what had been attained through previous trade accords, facilitating the subjugation of Third World peoples and the exploitation of their resources in the interests of US and other multinational corporations.

A Veritable Nightmare

A June 2000 UN-commissioned report, commenting on the Uruguay Round's most significant legacy, the formation of the WTO, asserted that the organization's rules "reflect an agenda that serves only to promote dominant corporatist interests that already monopolize the arena of international trade". For Third World populations, WTO policies were a "veritable nightmare", according to the report.[29]

The "nightmare" created by WTO policies and by globalization in general generated worldwide opposition and condemnation. The World Council of Churches (WCC) spoke out against "the present unjust economic system that is based on flagrant international inequality in the distribution of knowledge, power and wealth. . . The process of rapid globalization of national economies today has only increased social and economic injustice in the world and further widened the gap between the rich and the poor. . . . The globalization process has imposed inhuman working conditions on millions of people that are forced either into unemployment or casual labor with no social protections and thus into poverty and despair. It has increasingly undermined the participation of large sectors of society in the political process within their own states, making a mockery of democracy. It has eroded democratic participation at the international level as well."[30]

The WCC noted that under globalization the major decisions were being made by "thirty or so nations and sixty giant corporations. . . [Globalisation] contributes to the erosion of the nation state." The process had become an instrument "to gain more control over national budgets and create a profitable and safe environment for investments by the private sector at an unbearable cost for the people".

The Uruguay Round and NAFTA accords were negotiated over the heads of the world's electorates by government representatives who had not sought a mandate to participate in the negotiations. Populations in signatory nations had not been consulted and had not voted to approve their countries' ratification of the agreements, which were negotiated behind closed doors by governments whose dealings were protected from public scrutiny and accountability and from domestic pressure groups.

The Uruguay Round and NAFTA accords isolated the general public of participating nations from the actual negotiations and from accepting or rejecting the agreements. If we consider democratic undertakings as those that are an expression of the will of the majority, then the accords have little claim to being democratic. Advocates who portray them as the building blocks of a new more democratic global order demonstrate a remarkable facility for redefining the concept of democracy.

Coinciding with the completion of the Uruguay Round talks in April 1994, protests were held in numerous countries. In that month, South Korean students and farmers staged anti-GATT demonstrations throughout the country, and in India up to 500 workers were injured during violent clashes with police. In December 1994, riots occurred in the Philippines. In all European Union countries farmers held anti-GATT protests in the years before the agreement was finalized. In Brussels and Strasbourg, French farmers fought with police. Hundreds were arrested and many injured. In Ireland, farmers dumped cattle feed outside the US embassy.

Coinciding with the start-up of NAFTA in January 1994, an armed uprising of Indian peasants occurred in the Mexican state of Chiapas. According to a rebel leader, Subcomandante Marcos, NAFTA represented "a death sentence"[31] for Mexico's Indians, for whom the imposition of economic globalization in its regional framework, NAFTA, would mean further impoverishment, suffering, hunger and death.

Controlling the World's Food

The backlash mirrored widely held fears about the potentially pernicious implications of the corporate-friendly accords, especially the enforced enfeeblement of democracy and national sovereignty and a further loss of control over national resources.

Corporate control over the earth's resources is a long-standing phenomenon. In 1978, for instance, 81 per cent of Third World export earnings came from primary commodities, including oil.[32] However, Third World countries had little control over the price or the sale and marketing of the commodities. Some of the world's largest corporations exercised quasi-monopolistic control over trade in these goods. By the mid-1980s, around 75 per cent of world trade in crude oil and around 85 per cent of trade in copper, iron ore, bauxite, tobacco, wheat, coffee, cocoa and numerous other commodities was controlled by between three and six giant transnational corporations. Three American corporations accounted for over 60 per cent of world trade in bananas, and one US company controlled 40 per cent of the world cocoa market.[33]

An Independent Commission on International Development Issues established in 1977, known as the Brandt Commission, commented on the growing power and influence of transnationals. "Underlying many of the fears about multinational corporations, both in the South and the North, is the concern that they have been able to race ahead in global operations out of reach of effective controls by nation states or international organizations. . . that they constitute a network of transnational power which has provided a new element in the struggle of political and economic forces."[34]

Less than a quarter century later, the world had around 63,000 transnational corporations with perhaps 690,000 foreign affiliates. Their international production, a UN report noted, spanned "virtually all countries and economic activities, rendering it a formidable force in today's world economy". The size of the largest corporations was mind-boggling. The US-based Wal-Mart retailing chain had 910,000 employees, the motor manufacturer DaimlerChrysler some 441,000, electronics giant Siemens around 416,000 and General Motors 396,000. The assets of the US-headquartered General Electric amounted to around $356 billion and its sales to over $100 billion.[35] What the GATT Uruguay Round agreement achieved was to place the global operations of these transnationals and their affiliates almost completely "out of reach of effective controls by nation states or international organizations", thereby augmenting transnational power while curbing the power of nation states.

By the end of the 1960s, a number of giant corporations controlled all stages of the production chain of some foods from field to retail sales outlets. By 1980, five multinationals – Cargill, Continental, Louis Dreyfus, Bunge and Andre – had an overwhelming monopoly over the world's grain trade. By the mid-1980s, between 70 and 90 per cent of world trade in several food commodities was controlled by between three and six multinationals.[36]

To reinforce their control over the world's food supp[l]y
nationals launched a new strategy, whereby seeds fo[r]
became their patented property. David Weir and Mark Sch[u]
mented on this strategy in their 1981 book *Circle of Poison.* "[Of]
patents granted for beans. . . over three-quarters are held by j[ust]
corporations: Union Carbide, Sandoz, Purex and Upjohn. Two [US-]
based companies, Sandoz and Ciba-Geigy, alone control most o[f]
US alfalfa and sorghum seed supply. Chemical companies are buy[ing]
traditional seed supply firms, and their patentable 'commodities', a[t]
an alarming rate. . . the international pesticide giants Monsanto, Ciba-
Geigy, Union Carbide and FMC are ranked among the largest seed
companies in the United States. . . By cornering the global seed market, the companies apparently plan to ensure that farmers the world
over are dependent on their seeds, as well as their fertilizers and
pesticides."[37]

Corporate patenting of seeds reversed the traditional practice of
free access to seed varieties and restricted the right of farmers to develop, exchange and sow their own seeds. Since the ownership of patents
is concentrated in the richer countries, this widened inequalities
between rich and poor countries. As corporate oligopolies increase
their control over global trade in food crops, they can dictate to growers around the world what seeds to sow – usually ones whose patents
are owned by corporations. Growers who refuse to comply can be
blacklisted. They become hostages of corporate patent owners.

A UN-commissioned study referred to measures adopted by the
World Trade Organization relating to the issue of patenting, especially of plant varieties and life forms. "The granting of patents covering
all genetically engineered varieties of a species, irrespective of the
genes concerned or how they were transferred, puts in the hands of a
single inventor the possibility to control what we grow on our farms
and in our gardens. At a stroke of a pen the research of countless farmers and scientists has potentially been negated in a single, legal act of
economic highjack," it stated. "The implications of such a measure are
serious for the issue of food security, and its consequent relationship
to the right to food. Furthermore, it represents outright piracy and
appropriation of nature's bounty which has been designated for the
whole of humanity and not for a privileged and technologically
advanced few."[38]

Patents foster monopoly, allowing owners to control markets, the
converse of the "free-trade" system purportedly being fostered by the
globalization process. Staple foods are, more and more, becoming the
private property of multinationals. Whoever controls the patents for
the world's seeds, the first and most vital link in the food production
chain, controls the world's food. Whoever controls the world's food
supply has the power of life and death over the world's peoples.

atents, and hence control over food,
ιe globalization process, through the
ν Rights (TRIPs) provisions in the
ιlso copper-fastened the rights of
ιies. Although millions of people
ιuse they cannot afford the drugs
ιnpanies prevent others from manufac-
ςs. Significantly, many of the drugs are a direct
ιiopiracy". This entails the patenting of drugs
ι plants that have been freely used for generations for
ι purposes by indigenous peoples in areas such as the Amazon
ςion. Payments to the indigenous groups for the patents are rare or, at best, derisory.

Opposition to TRIPs led to protests in several countries. In mid-1993, farmers in southern India destroyed a premises owned by Cargill. This American company's global operations, perhaps, give us a look into the future – into a world increasingly being dominated by megacorporations. The compass of its operations has been summarized by *Corporate Watch* magazine. Cargill, it stated, was "one of the most powerful corporations on earth. Wealthier than many developing nations. . . in 1997 its global revenue was $56 billion. . . Now it is the largest grain trader. . . and malting barley producer in the world. . . Cargill is also the largest beef packer in Canada; the third largest beef packer and flour miller in the US; the fourth largest cattle feeder and sixth largest turkey producer in the US; and the second largest phosphate fertilizer producer in the world. Cargill is also a major power in salt, peanuts, cotton, coffee, truck transport, river/canal shipping, molasses, livestock feed, steel, hybrid seeds, rice milling, rubber, citrus, chicken and fresh fruits and vegetables. . .. In India, Cargill has tried to take control of the seed market by lobbying for intellectual property rights and patenting laws that would make it illegal for farmers to grow and sell their own seeds."[39]

MAI

The Uruguay Round and NAFTA accords gave corporations vast new powers. Nevertheless, the corporations and their political collaborators were not content. In 1995, member governments of the Organization for Economic Cooperation and Development (OECD) commenced secret negotiations on a Multilateral Agreement on Investment (MAI). Charles Derber, professor of sociology at Boston College, has pointed out the agreement's unparalleled concessions, writing that the "MAI requires that every country open every part of its economy – its banks, television stations, and all its vital industries – to unrestricted foreign investment or acquisition". Some critics, he remarked, were calling the MAI "a new economic constitution for the entire world".[40]

According to John Pilger – winner on two occasions of the journalist of the year award, the highest honour in British journalism – the "MAI 'negotiations' represent the most important imperial advance for half a century, yet they do not qualify as headline news. Once formalized, they will remove the last restrictions on the free movement of foreign capital anywhere in the world, while effectively transferring development policy from national governments to multinational corporations. At the same time, multinationals will be freed from the obligation to observe minimum standards in public welfare, the environment and business practices."[41]

The proposals were intended to remove almost all controls by sovereign states over multinationals and over investment capital. They would, critics pointed out, give multinationals the right to sue states whose policies – for example, environmental standards – were injurious to corporate profits, thereby giving corporations the power to frustrate government policies and decisions aimed at benefiting citizens' lives.

In Europe, Susan George, associate director of the Transnational Institute, described the proposed MAI as giving "all rights to corporations, all obligations to governments and no rights at all to citizens".[42]

In the United States, Noam Chomsky wrote of how the agreement would "allow corporations to sue governments while they remain immune from any liability".[43]

Political scientist Peter Henriot, SJ, director of the Jesuit Centre for Theological Reflection in Zambia, wrote that the MAI, "if implemented in Africa, would deprive governments of any ability to regulate the activities of transnational corporations (already limited in any case), and to guarantee minimum social and environmental protection for its citizens. Governments would also have an even more diminished role in shaping national development strategies and priorities."[44]

Angered at the secrecy and the implications of the MAI negotiations – which were carried out without being monitored by, or having any input from, members of the US Congress – twenty-five members of the House of Representatives queried how the agreement had "been under negotiation since May 1995, without any Congressional consultation or oversight, especially given Congress' exclusive constitutional authority to regulate international commerce".[45]

Incredibly, while US legislators were sidelined, Corporate USA was not. Its official liaison group to the MAI, the United States Council for International Business – which was formed in 1945 "to promote an open system of world trade, investment and finance" – was consulted at all stages of the negotiations, playing a key role in the formulation of MAI proposals. The organization has a membership of over 300 multinational companies, law firms and business associations, and is the US affiliate of the International Chamber of Commerce and of the Business and Industry Advisory Committee to the OECD.[46]

The twenty-five representatives queried the proposed terms of the MAI which, they claimed, "would allow a foreign corporation or investor to directly sue the US government for damages if we take any action that would restrain 'enjoyment' of an investment", and asked why the United States should "willingly cede sovereign immunity and expose itself to liability for damages under vague language".[47]

The negotiations were not conducted in the organization created to oversee international trade, the World Trade Organization, most of whose member states are from the Third World. They were held within the OECD, a forum for the world's leading industrial nations, where most of the world's multinationals originate. In late 1998, the talks were derailed following intense pressure, mainly from non-governmental organizations, and adverse media reaction in some countries. American newspapers and television and radio networks largely ignored the proposed agreement.

Speculation immediately began that the MAI's proposals would be transferred by stealth to the WTO and/or the International Monetary Fund. Noam Chomsky claimed that efforts were "already underway to change the IMF charter to impose MAI-style provisions as conditions on credits, thus enforcing the rules for the weak, ultimately others. The really powerful will follow their own rules."[48] The MAI's coercive provisions, if implemented, would entrench corporate control over national governments and over the world's peoples.

The Uruguay Round and NAFTA accords, the secret MAI negotiations and corporate patenting of seeds and drugs are just a few examples of how the US/corporate-driven globalization process is – with almost no consultation with, or approval from, the world's electorates – ceding global economic power to megacorporations and the masters of capital. There are other, equally startling, examples.

The Money Men

Traditionally, protectionism provided governments with a regulatory mechanism to control or stem the flow of trans-border commerce and capital, enabling them to shelter domestic sectors from powerful outside competitors and from rapacious carpetbaggers. Globalization, primarily through the Uruguay Round and NAFTA accords and through IMF structural adjustment programmes (which will be discussed later), undermined protectionism and capital controls, opening financial, industrial and other sectors to competition from outside. In this world of deregulated transfrontier flows, elected governments became marginalized, left to spectate impotently as currency and investment dealers freely moved vast sums of money across national borders, unhindered by tax authorities or any social concerns or responsibilities.

Concentrating enormous power and influence in the hands of the masters of capital, deregulation had obvious anarchic implications. According to a 1996 United Nations publication, "financial flows have reached unimaginable dimensions. More than a trillion dollars roam the world every 24 hours, restlessly seeking the highest return. This flow of capital. . . has opened the world to the operation of a global financial market that leaves even the strongest countries with limited autonomy over interest rates, exchange rates or other financial policies."[49] Just as easily as they can invest vast sums in selected countries, speculators and investors can also withdraw them at the touch of a computer key, at times with devastating consequences for the countries concerned. The vast majority of the $1.5 trillion now being traded daily across the world's frontiers is purely speculative, involving no commodities or manufactured products.[50] The speculation can undermine national economies, thereby hindering development, deepening poverty levels and precipitating social upheaval.

In 1997, an economic meltdown occurred in Asia, precipitating a crisis of global capitalism. The crisis began in Thailand in July of that year, when the country's purportedly miracle "Asian tiger" free-market economy became dangerously unstable. An attack by foreign hedge funds (used by speculators to profit from the acquisition and disposal of securities and currencies) on Thailand's national currency forced the government to devalue it. In a short space of time, numerous foreign speculators and investors disposed of their holdings of Asian currencies and stocks.

Within weeks the Thai baht had plummeted 40 per cent. It was followed by the Malaysian ringgit, the Indonesian rupiah, the South Korean won, the Philippine peso and the Japanese yen. By January 1998, the rupiah was in freefall, crashing to a quarter of its 1997 value. Amid fears that the unfolding Asian crises, contagion would spread elsewhere, in October 1997 the New York Stock Exchange experienced its largest ever single trading session point drop. The avarice of international money-capitalists and the tyranny of globalization and free-market economics erased two decades of spectacular economic growth in Asia, impoverishing millions. National currencies elsewhere were also attacked by speculators. Some countries, such as Brazil, successfully resisted the attacks, but often at a very high cost to its citizens.

One US-based multibillionaire financier and big-time speculator was especially vilified by Asian leaders, accused of being the prime mover behind the financial dealings that triggered Asia's crisis – George Soros. Soros' Quantum Fund and other speculators had earlier attacked one of the world's strongest currencies, sterling, forcing the British government to devalue it. The Quantum Fund profited to the extent of around $1 billion. The financial coup, Soros later told an interviewer, "was all in a day's work. It was not anything out of the ordinary."[51]

The enforced devaluations of sterling and Asian currencies revealed a dark, seldom spoken about facet of globalization. It is that the free movement of capital, made possible by the unfettering of capital from bothersome cross-border restrictions and from social obligations and ethical considerations, gives vast new powers to the owners and managers of capital in the global arena, since deregulation prioritized the privileges of capital, including the maximization of profits, over human rights in the broadest sense.

There are considerable dangers and social implications in giving such powers to moneyed elites. The ability of super-wealthy speculators to successfully attack sterling, one of the world's strongest currencies, and to profit from their venture raises the prospect of further recurrences of the exercise. Asia's 1997 experience exposed the link between the deregulation of capital controls and the vulnerability of the world's national economies to the pursuit of profits by private financial colossi, who sparked a chain reaction of devaluations, threatening the livelihoods and the future welfare of hundreds of millions of Asians.

There is another lesson to be learned from Asia's experience. As the region's crises deepened, foreign investors and speculators circled like vultures, sifting through the economic debris for devalued assets, particularly banks and other financial institutions. It amounted, critics claimed, to a recolonization of the countries by foreigners. The International Monetary Fund aided the takeover of assets in crisis-hit countries, demanding that governments agree to the disposal of companies and banks – many of which fell into the hands of cash-rich foreign bargain hunters – as a condition for receiving bailout loans.

The globalization of financial flows created a new global super-elite, the masters of capital. The scale of the financial resources controlled by these masters, such as the managers of hedge funds, have become so vast that they can alter prices in the world's markets upwards or downwards to meet their profit-making requirements. The transborder flow of their capital can take place almost as if national boundaries no longer exist, thereby engendering universal economic insecurity, sidelining governments, infringing on the sovereignty of countries at all levels of their economies and depriving nation states of the power to defend national interests.

Globalization has become the pervasive and defining economic and political model of the current era, fostering a diminution of democracy, national sovereignty and human rights, a widening disparity between the world's richest and poorest nations and an increasing cession of global economic and political power and influence to megacorporations and to other masters of capital.

Notes

1. *Foreign Policy in Focus*, Special Report no. 7, November 1999 (Interhemispheric Resource Center, Albuquerque, and Institute for Policy Studies, Washington, DC), p. 2. See also *Forbes*, 20 April 1998 and 27 July 1998, and *World Development Report 1998/99* (Washington, DC: World Bank, 1999), pp. 212–13.
2. Michael Moore, *Stupid White Men and Other Sorry Excuses for the State of the Nation* (New York: ReganBooks, 2001), p. 52.
3. *Human Development Report 1999* (New York: Published for UN Development Programme by Oxford University Press, 1999), pp. 3, 38.
4. *Ibid.*, pp. 2, 22, 28, 180–83. See also *The State of World Population 2001*, published by the UN Population Fund.
5. See *The State of World Population 2001*.
6. *A Future Without Child Labour* (Geneva: International Labour Organization, May 2002).
7. US State Department's annual *Trafficking in Persons* report, June 2002.
8. David C. Korten, *When Corporations Rule the World* (West Hartford, Conneticut: Kumarian Press/San Francisco: Berrett-Koehler, 1995), p. 54.
9. *Human Development Report* 1999, pp. 2, 26, 27.
10. Joseph Stiglitz, *Globalization and Its Discontents* (London: Allen Lane, 2002), p. 72.
11. World Trade Organization brochure, *Trading into the Future*, p. 1.11.
12. Peter Sutherland, "Trade Policy Debate Should Be Based on Objectivity", *The Irish Times*, 20 August 1993.
13. UNCTAD press release, 8 October 1996.
14. See *Trading into the Future*, p. 1.1.
15. "GATT Leader Forecasts New Era". *The Irish Times*, 12 April 1994.
16. *Semi-Annual Report to Congress by the Secretary of the Treasury, Pursuant to the Mexican Debt Disclosure Act of 1995.*
17. Speech at Latin America Bureau conference, London, March 1995.
18. Robert J. Samuelson, "The Limits of Immigration", *Newsweek*, 24 July 2000, citing World Bank estimates.
19. President Clinton, State of the Union address, 25 January 1994.
20. Samir Amin, *Capitalism in the Age of Globalization* (London: Zed Books, 1997), p. 30.
21. *Multinational Monitor* (Washington, DC), April 1995.
22. *The Realization of Economic, Social and Cultural Rights: Globalization and Its Impact on the Full Enjoyment of Human Rights*. Preliminary report submitted by J. Oloka-Onyango and Deepika Udagama to the UN Economic and Social Council, June 2000.
23. See *Trading into the Future*, p. 1.1.
24. *Ibid.*, pp. 3.2, 1.14.
25. *States of Disarray: The Social Effects of Globalization* (UN Research Institute for Social Development, 1995), p. 153.
26. Jeffrey J. Schott, assisted by Johanna W. Buurman, *The Uruguay Round: An Assessment* (Washington, DC: Institute for International Economics, 1994), p. 15.
27. Conor O'Clery, "Bush's Steel Gamble Has Won Little at Home and May Lose a Lot Abroad", *The Irish Times* 29 March 2002.

28. Ralph Nader et al, *The Case Against Free Trade* (San Francisco: Earth Island Press/Berkeley, California: North Atlantic Books, 1993), p. 4.
29. See *The Realization of Economic, Social and Cultural Rights*.
30. Written submission by the Commission of Churches on International Affairs of the World Council of Churches to the UN Commission on Human Rights, 57th session (March-April 2001).
31. "A Rebellion Born in the Mountains", *CovertAction Quarterly*, no. 48 (Washington, DC), Spring 1994, p. 36.
32. *North-South: A Programme for Survival. The Report of the Independent Commission on International Development Issues* (London: Pan Books, 1982), p. 141.
33. Neil Middleton, Phil O'Keefe and Sam Moyo, *Tears of the Crocodile* (London: Pluto Press, 1993), p. 100; Fidel Castro, *Address at the Inauguration of the Second Congress of the Association of Third World Economists* (Havana: Editora Politica, 1981), p. 7; "Whose Earth is This Anyway?", *One World* newsletter (Dublin: Trócaire, July 1982).
34. See *North-South: A Programme for Survival*, pp. 189–90.
35. UNCTAD, *World Investment Report 2000*.
36. Roger Burbach and Patricia Flynn, *Agribusiness in the Americas* (New York: Monthly Review Press and NACLA, 1980), pp. 221–29; See Neil Middleton et al, *Tears of the Crocodile*, p. 100.
37. David Weir and Mark Schapiro, *Circle of Poison: Pesticides and People in a Hungry World* (San Francisco: Institute for Food and Development Policy, 1981), p. 44.
38. See *The Realization of Economic, Social and Cultural Rights*, quoting Vandana Shiva.
39. "Cargill: the Invisible Giant", *Corporate Watch* (Oxford), issue 7.
40. Charles Derber, *Corporation Nation* (New York: St Martin's Griffin, 2000), p. 276.
41. John Pilger, *Hidden Agendas* (London: Vintage, 1998), p. 74.
42. Walden Bello, Nicola Bullard and Kamal Malhotra, eds, *Global Finance* (London: Zed Books, 2000), p. 34.
43. Noam Chomsky, *Profit Over People: Neoliberalism and Global Order* (New York: Seven Stories Press, 1999), p. 138.
44. Peter Henriot, "Adjusting in Africa: For Whose Benefit?", *Trócaire Development Review 1998* (Dublin), p. 160.
45. See Noam Chomsky, *Profit Over People*, p. 141.
46. USCIB leaflet.
47. See Noam Chomsky, *Profit Over People*, p. 141; Charles Derber, *Corporation Nation*, p. 278.
48. See Noam Chomsky, *Profit Over People*, p. 165.
49. *Human Development Report 1996*, p. 8.
50. "Robin Hood's Tax Return", *Journalist* (London), June/July 2002, p. 28; *Human Development Report 1999*, p. 1.
51. Rupert Steiner, "Who Broke the Bank?", *The Sunday Times* (UK), 15 April 2001.

Chapter 2
Jugular Diplomacy

Trade Expansion

From America's colonial period to today's age of globalization, trade has consistently been the country's most important foreign policy issue. During the colonial era, rich fishing grounds along North America's Atlantic coast provided merchants with an opportunity to engage in transatlantic commerce. Maritime trade became the linchpin of the economies of coastal towns and cities.

By 1801, American shippers had cornered almost three-quarters of all foreign trade with India and were successfully engaged in seaborne commerce elsewhere, including Europe, the West Indies and China.[1] As America's ocean-borne trade expanded, so also did threats to the trade. By the late 1790s, it had become necessary to use naval vessels for the protection of merchant ships trading in the West Indies. In the early 1800s, naval forces were sent to the Mediterranean region to safeguard American ships from Barbary pirates, culminating in the blockading and naval bombardment of the city of Tripoli and the signing in 1805 of a peace agreement. The protection of trade became the navy's principal responsibility.

Summarizing the benefits of this navy-protected trade, Allan R. Millett and Peter Maslowski noted in their book *For the Common Defense* how the "unofficial alliance between the Navy and American commercial interests produced astounding results. Between 1790 and 1860 total exports (including reexports) increased from $20,000,000 to $334,000,000; this helped to transform the United States into one of the world's foremost economic powers by the end of the nineteenth century."[2]

The use of US armed forces to protect commercial interests became commonplace, not only abroad but also on the American mainland. Territorial expansion – to meet the needs of colonial merchants for furs and other goods and to meet the demands of white settlers for land –

also required the use of armed forces. This early alliance between the region's armed forces and its commercial interests set a precedent for future US foreign policy. The country's armed forces became an instrumentality of a foreign policy that, more and more, focused on promoting US commercial interests abroad and on expanding US hegemony.

The centrality of trade and investment considerations, and the importance of coercive strategies, in the conduct of US foreign policy was hinted at in 1907 by Woodrow Wilson, who opined that since "trade ignores national boundaries and the manufacturer insists on having the world as a market. . . the doors of the nations which are closed against him must be battered down. Concessions obtained by financiers must be safeguarded by ministers of state, even if the sovereignty of unwilling nations be outraged in the process. Colonies must be obtained or planted."[3] It was a call for the US to intervene in the affairs of weaker countries to protect US trade and investments.

Since the colonial period, trade has been such an important foreign policy issue in the United States that its governments have waged wars and intervened militarily, economically and politically in the affairs of other countries to protect and expand the nation's trade and other corporate interests. Ultimately, as will be seen, this interventionism culminated in the attainment of globalization. Globalization represents the Americanization of the international economy through the imposition of a US-formulated global trading system and the emergence of Corporate USA as a global power.

To properly understand this Americanization/globalization process, we need to analyse the parallel roles of trade and interventionism in the history of the United States.

Predator Nation

A culture of militarism, self-interest and territorial aggrandizement or control has suffused the entire history of white rule in the region that today comprises the United States of America. It began with the arrival of European settlers, their appropriation of land and the concomitant near-genocidal slaughter of those occupying the land, the Native Americans. By 1880 almost all the land stretching from the Atlantic coastline to the Pacific had been acquired by whites through war, threats and chicanery. By then, government-sanctioned butchery and also disease and starvation had devastated the indigenous tribes. In 1600, there were, perhaps, four million Native Americans. By 1880 there were less than a quarter-million.

In the early years of white territorial expansion, the Native Americans frustrated the settlers' land-lust. To acquire land the whites resorted to legally approved theft and murder. The use of legislative measures to steal land and to justify the killing of Indians accorded the thefts and killings a veneer of legality and morality, thereby assuaging some whites' Christian sensibilities.

The Declaration of Independence – the birth certificate of the United States – collaborated in this process, demonizing the Native Americans as a sub-human species ("merciless Indian Savages"). In "appealing to the Supreme Judge of the world for the rectitude of our intentions", the Declaration's Christian framers disingenuously sought to give an appearance of divine sanction for deeds that were clearly unchristian.

The demonization of antagonistic and non-compliant regimes, movements and ethnic groups became almost a routine procedure in the conduct of Washington's foreign policy. The more diminished an enemy's humanity, the easier it would be to justify killing them, overthrowing them or invading and conquering their territory. It was a tactic later employed with considerable success against communist, socialist, Islamic and independent-minded Third World regimes.

By the early 1800s, shortly after achieving nationhood, the country's political leaders were already contemplating the possibility, even inevitability, of territorial or jurisdictional expansion throughout the entire landmass of the Americas. In November 1801, President Thomas Jefferson wrote of how it was "impossible not to look forward to distant times", when the US would "cover the whole northern, if not the southern continent, with a people speaking the same language, governed in similar forms, and by similar laws".[4]

In 1823, the United States signalled its intention to dominate the affairs and people of other countries with the launch in that year of the Monroe Doctrine, which arrogated to the United States the role of overlord or protector of all Latin America, henceforth to be considered the exclusive domain of US interests. The doctrine warned that any interference by European powers in the affairs of the region would be construed as a hostile act ("the manifestation of an unfriendly disposition") against the United States itself.

Enunciated unilaterally by the United States, the doctrine's objective was to protect the region from intervention by European powers, but not from US aggression, exploitation and control. The promulgation of the doctrine was a response to moves by Spain to regain control over its former colonies in Latin America and over trade with them, moves that threatened the increasingly lucrative regional trade of the United States. The doctrine was the first major foreign policy initiative formulated by Washington. Industry and trade-driven, it set a precedent for the future. Henceforth, US foreign policy would largely be determined by "national interests" – a term that became synonymous with big business interests.

By 1830, seven years after the proclamation of the Monroe Doctrine and around a half century after its birth as a vulnerable nation, the United States had established itself as the world's sixth leading industrial power. By 1860, it had moved up to fourth place. By the end of the century it held the premier position. Never before had a newly independent nation achieved such superiority so fast.[5]

This rapid rise to global pre-eminence was fuelled by a burgeoning manufacturing sector. By the late nineteenth century, as industrial output outstripped domestic demand, American manufacturers were looking outside the United States for new markets for their goods, creating a pressure to find such markets through acquiring control over foreign countries. In the late 1890s, Senator Albert Beveridge of Indiana articulated a mood then prevalent in the United States when he remarked how "American factories are making more than the American people can use; American soil is producing more than they can consume. Fate has written our policy for us; the trade of the world must and shall be ours. . . We will cover the ocean with our merchant marine. We will build a navy to the measure of our greatness. Great colonies, governing themselves, flying our flag and trading with us, will grow about our ports of trade." In such territories, he forecast, "American law, American order, American civilization and the American flag" would be planted.[6]

His speculation proved to be remarkably prescient. Control over foreign regions, US domination of "the trade of the world" and the expansion of the nation's armed forces in order to secure this control and domination – all became prime preoccupations of successive US administrations.

America's Manifest Destiny

By 1845, the United States' ill-concealed ambition to expand its hegemony and territorial jurisdiction had acquired a name, Manifest Destiny. This new doctrine argued that it was the "manifest destiny" of the country "to overspread the continent allotted by Providence for the free development of our yearly multiplying millions".[7] Divine licence was being invoked to sanctify future US aggression and to provide a façade of legitimacy for US expansionist ambitions and a justification for unbridled greed abroad.

The year 1845, when the concept of Manifest Destiny was launched, coincided with the inception of a new phase in the nation's territorial enlargement. In that year the United States annexed the Mexican province of Texas. The following year US forces invaded Mexico. War followed. Within a few years, US aggression had forced Mexico to cede all of its dominions north of the Rio Grande, amounting to around a half of its entire territory, to its northern neighbour.

In the 1850s, a naval fleet was dispatched to Japan. In an unprecedented display of gunboat diplomacy, the country was coerced into opening its ports to US trade. The event was an early manoeuvre towards achieving US commercial domination in the Pacific.

Spanish dominions were the next victims of US military aggression. Once again, commercial considerations were a prime causal factor. In February 1898, a blast destroyed an American battleship in the port of Havana, Cuba's capital, killing 260 crewmen. Blaming the explosion on the island's Spanish colonial rulers, the United States invaded Cuba and another Spanish colony, the Philippines. At war's end a few months later, Cuba became an American protectorate and the Spanish territories of the Philippines, Guam and Puerto Rico were annexed by the United States.

The Spanish-American War occurred at a time when the United States had just attained its pre-eminence as an industrial power and needed colonies or foreign territories of its own to consolidate this pre-eminence. The potential benefits of the war, particularly for American industrialists and investors, were summarized by Senator Thurston of Nebraska. "War with Spain would increase the business and earnings of every American railroad; it would increase the output of every American factory; it would stimulate every branch of industry and domestic commerce."[8] War was being accepted in Washington as a useful and effective instrument of US trade expansion.

The importance of the Philippines was noted by John Barrett, the US minister to Siam. "They are richer and far larger than Cuba, and in the hands of a strong power would be the key to the Far East," he stated.[9]

In 1900, after the fall of the Philippines, Senator Albert Beveridge reflected on how the acquisition of the archipelago would be a crucial step towards global US hegemony and in gaining access to Asian markets for US exports. "The Philippines are ours forever. . . And just beyond the Philippines are China's illimitable markets. We will not retreat from either. . ... The power that rules the Pacific is the power that rules the world. That power will forever be the American Republic."[10]

A Taste of Empire

The war with Spain marked the inception of a new approach in the conduct of US foreign policy. For the first time in its history, the US had waged a war outside of the Americas to acquire new territories, gaining control over a mini-empire that stretched from the Caribbean across the Pacific to Asia. In the process the US was changed from a mere hemispheric power to a major global power.

By then public support for US aggression and territorial acquisition overseas was growing. This support was reflected in an editorial in the *Washington Post* on the eve of the war, which observed that a "new consciousness seems to have come upon us – the consciousness of strength – and with it a new appetite, the yearning to show our strength. . . The taste of Empire is in the mouth of the people."[11]

The concept of an American empire appealed to many Americans, including historian Brooks Adams. "With the completion of the Panama Canal all Central America will become part of our system," he wrote in 1902. "We have expanded into Asia, we have attracted the fragments of the Spanish dominions, and reaching out into China. . . We are penetrating into Europe, and Great Britain especially is gradually assuming the position of a dependency. . . The United States will outweigh any single empire, if not all empires combined. The whole world will pay her tribute. Commerce will flow to her from both east and west, and the order which has existed from the dawn of time will be reversed."[12]

Created by military aggression, America's mini-empire required further military intervention to ensure continuing US subjugation of the annexed territories and populations. To impose US rule in the newly conquered Philippines, tens of thousands of American soldiers were sent to crush pro-independence rebels. An estimated 20,000 Filipino insurgents and up to 200,000 civilians were killed.

President McKinley depicted the intervention as an act of liberation, dictated by moral considerations. "We were obeying a higher moral obligation, which rested on us and which did not require anybody's consent," he stated. "We were doing our duty by them, as God gave us the light to see our duty, with the consent of our own consciences and with the approval of civilization. . . It is not a good time for the liberator to submit important questions concerning liberty and government to the liberated while they are engaged in shooting down their rescuers."[13]

Commenting in the 1960s on the intervention, J. William Fulbright, chairman of the Senate Foreign Relations Committee, wrote that the country had been annexed because some of Washington's leaders "wanted America to have an empire just because a big, powerful country like the United States *ought* to have an empire".[14]

Interventions in America's "Backyard"

Washington's proclivity for aggression against populations which were not at war with the United States, and which posed no threat to the people or territorial integrity of the US, is evident from a US government document *Instances of the Use of United States Armed Forces Abroad 1798–1945*, which lists over 150 US military interventions in foreign countries during this period.[15]

America's own "backyard" – Central America and the Caribbean – was especially targeted. Post-1890 interventions in this region included:

Nicaragua	1894, 1896, 1898, 1899, 1910, 1912–25, 1926–33
Panama/Colombia	1895, 1901, 1902, 1903–14, 1918–20, 1921, 1925
Honduras	1903, 1907, 1911, 1912, 1919, 1924, 1925
Dominican Republic	1903, 1904, 1914, 1916–24
Cuba	1898–1902, 1906–9, 1912, 1917–22, 1933
Haiti	1891, 1914, 1915–34.[16]

The frequency of US interventions in the region exposed Washington's fixation on controlling the affairs of other countries. Post-1890 interventions in the Central American isthmus, the waist of the Americas, reinforced Washington's near-absolute power, reducing countries to little more than US fiefdoms which had no democratic rule, no national sovereignty and no right of self-determination. Commenting on the extent of US power and influence there, Under Secretary of State Robert Olds wrote in 1927 that US "ministers accredited to the five little republics, stretching from the Mexican border to Panama. . . have been advisers whose advice has been accepted virtually as law in the capitals where they respectively reside. . . We do control the destinies of Central America and we do so for the simple reason that the national interest absolutely dictates such a course. . . Until now Central America has always understood that governments which we recognize and support stay in power, while those we do not recognize and support fall."[17]

In 1903, a new republic was born in the isthmus when Washington severed the province of Panama from Colombia in order to construct an interoceanic canal linking the Atlantic and Pacific, thereby facilitating US trade with other regions. It was a striking demonstration of America's growing power and its willingness to use that power, even to the extent of creating a country so that the US business sector could have a shorter trading route between two oceans.

In 1912, Washington's hegemonic ambitions in the hemisphere were spelled out by President Taft, who predicted that the time was approaching "when three Stars and Stripes at three equidistant points will mark our territory: one at the North Pole, another at the Panama Canal, and the third at the South Pole. The whole hemisphere will be ours." US foreign policy, he suggested, might need to be shaped "to include active intervention to secure for our merchandise and our capitalists opportunity for profitable investment".[18]

Twentieth century US foreign policy was being shaped to meet the trade needs of Corporate USA and the investment needs of American capitalists.

World Wars

US participation in the First and Second World Wars would, for the first time in its foreign wars and interventions, exact an enormous price in terms of American lives lost, with a total of around 350,000 US combatants dying on the world's battlefields.[19]

America's entry into the First World War, President Wilson told Congress, was being undertaken, not in search of conquest but rather "for democracy. . . for the rights and liberties of small nations".[20] Not so, according to a Senate committee. Chaired by Republican Senator Gerald Nye of North Dakota, the committee concluded that America had entered the war "to save the skins of American bankers", who had advanced substantial loans to the Allied nations in Europe. US participation in the conflict, the committee claimed, had been engineered by "munitions makers", Wall Street and the banks, all of which benefited enormously from war-generated profits.[21] The war was the most successful profit-making venture in the history of US export trade.

In the course of the Second World War, Washington's foreign policy tacticians continually crossed the boundaries of what is acceptable in times of conflict. This was especially true of the unconscionable US attacks on populated urban areas, including its role in the firebombing of the German cities of Dresden and Hamburg.

On 6 August 1945, the United States dropped the world's first atomic bomb on Hiroshima, a Japanese city of around 300,000 people, and three days later repeated the exercise on the city of Nagasaki. Between 125,000 and 250,000 civilians were killed. The bombings represented a new nadir in Washington's long history of unethical foreign policy strategies. They occurred at a time when Japan was on the verge of capitulating and had already made overtures to initiate peace negotiations with the United States.

The US bombings in Japan and Germany exposed a profound paradox in America's sense of righteousness and moral superiority, which discerned no ethical issues in the mass murder of so many noncombatants. The country's capacity for moral blindness became even more pronounced in the decades after the war.

Pax Americana

The hegemonic power of the United States was unrivalled in the decades after the war. The breadth of the power that could be wielded by the US in the post-war global arena has been outlined in Ronald Steel's book *Pax Americana*. The United States, he wrote, was "the strongest and most politically active nation in the world. Our impact reaches everywhere and affects everything it touches. We have the means to destroy whole societies and rebuild them, to topple governments and create others, to impede social change or to stimulate it, to protect our friends and devastate those who oppose us. We have a capacity for action, and a restless, driving compulsion to exercise it, such as the world has never seen."[22]

Prior to the Second World War, there were six major powers in the world – the United States, Great Britain, Germany, Japan, the Soviet Union and France. Uniquely among these nations, mainland US emerged unscathed by the war's devastation. At war's end, the wealth, industrial output, military might and political influence of the United States had become so predominant on the world stage that the nation had, in effect, assumed the role of managing director of the post-war global order.

Former State Department official Richard J. Barnet summarized the intentions of US policy makers in this new world order. They had, he argued, "a rather clear design for expanding American power. . . The maintenance of strategic territory occupied in World War II, the containment of the two great potential power rivals, Russia and China, the filling of 'power vacuums' left by the collapse of French and British imperial power, the expansion of American influence into all open areas of the 'developing world' and the maintenance of a world capitalist economic system dominated by the United States have been conscious policies. To accomplish any of them the United States has been prepared to use force."[23]

Enjoying a power superiority without historical precedent, the United States, for the first time in its history, had the means, economic and military, to control the destiny of almost all the world's nations. This near-global post-war US hegemony can be termed Pax Americana.

The post-war goal of the United States was to secure its globe-girdling dominance. Such a course of action was proposed in 1948 by George F. Kennan, the State Department's first director of policy planning. Noting that the United States had "about 50% of the world's wealth but only 6.3% of its population", Kennan argued that "Our real task in the coming period is to devise a pattern of relationships which will permit us to maintain this position of disparity. . . To do so, we will have to dispense with all sentimentality and day-dreaming; and our attention will have to be concentrated everywhere on our immediate national objectives. We need not deceive ourselves that we can afford today the luxury of altruism and world benefaction. . . We should dispense with the aspiration to 'be liked' or to be regarded as the repository of a high-minded international altruism. We should stop putting ourselves in the position of being our brothers' keeper. . . We should cease to talk about vague and – for the Far East – unreal objectives such as human rights, the raising of the living standards, and democratization. The day is not far off when we are going to have to deal in straight power concepts. The less we are then hampered by idealistic slogans, the better."[24]

Washington's post-bellum Cold War foreign policy would be fashioned to preserve America's "position of disparity"; that is, its control over around a half of the world's entire wealth. In doing so, Washington would, as Kennan suggested, dispense with considerations such as human rights, democracy and living standards. This new foreign policy would be both confrontational and interventionist. Its ostensible rationale would be anti-communism.

By stigmatizing communism as a form of political and ideological disease, contagious and deadly, which could sweep through and infect nation after nation, the United States provided itself with an endless succession of justifications for military interventions and other criminal activities abroad against innocent people, all purportedly undertaken in defence of freedom and democracy.

Vietnam's Calvary

The effects of this Cold War doctrine were seen most chillingly in the course of the US-waged Vietnam War, which converted a large part of Indochina into a vast human abattoir, where the US military killing machine rained death and destruction on civilian targets.

Waves of B-52 bombers devastated the cities of Hanoi and Haiphong in North Vietnam, destroying homes, factories, schools and hospitals. Napalm bombs dropped on civilian areas incinerated the inhabitants. South Vietnamese peasants were herded into virtual concentration camps in an effort to isolate enemy guerrillas. Entire villages were destroyed. In Mai Lai in March 1968, an American platoon rounded up an estimated 504 women, children and old men and then murdered them, some after being raped.

In the course of the war, bombs dropped by the United States on Vietnam exceeded the gross tonnage of bombs used in all earlier conflicts throughout history. The war left a terrible legacy: up to three million Vietnamese killed; an estimated 300,000 prostitutes; countless orphans, amputees and beggars; up to a third of South Vietnam's population displaced; an explosion of tuberculosis, venereal and other diseases; huge swaths of land and nearby rivers permanently poisoned with toxic defoliants; once-forested regions now virtually infertile; North Vietnam's industries and transport networks destroyed; hundreds of thousands of miscarriages and grotesquely malformed stillborn foetuses and babies born with spina bifida, liver problems, immune system disorders, cerebral palsy, cancers, mental retardation and other severe physical and mental handicaps caused by the millions of gallons of chemical defoliants sprayed by US aircraft.

The people in two of Vietnam's neighbouring countries, Cambodia and Laos, were also sacrificed by Washington in pursuit of victory in the Vietnam quagmire. Up to 600,000 died during the course of an undeclared war waged by the United States in Cambodia, in which the Western hegemon employed B-52 bombers and ground assault troops. Worse still, the US aggression precipitated the collapse of Cambodia's political and social orders, creating a vacuum which resulted in the seizure of power by communist Khmer Rouge forces, the subsequent enslavement of an entire population and the mass slaughter of the "killing fields" in which one to two million Cambodians were exterminated by the Khmer Rouge or died from torture, illness, forced labour or hunger. Almost all the villages and towns in northeast Laos were obliterated, many of their inhabitants being burnt alive by American napalm and white phosphorus bombs. Up to 350,000 Laotians were killed.

The US-directed wars in Vietnam, Cambodia and Laos were not waged for the betterment of the people in these countries. They were waged to secure US hegemony in the region and to transfer control over Indochina's valuable resources to American corporations.

America's entanglement in the region began in the 1950s, during the Truman and Eisenhower presidencies, when Washington supported France's Indochina War – waged to reclaim France's former colonies of Vietnam, Laos and Cambodia.

"Indochina is a prize worth a large gamble," a 1950 *New York Times* report suggested. "In the North are exportable tin, tungsten, zinc, manganese, coal, lumber, and rice, and in the South are rice, rubber, tea, pepper, cattle and hides."[25] Subsequently, President Eisenhower admitted that, in aiding France's war effort, Washington was simply availing of "the cheapest way. . . to get certain things we need from the riches" of the region.[26]

The CIA

In the years after the Second World War, new bodies were established and new strategies devised to provide the United States with additional interventionist options for projecting US power and promoting US corporate interests abroad. Among the bodies were some of the most secretive institutions in the world. One was the vast National Security Agency, an organization whose tens of thousands of employees use some of the world's most powerful computers and the most elaborate electronic surveillance system to eavesdrop on telephone conversations and other forms of electronic communication. Today it has the capacity to listen to every telephone conversation and to intercept all e-mail traffic in the world. Another organization was the Central Intelligence Agency. Established in 1947, the CIA would have responsibility for covertly countering threats and challenges to post-war US global hegemony. Third World populations would experience a contagion of CIA-fostered terror and butchery.

John Stockwell, former director of the CIA's task force in Angola, outlined in his book *The Praetorian Guard* the scope of the agency's remit: to kill, to manipulate elections, to topple governments, to foster civil strife, to form death squads. There "have been about 3,000 major covert operations and over 10,000 minor operations – all illegal, and all designed to disrupt, destabilize, or modify the activities of other countries", he wrote. The CIA, he continued, had "overthrown functioning constitutional democracies in over 20 countries. It has manipulated elections in dozens of countries. It has created standing armies and directed them to fight. It has organized ethnic minorities and encouraged them to revolt in numerous volatile areas. . . During the 1980s the CIA created, trained, and funded death squads."[27]

Describing the CIA's role in Indonesia in 1965, Stockwell wrote of how "the CIA organized an operation to discredit the Communist party. . . The result was a bloodbath. . . The CIA's own internal reporting estimated that 800,000 people had been killed."[28] The carnage amounted to the systematic annihilation of those deemed to be a threat to US interests in the country.

In 1955, the CIA spent $1 million in the country in a futile bid to thwart the Nationalist party of Achmed Sukarno in that year's national elections. When that ploy failed, the United States resorted to direct military intervention. Backed by unmarked US bombers, rebel officers launched an armed revolt. In May 1958, a CIA pilot, Allen Pope, was shot down and apprehended during a bombing raid, thereby exposing the central role of the CIA in the botched coup attempt. Almost a decade later, Sukarno was deposed by a military coup and replaced by Washington protégé General Suharto, the principal figure behind the slaughter of his fellow countrymen.

CIA covert operations elsewhere included successfully manipulating election results in Italy through funding political parties and individual politicians to the tune of $65 million over a twenty-year period; installing CIA-selected candidate Ramon Magsaysay as president of the Philippines in 1953; overthrowing the government of Mohammed Mossadegh in Iran in the same year, of Jacobo Arbenz in Guatemala the following year and of João Goulart in Brazil and Dr Cheddi Jagan in British Guyana in 1964; financing and directing the 1961 Bay of Pigs invasion in Cuba in an effort to remove Fidel Castro from power; and masterminding the 1973 coup in Chile, which led to years of military rule and repression.

New strategies for imposing Pax Americana were introduced by the CIA, including targeting Third World leaders for assassination. Among these were Patrice Lumumba in the Congo, Rafael Trujillo in the Dominican Republic and Fidel Castro in Cuba.

Angola

In October 1975, national elections were scheduled to take place in the newly independent African country of Angola. Three separate groups were to participate in the elections – the MPLA, FNLA and UNITA. Seven months before the proposed elections, the country was plunged into war following the killing of fifty-one MPLA activists by the FNLA. The elections were aborted.[29]

Shortly before the killings, the CIA had been authorized to channel $300,000 to the FNLA. Later, US military supplies flowed to the FNLA and UNITA, including surface to air missiles, mortars, recoilless rifles, rocket launchers, communications equipment and machine and sub-machine guns. Angolan villages became human slaughterhouses. Typical of UNITA butchery was the October 1976 killings at Canhala, where the insurgents hacked 287 villagers to death with machetes.

Following seventeen years of bloody conflict, national elections were finally held in September 1992, which the United Nations declared were free and fair. The US-backed UNITA rebels rejected their electoral defeat and resumed fighting. By then there were an estimated one million corpses, three million homeless and vast numbers of orphans and amputees.

Washington's covert war, although purportedly waged to curb Soviet influence in the strategically important region, was also conducted to enable Corporate USA to gain control over the country's oil and diamond wealth.

Latin America

More than any other region in the world, Latin America has been a target for US interventions. In general, these interventions have sought either to remove regimes deemed to be a threat to US corporate interests or to install or protect regimes favourably disposed towards these interests. US client regimes in Latin America have typically included right-wing military juntas, dictatorships, oligarchies and other forms of coercive government. Many were beholden to Washington for collaborating in their seizure of power. All were beholden for sustaining them in power.

A 1954 CIA-planned coup in Guatemala initiated three decades of rule by terror, during which up to 150,000 were killed, most of them Indian peasants. In that same year, General Alfredo Stroessner seized power in Paraguay in a military coup, retaining the presidency for thirty-five consecutive years. The longevity of his reign relied on US aid, the employment of terror as an instrument of government, the use of torture and the execution of opponents. A 1964 CIA-backed coup in Brazil was followed by two decades of military tyranny. In 1963, the government of Juan Bosch was overthrown in the Dominican Republic by military leaders. In April 1965, efforts to reinstate him were foiled by American forces sent to the country by President Johnson.

In the 1970s, El Salvador had a succession of military rulers, all of whom were supported by the United States, with Washington pouring military aid into the country and providing training for military personnel. Opposition to military rule was met by a wave of repression, including extra-judicial executions and "disappearances". Army officers formed death squads to murder dissidents. As the killings continued, millions of dollars of US taxpayers' money was given to the regimes. A fleet of assault helicopters and fixed-wing aircraft was furnished, and US military advisors helped to coordinate military offensives against the Salvadoran people.

Nicaragua

In 1979, nationalist Sandinista guerrillas ended over forty years of rule by the US-supported Somoza dictatorship in Nicaragua. A Sandinista-led government was formed. Shortly afterwards, a Contra (counter-revolutionary) force, most of whose leaders had been members of the Somozan National Guard, launched a war against the new regime and against the Nicaraguan people. Depicted by Washington as heroic patriots seeking to topple a totalitarian communist administration, the guerrilla force was financed, armed and trained by the CIA.

Others painted a less flattering picture, documenting a litany of Contra atrocities: women raped, stomachs hacked open, breasts cut off, eyes gouged out, testicles severed, throats slashed, farm animals slaughtered, crops burned and clinics, schools, homes and factories destroyed. Testimonies of Contra victims interviewed by Reed Brody, former assistant attorney general of the state of New York, indicated the horror of the US-backed campaign of terror. Typical was the testimony of Doroteo Tinoco Valdivia, who told of how Contras attacking his farming cooperative near Yali had taken "one boy about 15 years old, who was retarded and suffered from epilepsy... they had cut his throat, then they cut open his stomach and left his intestines hanging out on the ground like a string. They did the same to Juan Corrales who had already died from a bullet in the fighting. They opened him up and took out his intestines and cut off his testicles." Maria Bustillo Viuda de Blandon related how her husband, a lay pastor, and her five children had been forced out of their home near El Jicaro by Contras. When she found them later, they "were left all cut up. Their ears were pulled off, their throats were cut, their noses and other parts were cut off."[30]

The savagery of Contra terrorism prompted Rep. Samuel Gejdenson (D-Connecticut) to ask what "economic objective or military gain is there to be had in killing a five-year old child, or in raping a grandmother? What military objective can be found in slaughtering a young bride in front of her parents, or in burning the home of a coffee picker, or in slitting the throat of an old man? The only achievement is that of imposing a climate of total fear. And therein lies the Contra's objective: to blanket the population in fear."[31]

President Reagan denounced the Sandinista government as a totalitarian Marxist regime that had imposed a new dictatorship on the Nicaraguan people and was seeking to subvert democracy in neighbouring countries. Yet it included several Catholic priests in cabinet and sub-cabinet posts, the only government in the world to elevate so many priests to high political offices.

According to one of these, Minister of Culture Ernesto Cardenal, a monk, the revolution that Washington was seeking to derail was motivated by a spirit of Christian love. "And by love we mean love of neighbor – concern for adequate nourishment for everybody, improvement in the quality of life for the whole population, making sure everyone has decent housing, making sure there are medical services for everybody, education and culture for everybody, recreation, care of the elderly, child care – in other words, a society of brothers and sisters."[32]

The Reagan administration's hostility towards the Sandinistas ensured that World Bank and Inter-American Development Bank loans to Nicaragua ceased and that Contra attacks on isolated villages and small communities, farming cooperatives, clinics and other undefended or poorly defended rural facilities and centres of population were intensified. Oil installations at Puerto Sandino and Corinto were attacked in CIA-directed operations, forcing the evacuation of around 25,000 residents. In early 1984, the CIA mined the approaches to Nicaragua's main seaports.

A "warfare course" manual, *Psychological Operations in Guerrilla Warfare*, was supplied to the Contras by the CIA, providing advice on how to kidnap and assassinate public figures, engage in economic sabotage, destroy public buildings and recruit "professional criminals" to foment mob violence and clashes with the authorities.

The CIA-orchestrated Contra war in Nicaragua was of special significance. With its small population, scant resources, poorly armed military forces and struggling Third World economy, Nicaragua was of peripheral economic importance to Washington and posed no military threat to the United States. However, a Nicaraguan secession from Washington's sphere of influence would represent a diminution of US hegemony and, if unpunished and not reversed, could tempt other nations to follow suit in rejecting US domination, thereby curtailing the advantages, even monopoly, enjoyed by American industrialists, bankers and investors in such countries.

Ultimately, the US destabilization programme achieved its objective, the fall of a democratically elected government which had refused to become a US puppet regime. In February 1990, with pre-election polls indicating a clear-cut Sandinista victory, US-funded opposition parties defeated the Sandinistas in national elections. The electorate had voted with a loaded gun pointing at its head, with President George H. Bush warning that the decade-long Contra war would continue and that America's economic blockade of Nicaragua would remain in place unless the elections produced an outcome that was palatable in Washington. By then Contra terrorism had claimed around 30,000 lives and had displaced around 300,000 people.

After the election the Nicaraguan people were deserted by Washington, left to flounder helplessly in the degradation and poverty from which they had been slowly extricating themselves. The country's largely peasant population – like those in Angola, Vietnam, Cambodia and many other Third World countries – had become a mere pawn on the post-Second World War global Pax Americana chessboard.

School of the Americas

To counter threats to US hegemony and to the foreign interests of Corporate USA, US-run military schools were established to train Third World military and intelligence personnel. To date, hundreds of thousands of these have passed through the schools, including over 50,000 Latin American graduates of the School of the Americas.

Established in Panama in 1946, the School of the Americas (SOA) was formed to promote stability throughout Latin America after the Second World War, through providing training for Latin Americans in counter-insurgency and other strategies designed to maintain US client regimes in power and to topple those posing a threat to US hegemony and corporate interests.

Among its alumni were some of the hemisphere's most unsavory thugs, including dictators, murderers and torturers. *Latinamerica Press* listed some of these: "Among the graduates of the school are former Panamanian strongman Gen. Manuel Noriega, now in a US prison for drug trafficking, Bolivian Gen. Banzer, the head of a bloody military dictatorship from 1977 to 1978, Salvadoran death squad leader Roberto D'Aubuisson and former Argentine Gen. Leopoldo Galtieri, who oversaw the final two years of the country's 'dirty war' in which more than 30,000 people were either killed or disappeared. SOA graduates figure prominently in the UN's Truth Commission Report on El Salvador. Alumni of the school were implicated in the assassination of Archbishop Oscar Romero, the murders of four US church women, the assassination of six Jesuit priests, their housekeeper and her daughter and the El Mozote massacre on Dec 11, 1981, when more than 1,000 civilians were killed as the army wiped out a whole village. El Salvador is only part of the school's story. The three highest-ranking

Peruvian officers convicted in February 1994 of murdering nine students and a professor. . . were SOA graduates. Half of the 246 Colombian officers accused of war crimes by an international human rights tribunal last year [1993] were alumni of the school."[33]

Graduates of the School of the Americas displayed a remarkable aptitude for seizing political power by force. A 1967 Senate Foreign Relations Committee report noted that "most of the Latin American military leaders who conducted the nine coups between 1962 and 1966 had been recipients of US training".[34] Such has been the record of the SOA in spawning future dictators that it became known in Latin America as *"La Escuela de Golpes"*, the School of Coups.[35] It was Washington's principal base for destabilization in the continent.

The US lent its support to these coup-initiated military dictatorships, which became pliant surrogates of Washington. After the CIA-directed overthrow of President Allende in Chile in 1973, the US greatly increased its military assistance to such dictatorships. The assistance was used to increase the repressive and killing capacity of the regimes, not to promote human rights, freedom or democracy in the region or for defence against external threats.

By the end of 1976 – following coups in Brazil (1964), Chile (1973), Uruguay (1973), Argentina (1976) etc. – most of Latin America's population was being subjected to a reign of terror by US-backed military regimes. Armed and supported by the United States, such regimes remained in power through thwarting the legitimate aspirations of the people, suppressing popular movements and smothering demands for reforms, for justice and for a return to democracy.

Racketeers for US Capitalism

The mechanisms employed by the United States for imposing its near-global control often have horrific consequences for the populations of underdeveloped countries. Washington's willingness to countenance such repercussions in pursuing its goal of global US hegemony belies the country's self-projected image of a benign Uncle Sam, distressed by the suffering of so many of the world's people and determined to assuage the distress and pain.

Of course, wherever there are victims there are also, often, beneficiaries. If Third World populations are the principal victims of Washington's jugular diplomacy, who are the beneficiaries? Whose interests are served by Washington's foreign policy machinations?

American economist Scott Nearing was an early supporter of Eugene V. Debs' thesis that Washington's wars and interventions were being conducted at the behest and in the interests of a US "master class". Nearing argued that corporate influence in Washington was such that the country's business elites were framing US foreign policy, fostering war and imposing Washington's, and their own, will on other nations in order to protect the elites' foreign business interests. He alleged that American manufacturers, keen to boost their production, were active in promoting US participation in the First World War. Nearing's radical views led to his dismissal from university teaching posts, ending his academic career. For obstructing recruitment during the war he was arrested under the Espionage Act.[36]

Gerald Nye's Senate committee subsequently fuelled the debate on the issue, claiming that America's entry into the war had been masterminded by the country's bankers and manufacturers to protect their interests.

The thesis of a business-dominated, American, war-waging ruling class received further support in the 1930s from an unlikely ally – General Smedley Butler, one of America's most decorated military heroes. Recounting his military career, Butler told of how he had "spent thirty-three years and four months in active service as a member of our country's most agile military force – the Marine Corps. . . And during that period I spent most of my time being a high-class muscleman for Big Business, for Wall Street and for the bankers. In short, I was a racketeer for capitalism. . . Thus I helped make Mexico and especially Tampico safe for American oil interests in 1914. I helped make Haiti and Cuba a decent place for the National City Bank boys to collect revenues in. . . I helped purify Nicaragua for the international banking house of Brown Brothers in 1909–12. I brought light to the Dominican Republic for American sugar interests in 1916. I helped make Honduras 'right' for American fruit companies in 1903. In China in 1927 I helped see to it that Standard Oil went its way unmolested."[37]

The *raison d'être* for the marine invasions was the protection of American business interests, including loans from US banks to Central American and Caribbean countries. In 1909, General Butler led a marine force into Nicaragua. The invasion led to the overthrow of the government, and the installation of a Nicaraguan employee of an American-owned mining company as president of the country. Butler's intervention helped one US bank to maintain such dominance in the country that it became known in financial circles as the "Brown Brothers Republic".[38]

In December 1914, marines invaded Haiti. Government gold deposits were seized and handed over to the National City Bank in New York, then in dispute with the Haitian authorities over debt repayments. Opposition to the US occupation was brutally suppressed by Butler. In 1916, marines entered Haiti's neighbour, the Dominican Republic, ousted the government and placed a military dictatorship in power. To ensure the repayment of loans to US banks, the Dominican Republic's customs revenues were collected by a US-appointed official. The US occupation continued until 1924. In 1917, marines invaded Cuba. The operation was undertaken, according to Acting Secretary of State Frank Polk, to "aid in the protection of [US-owned] sugar properties and mining properties".[39] In 1927, at a time of considerable unrest in China, a marine force under Butler occupied Standard Oil's depot near Shanghai to protect it and other US interests.

The protection of corporate interests was at the very heart of such interventions. Many of the marine invasions had been undertaken, Butler argued, because American bankers "lend money to foreign countries and when they cannot repay, the President sends Marines to get it. I know – I've been in eleven of these expeditions." War, he claimed, was "largely a matter of money".[40] As the tramp of Marine Corps boots echoed through country after country, many became little more than colonies of the United States and victims of US corporate greed.

Later the CIA continued this tradition of pro-business interventions in the Third World. Early CIA operations included the 1953 overthrow of Mohammed Mossadegh in Iran, the 1954 overthrow of the Arbenz government in Guatemala, the 1961 landing of an armed force at Cuba's Bay of Pigs and the 1964 overthrow of João Goulart in Brazil.

These interventions followed, respectively, the nationalization by Mossadegh of Iran's rich oil resources, which had long been exploited by the British-owned Anglo-Iranian Oil Company (After Mossadegh's overthrow, the US returned the shah of Iran to power. Subsequently, US companies were granted a 40 per cent share of Iran's oil production); the expropriation in Guatemala by the reformist Arbenz government of huge swaths of unused land owned by the largest landholder in Guatemala, the American-owned United Fruit Company; the seizure by the Castro government of US-owned oil refineries, sugar mills, manufacturing industries, banks, landholdings and electricity and telephone networks; the takeover of a Brazilian subsidiary of the giant US-based International Telephone and Telegraph (ITT) and the passing of a law limiting the level of profits that foreign companies could repatriate.

The CIA was thus pursuing the same foreign policy goals, albeit employing different tactics, as General Butler's Marine Corps and the School of the Americas. The rights of sovereign nations were being subordinated to the interests of American businessmen, bankers and affluent investors.

The American people, without public approval or consultation, were being entangled in wars and interventions by a corporate-dominated ruling class for the benefit of that class.

Notes

1.   Walter LaFeber, *The American Age: US Foreign Policy at Home and Abroad, 1750 to the Present* (New York: W. W. Norton, 1994), p. 48; V. G. Kiernan, *America: The New Imperialism* (London: Zed Press, 1980), pp. 3–4.

2.   Allan R. Millett and Peter Maslowski, *For the Common Defense: A Military History of the United States of America* (New York: The Free Press, 1994), p. 140.

3.   Quoted in Michael Parenti, *Against Empire* (San Francisco: City Lights Books, 1995), p. 40.

4.   Thomas Jefferson to James Monroe, 24 November 1801, in Andrew A. Libscomb, ed., *The Writings of Thomas Jefferson* (Washington, DC: 1903), vol. 10, p. 296. Cited in LaFeber, *The American Age*, p. 53.

5.   Gordon Martel, ed., *American Foreign Relations Reconsidered 1890–1993* (London: Routledge, 1994), p. 2; John M. Blum et al, *The National Experience: A History of the United States* (Fort Worth, Texas: Harcourt Brace Jovanovich, 1993), p. 464.

6.   Jenny Pearce, *Under the Eagle: US Intervention in Central America and the Caribbean* (London: Latin America Bureau, 1982), p. 9; Paul S. Boyer et al, *The Enduring Vision: A History of the American People* (Lexington, Massachusetts: D. C. Heath, 1993), p. 718.

7.   John L. O'Sullivan, *United States Magazine and Democratic Review*, July-August 1845.

8.   W. E. Woodward, *A New American History* (New York: Garden City Publishing, 1938), p. 687.

9.   Walter Millis, *The Martial Spirit: A Study of Our War with Spain* (Boston: Houghton Mifflin, 1931), p. 182.

10.   George Brown Tindall and David E. Shi, *America: A Narrative History* (New York: W. W. Norton, 1996), p. 989.

11.   Quoted in William Miller, *A New History of the United States* (London: Paladin, 1970), p. 298.

12.   See Blum et al, *The National Experience*, p. 549, citing Brooks Adams, *The New Empire*, (New York/London: Macmillan, 1902).

13.   Noam Chomsky, *The New Military Humanism: Lessons from Kosovo* (London: Pluto Press, 1999), p. 77. See also Miller, *A New History of the United States*, p. 298.

14.   J. William Fulbright, *The Arrogance of Power* (Middlesex: Pelican Books, 1970), p. 18.

15.   *Instances of the Use of United States Armed Forces Abroad 1798–1945*. Presented to a Senate committee in 1962 by Secretary of State Dean Rusk and revised 1975 by the Foreign Affairs Division, Congressional Research Service, Library of Congress (Washington, DC: US Government Printing Office).

16.   Compiled from Pearce, *Under the Eagle*; Howard Zinn, *A People's History of the United States* (New York: Harper Perennial, 1990); *Instances of the Use of United States Armed Forces Abroad 1798–1945*; and other sources.

17.   See Pearce, *Under the Eagle*, p. 19; Holly Sklar, *Washington's War on Nicaragua* (Boston: South End Press, 1988), p. 299.

18.   Eduardo Galeano, *Open Veins of Latin America: Five Centuries of the Pillage*

of a Continent (New York: Monthly Review Press, 1997), p. 107. The first quotation is retranslated from Spanish.

19. See Millett and Maslowski, *For the Common Defense*, p. 653.

20. President Woodrow Wilson, address to Congress, April 1917.

21. W. J. Rorabaugh and Donald T. Critchlow, *America: A Concise History* (Belmont, California: Wadsworth Publishing, 1994), p. 516; Martel, *American Foreign Relations Reconsidered*, p. 40.

22. Ronald Steel in Stanley N. Katz and Stanley I. Kutler, eds., *New Perspectives on the American Past* (Boston: Little, Brown, 1969), vol. 2, p. 496. Reprinted from Ronald Steel, *Pax Americana* (Viking Press, 1967).

23. Ralph Stavins, Richard J. Barnet and Marcus G. Raskin, *Washington Plans an Aggressive War* (New York: Random House, 1971), p. 244.

24. *Policy Planning Study* 23, 24 February 1948. Reprinted in State Department's *Foreign Relations of the United States, 1948*, vol. 1.

25. Dorothy Buckton James, ed., *Outside, Looking In: Critiques of American Policies and Institutions, Left and Right* (New York: Harper and Row, 1972), p. 88, citing a *New York Times* report of 12 February 1950.

26. *Ibid.*, p. 89, citing *New York Times*, 3 August 1953.

27. John Stockwell, *The Praetorian Guard: The US Role in the New World Order* (Boston: South End Press, 1991), pp. 70–74.

28. *Ibid.*, pp. 72–73.

29. America's 1970s role in Angola is detailed in John Stockwell, *In Search of Enemies: A CIA Story* (London: Andre Deutsch, 1978). Stockwell was the head of the CIA's task force in Angola.

30. Reed Brody, *Contra Terror in Nicaragua* (Boston: South End Press, 1985), pp. 22–23.

31. *Ibid.*, p. 7.

32. Teofilo Cabestrero, *Ministers of God, Ministers of the People: Testimonies of Faith from Nicaragua* (Maryknoll, New York: Orbis Books/London: Zed Press, 1984), p. 17.

33. "USA: School for Dictators under Fire", *Latinamerica Press* (Lima, Peru), 1 September 1994. This publication is an independent and ecumenical weekly, dedicated to the service of the poor of Latin America and the Caribbean.

34. Richard R. Fagen, ed., *Capitalism and the State in US-Latin American Relations* (Stanford, California: Stanford University Press, 1979), p. 152, citing Edwin Lieuwen, *The United States and the Challenge to Security*, pp. 121–22.

35. *Latinamerica Press*, 1 September 1994.

36. Scott Nearing, *The Making of a Radical: A Political Autobiography* (New York: Harper and Row, 1972); Scott Nearing and Joseph Freeman, *Dollar Diplomacy: A Study in American Imperialism* (New York, 1925/reprinted New York: Monthly Review Press, 1966).

37. Butler's comments have been widely quoted since their publication in the 1930s. See Leo Huberman and Paul M. Sweezy, *Cuba: Anatomy of a Revolution* (New York: Monthly Review Press, 1968), p. 16; Sklar, *Washington's War on Nicaragua*, pp. 1–2; Pearce, *Under the Eagle*, p. 20; Jules Archer, *The Plot to Seize the White House* (New York: Hawthorn Books, 1973), pp. 118–19.

38. Frank Niess, *A Hemisphere to Itself: A History of US-Latin American Relations* (London: Zed Books, 1990), pp. 83–84.
39. Frank Polk, 18 July 1917, as quoted in Robert F. Smith, *The United States and Cuba: Business and Diplomacy, 1917–1960* (New Haven, Connecticut: College and University Press, 1960), p. 19.
40. See Archer, *The Plot to Seize the White House*, p. 130.

Chapter 3

The Power Elite

Pluralist Democracy

The framing and implementation of interventionist, pro-corporate US foreign policies is made possible by the country's unique multi-layer system of government. At the heart of this system are open competitive elections through which the electorate fills over a half-million local government and state posts, elects senators and representatives to the nation's bicameral legislature and, every four years, elects a president and vice president. Judged solely on the number of posts filled through the public exercising its voting franchise, the United States is, arguably, the world's most democratic country.

In approving the Declaration of Independence, the Continental Congress affirmed the importance of the public in the political process. Governments, the delegates held, derive "their just powers from the consent of the governed".[1] Alexander Hamilton commented on this principle of democratic government in *Federalist Paper No. 22*. "The fabric of American empire ought to rest on the solid basis of the consent of the people. The streams of national power ought to flow immediately from that pure, original fountain of all legitimate authority," he wrote.

According to the sanguine theorising of advocates of pluralism, widely held to be the model of representative democracy practised in the United States, political influence should be extensively and reasonably uniformly distributed in society among the diverse groups that comprise that society. In a pluralist democracy, the direction of the nation's political agenda should, ideally, be influenced by a plurality of competing organized interest groups from a broad spectrum of society, with no one group controlling or unduly dominating or benefiting from the decision-making process.

In theory, the executive, legislative and judicial branches of the US federal government conduct the nation's domestic and foreign affairs in the name and in the best interests of the broad mass of the American people. These branches may be considered as the board of directors of a giant America Inc., whose stockholders are the American people. Although the nation's poor and rich do not have equal holdings of stocks, theoretically they have equal voting rights and hence equal influence in determining the composition of the board and the direction taken by the board in the domestic and foreign policy-making spheres. Reality, however, can often prove to be very far removed from the ideal and from theory.

Government by Wealth

Many dissenters contend that America's national policy-making power structures are dominated by the nation's wealthy elite, by the corporate sector and by their surrogates, with the political participation of the great majority of the American people being confined to choosing between presidential and congressional candidates drawn from two near-identical parties which have, essentially, little ideological divergence. These candidates, it is claimed, are almost invariably very rich, have close corporate ties or are part-bankrolled by, and owe allegiance to, corporate or superrich elite paymasters. This two-party electoral system, critics argue, is run by just one party: Corporate USA.

The extraordinary degree of political power exercised in the United States by the corporate sector was referred to in the 1870s by Henry Adams, a grandson of President John Quincy Adams, who wrote that there was a widely held view in the country that the time was approaching when corporations "swaying power such as has never in the world's history been trusted in the hands of mere private citizens. . . will ultimately succeed in directing government itself".[2]

The sector's political power and influence was condemned by Rutherford B. Hayes, the nineteenth president of the United States (1877–81), who railed at how the nation's purported democratic model "is a government of the people, by the people and for the people no longer. It is a government of corporations, by corporations, and for corporations."[3]

In 1910, former President Theodore Roosevelt spoke of "a small class of enormously wealthy and economically powerful men whose chief object is to hold and increase their power". The citizens of the United States, he argued, "must effectively control the mighty commercial forces which they have themselves called into being".[4]

Woodrow Wilson, in the course of his first presidential election campaign, was even more outspoken: "The masters of the government of the United States are the combined capitalists and manufacturers of the United States. It is written over every intimate page of the records of Congress, it is written all through the history of conferences at the

White House, that the suggestions of economic policy have come from one source, not from many sources. . . the men really consulted are the men who have the biggest stake – the big bankers, the big manufacturers, the big masters of commerce, the heads of railroad corporations and of steamship corporations. . . The government of the United States at present is a foster child of the special interests."[5]

In 1901, the *Bankers' Magazine* commented that the business sector was "gradually subverting the power of the politician and rendering him subservient to its purposes".[6]

During the mid-1800s, American banks were accused of engaging in behind-the-scenes political manipulation, attempting to place their own nominees in the White House. This allegation resurfaced at Woodrow Wilson's nomination convention in 1912 when William Jennings Bryan, soon to become Wilson's secretary of state, sponsored a resolution that as "proof of our fidelity to the people, we hereby declare ourselves opposed to the nomination of any candidate for President who is the representative of or under obligation to [banker] J. Pierpont Morgan. . . or any other member of the privilege-hunting and favour-seeking class".[7]

In the scenarios outlined by some critics, US democracy is illusory, elections being merely a device to convince Americans that their governments have been chosen by them and represent their interests. A society, as Noam Chomsky has pointed out, "can have the formal trappings of democracy and not be democratic at all. The Soviet Union, for example, had elections." The United States, he argued, comprises "a business-run society. The political parties have reflected business interests for a long time."[8]

According to former US Attorney General Ramsey Clark, "the United States is not a democracy. It is a plutocracy. It is government by wealth."[9] William Allen White, a doyen of American editors, wrote of his dismay on discovering "the whole system of American politics wherein wealth controlled government".[10]

In his monumental three-volume *Elites in American History*, Philip H. Burch, Jr, a professor of political science, meticulously examined the class ties – in terms of socio-economic background and affiliations – of the country's most powerful political figures, holding that such an analysis "should reveal much about the nature and locus of power in a society". His findings were illuminating. He found that in the pre-Civil War period 1789–1861 a total of 95.8 per cent of all major cabinet and diplomatic posts were filled by appointees drawn from elite classes. For the period 1861–1933 the figure was 83.5 per cent and 64.4 per cent for the period 1933–1980.[11]

Such semi-monopolization of the most powerful cabinet and diplomatic posts by an elite class is, among the world's long-established democracies, unique to the United States, giving a tiny segment of American society virtual control over the affairs of the country and over the lives of all Americans and also over the lives of most of the world's peoples.

Such domination of political offices and power exists in the United States, made possible by the appointive nature of almost all the most powerful political offices and by an American mindset which endorses, almost exclusively, the practice of a two-party contest for the top elective political offices.

Funding Congressional Candidates

Money is a major factor in the process of rule by an elite class. It is generally synonymous with influence and power in all sectors of national politics in the United States. In congressional politics, money serves as a lubricant for gaining access to members of both houses and usually as a determinant of who gets elected and what transpires after their election.

The road to Congress is an expensive one. In the 1994 elections, Michael Huffington spent over $27 million of his oil fortune in pursuit of a Senate seat for California, yet lost. Six years later, investment banker Jon Corzine, former co-chairman of Goldman Sachs, spent double that amount to win a Senate seat for New Jersey. Gubernatorial and mayoral elections are also expensive affairs. In 2001, billionaire businessman Michael Bloomberg expended over $50 million in his successful bid for the office of mayor of New York.

Candidature for the House and Senate (the latter often called the Millionaires' Club) can, realistically, only be considered by those with immense personal fortunes and those having the patronage of individuals and forces of great wealth. Congressional seats have gone beyond the grasp of ordinary citizens. Although money cannot guarantee electoral success, nevertheless it is obvious that well-funded candidates enjoy a huge advantage over those with significantly smaller financial resources. For office-seekers to maximize their electoral prospects, they must maximize their funding, leaving candidates increasingly dependent on cash-rich donors, particularly the corporate sector, the largest contributor to congressional candidates' election campaigns.

The most controversial conduit for corporate contributions is Political Action Committees. PACs are special-interest groups, formed to funnel money into political campaigns. They have been established by individual corporations, labour unions, professional associations, business trade associations, farming organizations, civil rights bodies, women's organizations and a host of other disparate bodies. Their objective is to use campaign contributions to sway election results, to "buy" access to Congress and thereby to influence public policy.

PAC contributions have an enormous impact on campaign funding for the Senate and House. In 1986, 194 of the 435 representatives received 50 per cent or more of their campaign funds from PACs.[12] By mid-1997, there were 3,875 PACs, of which 1,720 (or 44 per cent) were corporate linked. PAC contributions to the 1998 congressional election campaigns totalled over $200 million.[13]

Corporate USA is, by far, the largest contributor of funds to candidates seeking Senate and House seats. Its contributions are not limited to PAC expenditure. Often channelled surreptitiously through an army of lobbyists, corporate executives and foundations, corporate munificence to candidates has also included "slush funds", soft loans, manning campaign offices, payments for attending or speaking at functions, insider stock market information and gifts of corporation stocks, all-expenses paid trips and holidays, employment for family members and directorships or employment after retirement from political office, often as high-rent lobbyists. In the nation's capital, registered lobbyists, most of them representing business interests, outnumber the 535 legislators in the houses of Congress by over twenty to one. At the start of the new millennium there were around 14,000 lobbyists.[14] A lobbyist, American humourist Will Rogers remarked, "is a person that is supposed to help a Politician to make up his mind, not only help him but pay him".[15]

In return for the corporate bounteousness, the lawmakers indulge the self-serving interests of their paymasters, shaping corporate-friendly tax codes and loopholes, defending corporate tax cheats and polluters, diluting labour legislation and remaining mute in the face of corporate wrongdoing. Financial gain can be a persuasive quencher of moral qualms.

Theoretically, the ever-present threat of being ousted from office by an electorate with the power to make or to break their political careers should ensure that members of both houses have what James Madison, the "Father of the Constitution", termed "an immediate dependence on, and an intimate sympathy with, the people"[16], obliging them to take cognizance of, and be responsive to, the wishes and needs of their constituents. In practice, large segments of the electorate have little or no influence on, or access to, their elected senators and representatives. In this category are the poor, the homeless and the unemployed – people who lack organization, cohesion and money.

Generally, corporate PAC money is paid to incumbents rather than to challengers. This selective patronage is induced by a pragmatic consideration – over 90 per cent of incumbents are usually re-elected. The incumbents that benefit most from corporate PAC funding are those sitting on congressional committees whose decisions impact most on corporate profitability, such as members of the tax-writing Senate Finance Committee and the House Ways and Means Committee.

A Den of Corruption

Addressing the Senate in April 1967, long-serving Sen. Russell Long (D-Louisiana), who served as chairman of the Senate Finance Committee, spoke at length on the manipulative influence within Congress of financial contributions from the business sector. "Most campaign money comes from businessmen. . . It would be my guess that about 95 per cent of campaign funds at the congressional level are derived from businessmen," he stated. "Merely by assiduously tending to the problems of business interests located in one's own state, a legislator can generally assure himself of enough financial support to campaign effectively for re-election."

Business funding, he argued, was highly selective. "A great number of businessmen contribute to legislators who have voted for laws to reduce the power of labor unions, to regulate unions, to outlaw the union shop. Many businessmen contribute to legislators who have voted to exempt their businesses from the minimum wage. Businessmen contribute to legislators who have fought against taxes that would have been burdensome to their businesses. . . Bankers, insurance company executives, big moneylenders generally contribute to legislators who vote for policies that lead to high interest rates. Many large companies benefit from research and development contracts which carry a guaranteed profit. . . Executives of such companies contribute to those who help them get the contracts. . . Executives of regulated companies contribute to legislators who vote to go easy on the regulation, and ask no more questions than necessary about their rates."[17] The distinction between large corporate contributions and bribes is usually tissue thin.

The transformation of financial muscle into political power and influence is a long-standing phenomenon in the United States. Matthew Josephson's book *The Robber Barons* recorded how during the late 1800s, the heyday of banker J. P. Morgan and oil monopolist John D. Rockefeller, the "halls of legislation were transformed into a mart where the price of votes was haggled over and laws, made to order, were bought and sold".[18] Congress had become a festering den of corruption.

In 1892, social reformer Ignatius Donnelly (a founder of the Populist party, probably the largest people's political movement in the history of the United States) wrote of how "Corruption dominates the ballot box, the legislatures, the Congress and even touches the ermine of the bench. . . The fruits of the toil of millions are boldly stolen to build up colossal fortunes of the few."[19]

For many legislators, their aides and friends, political corruption is an extremely profitable enterprise. In 1955, Robert Gene (Bobby) Baker became secretary to the Senate majority leader. Eight years later his net personal wealth had soared from around $11,000 to an estimated $2 million-plus.[20] In 1879, Nelson W. Aldrich became a congressman. After thirty-two years in the two houses of Congress, his wealth had risen from, perhaps, $50,000 to an estimated $12 to $30 million.[21]

Congressional politics has become a money-procuring racket, the votes of many senators and representatives being a saleable commodity. Financial contributions to money-hungry legislators can surmount legislative obstacles. If a donation can buy a degree of influence, then it follows that large donations can buy a lot of influence and a lot of votes. Big favours demand big contributions. Thus, the community of wealth, most notably the corporate sector, can usually prevail, time after time, to initiate or block legislative proposals and thereby protect their vested interests. America's political system is overwhelmingly compromised in favour of vested interests because vested interests fund the system. Power and influence belong to those who can buy it.

Corporate money is dislodging the electorate's votes as the determinant of what transpires on Capitol Hill. With so many corporate servitors in both houses of Congress, corporate contributions are equivalent to almost risk-free financial investments. The Senate and House of Representatives have become virtual subsidiaries of Corporate USA.

America's political model is no longer a paragon of democracy – defined by Abraham Lincoln in his Gettysburg Address as "government of the people, by the people, for the people".

Corporate USA and the Presidency

The alliance of big business with politicians has poisoned the body politic at all levels. The corporate sector's corrupting influence has even reached into the very nucleus of American political power, the White House.

Post-Watergate investigations into corporate contributions to President Nixon's 1972 re-election campaign unearthed evidence of extensive graft and malpractice.[22] What was startling about many contributions were the precautions taken to "launder" them to conceal the identities of corporate donors. Among these were American Airlines, Ashland Oil, Braniff Airways, Goodyear Tire and Rubber Company, Gulf Oil, Minnesota Mining and Manufacturing and Phillips Petroleum. Contributions from individual businessmen included $2 million from insurance magnate W. Clement Stone. Gulf Oil vice president Claude C. Wild explained that his firm had contributed $100,000, fearing that it might otherwise "end up on a blacklist or bottom of the totem pole".[23]

For some donors their contributions, made in expectation of a quid pro quo, proved to be gilt-edged investments. In December 1970, a section of the dairy industry pledged $2 million to Nixon's re-election campaign. Shortly afterwards government dairy subsidies were unexpectedly increased.

William A. Powell, president of Mid-America Dairy, explained the rationale behind the industry's political contributions: "I have become increasingly aware that the sincere and soft voice of the dairy farmer is no match for the jingle of hard currencies put in the campaign funds of the politicians by the vegetable fat interests, labor, oil, steel, airlines and others. We dairymen as a body can be a dominant group. On March 23, 1971, along with nine other dairy farmers, I sat in the Cabinet room of the White House, across the table from the President of the United States. . . Two days later an order came from the US Department of Agriculture increasing the support price of milk to 85 per cent of parity, which added from $500 to $700 million to dairy farmers' milk checks. . .Whether we like it or not, this is the way the system works."[24]

In 1971, the anti-trust division of Nixon's Justice Department dropped its opposition to a giant merger, the takeover of the Hartford Fire Insurance Company by the International Telephone and Telegraph Corporation, shortly after ITT had secretly pledged $400,000 towards the cost of the Republican national convention.[25]

Thirty years later, political donations again became headline news. In January 2001, shortly before leaving the White House, President Clinton unconditionally pardoned billionaire fugitive financier Marc Rich, who had fled abroad in 1983 while facing charges of massive tax fraud and racketeering. The pardon was secured after Rich's ex-wife contributed heavily to the Democratic party, to Bill Clinton's presidential library and to Hillary Clinton's Senate race.

Like the legislative branch, corporate finance not only buys influence within the executive branch but also is a determinant of the viability of presidential candidates. In October 1999, over a year before the November 2000 presidential election and before any primaries were held, Republican contender Elizabeth Dole withdrew from the campaign, having failed to acquire an adequate level of funding from the corporate sector. Corporate finance had become the de facto primary process. The winner of the race for the White House was George W. Bush, whose entire political career owed its success to corporate funding and his family's fortune, earned from Texas oil.

In his 1996 book *The Buying of the President*, Charles Lewis of the Center for Public Integrity commented on the key role played by the corporate sector in the choice of presidential candidates. "Before the first vote is cast in a presidential primary, a private referendum has already been conducted among the nation's financial elites as to which candidate shall earn his party's nomination," he wrote.[26] In *The Buying of the President 2000*, he returned to the same theme. "The dirty secret of American presidential politics is that the nation's wealthiest interests largely determine who will be the next President of the United States in the year *before* the election. As political fund-raising consultant Stan Huckaby has noted, without exception, in every election since 1976, the candidate who has raised the most money by the end of the year preceding the election, and who has been eligible for federal matching funds, has become his party's nominee for President."[27]

Redistributing Wealth – Upwards

In most democratic societies, there is a commitment to social justice. This requires prioritizing the needs of those at the very bottom of the social ladder, including levying taxes on the principle of ability to pay. In the United States, as a rule, taxes favour those already holding the lion's share of the nation's wealth, notably the giant corporations and superaffluent elite classes. Taxes paid by the less well off subsidize the lavish lifestyles of the rich. The tax burden is transferred from wealthy individuals to the less affluent and from giant corporations to smaller business enterprises.

Time magazine commented on this phenomenon in April 1994: "Corporations and the very rich have seen their taxes decline about a third in the past few decades, while the middle class now pays 329% more than it did 20 years ago. The result is a quiet, ongoing upward redistribution of wealth."[28]

Arthur M. Schlesinger, Jr, special assistant to President Kennedy, wrote of how the president "was outraged to discover that an oil man reputed to be among the richest living Americans had in certain years paid income taxes of less than $1000; that, of the nineteen Americans with incomes of more than $5 million a year, more than twenty-five per cent had paid no income tax at all in 1959".[29] The corporate sector has been similarly fortunate, benefiting financially on a huge scale from a raft of tax privileges, tax loopholes, subsidies and other measures.

The upward redistribution of wealth represents a transfer of public wealth to corporations and the superwealthy. When new tax proposals are framed by Washington administrations, it is the richest, the very people who least need tax windfalls, who benefit most. An "economic stimulus" package proposed by President George W. Bush was designed to feed tens of billions of taxpayers' dollars to Corporate USA elites, including oil sector intimates of the president and Vice President Cheney, while being of little help to those struggling to make ends meet.

Campaigns seeking equitable reform of the nation's tax system have generally been ignored by the ruling elite. Lacking financial, media and political muscle, numerical strength, cohesiveness and persistence, most campaigns quickly peter out.

The upward redistribution of wealth is just one manifestation of rule by an elite class in the United States.

Monopolizing Power

The implementation of policies that benefit Corporate USA and America's superrich is made possible by the corruption of the legislative branch of the federal government, the dependence of presidential candidates on corporate funding and, especially, the monopolization or semi-monopolization of the most important cabinet and sub-cabinet posts by corporate-linked figures.

The president of the United States, the most powerful individual in the world, is the nation's chief executive, presiding over the executive branch of government. The branch includes thirteen or more departments run by members of the president's cabinet, the foremost policy-makers within the federal government. However, the president is the only officer of the government directly elected by the people, the vice president merely riding into office on the president's coat-tails, while the secretaries in charge of each of the departments are appointed by the president with the consent of the Senate.

The appointive/non-elective nature of key offices within the executive branch has profound implications for the formulation and conduct of US domestic and foreign policies. Not having to seek a mandate from the electorate, these executive members are not directly dependent on the public for their accession to political office and hence are not compelled, to any great degree, by electoral considerations to be sensitive to the wishes and needs of the people.

What is extraordinary about executive branch appointees is the number recruited from the corporate sector.[30] During the period 1947 to late 1979, there were eleven secretaries of the treasury and sixteen secretaries of commerce. Twenty-six of these twenty-seven cabinet-level appointees had served as a chairman, president, vice president, director, partner or senior official in the corporate sector prior to their cabinet appointments. The only one with no overt close ties to the corporate community was Henry Fowler, treasury secretary 1965–69. Such is the impact of policies formulated by holders of these two offices on the corporate sector that the appointment to these posts of figures drawn on loan from big business might be construed as allowing the corporate sector to regulate itself.

Corporate figures have also dominated the chairmanship of the Federal Reserve System, which is responsible for setting the nation's monetary and credit policies. The most recent appointees were Paul A. Volcker, chairman of the Fed from 1979–87, who was a Chase Manhattan Bank alumnus, and his successor in the Fed, Alan Greenspan, president of Townsend-Greenspan Inc., an economic consultancy firm.

Corporate semi-monopolization of the posts of secretary of the treasury, secretary of commerce and chairman of the Federal Reserve System enables corporate-linked appointees to virtually control the national economy. This control is a mainspring of the sector's continuing success and prosperity. Corporate figures also semi-monopolize the key foreign policy posts – those of the secretary of state, secretary of defense, national security adviser and director of the CIA.

In the post-war period 1947 to late 1979, there were fourteen secretaries of defense: James V. Forrestal (1947–49), a senior official in investment bankers Dillon Read and Co.; Louis Johnson (1949–50), a bank director; George Marshall (1950–51), a board member of Pan-American World Airways; Robert A. Lovett (1951–53), a partner in investment bankers Brown Brothers Harriman; Charles E. Wilson (1953–57), president of General Motors; Neil McElroy (1957–59), president of Procter and Gamble; Thomas S. Gates (1959–61), a partner in investment bank Drexel and Co.; Robert McNamara (1961–68), president of the Ford Motor Co.; Clark Clifford (1968–69), a director of the National Bank of Washington; Melvin Laird (1969–73); Elliot Richardson (1973), a director of the New England Trust Co.; James R. Schlesinger (1973–75), a former director of the CIA; Donald Rumsfeld (1975–77), an investment bank official; and Harold Brown (1977–81), a director of IBM and the Times-Mirror Co.[31]

Of the fourteen appointees, only Laird and Schlesinger had no overt close ties to the corporate sector, although Schlesinger had served as a senior staff member in the Rand Corporation, a research organization of America's power elite whose board of trustees is dominated by corporate executives.

In his book *The Roots of American Foreign Policy: An Analysis of Power and Purpose*, historian Gabriel Kolko analysed the backgrounds of the most powerful of America's foreign policy decision-makers within the State, Defense (or War), Treasury and Commerce Departments and within relevant executive-level agencies. He found that "men who came from big business, investment and law held 59.6 percent of the posts" from 1944 through 1960. The net result of the study, he wrote, "revealed that foreign policy decision-makers are in reality a highly mobile sector of the American corporate structure. . . The very top foreign policy decision-makers were. . . intimately connected with dominant business circles and their law firms."[32]

Richard J. Barnet, formerly a State Department official and an adviser to the Department of Defense, has written about the appointment of national security managers who, he noted, "have been primarily recruited from the world of big business and high finance." Looking at the holders of the top positions – the secretaries and under secretaries of state and defense, the secretaries of the three services (army, air force and navy), the chairman of the Atomic Energy

Commission and the director of the CIA – Barnet found that "of ninety-one individuals who held these offices during the period 1940 to 1967, seventy of them came from major corporations and investment houses. This includes eight out of ten secretaries of Defense, seven out of eight secretaries of the Air Force, every secretary of the Navy, eight out of nine secretaries of the Army, every deputy secretary of Defense, three out of five directors of the CIA, and three out of five chairmen of the Atomic Energy Commission."[33] Such semi-monopolization of power constitutes rule by a corporate elite.

The Rise of Corporate Power

In a letter written shortly before his death, President Lincoln expressed his unease at the growing power and influence of the corporate sector, warning of "a crisis approaching that unnerves me and causes me to tremble for the safety of my country. . . Corporations have been enthroned and an era of corruption in high places will follow, and the money power of the country will endeavor to prolong its reign by working upon the prejudices of the people until all wealth is aggregated in a few hands, and the Republic is destroyed. I feel at this moment more anxiety for the safety of my country than ever before even in the midst of war."[34]

The "money power" of the post-Civil War elite was demonstrated in 1895 when President Cleveland, facing a potentially disastrous drain of gold from the US treasury, was forced to accede to the terms demanded by banker J. P. Morgan and his associates for a bailout. It was a humiliating experience for the president and for many Americans – the world's leading industrial nation being saved from bankruptcy by private bankers intent on profiting handsomely from the transaction. Some regarded the bankers' role as treasonable and their profits as unconscionable. Later, President Theodore Roosevelt issued his famous denunciation of ultra-rich monopolists such as Morgan and oil tycoon John D. Rockefeller as "malefactors of great wealth".[35]

By early in the twentieth century, a small oligarchy headed by bankers J. P. Morgan and George F. Baker and by James Stillman of the Rockefeller-linked National City Bank of New York had acquired control over a vast portion of the nation's wealth. A US Congress House Committee on Banking and Currency, set up to investigate "the concentration of money and credit" in the United States, noted the economic power of the three bankers and their close associates. A key finding of the committee was later summarized by Thomas Cochran and William Miller in their book *The Age of Enterprise: A Social History of Industrial America*. These three bankers and their financial associates, Cochrane and Miller wrote, "occupied 341 directorships in 112 great corporations. The total resources of these corporations in 1912 was

$22,245,000,000, more than the assessed value of all property in the twenty-two states and territories west of the Mississippi River, more than twice the assessed value of all property in the thirteen southern states."[36]

The concentration of these huge resources in the hands of corporate leviathans gave them influence within both the executive and legislative branches of government. Cabinet appointees recruited from the upper echelons of the financial and non-financial corporate sectors came to dominate the country's executive policy-making hierarchy. Even the judiciary, the third cornerstone of the American political model, was also dominated by corporate-linked figures. Many of the appointees to the Supreme Court, America's highest court and composed normally of nine unelected justices with life tenure, were drawn from men and women associated with corporate interests

The consequential pro-corporate bias of the judicial branch is a very important consideration in understanding the nature of elite rule. This bias was alluded to by Eugene V. Debs in 1918. "Who appoints our federal judges? The people?" he asked rhetorically. "In all the history of the country, the working class have never named a federal judge. There are 121 of these judges and every solitary one holds his position, his tenure, through the influence and power of corporate capital. The corporations and trusts dictate their appointment. And when they go to the bench, they go not to serve the people but to serve the interests that place them and keep them where they are. Why, the other day, by a vote of five to four. . . they declared the child labor law unconstitutional – a law secured after twenty years of education and agitation on the part of all kinds of people. And yet, by a majority of one, the Supreme Court, a body of corporation lawyers, with just one exception, wiped that law from the statute books, and this in our so-called democracy, so that we may continue to grind the flesh and blood and bones of puny little children into profits for the Junkers of Wall Street. And this in a country that boasts of fighting to make the world safe for democracy. The history of this country is being written in the blood of the childhood the industrial lords have murdered."[37]

The monopolization or semi-monopolization, by a tiny corporate-linked class, of key offices within the executive and judicial branches of the federal government and the corporate sector's corruption of the legislative branch amounts to a form of tyranny in which the affairs of the United States are conducted in the interests of Corporate USA and superrich American elites.

Notes

1.   Declaration of Independence, 4 July 1776.

2.   John A. Garraty, *The American Nation: A History of the United States* (New York: HarperCollins, 1995), p. 506.

3.   Harvey Wasserman, *America Born and Reborn* (New York: Collier Books, 1983), p. 291. See also Charles Derber, *Corporation Nation* (New York: St Martin's Griffin, 2000), p. 17.

4.   Robert E. Sherwood, *Roosevelt and Hopkins* (New York: Bantam Books, 1950), vol. 1, p. 50.

5.   Woodrow Wilson, *The New Freedom* (New York: Doubleday, 1913), pp. 57–58.

6.   William Miller, *A New History of the United States* (London: Paladin, 1970), p. 259; Howard Zinn, *A People's History of the United States* (New York: Harper Perennial, 1990), p. 342.

7.   Edith Gittings Reid, *Woodrow Wilson: The Caricature, the Myth and the Man* (New York: Oxford University Press, 1934), p. 130; Jean Strouse, *Morgan: American Financier* (London: Harvill Press, 1999), p. 664.

8.   Noam Chomsky, interviewed by David Barsamian, *Secrets, Lies and Democracy* (Tucson, Arizona: Odonian Press, 1995), p. 7.

9.   Interview, *Granma International* (Cuba), 15 February 1995.

10. William Allen White, *The Autobiography of William Allen White* (New York: Macmillan, 1946), p. 440.

11. Philip H. Burch, Jr, *Elites in American History* (New York: Holmes and Meier, 1980), vol. 3, pp. 2, 383.

12. Jeffrey M. Berry, *The Interest Group Society* (New York: HarperCollins, 1989), p. 122.

13. Philip John Davies, *US elections today* (Manchester: Manchester University Press, 1999), pp. 118–19.

14. Charles Lewis and the Center for Public Integrity, *The Buying of the President 2000* (New York: Avon Books, 2000), p. 5.

15. Jay M. Shafritz, *The HarperCollins Dictionary of American Government and Politics* (New York: Harper Perennial, 1993), Concise Edition, p. 279.

16. James Madison, *Federalist Paper No. 52*.

17. *Congressional Record*, 4 April 1967, pp. S4582–83. See Ferdinand Lundberg, *The Rich and the Super-Rich* (Secaucus, New Jersey: Lyle Stuart, 1988), pp 717–18; Morton Mintz and Jerry S. Cohen, *America, Inc.: Who Owns and Operates the United States* (New York: Dial Press, 1971), pp. 184–85.

18. Quoted in David C. Korten, *When Corporations Rule the World* (West Hartford, Connecticut: Kumarian Press/San Francisco: Berrett-Koehler, 1996), p. 58.

19. Harold Evans, *The American Century* (London: Jonathan Cape/Pimlico, 1998), p. 29.

20. Robert N. Winter-Berger, *The Washington Pay-Off* (New York: Dell, 1972), p. 54; Phyllis Schlafly, *A Choice Not an Echo* (Alton, Illinois: Pere Marquette Press, 1964), pp. 18–19.

21. Nelson W. Aldrich, Jr, *Old Money: The Mythology of Wealth in America* (New York: Allworth Press, 1996), p. 8; Peter Collier and David Horowitz, *The Rockefellers: An American Dynasty* (New York: Signet, 1977), p. 91; Ferdinand Lundberg, *America's 60 Families* (New York: Halcyon House, 1939), p. 61.

22. Useful sources of information on the post-Watergate political funding investigations and scandals include David Vogel, *Fluctuating Fortunes: The Political Power of Business in America* (New York: Basic Books, 1989), pp. 115–20; Ovid Demaris, *Dirty Business: The Corporate-Political Money-Power Game* (New York: Avon Books, 1975), pp. 375–432; Richard J. Barnet and Ronald E. Müller, *Global Reach: The Power of the Multinational Corporations* (New York: Simon & Schuster, 1974), pp. 248–50.

23. See Demaris, *Dirty Business*, p. 431; Barnet and Müller, *Global Reach*, p. 439, citing *Newsweek*, 26 November 1973.

24. See Demaris, *Dirty Business*, p. 416.

25. ITT's takeover is detailed in Anthony Sampson, *The Sovereign State: The Secret History of ITT* (Kent, UK: Coronet, 1985); Demaris, *Dirty Business*, p. 58–79.

26. Quoted in Lewis, *The Buying of the President 2000*, p. 3.

27. *Ibid.*, p. 3.

28. Barbara Ehrenreich, 'Helping America's Rich Stay that Way', *Time*, 18 April 1994.

29. Arthur M. Schlesinger, Jr, *A Thousand Days: John F. Kennedy in the White House* (London: Mayflower-Dell, 1967), p. 768.

30. Among the best sources of information on the corporate ties of cabinet members is Philip H. Burch, Jr's three-volume *Elites in American History*. See also Edward S. Greenberg, *The American Political System: A Radical Approach* (Glenview, Illinois: Scott, Foresman, 1989), pp. 146–48.

31. See Burch, *Elites in American History*, vol. 3.

32. Gabriel Kolko, *The Roots of American Foreign Policy: An Analysis of Power and Purpose* (Boston: Beacon Press, 1969), pp. 16–19.

33. Richard J. Barnet in Dorothy Buckton James, ed., *Outside, Looking In: Critiques of American Policies and Institutions, Left and Right* (New York: Harper and Row, 1972), p. 316.

34. Letter from President Lincoln to William Elkin, 21 November 1864, as quoted by Gurudas, *Treason: The New World Order* (San Rafael, California: Cassandra Press, 1996), p. 263. See also Korten, *When Corporations Rule the World*, p. 58; Kevin Danaher, *10 Reasons to Abolish the IMF and World Bank* (New York: Seven Stories Press, 2001), p. 42.

35. This 1907 denunciation has been widely quoted. See Ron Chernow, *The Death of the Banker* (London: Pimlico, 1997), p. 102; George Donelson Moss, *The Rise of Modern America: A History of the American People, 1890–1945* (Englewood Cliffs, New Jersey: Prentice Hall, 1995), p. 77.

36. Thomas Cochran and William Miller, *The Age of Enterprise* (New York: Macmillan, 1942/revised edition, New York: Harper Torchbooks, 1961), p. 194.

37. Speech at Canton, Ohio, 16 June 1918.

Chapter 4

The Rockefeller Connection

America's Plutocratic Circle

The question of who really rules America was analysed in Ferdinand Lundberg's best-selling 1937 book *America's 60 Families*. Its findings were summarized in the book's opening lines: "The United States is owned and dominated today by a hierarchy of its sixty richest families, buttressed by no more than ninety families of lesser wealth. Outside this plutocratic circle there are perhaps three hundred and fifty other families. . . These families are the living center of the modern industrial oligarchy which dominates the United States, functioning discreetly under a *de jure* democratic form of government behind which a *de facto* government, absolutist and plutocratic in its lineaments, has gradually taken form since the Civil War. This *de facto* government is actually the government of the United States – informal, invisible, shadowy. It is the government of money in a dollar democracy."[1]

This "modern industrial oligarchy", born around the Civil War period, had consolidated by the early 1900s with the emergence of giant manufacturing companies, railroad monopolies and powerful finance houses. By 1910, over 60 per cent of all American workers were employed by just 5 per cent of the country's manufacturing corporations.[2]

Two figures dominated the country's economic sector: oil monopolist John D. Rockefeller and, especially, investment banker J. Pierpont Morgan, who controlled more economic power in the United States than anyone else. Holding vast sums of investment capital, Morgan could choose which companies and industries to nurture with funding or to starve into submission or even into bankruptcy. Using investment capital as a lever, he demanded places on corporate boards and often the right to direct the corporations' operations. By early in the twentieth century, Morgan, together with two other bankers and their financial associates, occupied 341 directorships in 112 giant corporations, fostering a concentration of economic power in the United States greater than ever existed before. Only Rockefeller, the creator of America's first and most powerful monopoly, came close to matching Morgan's economic power.

The Rockefellers

In 1863, as the Civil War raged, John D. Rockefeller, a trader in farm produce, had invested in his first oil refinery. Soon he controlled the largest oil-refining group in the world, Standard Oil – the progenitor of Exxon/Esso, Chevron and Mobil, three of the world's largest oil companies – and also wielded considerable power and influence in America's political sphere.

His political involvement had an inauspicious start. In 1894, crusading journalist Henry Demarest Lloyd accused Rockefeller of buying the loyalty of politicians in the oil-producing states of Pennsylvania and Ohio.[3] Corroborative evidence was provided by Ida Tarbell, the most prominent female journalist of her time.[4] The revelations helped to unseat a number of the bribe-taking officeholders.

Denounced by political reform campaigner Robert La Follette as the "greatest criminal of the age"[5] and by Eugene V. Debs, who spoke of "Rockefeller's bloodstained dollars",[6] John D. Rockefeller was the most infamous and hated of America's "robber barons". President Theodore Roosevelt publicly denounced Rockefeller and his circle of businessmen. "Every measure for honesty in business that has been passed in the last six years has been opposed by these men," he stated.[7]

An anti-trust suit initiated by Roosevelt, which had Standard Oil as its target, culminated in a 1911 Supreme Court directive ordering the oil giant to divest itself of its constituent parts, thus splitting Standard Oil into over thirty separate companies. However, the divested companies were still owned by the same shareholders who had previously owned Standard Oil stock, headed by Rockefeller who held a quarter of the total, probably making him the richest person in the United States.

Two years after the court's ruling, John D. Rockefeller was again in the spotlight. In September 1913, miners in Colorado went on strike at Colorado Fuel and Iron Company (CFI) coal mines. They were rebelling against poverty-level wages; working conditions which caused a spate of deaths (over 300 were killed in local mines in 1910, including 79 miners killed in an explosion in a CFI mine in January 1910); the use of terror tactics to prevent miners uniting under a union banner; and the company's feudal near-total control over the lives of miners and their families.

CFI miners lived in company-owned shacks in towns that operated like corporate fiefdoms, where workers were reduced to a state of serfdom. The towns were patrolled by armed company guards who dictated affairs with impunity, quarantining the towns from outside union influence, suppressing dissent with brutal efficiency and imposing the company's fiat. Spies mingled with the miners, identifying union sympathisers and organizers, who were then fired. John D. Rockefeller had a controlling 40 per cent interest in the company.

Denouncing the strike as an "organized and deliberate war on society", senior Rockefeller aide Frederick Gates argued that the "officers of the Colorado Fuel and Iron Company are standing between the country and chaos, anarchy, proscription and confiscation and in so doing are worthy of the support of every man who loves his country".[8]

As the strike commenced, the CFI hired gunmen, who were immediately deputized by the local sheriffs. On the morning of 20 April 1914, seven months after the commencement of the strike, militiamen attacked an encampment of mining families at Ludlow, Colorado. Machine-gun fire ripped through the tents, which were later torched by the attackers. When the shooting ceased, the bodies of two women and eleven children were found in one tent. A public relations debacle for the Rockefellers, the killings became known internationally as the Ludlow Massacre.

During strikes around the same time at another Rockefeller-linked industrial facility, the Standard Oil refinery at Bayonne, New Jersey, armed guards killed several workers.[9]

By the time of John D. Rockefeller's demise in 1937, control of the family's business interests had already been passed on to his only son, John D., Jr. In turn, the baton was passed on to the latter's five sons – John D. III, Nelson, Laurance, Winthrop and David – who inherited one of the largest family fortunes in history and a vast business empire comprising a vast network of banks, industrial corporations, property and other wealth-generating assets.[10]

Two of the country's largest banks, the Chase and the National City Bank of New York (later Citibank) became known as the "Rockefeller banks". Rockefeller influence in the First National City Bank began with a friendship between the bank's head, James Stillman, with William Rockefeller, a brother of Standard Oil's founder, and was sealed by the marriage of two of Stillman's daughters to two of William's sons. In the 1950s, James Stillman Rockefeller, a grandson of William Rockefeller, became president of the bank. Rockefeller control over the Chase bank was attained through a merger between the family's Equitable Trust and the Chase National Bank in 1930. A succession of Rockefeller nominees filled the top posts in the new bank, including David Rockefeller, who became chairman after the Chase National – called "the mighty bastion of the Rockefeller family" by *Newsweek* magazine[11] – merged in 1955 with the Manhattan Bank to create the Chase Manhattan.

Rockefeller pre-eminence in banking was paralleled by a similar domination of the oil industry. By the mid-1970s, Exxon/Esso (earlier called Standard Oil of New Jersey) had outstripped General Motors to become the world's largest industrial corporation and the greatest corporate profit earner in history. Two other Standard Oil companies, Mobil (Standard Oil of New York) and Chevron (Standard Oil of California), were also among the world's largest corporations.

Rockefellers and Politics

The Rockefellers' financial power was converted into political power. Nelson Rockefeller was particularly successful. His political career began in 1940 with his appointment by President Franklin D. Roosevelt as coordinator of inter-American affairs. In 1944, he became Roosevelt's assistant secretary of state for Latin America. During the Truman presidency, he was appointed chairman of the International Development Advisory Board; during the Eisenhower presidency under secretary for health, education and welfare and, later, special assistant for cold war strategy; and during the Nixon presidency a special adviser to the president, heading a mission to Latin America with the goal of formulating recommendations for a new policy towards the region.

In 1958, Nelson entered elective politics, successfully campaigning for the governorship of New York, a position he held for four consecutive terms (1958–73). Following three unsuccessful bids for the Republican party's nomination for the presidency of the United States, he reached the zenith of his political career in 1974 when selected as vice president of the United States by President Ford. His gubernatorial successes were achieved through the expenditure of, reportedly, over $25 million of family money, an enormous fortune in those years.[12]

Nelson's younger brother, Winthrop, won the gubernatorial election in Arkansas in the 1960s on two consecutive occasions.

Another brother, Laurance, was able to indulge in his enthusiasm for conservation when President Eisenhower appointed him to head the Outdoor Recreation Resources and Review Commission. He continued this work during the Kennedy presidency. President Johnson chose him to head a White House Conference on Natural Beauty and as chairman of a Citizens' Advisory Committee on Recreation and Natural Beauty. President Nixon gave him the chairmanship of the Citizens' Advisory Committee on Environmental Quality.

A fourth brother, John D. III, was less active politically. However, his son John D. (Jay) Rockefeller IV became another of the family's political success stories. In 1961, he was selected by the Kennedy administration to become a member of the advisory council to the Peace Corps. He was twenty-four years old at the time. In 1966, he became an elected member of West Virginia's legislature, subsequently becoming the state's secretary of state (1968–72), its governor (1977–84) and senator in 1984. In 1988, the respected *Almanac of American Politics* wrote of how he had "been mentioned as a possible presidential candidate almost from the time he ran for the House of Delegates in Kanawha County" in West Virginia in the mid-1960s, when he was still in his twenties.[13]

Winthrop W. Aldrich, an uncle of Nelson and his four brothers and a former chairman of the Chase National Bank, was appointed ambassador to Great Britain by President Eisenhower.

Rockefeller in-law Gerard Smith,[14] the first chairman of the Trilateral Commission in North America, served in appointive offices under seven presidents, from Truman to Carter, including as President Eisenhower's assistant secretary of state for policy planning, President Nixon's director of the US Arms Control and Disarmament Agency and chief SALT (strategic arms limitation talks) negotiator and President Carter's ambassador at large for non-proliferation matters.

David Rockefeller could also have served in political office. Shortly after his election as president, Ronald Reagan sought David's assistance in developing an economic programme for Latin America, where the Rockefeller family had made enormous investments, and profits.[15] David was also, it seems, offered the post of treasury secretary by four US presidents – Kennedy, Johnson, Nixon and Carter – and the chairmanship of the Federal Reserve by Carter.[16] In 1965, the *New Yorker* reported that "Several highly placed Republicans have privately indicated that they would be delighted to support him [David Rockefeller] if he should ever indicate an interest in the Presidency."[17]

Despite his aversion to occupying key appointive political offices, David Rockefeller became the family's most accomplished wielder of power and influence in the political sphere. The principal instrumentalities employed in attaining this power and influence were the family's vast wealth and a number of Rockefeller and corporate-funded private organizations, such as the Council on Foreign Relations.

Council on Foreign Relations

The prosperity of Corporate USA and of superrich Americans is contingent on the framing of favourable domestic and foreign policies in Washington. Throughout the early years of the twentieth century, this was accomplished, in one administration after another, by corporate-linked figures who filled key cabinet-level and sub-cabinet posts and also posts in the judiciary and the diplomatic service. However, lacking cohesion and a shared focus, appointees tended to pursue different agendas, which were usually determined by their own interests and those of their individual corporate paymasters.

Such political rivalry between favour-seeking appointees from the corporate sector ensured that within the corridors of political power in Washington, Corporate USA was then an ill-organized conglomeration of competing corporations. These had no institutional structure or satisfactory mechanism for resolving conflicts between corporations, for achieving agreement on corporate-friendly policies and for transferring these policies to Washington's rulers for implementation.

The corporations, ideally, needed a consensus-seeking, policy-planning forum whose members could, with some confidence, aspire to gain control over the levers of political power. Successful aspirants from such a forum could then collaborate in bringing similar pro-corporate and pro-wealth views to bear on the decision-making processes during their periods in political offices, thereby benefiting the corporate sector as a whole, including the sector's wealthy elites. The formation of the Council on Foreign Relations in 1921 created such a body.

The CFR is a New York-based, corporate-dominated organization that has close ties to the Rockefellers. The organization's headquarters is located in a former stately residence of the Pratt family at 58 East 68th Street in New York, which was donated in 1944 to the council. Charles Pratt, the originator of the family's wealth, built up an oil refining business and then sold it to Standard Oil, whose fold he joined, becoming an associate of the company's founder, John D. Rockefeller.

Among the early patrons of the CFR was John D. Rockefeller, Jr, who part-funded the conversion of the Pratt residence into the CFR's HQ. In the 1950s, the family's Rockefeller Foundation donated $500,000 to the organization.[18] By 1953, the CFR's key offices of chairman, president, vice president, secretary, treasurer and executive director were all filled by individuals with ties to Rockefeller interests.[19] For thirty-two consecutive years, from 1953 to 1985, two heads of the Chase bank, John J. McCloy and David Rockefeller, held the office of chairman of the CFR.

According to its own reports, it is an "organization dedicated to improved understanding of American foreign policy and international affairs. . . The Council's membership is composed of men and women with experience in American foreign policy who are leaders in academe, public service, business, and the media. . . The Council takes no institutional position on issues of foreign policy; it is host to many views, advocate of none."[20]

It is a facile description. A discussion forum and by-invitation-only cabal of America's most elite inner circle, CFR members, together with other associated elites, constitute a collective form of supra-government. Regardless of which political party or administration is in power, council members and associated elites play pivotal roles in the construction and implementation of US national policies, particularly the country's foreign policy.

The council's fig-leafed political ambitions became apparent just three years after its formation with the candidature of the organization's first president, John W. Davis, for the presidency of the United States. Running on the Democratic ticket, he was defeated by Republican candidate Calvin Coolidge. The political fortunes of the council soon changed. Many of the nation's foremost political offices became virtual council dominions.

A council report for the year 1949–50 hinted at the growing influence of its members within US administrations. The council's private discussion groups, it stated, were a "training ground for members called upon to serve the government in important positions. Such instances are too numerous to record here."[21] A 1971 CFR report was more forthright about the organization's success in the political sphere: "Over a third of the Council's 1,500 members have been called on by the government during the last twenty years to undertake official responsibilities."[22]

The chairman of the council for seventeen of those twenty years, John J. McCloy – himself an appointee to several political offices, including assistant secretary of war, and an adviser to eight presidents of the United States – commenting on the process employed in the government's selection of defence-related appointees during the Second World War, admitted that "Whenever we needed a man, we thumbed through the roll of Council members and put through a call to New York," to the council's headquarters.[23]

The importance of the council as a reservoir of future high-level political leaders has been commented on by journalist Joseph Kraft, himself a CFR member. The CFR, Kraft posited, "comes close to being an organ of what C. Wright Mills has called the Power Elite – a group of men, similar in interest and outlook, shaping events from invulnerable positions behind the scenes", adding that the council "has been the seat of. . . basic government decisions, has set the context for many more and has repeatedly served as a recruiting ground for ranking officials".[24] CFR member and former State Department official Richard Barnet wrote that council membership could be considered "a rite of passage for an aspiring national security manager".[25]

In his book *The Making of the President 1964*, Theodore H. White referred to the political success of CFR members. The council, he wrote, "has for a generation, under Republican and Democratic administrations alike, been the chief recruiting ground for Cabinet-level officials in Washington. Among the first eighty-two names on a list prepared for John F. Kennedy for staffing his State Department, at least sixty-three were members of the Council" – an astonishing 77 per cent.[26]

The CFR's political influence was referred to by political scientist Lester Milbrath, who wrote that the organization "while not financed by government, works so closely with it that it is difficult to distinguish Council actions stimulated by government from autonomous actions".[27] Kraft dubbed the CFR a "School for Statesmen".[28] *Newsweek* called its leadership the "foreign-policy establishment of the US".[29]

In their 1977 book *Imperial Brain Trust: The Council on Foreign Relations and United States Foreign Policy*, Laurence H. Shoup and William Minter examined the role of American elites in one sector of government – foreign affairs. They found that 57 per cent of the "top foreign policy officials" in the Johnson administration were members of the CFR. The figure for the Kennedy administration was 51 per cent, 40 per cent for the Eisenhower administration and 42 per cent for the Truman administration.[30] Such statistics signify a semi-monopolization of control over the nation's foreign affairs by people associated with just one private organization, the corporate-dominated CFR.

The Business Advisory Council and the Committee for Economic Development

On its own the CFR could not fulfil the wide-ranging political ambitions of Corporate USA, since its narrow-focused agenda was largely restricted to American foreign policy and international affairs. Other consensus-seeking corporate planning forums were needed, capable of formulating economic policies and providing political leaders from their membership rosters to oversee the implementation of the policies in government.

In 1933, a Business Advisory Council (later called the Business Council) was formed. Dominated by the country's leading industrialists and bankers, it functioned in an advisory capacity to the Department of Commerce. This gave its members unique access to top policy-makers, a privilege not granted to other sectors of society and of the economy.

During the Second World War, Corporate USA formed another organization, the Committee for Economic Development (CED) to draft proposals for the post-war world order. Of 150 CED trustees during its first fifteen years, "38 served in government posts in both Republican and Democratic administrations",[31] political sociologist G. William Domhoff observed. In the Business Council, "as of 1963 some 86 of 175 members had worked in the government on a fulltime basis".[32]

The Bilderberg Group

In 1954 another corporate-dominated, consensus-seeking body, the Bilderberg Group, was formed. Like the CFR, it also has ties to the

Rockefellers. Among the attendees at its inaugural meeting in May 1954 was David Rockefeller, who became a member of the organization's steering committee. Between 1955 and 1957, Dean Rusk was co-chairman of Bilderberg's American branch, at a time that he was also president of the Rockefeller Foundation.

Unlike the all-American CFR, CED and Business Council, the Bilderberg Group drew its members (called "alumni" or Bilderbergers) from the United States, Canada and western Europe. At its meetings – attended by corporate leaders, politicians, academics, military figures, news media chiefs and corporate-linked lawyers – no resolutions are proposed and no votes are taken. According to the group, it is "an international forum in which different viewpoints can be expressed and mutual understanding enhanced".[33]

Attendees are handpicked by the group's steering committee, which also determines the meetings' agendas. Since committee members are either corporate leaders or pro-corporate in their orientation, this enables the committee to ensure that like-minded individuals are invited to discuss the meetings' pre-set topics, which particularly reflect the interests and priorities of the corporate sector.

The meetings provide representatives of Corporate USA with an opportunity to commune with their European and Canadian counterparts and to achieve a considerable degree of coherence on economic and foreign policy issues. An alliance of North American and European corporations, controlling a vast amount of the world's wealth and resources, has the potential to exercise enormous influence and power throughout the world, provided they can concur on major policy issues.

The influence and power-projecting potential of Bilderberg meetings was outlined in a 1980 book. "Top executives from the world's leading multinational corporations meet with top national political figures. . . to consider jointly the immediate and long-term problems facing the West. . . when Bilderberg participants reach a form of consensus about what is to be done, they have at their disposal powerful transnational and national instruments for bringing about what it is they want to come to pass," it reported.[34]

The Trilateral Commission

In 1973, yet another corporate-dominated organization, the Trilateral Commission, was formed, its members drawn from similar sources as Bilderberg, mainly corporate leaders, politicians, academics, media chiefs and corporate-linked lawyers. The Trilateral Commission, the CFR, the Business Council, the Committee for Economic Development, the Bilderberg Group and other organizations such as the National Association of Manufacturers and the US Chamber of Commerce are part of what may be termed the nation's "business establishment", the most powerful and cohesive interest group in America's political sphere.

The Trilateral Commission, the CFR and the Bilderberg Group may be considered as sister organizations. The three are foreign policy forums, although the commission's and the Bilderberg Group's range of interests also encompasses economic policies and other issues. Their most striking features are their corporate ties, the political success of their members in the United States and elsewhere and the number of members they have in common.

The Trilateral Commission's ties with the CFR and the Bilderberg Group began in 1973 when the commission recruited many of its first members from the two existing foreign policy forums. There have also been close ties between the CFR and Bilderberg. These were so close in the latter's earliest years that they amounted to CFR control over Bilderberg's affairs in the United States. During Bilderberg's first fourteen years, every US participant who served as honorary secretary-general, chairman, co-chairman, advisory committee member and steering committee member was, without exception, also a member of the CFR,[35] prompting speculation that Bilderberg was nothing more than a European-based wing of the CFR.

The three organizations are forums of Corporate USA and associated elites, particularly elites linked to the Rockefellers. The Trilateral Commission's founder was David Rockefeller.[36] During its early existence, the commission was almost a Rockefeller family monopoly. Most of its early members were personally selected and recruited by David, including his nephew John D. Rockefeller IV, governor of West Virginia. Between its formation in 1973 and the end of the century, the commission's North American branch had three chairmen. All had close ties to the Rockefellers. The first chairman was Gerard C. Smith, a Rockefeller in-law. In 1977, David Rockefeller succeeded him as chairman. In turn, he was succeeded in 1991 by Paul A. Volcker, who had served as a trustee of the Rockefeller Foundation and was a former Chase Manhattan Bank executive. The first secretary of the commission's North American branch was George S. Franklin, another Rockefeller in-law, who was executive director of the CFR from 1953 to 1971. In 1991, David Rockefeller became honorary chairman of the commission.

Much of the initial funding for the commission was provided by David Rockefeller himself and by the Ford Foundation. Additional finance was provided by the Rockefeller Foundation, the Rockefeller Brothers Fund and the oil giants Exxon (or Esso) and ARCO, which were offspring of the Rockefeller-founded Standard Oil. Corporate interest in the project was mirrored in the sector's level of financial contributions. Corporate contributors in the commission's early or subsequent years comprised a litany of America's largest corporations, including another Rockefeller-linked oil giant, Mobil, together with the Bechtel Group, Xerox, General Motors, Ford, Coca-Cola, ITT, W. R. Grace, Goldman Sachs, Boeing, BankAmerica, Northrop, the *Washington Post*, United Brands and Cargill. Corporate USA was also a generous financial patron of the CFR and Bilderberg.

The Corporate Connection

The triad of foreign policy forums, together with associated organizations, constitute a policy-planning network tied to the corporate community and to the most influential elements of the upper class. The economic forces represented within the organizations are, for the most part, associated with big business. Within the Trilateral Commission, Professor Stephen Gill wrote in his book *American hegemony and the Trilateral Commission*, the "economic interests represented are predominantly those of internationally mobile forms of capital. . . Firms represented are at the apex of world economic hierarchies and at the vanguard of the transnationalization process." Within a decade of its creation, around two-thirds of the world's 100 largest public companies were represented in the commission's membership.[37]

The elitist nature of the three organizations is evident from their membership lists. In January 2002, the Trilateral Commission's European membership included seven British lords, one German count, one Czech prince, one Belgian count, two Belgian barons and one Belgian viscount. The Bilderberg Group's first chairman was Prince Bernhard of the Netherlands, who was succeeded by Alec Douglas Home, the fourteenth earl of Home. Later, Lord Peter Carrington became its chairman.

Bankers, industrialists, corporate consultants, corporate lawyers and trustees of corporate-linked foundations dominate the CFR. During its first quarter-century, it had fifty-five officers and directors, who held seventy-four corporate directorships.[38] An analysis by political sociologist G. William Domhoff of the council's 1978–79 membership found that twenty-one of the leading twenty-five US banks, sixteen of the top twenty-five insurance companies and 70 per cent of the top 100 industrial corporations had at least one officer or director who was a CFR member.[39]

All the holders of the office of chairman of the CFR's board from the creation of the post in 1946 to the end of the century were bankers. Bankers, and leading industrialists, are also hugely influential figures within the Bilderberg Group.

The most influential of the three Rockefeller-linked foreign policy forums at international level is the Trilateral Commission. Unlike the CFR, whose membership is restricted to "US citizens or permanent residents who have made application to become citizens",[40] David Rockefeller's Trilateral Commission recruited its members from the three major industrialized regions of the world, namely North America (US and Canada), Japan and western Europe.[41]

There is an important facet of the overlapping memberships of the commission, the CFR and the Bilderberg Group. Many members of these three forums have also been members of the Business Roundtable, the Business Council and the Committee for Economic Development (CED), consensus-seeking and policy-planning American business organizations whose membership rosters comprise representatives of the country's largest banks and non-financial corporations.

The Carter Administration and the Trilateral Commission

The CFR and the Trilateral Commission are immensely important bodies. In the entire history of the United States, no private organization has been able to seriously rival the records of the two organizations as incubators of US foreign policy and as informal talent-spotting, training and recruitment centres for America's future most powerful political leaders. Simply stated, both corporate-led bodies originate foreign policy proposals and furnish the political leaders to implement these in government. Both also provide leaders to shape and direct domestic policy.

A useful starting point for analysing the extent of the organizations' politico-economic influence and power is the Carter presidency. The Trilateral Commission has acknowledged that one of its aims is to attain a position of influence in the political realm in the three (hence 'Trilateral') regions where it established branches. An early commission document explained that the organization proposed to "foster understanding and support of Commission recommendations both in governmental and private sectors in the three regions".[42]

However, nowhere in its publications is it stated that it is an objective of the organization to secure political offices for members. The commission's founder bluntly denied such a goal. The commission, David Rockefeller asserted, "does not take positions on issues or endorse individuals for office". (One may query the apparent contradiction between the founder's claim that the commission "does not take positions on issues" and the organization's stated objective of fostering "support of Commission recommendations" within governments.) The filling of so many political offices by Trilateralists, its founder claimed, was "not surprising" since the body's "membership has always consisted of some of our most outstanding citizens".[43]

The political success of commission members in the United States is unparalleled. Between 1977 and the end of the century, three (Carter, George H. Bush and Clinton) of the four presidents of the United

States and two vice presidents (Mondale and Bush) were Trilateralists. Could these successes have been attained with no element of manipulation or behind-the-scenes coordination? A look at Jimmy Carter's accession to the presidency is revealing.[44]

Among the earliest recruits to the Trilateral Commission after its formation in 1973, Jimmy Carter was almost unknown outside Georgia, where he was governor. Public opinion polls conducted in late 1975 to identify potential participants and the likely victor in the following year's race for the White House almost ignored the peanut farmer. A year later, he defeated White House incumbent President Gerald Ford in the election.

How can one explain this rise from national near-obscurity to the most powerful office in the world? Money, much of it obtained from the corporate sector, obviously played a role. Favourable media coverage during the election campaign played an even greater role. The media can make or break political careers. They made Carter's. Most notable in this respect was the support accorded him in the media organs of the "establishment", many of whose leading figures were members of the CFR or the Trilateral Commission. However, probably the most important factor in his success was the support he received from America's most powerful establishmentarian, David Rockefeller, founder of the Trilateral Commission. Political hopefuls nurtured by Rockefeller, within the commission and other forums linked to the family, have had an extraordinary record of success in attaining the nation's highest political offices.

Commenting on the importance of the commission to Carter's candidacy, Gerald Rafshoon, Carter's media adviser since his gubernatorial campaign, told a reporter that the presidential candidate's ties to the commission were "critical to his building support where it counted".[45]

The commission's rise to national prominence was phenomenal. Less than four years after its establishment, one of its members had become president of the United States, and twenty-three appointees recruited by Carter from the commission had *total* control over the country's foreign policy. (See Appendix A.) Carter's personal success was especially astounding – a little-known rank outsider in the presidential race transformed into a viable and ultimately successful candidate for the nation's highest, and the world's most powerful, political office.

Incredibly, Jimmy Carter and his twenty-three appointees (including his vice president, secretary of state and national security adviser) comprised almost 40 per cent of the total American membership of the recently formed commission. In the mid-1970s, it had around sixty-five American members. Other Carter appointees also had ties to the organization. Assistant Secretary of the Treasury C. Fred Bergsten had helped in the commission's formation and subsequently became an executive member. Samuel Huntington, appointed coordinator of security planning at the National Security Council, was a Trilateral Commission analyst. David Rockefeller, reportedly, was offered the posts of treasury secretary and chairman of the Federal Reserve, but declined the offers.[46]

The Reagan, George H. Bush, Clinton and George W. Bush Administrations

In 1980, Carter's bid for re-election was stymied by Ronald Reagan, who was not a Trilateralist. Nevertheless, commission members were chosen to fill many of the principal offices in the new administration, including Vice President George H. Bush. (Lists of senior political appointees recruited by a succession of Washington administrations from the Trilateral Commission, the CFR and other Rockefeller-linked organizations and also directly from Corporate USA are included in Appendix A).

In 1989, when the Reagan era ended, George H. Bush succeeded him as president. Once again numerous Trilateralists were appointed to important posts. He was a member of the Trilateral Commission and a former director of the CFR (1977–79).

The 1992 presidential race between incumbent George H. Bush and challenger Bill Clinton once again demonstrated the commission's capacity for executing statistically astonishing feats. Both presidential contenders were Trilateralists. Regardless of who won the race, the commission would have a member in the White House.

Bill Clinton – who was a member of the Trilateral Commission, the CFR and the Bilderberg Group – won, subsequently filling his two administrations with a plethora of appointees drawn from the three organizations. Altogether, well over sixty members of the three bodies accepted appointments to key posts and dozens of others to less important ones. The appointments gave members of the sister organizations total control over US foreign policy.

In January 2001, Clinton was succeeded by George W. Bush. The new president's most senior appointees were overwhelmingly drawn from the same three organizations and from Corporate USA.

Possibly the wealthiest executive branch in the history of the United States – the president, vice president and over a half of the cabinet appointees were multimillionaires or millionaires – it could reasonably be dubbed the Oil and Monsanto Executive Branch. Four members had close ties to the oil industry and three to Monsanto.

The oil industry had been a patron of George W. Bush throughout his entire political career. In his younger days, following in the footsteps of his father, founder of Zapata Petroleum, he had made a foray into the industry, setting up Arbusto Energy. His ties to the energy sector were reflected in his appointments. His vice president, national security adviser, commerce and army secretaries and numerous other appointees were recruited from the energy sector. (See Appendix A.)

The Bush administration had especially close ties with Enron, the world's largest energy-trading company. Not only had the new president's trade representative and army secretary been employed by the corporation, his most prominent economic adviser, Larry Lindsay, had also been on Enron's payroll. Bush's senior political strategist, Karl Rove, had held Enron stock. US Attorney General John Ashcroft had accepted large donations from Enron and its chairman Kenneth Lay in his campaign for a Senate seat. Enron and Lay, a Trilateral Commissioner, had been George W. Bush's most generous financial patrons during his Texas and presidential election campaigns.

In December 2001, Enron, which had been America's seventh largest corporation, filed for bankruptcy, the biggest in US history. Subsequently, it was revealed that in the preceding years the company had poured dollars into the pockets of those responsible for policing it, including up to 71 per cent of the members of the Senate and 43 per cent of the House of Representatives. According to the Center for Responsive Politics, 70 per cent of the members of the House Commerce Committee had accepted Enron money, as had several members of the Senate Banking Committee, among them Senator Phil Gramm whose wife was an Enron board member.[47]

Enron's largesse was amply rewarded. It was exempted from numerous local and state regulations, given access to the nation's most powerful decision-makers and regulators, and Enron employees and nominees were appointed to key offices. Shortly after the election of George W. Bush as president, Enron's chairman gave a list of suggested nominees for posts in the Federal Energy Regulatory Commission to Bush's personnel director. Subsequently, two of these nominees, Pat Wood and Nora Brownell, were appointed to the commission, Wood becoming its chairman.[48]

Figures linked to Monsanto were similarly fortunate. Defense Secretary Donald Rumsfeld and Secretary of Agriculture Ann Veneman had both been directors of Monsanto companies. Attorney General John Ashcroft had been a beneficiary of Monsanto election campaign funding. In March 2001, President Bush nominated Linda J. Fisher as deputy administrator of the Environmental Protection Agency. She had been vice president of government affairs in Monsanto, arguably the world's master seed engineer of genetically modified foods. Condemned as "Frankenstein Foods" by European consumers, fears about their safety compelled EU governments to oppose their importation and sale.

The control exercised by corporate-linked appointees over America's affairs was so overpowering that the Bush administration had become the most compromised in living memory.

Rockefellerian Elites

The Trilateral Commission and its two sister organizations facilitate this corporate political control and Rockefeller political power and influence. The Rockefellers have other forums which perform a similar function, providing members for service in the highest echelons of government. Of President Carter's appointees, three are particularly noteworthy: Cyrus Vance (secretary of state), W. Michael Blumenthal (secretary of the treasury) and Paul A. Volcker (chairman, Federal Reserve Board). All three were trustees of the Rockefeller Foundation, Vance being its chairman from 1975–77. Volcker had been a senior figure within the Chase Manhattan Bank, a cornerstone of the Rockefellers' business empire. The elevation of three members of a numerically miniscule Rockefeller board of trustees to three of the nation's most powerful posts represented an awesome and statistically inexplicable achievement.

Rockefeller influence was also considerable in other administrations. During the Eisenhower presidency, John Foster Dulles, chairman of the Rockefeller Foundation 1950–52, was secretary of state, usually considered the most powerful foreign policy post after the presidency. After John F. Kennedy replaced Eisenhower in the White House, he appointed Dean Rusk as secretary of state. Rusk was president of the foundation at the time of his appointment. When Lyndon B. Johnson assumed the presidency after the assassination of President Kennedy, he retained Rusk at State.

The next four US presidents were Richard Nixon, Gerald Ford, Jimmy Carter and Ronald Reagan. Rockefeller acolyte Henry Kissinger served as secretary of state under Nixon and Ford. Rockefeller Foundation chairman (1975–77) Cyrus R.Vance was Carter's secretary of state. Chase Manhattan Bank director Alexander Haig took over the reins at State under Reagan. Thus, secretaries of state under seven consecutive presidents had close ties to the Rockefellers. The degree of political power attained by trustees of Rockefeller foundations has never been equalled by figures drawn from any other family-connected foundation.

Established in 1913, the Rockefeller Foundation's professed goal was to "promote the well-being of mankind throughout the world".[49] In pursuing this objective, the foundation claimed, it had "sought to identify, and address at their source, the causes of human suffering and need" and was committed to "a more equitable sharing of the world's resources" and to "building democracy".[50]

Ironically, several foundation trustees, while in high government offices, would be responsible for inflicting horrendous suffering and death on peasant populations and for pursuing policies that exploited the resources of underdeveloped countries, thereby stripping the people of these countries of the means to escape from their impoverished existence.

Another Rockefeller philanthropic foundation also exercised enormous political power and influence in Washington. Prior to John F. Kennedy's inauguration in 1961, a number of reports had been published on foreign and domestic issues by the Rockefeller Brothers Fund. These reports were prepared by six panels in the fund's Special Studies Project, which sought to identify, and to provide viable solutions for, the critical problems facing the United States. Financed by the Rockefellers, the project was chaired by two brothers of David Rockefeller, Nelson and Laurance. The panels' proposals influenced the direction of national policies, especially the future increased militarization of US foreign policy. Many of those responsible for formulating the proposals would, as appointees in subsequent administrations, be in a position to implement them. At least fifteen of the project's panellists, advisers and staff members were appointed by President Kennedy, including his secretary of state and national security adviser.[51] (See Appendix A.)

Several of Kennedy's appointees from the Rockefeller Foundation and the Rockefeller Brothers Fund were also members of the Council on Foreign Relations and/or the Bilderberg Group. In recruiting so many of his appointees from these four bodies, President Kennedy vested near-total control over foreign policy, and over much of domestic policy, in men associated with the Rockefeller family and with Rockefeller-linked bodies. These may be termed "Rockefellerian elites".

The term "Rockefellerian elites" is employed, for the purpose of brevity, to encompass American members of Rockefeller-linked foreign policy forums (particularly the Trilateral Commission, CFR and the Bilderberg Group), trustees, advisers and panel members associated with the Rockefeller Foundation, the Rockefeller Brothers Fund and other family-controlled foundations, and the heads of Rockefeller-dominated corporations such as the Chase Manhattan Bank, who determine the direction of US foreign and domestic policies through serving as president or vice president of the United States, filling the highest appointive offices in the executive branch of government and the most influential sub-cabinet posts and through securing ambassadorial appointments, White House advisory responsibilities and other key appointive positions of political power and influence within Washington's decision-making structures or who fill the highest offices in the world's most powerful international and regional institutions, particularly the United Nations, the World Bank, the International Monetary Fund, the World Trade Organization, GATT and NATO.

Rockefellerian elites also include foreign members of the Rockefeller-linked foreign policy forums, foundations and corporations who attain the highest elective and appointive posts within their nations' governmental structures and within key institutions such as the United Nations and the World Bank.

Building a Consensus

One aspect of the political power wielded in the United States by Rockefellerian and corporate elites is particularly noteworthy. It is that – apart from those who fill the elective offices of president and vice president of the country – the key posts they semi-monopolize are appointive ones, especially the chairmanship of the Federal Reserve Board, the secretaryships of state, the treasury, defense and commerce and other important cabinet and sub-cabinet offices. Overall, this represents a transfer of political and economic power from just two political figures elected by the people to numerous elite appointees having no direct elective mandate from the people and little accountability to the people.

Even during periods when the presidency of the US is not held by a Rockefeller-linked person, the president's top foreign and domestic policy appointees are generally drawn from among members of the three Rockefeller and corporate-dominated foreign policy forums, from Rockefeller foundations or directly from the corporate sector or from among corporate lawyers and lobbyists. These appointees, together with corporate-funded legislators in Congress, help to shape a corporate-friendly and pro-wealth economic climate in the United States and abroad. The ultimate outcome – globalization.

Two of the most important functions of the three sister organizations and of associated corporate bodies are to provide forums where conflicts between corporate-linked elites can be considered and compromised and to talent-spot like-minded figures to implement pro-corporate agendas in government. The goal of these bodies is thus to act as catalysts in the evolution of a consensus among their members, and especially among those fated to fill high political offices, on a multiplicity of issues affecting the interests of the organizations' corporate and super-wealthy bankrollers.

Private meetings are indispensable mechanisms for achieving uniformity and conformity on matters of foreign and domestic policies among the organizations' members. The attainment of a consensus in the CFR is, especially, fostered through its discussion and study groups. Their relevance has been commented on by G. William Domhoff, who argued that within the groups "members of the power elite study and plan as to how best to attain American objectives in world affairs. It is here that they discuss alternatives and hash out differences."[52] The corporate sector's pre-eminence within the CFR ensures that the sector's interests are always to the fore, thus facilitating the discussion, and resolution, of differences within broadly based pro-corporate assumptions.

Within the Trilateral Commission, the most important discussion forum is its annual plenary meetings, where the elites of the commission's three regional groups interact. Stephen Gill, associate professor of political science at York University in Toronto, who has interviewed numerous leading Trilateralists, has written on the importance of the plenaries, noting that their "proponents argue that the meetings develop a sense of collegiality and mutual confidence among the members, building the trust and predictability stressed in public choice theory as being important for the development of international agreements. Despite the collegial flavour of the meetings, discussion is open, frank and often heated, and differences over vital aspects of policy are confronted and explored, even when agreement or consensus seems unlikely or impossible."[53]

Achieving a consensus within the Bilderberg Group is, like the CFR and Trilateral Commission, facilitated by the organization's selection process. "The key factor of inclusion" in the Bilderberg Group, Professor Gill noted, "was the degree to which an influential individual was, or could become, sympathetic to the basic purposes of the meetings. Prominent in the American section were the network of Rockefeller interests."[54]

In attempting to forge a consensus, the intention of corporate patrons of the three sister organizations is to promote the emergence of a cohesive, corporate-led elite, whose members, for the most part, will view the world, its nations, its populations and its resources through similar ideologically tinted spectacles.

Diluting Democracy

A feature of the policies pursued by America's ruling elites is the degree to which the policies coincide with the interests of the ruling class. This is especially tangible in the sphere of taxation policies instituted by the elites, which facilitate an upward redistribution of wealth, transferring the tax burden from wealthy individuals and large corporations to the less affluent and smaller business enterprises. This represents a transfer of public wealth to corporations.

The ability of Washington to persist with inequitable tax policies and other unpopular courses of action, such as the Vietnam War, constitutes a form of tyranny in which democracy is diluted to accommodate the interests of the corporate class. Such a system of domination and privilege is made possible by confining the public's mass participation in the nation's decision-making to electing political leaders who have, in general, been hand-picked and bankrolled for the elections by Corporate USA.

The question of diluting democracy in the United States was discussed in one of the Trilateral Commission's earliest major task force reports, *The Crisis of Democracy*, which was published just two years after the organization's formation. Disputing the validity of Al Smith's remark that "the only cure for the evils of democracy is more democracy", the commission's report concluded that "some of the problems of governance in the United States today stem from an excess of democracy. . . Needed, instead, is a greater degree of moderation in democracy."[55]

The report argued that for a democratic political system to function effectively "usually requires some measure of apathy and noninvolvement on the part of some individuals and groups". A breakdown of democracy could occur when sectors of society, particularly oppressed and marginalized groups, begin to mobilize and to seek redress for their grievances and for injustices perpetrated against them. In the 1960s, there was a democratic surge and a consequential "substantial decrease in governmental authority", the report argued, when previously "passive or unorganised groups in the population now embarked on concerted efforts to establish their claims to opportunities, positions, rewards, and privileges, which they had not considered themselves entitled to before". These groups included blacks, Indians, Chicanos, white ethnic groups, students and women.[56]

This democratic surge was "a general challenge to existing systems of authority, public and private. . . People no longer felt the same compulsion to obey those whom they had previously considered superior to themselves in age, rank, status, expertise, character, or talents."[57]

The moderation of this "excess of democracy", the report concluded, would necessitate a diminution of public influence. Democracy was "only one way of constituting authority, and it is not necessarily a universally applicable one. In many situations the claims of expertise, seniority, experience, and special talents may override the claims of democracy as a way of constituting authority."[58]

The message was unambiguous. Regardless of public opinion, the American electorate should, "in many situations", be willing to defer to the alleged superior knowledge and expertise of the ruling elites.

The primary threat to democratic government in the United States was deemed to come not from external sources, "but rather from the internal dynamics of democracy itself in a highly educated, mobilized, and participant society".[59] The more participative a society is in its nation's decision-making process, the greater is the threat to the operation of democracy. What is required, according to the Trilateral

Commission report, is that large segments of society be reduced to a state of apathy and acquiescence, which would isolate them from the centres and the wielders of power.

Since the centres of national political power in the United States are largely corporate and Rockefeller dominions, curbing the "excess of democracy" insulates these wealthy ruling elites from challenges from the working class, the marginalized and other unorganised sectors of society, which already account for a disproportionately large percentage of non-voters in the United States. Such a policy is anti-majoritarian. But then rule by a small elite class is by its very nature anti-majoritarian, since it seeks to exclude the vast majority of the population from participating in or even influencing the decision-making process.

Corporate and Rockefeller domination of the executive branch of government, their manipulation of the legislative branch and the isolation of sectors of an already apathetic society from a participative role in the political sphere corrodes the democratic process, transforming America's model of democracy into one that is oligarchic in character. An oligarchy is a form of government in which power is controlled by a small group of people or by a dominant class or clique.

America's oligarchs comprise a national elite of industrialists, bankers, corporate lawyers and others whose primary loyalty is to their elite class and to corporate interests rather than to the electorate. This elite class constitutes what Eugene V. Debs termed the "master class". At its helm are the Rockefellers, the country's most powerful establishmentarians.

"We Own America."

The near-monopolization of power by Corporate USA and associated moneyed elites such as the Rockefellers is, inevitably, self-serving. In 1911, Frederick Townsend Martin, heir to a large fortune, wrote with astonishing candour on the nature of elite rule in the United States: "It matters not one iota what political party is in power or what President holds the reins of office. . . we are the rich; we own America. . . we intend to keep it if we can by throwing all the tremendous weight of our support, our influence, our money, our political connections, our purchased senators, our hungry Congressmen, our public-speaking demagogues into the scale against any legislature, any political platform, any presidential campaign that threatens the integrity of our estate."[60]

The Rockefellers have been particularly successful in converting financial power into political control. Rockefeller wealth has been the primary factor behind the family's political power and influence, enhancing the possibility of success for family members and family-approved aspirants in electoral contests, facilitating the procurement of appointive offices for them and aiding Rockefeller domination of forums such as the CFR and David's Trilateral Commission. However, the family's political power and influence cannot be attributed to wealth alone. If this were the case, then, clearly, other superrich families could also enjoy a comparable degree of success in filling elective and appointive political offices with family members and could also exercise a comparable level of control over "business establishment" forums. What sets the Rockefellers apart? It is that they have contrived to become the acknowledged doyens and representatives of, and planners for, a power-hungry, super-affluent and corporate-linked elite that subscribes to John Jay's maxim that those "who own the country ought to govern it".[61]

Jay's utterance was an early justification for the stratification of American society and for rule by a moneyed elite. He was the first chief justice of the Supreme Court.

Ruling the World

By the start of the twenty-first century, the power and influence of elites associated with Corporate USA and, especially, with the three Rockefeller-linked sister foreign policy forums had become so universal that the elites not only controlled the destiny of the United States; they also controlled, to an enormous extent, the world's destiny.

Such elites occupied key posts in the world's most important multilateral organizations, most notably in the three bodies that, under Washington's guidance, were setting the economic agenda for the twenty-first century: the International Monetary Fund (IMF), the World Bank and the World Trade Organization. At the start of the new century, the acting head of the IMF was a Zambian-born US citizen, Stanley Fischer (Trilateral Commission, CFR and Bilderberg Group). In March 2000, he was succeeded by another Trilateralist, Horst Köhler from Germany. Fischer became the IMF's first deputy managing director, the second most powerful office. He held this post until June 2001, when he was replaced by Anne O. Krueger, a CFR member. At the same time, Timothy Geithner was appointed director of policy development and review in the IMF. He was a senior fellow for international economics at the CFR.

The president of the World Bank was James D. Wolfensohn (CFR, Bilderberg Group steering committee, Rockefeller Foundation trustee). Rockefellerian elites holding office under Wolfensohn included David de Ferranti, World Bank vice president for Latin America and the Caribbean, a Rockefeller Foundation trustee.

Heading the World Trade Organization was Michael Moore, a member of the Eminent Persons Group on World Trade, a forum for Rockefeller-linked figures and other devotees of globalization.

Heading the United Nations was Kofi Annan from Ghana, Washington's choice for the UN post. Annan's ties to the US began in the late 1950s when he was talent-spotted by the Ford Foundation – which had helped to fund the Trilateral Commission in its early years – as part of its programme for identifying and nurturing potential future leaders. A Ford Foundation grant enabled him to study at Macalester College in Minnesota. (Established in 1936, the foundation's funds derive from an investment portfolio that began with gifts and bequests of Ford Motor Company stock by the company's founder Henry Ford and his son Edsel.) Rockefellerian elites under Annan included UNICEF Executive Director Carol Bellamy (CFR), the UN High Commissioner for Refugees Sadako Ogata (Trilateral Commission) and the High Commissioner for Human Rights Mary Robinson (Trilateral Commission). A list of attendees at the annual meeting of the Bilderberg Group in June 2000 included Louise Frechette, the UN's deputy secretary-general. In early 2001, Ogata was replaced as UN high commissioner for refugees by Ruud Lubbers, a Bilderberg alumnus.

The European Union, despite internal divisions, is the world's second most powerful hegemon. Heading the European Commission (Euro commissioners are the EU's counterparts of secretaries of departments in the United States – like their US counterparts they are appointed, not elected by the people) was Romano Prodi, who had served on the Bilderberg Group's steering committee in the 1980s. Of the nineteen Euro commissioners serving under Prodi, seven were Bilderbergers:[62]

- Pedro Solbes (commissioner for economic and monetary affairs)
- Mario Monti (competition)
- Erkki Liikanen (enterprise and information society)
- Günter Verheugen (enlargement)
- Frits Bolkestein (internal market)
- Antonio Vitorino (justice and home affairs)
- Pascal Lamy (trade).

Mario Monti was a former executive member of the Trilateral Commission and a former member of Bilderberg's steering committee. Solbes was a Trilateralist. Lamy was a director of the Overseas Development Council, whose establishment was made possible by Ford and Rockefeller Foundation funding. Its chairman was Peter Sutherland, a Trilateralist and Bilderberger. As head of GATT (General Agreement on Tariffs and Trade) and of the World Trade Organization, Sutherland was a central figure in progressing the process of globalization. The European commissioner for external relations was Chris Patten (Trilateral Commission). The coordinator of the EU's foreign and security policy was Javier Solana (Bilderberg Group).

At the time that Romano Prodi was on Bilderberg's steering committee, its treasurer was Willem F. (Wim) Duisenberg, who became the first ever president of the European Central Bank, a post equivalent in Europe to the chairmanship of the Federal Reserve System in the United States. Sharing power with Duisenberg in the bank was a five-member executive board, which included Otmar Issing (Germany), a Bilderberger, Italian Tommaso Padoa-Schioppa (Bilderberg) and Sirkka Hämäläinen from Finland (Trilateral Commission). Padoa-Schioppa was on the advisory committee of the Rockefeller-linked Institute for International Economics, a coterie of free-trade and globalization devotees. Its recent chiefs have included Director David Rockefeller, the chairman of the board of directors Peter G. Peterson (who was concurrently Chairman of the CFR) and Renato Ruggiero (Trilateral Commission), who succeeded Sutherland as head of the World Trade Organization.

In January 2002 an Irish Bilderberger, Pat Cox, was elected president of the European Parliament.

Chairman of the board of governors of the European Bank for Reconstruction and Development (EBRD) was Laurent Fabius, a Trilateral Commissioner. Its president, until his appointment as managing director of the IMF in early 2000, was Horst Köhler (Trilateral Commission). After Köhler's IMF appointment, the EBRD's acting president and first vice president was Charles R. Frank, Jr, (CFR).

The EBRD is an enormously powerful multilateral agency, in which the United States is a shareholder. Founded in 1991, the year the Soviet Union ceased to exist, it dominates, usually with the IMF and World Bank, the economic affairs of almost all the former communist countries in Eastern and central Europe and of the post-Soviet Union Commonwealth of Independent States.

The secretary-general of NATO was Lord Robertson (a Bilderberger and council member of the Royal Institute of International Affairs in Britain, a sister organization of the Council on Foreign Relations in the United States). NATO's commander-in-chief was General Joseph Ralston (CFR).

Leading national political figures (see Appendix A) around the world were also members or alumni of Rockefeller-linked bodies, including British Prime Minister Tony Blair, a Bilderberger.

Responsible for the drafting of an Earth Charter to "effect a global transition to a new development pathway that is sustainable in environmental and human as well as economic terms" was a team led by Steven Rockefeller, chairman of the Rockefeller Brothers Fund. Coordinating the project was the Earth Council, headed by Maurice Strong, a former Trilateral commissioner and Rockefeller Foundation trustee.[63]

Deputy secretary-general of the Organization for Economic Cooperation and Development (OECD), a forum for the world's richest countries, was Sally Shelton-Colby, widow of William Colby, director of the CIA 1973–76. Like her husband, she was a member of the CFR.

At the head of the world's elite rulers at the start of the century stood one individual, the president of the United States, Bill Clinton. He was a member of all three principal Rockefeller-linked foreign policy forums. With the disintegration of the Soviet Union, the collapse of communism, the imposition of globalization and the concomitant global dominance of the Stars and Stripes, President Clinton had become the CEO of almost all the world's people, although elected to office by less than 1 per cent of these people.

His successor, George W. Bush, was an even more illogical and illegitimate global CEO. Described by one commentator as a functional illiterate and failed business executive who was bequeathed a life of privilege through family and corporate connections,[64] George W. stole the presidency of the United States, an office he would use to enrich his corporate friends and patrons and to further the imposition of globalization and US hegemony on the world's peoples.

Rockefellerian and corporate elites semi-monopolized executive branch and key sub-cabinet posts in the Clinton and George W. Bush administrations. The perceived orchestrator of the world economy and, probably, the second most powerful figure in the world was Alan Greenspan, chairman of the Federal Reserve. He was a Trilateral commissioner and a former CFR director [1982–88].

Such elite control of key offices in the Clinton and Bush administrations, in foreign governments, the World Trade Organization, the IMF, World Bank, United Nations, the European Commission, the European Central Bank, the European Bank for Reconstruction and Development, NATO, the OECD, the Earth Council and a plethora of other powerful international forums gave Rockefellerian and corporate elites the power to determine the fate of the planet's six billion inhabitants at the start of the new century.

Notes

1. Ferdinand Lundberg, *America's 60 Families* (New York: Halcyon House, 1939 edition), p. 3.
2. W. J. Rorabaugh and Donald T. Critchlow, *America: A Concise History* (Belmont, California: Wadsworth Publishing, 1994), p. 438.
3. Henry Demarest Lloyd, *Wealth Against Commonwealth* (published 1894/reprinted Englewood Cliffs, New Jersey: Prentice Hall, 1963).
4. Ida Tarbell, *History of the Standard Oil Company* – serialized in *McClure's Magazine* between 1902–1904 and published in book form in 1904.
5. Peter Collier and David Horowitz, *The Rockefellers: An American Dynasty* (New York: Signet, 1977), p. 4; Ron Chernow, *Titan: The Life of John D. Rockefeller, Sr* (London: Warner, 1999), p. 498.
6. Speech at Canton, Ohio, 16 June 1918.

7.   Quoted in Daniel Yergin, *The Prize: The Epic Quest for Oil, Money and Power* (New York: Touchstone, 1993), p. 108.

8.   Quoted in Collier and Horowitz, *The Rockefellers*, p. 108. See also Chernow, *Titan*, pp. 580–81.

9.   See Harold Evans, *The American Century* (London: Jonathan Cape/Pimlico, 1998), p. 125; Joel Andreas, *The Incredible Rocky* (New York: NACLA, 1979), p. 7.

10.   Numerous books have provided in-depth analyses of the Rockefellers' business, political and philanthropic pursuits, including Collier and Horowitz, *The Rockefellers*; Chernow, *Titan*: John Ensor Harr and Peter J. Johnson, *The Rockefeller Conscience* (New York: Charles Scribner's Sons, 1991); Gerard Colby with Charlotte Dennett, *Thy Will Be Done: The Conquest of the Amazon: Nelson Rockefeller and Evangelism in the Age of Oil* (New York: HarperCollins, 1995); E. Richard Brown, *Rockefeller Medicine Men* (Berkeley, California: University of California Press, 1980); Michael Kramer and Sam Roberts, *I Never Wanted to Be Vice President of Anything: An Investigative Biography of Nelson Rockefeller* (New York: Basic Books, 1976).

11.   "Dirty Business", *Newsweek*, 14 December 1998.

12.   See Andreas, *The Incredible Rocky*, p. 9; Collier and Horowitz, *The Rockefellers*, p. 452.

13.   Michael Barone and Grant Ujifusa, *The Almanac of American Politics 1988* (Washington, DC: *National Journal*), p. 1271.

14.   Gerard Smith is identified as a Rockefeller in-law in Stephen Gill, *American hegemony and the Trilateral Commission* (Cambridge: Cambridge University Press, 1991), p. 138. No reply was received to written queries to the Trilateral Commission by the author of *America Rules* to confirm Smith's marriage ties.

15.   Ronald Reagan, *An American Life* (New York: Simon & Schuster, 1990), pp. 239–40.

16.   The offers of the post of treasury secretary are referred to in Gill, *American hegemony and the Trilateral Commission*, p. 151; Collier and Horowitz, *The Rockefellers*, p. 403; Robert Eringer, *The Global Manipulators* (Bristol, UK: Pentacle Books, 1980), p. 72; Leonard Silk and Mark Silk, *The American Establishment* (New York: Avon Books, 1981), p. 207.

17.   William Hoffman, *David* (New York: Dell, 1972), p. 2, citing the *New Yorker*, 9 January 1965.

18.   The patronage of John D. Rockefeller, Jr, and the Rockefeller Foundation is referred to in Peter Grose, *Continuing the Inquiry: The Council on Foreign Relations from 1921 to 1996* (New York: CFR, 2001).

19.   The CFR's key officeholders in 1953 with ties to Rockefeller interests included CFR chairman John J. McCloy, its president Henry M. Wriston, vice president David Rockefeller, vice president and secretary Frank Altschul, treasurer Elliott V. Bell and executive director George S. Franklin. John J. McCloy became chairman of the CFR in 1953, the same year he became chairman of the Rockefeller-controlled Chase National Bank (post-1955, the Chase Manhattan Bank). McCloy was a trustee of the Rockefeller Foundation and a partner in a law firm whose leading clients included the Rockefellers and their associated business interests.

In 1945 the Rockefellers had offered him the presidency of the Standard Oil Company of California.

David Rockefeller became a CFR vice president in 1950. He succeeded McCloy as chairman of the CFR and of the Chase Manhattan

George S. Franklin was a Rockefeller in-law.

Frank Altschul had been a director of the Chase National Bank.

Elliott V. Bell became a Chase Manhattan director.

In 1951, Henry M. Wriston became president of the CFR, a post he retained until 1964. His son Walter was a senior official in another Rockefeller-linked bank, the First National City Bank of New York, and later became chairman of its successor, Citibank.

These ties are outlined in Philip H. Burch, Jr, *Elites in American History* (New York: Holmes and Meier, 1980), vol. 3, p. 125.

20.   CFR Annual Report, July 1, 1987–June 1, 1988, pp. 4, 6.
21.   Report of CFR's executive director for the year 1949–50, as quoted in Emanuel M. Josephson, *Rockefeller "Internationalist"* (New York: Chedney Press, 1952), p. 245.
22.   *Programs and Purposes: Studies on Foreign Policy 1970–1971* (New York: CFR, 1971). Cited in G. William Domhoff, *The Powers That Be: Processes of Ruling Class Domination in America* (New York: Vintage Books, 1979), p. 66.
23.   Joseph Kraft, *Harper's*, July 1958, p. 67. Quoted in G. William Domhoff, *The Higher Circles: The Governing Class in America* (New York: Random House, 1970), p. 117.
24.   See Kraft, *Harper's Magazine*. Quoted in Domhoff, *The Higher Circles*, p. 113, and Gary Allen, *Kissinger: The Secret Side of the Secretary of State* (Seal Beach, California: '76 Press, 1976), p. 29;
25.   Laurence H. Shoup and William Minter, *Imperial Brain Trust: The Council on Foreign Relations and United States Foreign Policy* (New York: Monthly Review Press, 1977), p. 5, quoting Richard J. Barnet, *Roots of War* (New York: Athemeum,1972), p. 49.
26.   Theodore H. White, *The Making of the President 1964* (London: Jonathan Cape, 1968), p. 67.
27.   See Domhoff, *The Higher Circles*, p. 114, citing James N. Rosenau, ed., *Domestic Sources of Foreign Policy* (New York: Free Press, 1967), p. 247.
28.   See Kraft, *Harper's*, July 1958, cited in Domhoff, *Higher Circles*, p. 113.
29.   See Shoup and Minter, *Imperial Brain Trust*, p. 4, citing *Newsweek*, 6 September 1971.
30.   *Ibid.*, pp. 62, 64.
31.   See Domhoff, *The Powers That Be*, p. 68.
32.   G. William Domhoff, *The Bohemian Grove and Other Retreats* (New York: Harper and Row, 1974), p. 101.
33.   Bilderberg Group press release, 24 May 2001.
34.   Holly Sklar, ed., *Trilateralism: The Trilateral Commission and Elite Planning for World Management* (Boston: South End Press, 1980), p. 158.
35.   *Congressional Record* (Washington, DC), 15 September 1971, p. E9616. See *Spotlight on the Bilderbergers: Irresponsible Power* (Washington, DC: Liberty Lobby), p. 17.
36.   Excellent analyses of the Trilateral Commission are provided by Gill, *American hegemony and the Trilateral Commission,* and Sklar, *Trilateralism.*

37. See Gill, *American hegemony and the Trilateral Commission*, pp. 157–58.

38. See Grose, *Continuing the Inquiry*.

39. G. William Domhoff, *Who Rules America Now?* (New York: Touchstone, 1986), p. 86.

40. CFR Annual Report, July 1, 1987 – June 1, 1988, p. 6.

41. Following the collapse of the Soviet Union, the Trilateral Commission broadened its membership base. In 1998, its European group was enlarged to include Poland, Hungary, Slovenia, Estonia and the Czech Republic. Two years later, the commission was further enlarged by the addition of Mexico to the North American group and the formation of a Pacific Asian group which retained Japan and recruited Korea, Australia, New Zealand, Indonesia, Malaysia, the Philippines, Singapore and Thailand. The new Pacific Asian group also includes participants from China, Hong Kong and Taiwan. Since 1998, the commission has also liaised with "a group of selected leaders from Other Areas – East Asia, Latin America, Turkey, Russia, Ukraine, Middle East, Africa, India – who share our vision and goals: strong democracies and open market economies". (Commission leaflet).

42. Sklar, *Trilateralism*, p. 204, citing Trilateral Commission memo of 15 March 1973.

43. See Sklar, *Trilateralism*, p. xi, citing report in *Wall Street Journal*, 30 April 1980.

44. The identities of appointees within the Carter and other administrations who were members of the Trilateral Commission and/or the CFR can be ascertained by referring to the organizations' membership lists. CFR membership lists are published in the body's annual reports – which are difficult to obtain. Lists of Trilateral Commission members are generally available on request from the commission. The names of commission members during its first six years are printed in Sklar, *Trilateralism*.

   Lists of Bilderberg alumni are available on the internet, on several sites. They are also published by the Washington, DC-based Liberty Lobby group. Strictly speaking, the Bilderberg Group is not an organization, since it has no formal membership. Its alumni consist of invited participants at its annual meetings. (It should be noted that there is a very small possibility that one or more of the members of the CFR whose names appear in *America Rules* may be misidentified, being ascribed a membership that belongs to another individual having the same or a similar name. This is due to the fact that members of the CFR are listed in that body's annual reports with no identification other than their names. Written queries to the CFR by the author of this book to confirm the CFR membership of some of Washington's cabinet and sub-cabinet appointees went unanswered.)

45. See Sklar, *Trilateralism*, p. 203, citing *Playboy* report of November 1976.

46. Carter's alleged offer to David Rockefeller of the post of treasury secretary is reported in Gill, *American hegemony and the Trilateral Commission*, p. 151, and Eringer, *The Global Manipulators*, p. 72. The Fed offer is reported in Burch, *Elites in American History*, vol. 3, p. 356, and Sue Branford and Bernardo Kucinski, *The Debt Squads: The US, the Banks, and Latin America* (London: Zed Books, 1990), p. 101.

47.   Reported in *The Irish Times*, 15, 18, 19 January 2002.
48.   Report by Associated Press business writer Marcy Gordon, "Enron Choices Received Bush Posts", 1 February 2002. See newspaper reports on that and subsequent days, and also http://www.usatoday.com/ news/nation/2002/02/01/enron.htm
49.   *The Rockefeller Foundation: A History* (New York: Rockefeller Foundation), p. 6.
50.   *Rockefeller Foundation 1998 Annual Report*, p. 2.
51.   See Gerard Colby with Charlotte Dennett, *Thy Will Be Done*, pp. 337–39.
52.   See Domhoff, *The Higher Circles*, p. 120.
53.   See Gill, *American hegemony and the Trilateral Commission*, p. 147.
54.   *Ibid.*, p. 132.
55.   Samuel P. Huntington in Michel Crozier, Samuel P. Huntington and Joji Watanuki, *The Crisis of Democracy* (New York: Trilateral Commission, 1975), p. 113.
56.   *Ibid.*, pp. 61–62, 64, 114.
57.   *Ibid.*, pp. 74–75.
58.   *Ibid.*, p. 113.
59.   *Ibid.*, p. 115.
60.   F. T. Martin, *The Passing of the Idle Rich* (Garden City, New York: Doubleday, Page, 1911). Quoted in W. E. Woodward, *A New American History* (New York: Garden City Publishing, 1938), p. 626.
61.   Joseph R. Fiszman, ed., *The American Political Arena* (Boston: Little, Brown, 1966), p. 3.
62.   Written questions to the European Commission tabled by Irish MEP Patricia McKenna have identified Euro commissioners who were/are Bilderbergers and/or Trilateral commissioners.
       See   http://www.cetrexnews.com/members/bilderberg/bilder.htm and http://www.centrexnews.com/members/bilderberg/2000.htm
63.   See the Earth Council's website, http://www.ecouncil.ac.cr/about/ backgrnd.htm
64.   Michael Moore, *Stupid White Men and Other Sorry Excuses for the State of the Nation* (New York: ReganBooks, 2001).

Chapter 5

Cold Warriors

Containing the Soviet Union

Although the CFR was formed less than three years after the First World War had ended, it was not until after the Second World War had begun that this forum assumed its now customary role as a premier incubator of US foreign policy.

Shortly after this war had erupted in 1939, three CFR members met in Washington for secret discussions. They were Assistant Secretary of State George S. Messersmith, Walter H. Mallory (executive director of the CFR 1927–59) and Hamilton Fish Armstrong (CFR director 1928–72 and executive director 1922–28). Their deliberations resulted in the CFR being commissioned to undertake a quite astounding mission for a private organization – to establish a CFR War and Peace Studies Project whose constituent groups would, on behalf of the Department of State, design a blueprint for a controllable and responsive post-war global order compatible with American interests.[1]

A council publication noted that in proposing the project, the CFR had "conceived a role for the Council in the formulation of national policy", the project's intended goal being to "guide American foreign policy in the coming years of war and the challenging new world that would emerge after". The group's proposals provided a framework for post-bellum US foreign policy and for the attainment of US global hegemony. The project was financed to the tune of nearly $350,000 by the Rockefeller Foundation.[2]

By the time the war drew to a close, the United States had become the world's supreme hegemon. Its military, political and economic power was unrivalled, its allies were near-bankrupt, its enemies crippled, pre-war colonial empires were shattered and the US alone possessed the world's most fearsome weapon of mass destruction, the atomic bomb. The objective of Washington, and of the CFR, was to preserve this US panoply of power through imposing a US-fashioned and

US-dominated capitalist order on the post-war world. With "about 50% of the world's wealth but only 6.3% of its population", America's ambition, as George F. Kennan, director of the Policy Planning Staff, pointed out, should be "to maintain this position of disparity".[3]

However, the country's post-war hegemonic ambitions faced a challenge from a wartime ally, the Soviet Union. With over 20 million dead, thousands of towns and villages in ruins, parts of cities no more than giant blankets of rubble and skeletons of gutted buildings, countless millions of homeless forced to live in holes in the ground, the nation's infrastructure devastated in many areas and tens of millions of livestock butchered by the Germans, the Soviet Union's war deaths and damage were, by far, the worst sustained by any one country.

Twice in three decades, in both World Wars, it had endured aggression from German forces. The First World War occurred at a time of immense mass discontent and political instability in Russia, which later, after expanding territorially, became the Soviet Union. In 1917, as the war raged, communist Bolshevik forces toppled the Russian monarchy, creating the world's first communist state. The birth of communist Russia was followed by a civil war. In 1918, before the guns fell silent on First World War battlefields, Allied forces, including Americans, landed in Russia, where they supported anti-communist forces in the civil war. US participation in the intervention marked the start of Washington's seven-decade campaign to topple the communist regime.

The scale of the human losses and suffering and the vast devastation inflicted on the country during the two World Wars, the civil war and in 1812, when Napoleon invaded Russia and Moscow burned, aroused deeply rooted anti-war emotions in the Russian population, fostering a resolve that never again should the country and its people be subjected to the horrors of armed intervention by foreign forces.

Second World War exigencies had compelled Washington and London to enter into an alliance with the Soviet Union. However, when the war ended, the weakened Soviet Union found itself in an extremely precarious position. As the world's first and only communist nation, it had no natural allies in a post-war, capitalist-dominated world. One nation was especially perceived to pose a military threat to Soviet territorial integrity, the United States. Soviet leaders viewed the US as an expansionist, nuclear-armed hegemon whose chain of overseas military bases represented an ominous military encirclement.

To counter this potential threat, and also the threat posed by neighbouring countries, the Soviet dictator Joseph Stalin planned to form a cordon sanitaire of Soviet-dominated buffer states along his country's frontiers in Europe in order to protect Soviet national sovereignty and territory. To Stalin there was little difference between his plans for Soviet puppet regimes to hold power in neighbouring

European countries and Washington's pliant client regimes in Latin America and elsewhere, which the United States kept in power against the will of the people through armed aggression, economic assistance and the provision of weapons and other instruments of repression.

Fearing that the formation of a sphere of Soviet influence in eastern Europe might beget a militarily and economically powerful communist state capable of challenging America's status as the premier superpower in the post-war world, President Truman resolved that there should be no expansion of Soviet rule or domination in Europe beyond its own borders and thus no diminution of US post-war hegemony. Washington embarked on a campaign to counter the Soviet threat to US hegemony. The subsequent hostile relations between the two countries became known as the Cold War. Its goal was to secure US global supremacy.

Shaping the Post-War World

There were three main architects of Washington's Cold War doctrine:

- State Department official George F. Kennan, whose thesis that Soviet expansionism could and should be blocked by the United States through a strategy of "containment" became a fundamental principle of US Cold War foreign policy. (His thesis was first published in the CFR's *Foreign Affairs* publication in July 1947).

- Under Secretary of State (later Secretary of State) Dean Acheson, the principal author of the Truman Doctrine, which depicted an evil ideology, communism, whose tentacles sought to envelop "free peoples" everywhere, entrapping them within a tyrannical system which relied on "terror and oppression" for its survival.

- Paul H. Nitze, the successor to Kennan as director of the State Department's Policy Planning Staff, who supervised the compilation of fresh guidelines and justifications for Washington's agenda of hostility towards the Soviet Union. These were set forth in April 1950 in Nitze's National Security Council Directive 68 (NSC–68), which proposed a formula "to foster a world environment in which the American system can survive and flourish" through containing and undermining the Kremlin's "inescapably militant. . . totalitarian dictatorship" and thus "foster the seeds of destruction within the Soviet system".

Nitze's document, Kennan's containment strategy and the largely Acheson-authored Truman Doctrine launched one of the most bloody, confrontational and interventionist periods in the history of the United

States, being the cornerstones of the country's Cold War foreign policy for four decades. They provided a rationale and pretext for relentless hostility towards the Soviets and for undermining communism and socialism in the Soviet Union and its satellite countries; placed the United States in a state of constant war preparedness; promoted the development of programmes "to wage overt psychological warfare" against the Kremlin; intensified "operations by covert means in the fields of economic warfare and political and psychological warfare with a view to fomenting and supporting unrest and revolt in selected strategic satellite countries"; increased expenditure for military purposes, including military assistance programmes; facilitated the concoction of crises, under the guise of combating communism, to justify US interventionism and criminal behaviour in Third World countries; and cajoled the American public to support, and to pay for, this aggressive and, at times, murderous foreign policy.[4] Ultimately, the Cold War cost US taxpayers the equivalent of at least $13 trillion.[5]

The principal architects of the Cold War – Kennan, Acheson and Nitze – were all CFR members, as also was journalist Herbert Bayard Swope, who coined the phrase "Cold War".

The important role of the CFR in the formulation of Cold War policies was hinted at in a council publication, which noted that the CFR "functioned at the core of the public institution-building of the early Cold War, but only behind the scenes. As a forum providing intellectual stimulation and energy, it enabled well-placed members to convey cutting-edge thinking to the public – but without portraying the Council as the font from which the ideas rose." The council's study and discussion groups, it added, "served as an important breeding ground for the doctrines of strategic stability, mutual deterrence, arms control and nuclear nonproliferation that guided American foreign policy for the years of the Cold War".[6]

The Cold War was largely a creation of CFR members. It would be waged by council members and other Rockefeller and corporate-linked elites.

Covert Cold Warfare

The formulation and direction of US foreign policy is the province of a powerful multi-departmental hierarchy. At its apex is the president of the United States, followed, as a rule, by his secretary of state. In the Cold War era, all presidents and secretaries of state shared foreign policy decision-making with others, notably the national security adviser, the secretary of defense and the director of the CIA.

During the Cold War years, these posts were dominated by members of the Council on Foreign Relations, alumni of the Bilderberg Group, trustees of the Rockefeller Foundation and by Trilateral commissioners. The success of corporate figures in filling these offices enabled them to shape and conduct the nation's Cold War foreign policy, with its emphasis on confrontation and intervention, often covert.

The mandate for covert operations and political warfare was provided by a National Security Council directive, NSC 10/2, of 18 June 1948. The result of a George Kennan proposal, the directive sanctioned a range of clandestine activities, including secret wars and overthrowing governments. It encompassed "propaganda; economic warfare; preventive direct action, including sabotage, anti-sabotage, demolition and evacuation measures; subversion against hostile states, including assistance to underground resistance movements, guerrillas and refugee liberation groups".[7]

Clandestine operations became a responsibility of the CIA and of a succession of CIA directors who were members of the triad of foreign policy forums, most notably the CFR, whose members often collaborated with the agency. The close ties between the CFR and CIA covert operations were referred to in a book, *The CIA and the Cult of Intelligence*. Written by Victor Marchetti, a former CIA official, and John D. Marks, it described how the council had "long been the CIA's principal 'constituency' in the American public. When the agency has needed prominent citizens to front for its proprietary companies or for other special assistance, it has often turned to Council members."[8] A proprietary company is one secretly run by the CIA and used in the agency's covert operations.

Clandestine operations became a linchpin of US Cold War interventionism, which included assassinating political leaders, fomenting civil disorder, overthrowing democratically elected governments and creating terrorist groups and death squads. Collaborating with the CIA in its Cold War projects was the Rockefeller Foundation, which was used as a cover by agency operatives for covert foreign operations. In its exposé of CIA covert activities, a Senate committee report of 1976 stated that such foundations were regarded as being "the best and most plausible kind of funding cover", facilitating the agency in secretly financing a wide range of covert action programmes. At times, CIA money was funnelled through Chase bank accounts.[9]

The Rockefeller family was a patron of the Cold War. The Rockefeller Foundation and the family-dominated Chase bank facilitated CIA covert activities. Nelson Rockefeller became special assistant for Cold War strategy in the Eisenhower administration, in effect a presidential coordinator for the CIA.

Rockefellerian and Corporate Elites and the Cold War

During the Cold War era there were eight US presidents. Secretaries of state under all eight presidents were CFR members and/or members of its sister organization, the Trilateral Commission. Three of these secretaries of state (John Foster Dulles, Dean Rusk and Cyrus Vance) were chairmen or presidents of the Rockefeller Foundation. President Reagan's first secretary of state, Alexander M. Haig, Jr, had been a director of the Rockefellers' Chase Manhattan Bank immediately prior to his cabinet appointment.[10]

Such individuals also dominated the affairs of other key State Department offices during the Cold War. The first three directors of the Policy Planning Staff were all CFR members, namely Cold War architects George F. Kennan and Paul H. Nitze, and Robert R. Bowie. Its fourth director was Rockefeller in-law Gerard C. Smith, who became the first chairman of the Trilateral Commission in North America.

To justify interventionist Cold War strategies, these people systematically nurtured a climate of anti-communism, through depicting a terrorist regime intent on imposing a global Pax Russiana. For four decades, the Cold War foreign policies devised by CFR members, and later revised and implemented by CFR and Trilateral Commission members, were responsible for death and destruction, not in the Soviet Union, the purported target of Washington's Cold War interventionism, but rather in the Third World. Millions died, most of them civilians with little knowledge of, or interest in, communist ideology. The CFR, Alexander Cockburn and Ken Silverstein remarked in their book *Washington Babylon*, had become a "tranquil watering-hole for senior mass murderers".[11]

The objectives of the Cold War coincided with the interests of the CFR's bankrollers. A primary goal was to prevent the development of a political and economic system in the Soviet Union that might, if allowed to grow unhindered, serve as a viable alternative to the capitalist model. The spread of communism outside the Soviet Union might create a Pax Russiana to challenge Pax Americana. However, in the tangled turmoil of the closing stages of the Second World War, strategic exigencies and military practicalities obliged Washington to treat the communist state as an ally. Among the temporary expedients resorted to by the Western power was a proposal for a period of joint Soviet and American trusteeship of Korea, following the defeat of Japan's forces of occupation. It was here that the first major confrontation of the Cold War era occurred.

Pending elections and the reunification of the country, Korea was split in two by the US and the Soviet Union, with the 38th parallel serving as an arbitrary demarcation line between Soviet-controlled territory to the north of the line and American-controlled territory to the south. However, the onset of the Cold War destroyed prospects for Korea's reunification. The withdrawal of Soviet and US troops from the country was followed by conflict between the two regions in 1948–49, which culminated in the Korean War. A striking feature of the war and of other US wars and interventions was the number of US foreign policy strategists who were associated with the CFR, the Bilderberg Group, the corporate sector and with the Rockefellers.

The Korean War began in June 1950 with an invasion of South Korea by armed forces from communist North Korea. Directing the US war effort were Secretary of State Dean Acheson, a CFR member, Defense Secretary Robert A. Lovett, a trustee of the Rockefeller Foundation, and CIA Director Walter Bedell Smith, one of the small group of people instrumental in forming the Bilderberg Group. In 1955, Smith became co-chairman, with Dean Rusk, of Bilderberg's US branch. The war drew to a close in 1953. The chief US negotiator at the peace talks was Arthur H. Dean, a CFR member and later a director of the CFR (1955–72). In 1957 he became co-chairman of the US branch of the Bilderberg Group.

In 1952, the Cold War entered a chillier phase with the election of CFR member General Dwight D. Eisenhower to the White House and his selection of CFR members John Foster Dulles and Allen Dulles as his secretary of state and director of the CIA, respectively. The corporate-dominated cabinet and government agencies pursued pro-corporate programmes.[12]

Under the CFR troika of Eisenhower and the Dulles brothers, the Cold War was intensified. Seven months after General Eisenhower's inauguration, the triumvirate orchestrated the overthrow of Mohammed Mossadegh in oil-rich Iran. A month later, Ramon Magsaysay was elected president of the Philippines. His candidacy and election campaign had been secretly coordinated and funded by the CIA. In mid-1954, through a CIA-directed military coup, the threesome toppled the Arbenz government in Guatemala. Only the second democratically elected government in the country's history, it had expropriated land held by the largest landholder in Guatemala, the American-owned United Fruit Company. In 1958, the three aided an armed revolt against Indonesian President Achmed Sukarno, supplying planes and pilots for bombing raids within the country.

Lethal poisons were prepared by the Dulles-directed CIA with the intention of assassinating Third World leaders, including Fidel Castro in Cuba and the prime minister of the Congo, Patrice Lumumba.

The interventionist Cold War roles of Rockefellerian and corporate elites continued after the departure of President Eisenhower from the White House. Prior to Eisenhower's departure, the Allen Dulles-headed CIA had prepared plans for an armed invasion of Cuba. Shortly after John F. Kennedy became president, the invasion was launched. Kennedy's principal strategists for the intervention were almost all members of the CFR and/or of the Bilderberg Group.

In 1964, Kennedy's successor, Lyndon B. Johnson, authorized the overthrow of João Goulart in Brazil in a CIA-aided coup. The following year, US forces were sent to the Dominican Republic to prevent Juan Bosch being reinstated as president. Almost 60 per cent of Johnson's top foreign policy officials were CFR members, including Secretary of State Dean Rusk and National Security Adviser McGeorge Bundy. By then the United States had become mired in a far bloodier Cold War theatre of operations, Vietnam.

The Vietnam War

The Vietnam War, the most catastrophic and bloody military intervention of the Cold War, was from start to finish waged by Rockefellerian elites, especially CFR members and former heads of the Rockefeller Foundation.

Washington's interference in the affairs of Vietnam had its origins in France's Indochina War, through which France attempted to reclaim its former colonies of Vietnam, Laos and Cambodia. In late 1949, as support grew within the State Department for the provision of US aid for France's war effort, Deputy Under Secretary of State Dean Rusk stated that the United States intended to deploy its resources "to reserve Indochina and Southeast Asia from further Communist encroachment".[13] A few months later, President Truman assented to American economic and military assistance for the European power. America's entanglement in the bloody debacle of the Vietnam War had begun.

By 1954, through President Eisenhower and his secretary of state, John Foster Dulles, the United States had become paymaster and arms supplier for France's war, American aid comprising almost 80 per cent of France's military spending in the region.[14] According to President Eisenhower, Washington aided France in Indochina because it was "the cheapest way. . . to prevent the occurrence of something that would be of a most terrible significance to the USA, our security, our power and ability to get certain things we need from the riches of. . . Southeast Asia".[15]

America's support for France's futile recolonization war was notable for the leading roles played by CFR members, particularly by President Eisenhower, John Foster Dulles and his CIA director, Allen Dulles, and earlier by Secretary of State Dean Acheson and Dean Rusk.

Three Washington administrations – those of John F. Kennedy, Lyndon Johnson and Richard Nixon – subsequently made the Vietnam War an American war, directed by political appointees recruited from the CFR, the Bilderberg Group, Rockefeller foundations and the corporate sector.

Two appointees left indelible legacies, Dean Rusk and Henry Kissinger. Dean Rusk (secretary of state for the entire duration of both the Kennedy and Johnson administrations, 1961–69, and assistant secretary of state and deputy under secretary in the late 1940s and early 1950s) was engaged in planning the war at the highest level longer than any other appointee.

Such was the influence of Henry Kissinger (national security adviser 1969–73 and secretary of state 1973–77) over the conduct of the war in its final years, that it could reasonably be called "Kissinger's War". Rusk was president of the Rockefeller Foundation (1952–61), a member of the Rockefeller Brothers Fund Special Studies Project in the late 1950s, a co-chairman of the US branch of the Bilderberg Group (1955–57) and a CFR member. Kissinger's ties to the Rockefeller family and to the three Rockefeller foreign policy forums were even closer than those of Dean Rusk.

Under President Kennedy, CFR members took almost total control over the waging of Washington's war in Vietnam. An estimated 51 per cent of his top foreign policy planners were CFR members, including Secretary of State Rusk.[16] Other important figures in the war were President Kennedy's defense secretary, Robert McNamara, former president of the Ford Motor Company, and the assistant secretary of state for far eastern affairs, Roger Hilsman, a former adviser to the Rockefeller Brothers Fund Special Studies Project.

Rusk's principal aide for the first eleven months of the Kennedy presidency was Chester Bowles. Like Rusk, he was a former member of the board of trustees of the Rockefeller Foundation and a former participant in the Rockefeller Brothers Fund Special Studies Project. Kennedy's treasury secretary, C. Douglas Dillon, was a trustee of the Rockefeller Foundation, as was the president's disarmament adviser, John J. McCloy.

Lyndon Johnson's accession to the presidency in November 1963 further strengthened the role of CFR members in determining the fate of Vietnam and its people. Kennedy's leading foreign policy decision-makers were all retained. The percentage of top foreign policy officials who were CFR members rose from an estimated 51 per cent under Kennedy to 57 per cent under Johnson.[17]

By early 1968, North and South Vietnam were being subjected to the heaviest aerial bombardment in the history of warfare, and neighbouring Laos had endured a comparable level of bombing.

A bipartisan group of elder statesmen, public officeholders and members of the corporate sector's inner circle, dubbed the Wise Men, was assembled by Johnson to act as foreign policy advisers. Twelve of the group's fourteen members were CFR members. Two (Douglas Dillon and John J. McCloy) were trustees of the Rockefeller Foundation. McCloy was a former chairman of the Chase Manhattan Bank.

The influence of the Wise Men over the direction of the Vietnam War during the Johnson presidency was enormous. One publication reported how "the most significant policy change in the American Vietnam War effort was made without any elaborate official policy planning. The government bureaucracy was not involved. The cabinet was not even involved. The decision was made by representatives of business – by an informal group that combined experience in government with inner circle affiliations. It appears, in fact, that the Wise Men met at every critical juncture in the war and that its opinion consistently prevailed."[18] Among the businessmen in the group of Wise Men were men associated with some of the country's largest banks and non-financial corporations.

In 1965, a pro-war group, the inappropriately named Committee for an Effective and Durable Peace in Asia, was formed to support President Johnson's war. Around one half of the committee members were CFR members, including the CFR chairman John J. McCloy, the CFR vice president David Rockefeller, CFR treasurer Gabriel Hauge and CFR director C. Douglas Dillon. McCloy, Rockefeller, Dillon and another committee member, Eugene Black, were all board members of the Chase bank.[19]

As the bankers and council members beat their patriotic war drums from their safe havens in the United States, the number of Americans fighting and dying in Vietnam was rising alarmingly. Most of them were still in their teens or early twenties and drawn disproportionately from the less affluent sectors, especially from working-class whites and poor blacks. Meanwhile, the elites' draft-age sons were safely ensconced in the United States or in non-combat posts overseas. Patriotism was a principle that the ruling class would resolutely uphold to the last drop of other people's blood. The truancy of members of the elite stratum of American society from Vietnam's theatre of war was conspicuous. Of 1,200 males in Harvard's 1970 class, only two served in the military in Vietnam.[20]

In his 16 June 1918 anti-war speech at Canton, Ohio, Eugene V. Debs spoke of how Americans had been conditioned by the "master class. . . to believe it to be your patriotic duty to go to war and to have yourselves slaughtered at their command. But in all the history of the world you, the people, have never had a voice in declaring war. . . the working class, who freely shed their blood and furnish the corpses, have never yet had a voice in either declaring war or making peace. It is the ruling class that invariably does both. They alone declare war and they alone make peace."

Class divisions and privileges in times of war have been a feature of the history of the United States. In America's colonial era, militia laws enabled rich draftees to shirk military duty through paying for substitutes to serve in their place, an option rarely feasible for poorer recruits due to the prohibitive cost involved. Similar schemes were employed during the Civil War in both the Confederate and Union forces. The Confederacy permitted the use of hired substitutes and exempted wealthy slave-owning plantation holders from being drafted. Exemption from service in the Union forces could be purchased by payment of a $300 fee. Among the host of wealthy Americans who dodged military service was John D. Rockefeller, the founding father of the family's fortune.

Henry Kissinger: War Criminal

In January 1969, Richard Nixon entered the White House. To implement his proposed strategy for the war in Vietnam, he chose a foreign policy team headed by William P. Rogers (secretary of state), Henry Kissinger (national security adviser and later secretary of state), Melvin R. Laird (defense secretary) and Richard Helms (CIA director). Kissinger and Helms were CFR members. Appointed a special assistant to Kissinger was Winston Lord, who became director of the Policy Planning Staff in Kissinger's State Department in 1973. Lord was a CFR member and its president from 1977–85.

Together, Nixon and Kissinger created a foreign policy monster that inflicted death and suffering on such a massive scale that they can be considered as two of the worst mass murderers of the twentieth century. Civilian areas were targeted in Vietnam. At Christmas 1972, they sanctioned around-the-clock air strikes against the northern cities of Hanoi and Haiphong, forcing a mass evacuation of residents to the countryside. In some areas all that was left after the bombing blitz were piles of rubble and pock-marked, lunar-like landscapes. Among the buildings destroyed was Hanoi's Bach Mai hospital. In South Vietnam, thousands of civilians were captured and murdered during the CIA-conceived Phoenix counter-insurgency programme. The duo waged similar murderously indiscriminate wars within Cambodia and Laos. Hundreds of thousands of civilians were killed. Millions fled the slaughter, creating a region of refugees.

Following Nixon's August 1974 resignation and Gerald Ford's accession to the presidency, Kissinger was retained as secretary of state and Kissinger's mentor, Nelson Rockefeller, became vice president.

America's Vietnam War drew to a close in April 1975. Before this occurred, Kissinger had begun to covertly intervene in the affairs of another faraway country, Angola, on the west coast of Africa, where a civil war began after US-funded FNLA guerrillas attacked and killed members of a rival movement. John Stockwell, who directed the CIA's covert operations in Angola, recalled how Kissinger "had overruled his advisors and refused to seek diplomatic solutions" and had "ordered us [the CIA] to seek every means to escalate the Angolan conflict".[21] Around one million died in the ensuing armed struggle, many tortured and butchered by the US-aided guerrillas.

In 1973, Henry Kissinger, who sacrificed the lives of Vietnamese, Cambodians, Laotians, Chileans and later Angolans and East Timorese on the altar of US foreign policy expediency, was the ludicrously incongruous joint recipient of the Nobel Peace Prize. Later, he was presented with a Nelson Rockefeller award for public service.

Kissinger and the Rockefellers

The presentation of a Nelson Rockefeller award to Kissinger was, in one sense, singularly appropriate. Throughout his political career, Nelson had been his mentor, a fact that Kissinger acknowledged in his autobiography, *The White House Years*, which he dedicated to the memory of his patron. It was Nelson, he wrote, who "introduced me to public life and sustained me throughout" and had "introduced me to high-level policymaking in 1955". Nelson Rockefeller, he admitted, was "the single most influential person in my life".[22] Kissinger the "statesman" was a Rockefeller creation.

In 1938, Kissinger, a fifteen-year old Jewish refugee, had arrived in the United States from Nazi Germany. In 1952, he was appointed head of the Harvard International Seminar, a summer programme for potential future foreign political leaders and figures of influence. The programme was funded covertly by the CIA and overtly by the university and the Rockefeller Foundation. The seminar appears to have been Kissinger's first contact with an organ of the Rockefeller family.[23]

In 1955, he was appointed by the CFR, now controlled by Rockefeller-linked officers, as staff director of a council study group. Among the group's members was David Rockefeller. For a twelve-year period, beginning in 1956 and lasting until his nomination as Nixon's national security adviser at the end of 1968, Kissinger served as a paid consultant to Nelson Rockefeller.

Kissinger became one of the Rockefeller brothers' most valued advisers and one of their closest friends. He was a member of all three of the Rockefeller-controlled foreign policy forums, the CFR, Trilateral Commission and the Bilderberg Group. In 1977, he became a director of the CFR. He also served on the International Advisory Committee of the Rockefellers' Chase Manhattan Bank. In 1974, he married Nancy Maginnes, a former aide to Nelson Rockefeller.

His record of war crimes places Rockefeller protégé Henry Kissinger on a par with many of the world's worst mass murderers of recent decades.

Securing Rockefeller Interests: Chile

The superintendence by Rockefellerian and corporate-linked elites of Cold War interventionist foreign policies was marked by some of the twentieth century's worst acts of state-directed terrorism against constitutional and popular governments, by Washington's brutalization of entire populations and by its support for some of the world's most criminal and undemocratic regimes.

Chile provides a revealing case history of America's corporate-political partnership, demonstrating the alliance's willingness and capacity to resort to interventionist strategies to protect corporate interests abroad.

In late 1970, Salvador Allende became president of Chile. The first Marxist to accede to such high political office in the continent by constitutional means, Allende had promised sweeping economic and social reforms to rescue the country from its entrapment in a quagmire of poverty, hunger, underdevelopment and indebtedness. In September 1973, he was killed in a CIA-aided military coup, ending the country's long tradition of democratic rule. Over three thousand civilians, possibly as many as 20,000, were murdered during the next sixteen years of military dictatorship, a form of government more compatible with US corporate interests abroad.

In September 1970, Henry Kissinger, then President Nixon's national security adviser, met privately with Donald Kendall, the head of Pepsico, and CIA collaborator Agustin Edwards, owner of the *El Mercurio* newspaper in Chile. Kissinger also met privately with David Rockefeller, chairman of the CFR and of the Chase Manhattan Bank.[24] The purpose of the meetings was to discuss strategies aimed at blocking the inauguration of Salvador Allende as president. Pepsico and the Rockefellers had considerable business interests in Chile.

The realization of Allende's promised reforms was contingent on stanching the haemorrhaging of wealth from the Chilean economy, which bled the country of the financial resources necessary for economic and social development. Especially important in this regard was the necessity to reduce or halt the outflow of profits being repatriated by American corporations with Chilean subsidiaries.

The degree of control exercised by these corporations over the Chilean economy and the Chilean people was outlined in Allende's reform programme, which noted how "American monopolies. . . have succeeded in acquiring virtually all our copper, iron and nitrate. They control our foreign trade and dictate our economic policy through the International Monetary Fund and other bodies. They dominate important branches of industry and the services. They themselves enjoy statutory privileges, while enforcing monetary devaluation and wage reductions."[25]

The economic well-being of Chile was tied to the mining and export of copper, the country's principal source of revenue. However, two US corporate giants, Kennecott and Anaconda, dominated Chile's copper-mining sector. Among Allende's main reform proposals was the nationalization of their Chilean operations. In 1899, John D. Rockefeller's brother William and others had acquired control over

Anaconda. At the time of Allende's accession to the presidency, Anaconda Copper was controlled by the Rockefellers' Chase Manhattan
Bank.[26] Also at risk of expropriation were other US-owned business
enterprises in Chile, including some owned by the Chase bank and the
Rockefeller-established International Basic Economy Corporation,
whose assets in Chile included a ready-mix cement company, a construction firm, investment and management companies and interests
in the oil sector.

The Rockefellers faced huge losses if President Allende's proposed
nationalization programme went ahead. Revelations that emerged at US
Senate hearings after the 1973 military coup cast light on the oppro-
brious covert roles played by the CIA, American corporations and
Rockefellerian elites in attempts to block Allende's bid for the presidency and in aiding coup attempts.[27]

Funding provided by the CIA and US corporations was an important element of US anti-Allende interventionist strategies. CIA money
funded propaganda manipulation of the Chilean press, the election
campaigns of political parties, public opinion polls and direct attempts
to foment a military coup. Over $3 million was spent by the CIA on a
successful scheme to prevent Allende's election to the presidency in
1964. After Allende's election in 1970, the 40 Committee, which is
responsible for approving major US covert operations, approved the
payment of over $1.5 million to the *El Mercurio* newspaper, whose anti-
Allende propaganda helped to set the stage for the 1973 military coup.
Between Allende's election in 1970 and the September 1973 coup, $8
million was spent by Washington on anti-Allende programmes.

Corporate USA collaborated in these programmes. In Chile's 1964
presidential election campaign, the Business Group for Latin America, comprised of the heads of American blue chip corporations with
operations in the region, donated funds to Allende's successful rival.
The group was established by David Rockefeller and other corporate
leaders.[28]

In 1965, David Rockefeller merged the Business Group with two
other business forums. The new body, whose 200 or so corporate members accounted for over 80 per cent of all US investment in Latin America, was called the Council for Latin America, later the Council of the
Americas. In 1970, ten of the new body's twenty directors were members of the Council on Foreign Relations.

In the 1970 election year, the new body offered to donate at least
$500,000 in a bid to scuttle Allende's presidential aspirations. The giant
US corporation ITT, which had extensive assets in Chile, offered to
give up to $1 million to part-fund an operation which it proposed to
mount jointly with the CIA to prevent Allende becoming president.
The CIA declined the offer.[29]

Among the US ruling elites who participated in the successful

1973 CIA-aided coup were Henry Kissinger and CIA Director Richard Helms. Former CIA Director John McCone, who was an ITT director, also collaborated. The three were CFR members. McCone had been a director of the Rockefeller-linked Standard Oil of California.

Securing Rockefeller Interests: Brazil

In 1964, the government of João Goulart was overthrown in Brazil, through another CIA-aided coup. The director of the CIA at the time was John McCone. As in Chile, Rockefeller interests were also at risk in Brazil. These included Standard Oil of New Jersey's lucrative position in the marketing of oil products; Chase bank subsidiaries; the Rockefeller brothers' 40 per cent share in one of Brazil's largest ranching and agribusiness operations (the million-acre Fazenda Bodoqueña Ranch); and the Brazilian holdings of the International Basic Economy Corporation (IBEC), which was established by Nelson Rockefeller in 1947 and later controlled by his son Rodman.

Among the bodies directing anti-Goulart schemes was the Brazilian Institute for Democratic Action (IBAD), a CIA front organization. Among the American corporations later named as sponsors of IBAD were two Rockefeller-linked corporations with interests in Brazil – IBEC and Standard Oil of New Jersey (Exxon/Esso).[30]

Philip Agee, who had worked in Latin America for twelve years as a CIA secret operations officer, later wrote of how a Brazilian parliamentary investigation revealed that IBAD, one of the CIA's "main political-action operations" in Brazil, and a related organization had spent "possibly as much as twenty million" dollars on anti-Goulart candidates in the 1962 electoral campaign, and that funds "of foreign origin were provided in eight of the eleven state gubernatorial races, for fifteen candidates for federal senators, 250 candidates for federal deputies and about 600 candidates for state legislatures".[31]

The military coup against Goulart had "Made in the USA" written all over it. The CIA financed not only anti-Goulart candidates but also anti-Goulart propaganda campaigns and "mass urban demonstrations",[32] as Philip Agee later revealed. Washington's principal channel of communication with the military conspirators was army attaché Vernon A. Walters, later deputy director of the CIA (1972–76), who was denounced by the Brazilian daily *Novos Rumos* as "the Pentagon's chief specialist in military coups. . . sent to Brazil for the sole purpose of overthrowing President Goulart and establishing a regime that would be a puppet of the US".[33]

At the time of the coup, Rockefellerian and corporate elites dominated US foreign policy: CIA Director John McCone had served as a director of Standard Oil of California; Secretary of State Rusk was a former president of the Rockefeller Foundation; National Security

Adviser McGeorge Bundy and the US Ambassador to Brazil Lincoln Gordon had been participants in the Rockefeller Brothers Fund Special Studies Project; Defense Secretary Robert McNamara was a former president of the Ford Motor Co. McCone, Rusk and Bundy were CFR members.

The years of military dictatorship that followed the coup were marked by the closure of Congress, the crushing of opposition parties, media censorship, the arrest of labour leaders, journalists and student activists and the emergence of death squads. Human rights campaigners were killed. The use of torture became routine.

Renowned Uruguayan writer Eduardo Galeano outlined the benefits of the US-aided coup for Corporate USA. "Between 1964 and mid-1968 fifteen auto and auto parts factories were swallowed up" by foreign giants such as Ford and Chrysler. Drug manufacturing companies were "gobbled" by foreign corporations, "reducing national production of drugs to one-fifth the market. Anaconda pounced on nonferrous metals and Union Carbide on plastics, chemicals, and petrochemicals; American Can, American Machine and Foundry, and other colleagues took over six Brazilian machine and metallurgical concerns; the Companhia de Mineracao Geral, owner of one of Brazil's biggest metallurgical plants, was bought for a song by a Bethlehem Steel-Chase Manhattan-Standard Oil consortium." A parliamentary commission, he wrote, subsequently found that "in 1968 foreign capital controlled 40 percent of the capital market in Brazil. . . 100 percent of motor vehicle production, 100 percent of tire manufacturing, more than 80 percent of the pharmaceutical industry, about 50 percent of the chemical industry. . . 48 percent of aluminium and 90 percent of cement production. Half of the foreign capital was that of US concerns."[34]

The CIA had, once again, been used as the investment security arm of Corporate USA and the Rockefellers.

Securing Rockefeller Interests: Cuba

In April 1961, a CIA-armed force invaded Cuba, fourteen months after a trade agreement was signed between Cuba's ruling government of Fidel Castro and the Soviet Union. The agreement constituted a barter arrangement whereby Moscow undertook to exchange oil for Cuban sugar, thereby enabling Cuba to conserve its scarce hard currency reserves. The deal represented a lifeline – Che Guevara called it "economic liberation"[35] – for the infant revolution.

However, the importation of Soviet crude oil would slash the profits of Standard Oil of New Jersey, Texaco and Shell, which up until then had imported their own oil for refining in their Cuban plants. Shortly after the signing of the agreement, President Eisenhower gave his approval for the training of an armed force of Cuban exiles to invade the island nation. Eisenhower's presidential election campaign had benefited from Rockefeller largesse.[36]

When the three oil companies were asked to refine Soviet crude oil, they refused to do so. At the end of June, the Cuban authorities seized the refineries. Within days, President Eisenhower cut Cuba's sugar quota. Castro retaliated by nationalizing thirty-six US-owned sugar mills, telephone and electric power companies and the oil refineries, including the Rockefeller-linked Standard Oil of New Jersey refinery.

On 17 April 1961, over 1,400 Cubans who had been trained, armed, financed and transported by the United States, landed at the Bay of Pigs in a vain bid to overthrow Castro. Plans for the invasion had been drawn up under the direction of two CFR members, President Eisenhower and Allen Dulles.

The invasion was mounted by President Kennedy, whose principal advisers for the invasion were Secretary of State Rusk, CIA Director Allen Dulles and National Security Adviser McGeorge Bundy. Treasury Secretary C. Douglas Dillon was also consulted. All were CFR members.

Three of these had very close ties to the Rockefeller family. Rusk had been president of the Rockefeller Foundation (1952–61) and Dillon a Foundation trustee (1960–61) and later its chairman (1971–75). Allen Dulles and David Rockefeller had served together as directors of the CFR since 1949.

Whenever Rockefeller interests were threatened abroad, there always seemed to be Rockefeller Foundation leaders and CFR members in the seats of political power in Washington eager to protect these interests.

Securing Rockefeller Interests: Peru

Since 1918, when the company cut off oil supplies to coerce the government to comply with its demands, Standard Oil of New Jersey operations were a political hot potato in Peru.[37] Using a local subsidiary, the International Petroleum Company (IPC), Standard Oil dominated the country's oil sector. This dominance and the company's repatriation of enormous profits, with little benefit accruing to Peru, aroused nationwide discontent.

By the 1960s, IPC's operations in Peru had become an explosive issue. When its government sought a more equitable deal with the company, an intransigent Standard Oil privately lobbied the Johnson administration's foreign policy decision-makers, most of whom were Rockefellerian elites. Washington's response was to halt US aid to the country.

In 1968, Peru's government backed down. Its generous new concessions to IPC lit the fuse on an already explosive controversy. As public anger escalated and internal divisions rent the government, Peru's armed forces seized power. IPC's holdings and the Chase Manhattan's Banco Continental were expropriated by the new junta.

The response of the Nixon administration's Henry Kissinger-dominated foreign policy team was to pressurize multilateral agencies such as the World Bank to curtail funds to Peru. Foreign investment capital was reduced to a trickle. Peru's economic situation rapidly deteriorated because of the US economic blockade and junta mismanagement. In 1975, the junta was toppled in a coup. Once more Rockefeller and Corporate USA interests had taken precedence over the needs of the population of a Third World country in the conduct of Washington's foreign policy.

Standard Oil in Indonesia

In 1945, Achmed Sukarno became the first president of newly independent Indonesia. Ten years later, the United States attempted to frustrate Sukarno's Nationalist party in that year's national elections, with the CIA giving $1 million to the centrist Masjumi party. Three years later, unmarked US bombers participated in an unsuccessful military coup attempt against him.

In April 1963, Sukarno took a major step towards breaking the dominance of some foreign multinationals in Indonesia when he gave an ultimatum to three foreign oil companies: agree to pay a fair share of their profits from their operations in the country to the Indonesian government or face expropriation of their assets. Two of the companies were American, Caltex and Stanvac. Following the ultimatum, the two companies sought assistance from Under Secretary of State Averell Harriman and Assistant Secretary of State for Far Eastern Affairs Roger Hilsman.[38]

Stanvac was a Far Eastern joint venture company of two offspring of the Rockefellers' Standard Oil Company – Standard Oil of New Jersey (Exxon/Esso) and Standard Oil of New York. Caltex was a joint enterprise between another Rockefeller-linked company, Standard Oil of California, and Texaco.

Sukarno was compelled to back down. Later he was toppled in a coup, being replaced by his Washington-approved successor, General Raden Suharto, who had played a leading role in the slaughter of an estimated 800,000 Indonesians.

At every important phase of the Sukarno saga, Rockefellerian elites had directed US foreign policy.[39] In the 1950s, when the CIA spent $1 million on an anti-Sukarno campaign during national elections, aided an armed revolt and mounted bombing raids within

Indonesia, the CFR triumvirate of President Eisenhower, Allen Dulles and John Foster Dulles were determining US foreign policy. Later, when the Rockefeller-linked oil companies in Indonesia experienced difficulties they turned to Averell Harriman, a former director of the CFR (1950–55) and Roger Hilsman, who a few years earlier had been an adviser to the Rockefeller Brothers Fund Special Studies Project. The secretary of state at the time was former Rockefeller Foundation president Dean Rusk. When Sukarno was deposed by Suharto and when Suharto's forces engaged in its massacre of Indonesians, Rusk was still secretary of state.

Rockefeller Interests in Iran

The convergence of US foreign policy and Rockefeller interests was also evident in Iran. In 1953, the ruling regime of Mohammed Mossadegh was overthrown in a CIA-coordinated coup. Mossadegh had chosen to nationalize his country's rich oil resources, then controlled by the British-owned Anglo-Iranian Oil Company. After the coup, Mossadegh was replaced by Mohammed Reza Shah Pahlavi, who rewarded the United States for its help in installing him as ruler by granting a 40 per cent share (later reduced to 35 per cent) of Iran's oil production to five US companies, three of which were daughters of the Rockefeller-founded Standard Oil Company. Responsible for Mossadegh's overthrow was the CFR triad of Eisenhower and the Dulles brothers, Secretary of State John Foster Dulles being a former chairman of the Rockefeller Foundation.

In January 1979, as Islamic fundamentalists fomented revolution within the country, its US-installed ruler, Shah Pahlavi, was forced to flee abroad. Warned that his admission into the United States could lead to the seizure of American hostages in Iran, President Carter rebuffed the shah's requests for asylum. When country after country followed suit, Carter and Secretary of State Cyrus Vance (earlier chairman of the Rockefeller Foundation) turned to their fellow Trilateral commissioners David Rockefeller and Henry Kissinger for help.

Rockefeller interests in Iran were not limited to oil.[40] The Chase Manhattan Bank, chaired by David Rockefeller, was a financial adviser to the shah and bankers to the government. During the shah's exile, Rockefeller associates acted as his advisers and assistants. When he became seriously ill with cancer, David Rockefeller "sent his personal physician to Mexico" to examine the shah, Carter revealed in his autobiography.[41]

In October 1979, the US president bowed to pressures from Rockefeller, Vance, Kissinger and former Chase chairman John J. McCloy to admit the shah to the United States. On 4 November, incensed Iranians stormed the US embassy in Tehran, seized over sixty embassy staff as hostages and demanded that the shah and his fortune be returned to Iran. Eight months later the shah died.

Under the shah, Iran had been a land ruled by fear, violence, torture and death. Informers recruited by SAVAK, the shah's secret police, were everywhere. Dissension was brutally crushed. Describing the fate that could befall those tortured by SAVAK, Iranian poet Reza Baraheni told of how interrogators might first beat prisoners with sticks and clubs, then hang them upside down, rape them, pass electric current through their bodies, extract nails and, on occasions, all their teeth. Sometimes a hot iron rod was pushed through a face, from one side to the other, he claimed. Other procedures employed by SAVAK, included broken bottles pushed into the anus and boiling liquids poured into the same orifice.[42]

David Rockefeller painted a contrasting picture of life under the shah. In time, he opined, the ruler would be viewed as "a modernizing leader who worked assiduously over several decades to bring economic and social progress for his beloved Iran".[43]

President Carter was similarly laudatory in his comments, speaking of "the great leadership of the Shah" and of "the respect and the admiration and the love which your people give you".[44]

Rockefeller Interests in Afghanistan

America's final and decisive Cold War conflict was in Afghanistan. The conflict followed the December 1979 invasion of the country by Soviet forces. President Carter's national security adviser, Zbigniew Brzezinski, subsequently revealed that the Soviet invasion had been deliberately orchestrated by Washington, beginning on 3 July 1979, almost six months before the Soviet invasion, when President Carter authorized the provision of covert US aid to opponents of Afghanistan's pro-Soviet ruling regime. On that July day, Brzezinski later disclosed, "I wrote a note to the President in which I explained to him that, in my opinion, this aid was going to induce a Soviet military intervention." Washington's covert operation in the Soviet Union's neighbouring country, he opined, "was an excellent idea. It had the effect of drawing the Russians into the Afghan trap", giving the Soviet Union its own ten-year Vietnam-type war that ultimately, he claimed, resulted in the breaking up of the Soviet empire.[45]

Washington's war-promoting efforts in Afghanistan in the 1980s became its most extensive and expensive covert operation of the Cold War. The recipients of the enormous US aid were Islamic fundamentalist mujahedin forces, which were supplied with weapons, including Stinger missiles, and were trained by US military instructors. Ultimately, the United States' mujahedin allies were victorious. The Soviet forces were withdrawn and, shortly afterwards, the Soviet Union and its empire collapsed. A fundamentalist Taliban regime seized power in Afghanistan, beginning an era of repression and executions.

The Taliban victory and the emergence of Osama bin Laden as a powerful extremist Islamic leader were consequences of US foreign policies. The US-induced Soviet invasion gave Washington an excuse to arm and train the mujahedin forces, which became useful collaborators in America's anti-Soviet Cold War. The CIA, with the collaboration of Saudi Arabia and Pakistan's Interservices intelligence agency, encouraged the recruitment of Muslims from around the world to fight against the Soviet forces. In the decade after 1982, an estimated 35,000 Muslims from forty-three Islamic countries took up arms with the mujahedin, many after training in military schools on the Pakistan-Afghan frontier.[46] It was from these CIA-armed and US and Saudi-funded training camps that bin Laden's al-Qaeda emerged. After the US-assisted Taliban victory, thousands of the mujahedin fighters dispersed to other countries to foment wars against infidels, and especially against their former sponsor, the United States. Al-Qaeda terrorists went to live in the US to make preparations for the World Trade Center and Pentagon attacks.

It is improbable that these attacks would have occurred if President Carter and his cabinet of Trilateral commissioners (including Brzezinski, David Rockefeller's closest collaborator in the commission's formation – together they had launched the idea of a Trilateral body at the 1972 Bilderberg Group annual meeting) had not successfully conspired to push a reluctant Soviet Union into intervening militarily in Afghanistan. 11 September was almost certainly the consequence of "blowback" – a term coined by the CIA to describe US foreign policies which end up having outcomes directly opposite to what Washington had planned.

The Soviet invasion and the ensuing war against the Soviet forces of occupation were thus consequences of Cold War scheming by Washington. An estimated one million Afghans were killed, probably at least twice that number were wounded or maimed, and further millions became refugees – all sacrificed in the pursuit of US foreign policy goals.

The 11 September 2001 attacks on the World Trade Center and the Pentagon, masterminded by Osama bin Laden, the leader of the al-Qaeda movement, provided Washington with a justification for intervening once again in Afghanistan. The ostensible rationale for the US war there was the Taliban government's refusal to hand over bin Laden for trial. Significantly, none of the nineteen 11 September suicide bombers, or the Saudi-born bin Laden himself, were Afghans. Fifteen of the bombers were citizens of Saudi Arabia, Washington's closest ally in the Muslim world. A veritable training school and recruiting ground for al-Qaeda due to the influence there of religious leaders that preached poisonous revanchist Islam and the nursery for most of the suicide bombers, oil-rich Saudi Arabia, unlike Afghanistan, escaped the horrors of Washington's retributive war. It was an absurd paradox. The country most responsible for promoting Islamic extremist ideology and for the funding and growth of Islamic terrorist bodies, including al-Qaeda, is a quasi-totalitarian US client state whose stability is guaranteed by US political and military support. A July 2002 briefing for a top Pentagon policy advisory panel, the Defense Policy Board, described Saudi Arabia as "the kernel of evil" in the Middle East, "active at every level of the terror chain. . . [it] supports our enemies and attacks our allies".[47]

Nevertheless, due to America's dependence on Saudi oil, Washington chose, at least temporarily, to ignore the country's culpability for the 11 September bombing. Three of the other four bombers came from the United Arab Emirates and Egypt, both US allies. The remaining bomber came from Lebanon. Although no Afghan had been directly linked to any act of terrorism against the United States, civilians in Afghanistan were bombed and killed by the hegemon, ostensibly because their government was sheltering bin Laden. His mere presence served as a flimsy pretext for waging war and overthrowing a hostile government in a strategically located country.

Afghanistan's strategic importance derived from its location close to former republics of the Soviet Union, which became independent as the Soviet Union disintegrated. The republics possessed vast untapped oil and gas deposits. Soon after the fall of the Soviet Union, four offspring of the Rockefellers' Standard Oil – Exxon, Mobil, Chevron and Amoco – were seeking access to the oil and gas in these republics. In the Caspian region, the Azerbaijan International Operating Company consortium, which included the Rockefeller-linked Exxon and Amoco and the American energy giant Unocal, gained control over estimated reserves of more than four billion barrels of oil. Among Amoco's paid consultants was Zbigniew Brzezinski, co-founder with David Rockefeller of the Trilateral Commission and the person who had precipitated the 1979 Soviet invasion and ensuing war in Afghanistan. In October 1995, the president of Turkmenistan announced the selection of Unocal to construct a pipeline across Afghanistan to Pakistan. Present at the announcement was Henry Kissinger, a Unocal consultant.

The subsequent war against terrorism in Afghanistan served as a veil for the US to secure dominance in the region and to gain access to its oil riches. Directing the war was President George W. Bush's oil cabinet, especially Secretary of State Colin Powell (CFR), National Security Adviser Condoleezza Rice (CFR) and Vice President Richard Cheney (CFR director and Trilateral commission). Rice was a former board member of Chevron (formerly the Rockefellers' Standard Oil of California). In 1992, Chevron had signed a joint venture agreement with one of the newly independent former Soviet republics, Kazakhstan, to develop the Tenghiz oil field. Kazakhstan is believed to have the world's largest untapped oil reserves.

As in Chile, Brazil, Peru, Cuba, Indonesia and Iran, Rockefeller and other US corporate interests were a major factor in Washington's post-11 September intervention in Afghanistan. Guided by Washington, a new regime was installed there, with many of its cabinet and sub-cabinet posts being filled by former US-supported warlords and guerrillas with dismaying records of gross barbarity.

Flirting With Dictators

Throughout and after the Cold War, repressive right-wing regimes had an ally in the Rockefeller family and its associated ruling Washington elites. In 1984, investigative reporter Penny Lernoux wrote that in Argentina, David Rockefeller was "remembered by thousands of victims of the military's repression as the American banker who told Argentina's generals not to worry about human rights".[48] A 1986 visit by him to the country provoked riots in which dozens were arrested.

In March 1976, military officers had seized power there. During the ensuing years of repression, a new phrase entered the nation's lexicon, "*los desaparecidos*", "the disappeared" who were kidnapped and murdered by government-linked death squads or tortured and killed in secret detention camps. The labour movement was systematically crippled. Strikes were forbidden, trade union leaders were killed and workers arrested. Around 30,000 civilians were murdered.

David Rockefeller's support for the military rulers was expressed in a very tangible form. Shortly after their seizure of power, the new rulers encountered severe debt repayment problems. A consortium of banks came to its aid, led by the David Rockefeller-chaired Chase Manhattan Bank.[49]

The Rockefellers were not popular in Argentina. A 1969 visit there by Nelson Rockefeller sparked a general strike and an explosion of violence in which around a dozen Rockefeller-controlled supermarkets were torched. Nelson's visit was part of a tour of Latin America. The purpose of the tour was to enable him, as chairman of a commission appointed by President Nixon, to devise new foreign policy proposals for a region where, by coincidence, the Rockefellers had very large investments. The tour was met with the most widespread public display of anti-American and anti-Rockefeller rage ever witnessed in the continent.

The riot-plagued tour began in Honduras, where a student was killed during the disturbances. Bolivia was another violence-marred venue, concern for his safety compelling the authorities to restrict Rockefeller's visit to a stopover at a heavily guarded airport. Visits to

Venezuela and Chile were cancelled due to the level of civil unrest. Peru's government, which was engaged in expropriating the holdings of Standard Oil of New Jersey and the Chase bank, let it be known that a visit by Rockefeller would not be welcome. In strife-convulsed Uruguay and in Ecuador's capital city, students clashed with troops. Ten students were killed in Ecuador. In Costa Rica, Colombia and Panama, the public also vented its anger at his visit. In Brazil dissidents were rounded up prior to his arrival. In the Dominican Republic, four demonstrators were killed.

Rockefeller's tour was perceived by Latin Americans as a very overt manifestation of Washington's, and Rockefeller's own, endorsement of repression in the region. In country after country, Nelson Rockefeller embraced, either literally or figuratively, authoritarian and undemocratic rulers, including some of the continent's worst human rights violators. Photographs taken in Haiti show him with his arm around "Papa Doc" Duvalier, the self-declared "president for life". Duvalier's fourteen years in power were marked by an all-pervasive climate of terror, created by his Tontons Macoutes "bogeymen" who abducted, tortured and killed opponents.

Repressive US-backed military regimes in Latin America were propped up with loans provided by the David Rockefeller-chaired Chase Manhattan Bank, as were undemocratic and tyrannical right-wing regimes elsewhere.

Rockefeller support of unpopular and illegal regimes has, almost always, mirrored Washington's support for them. Conversely, the degree to which White House-approved interventions (such as those in Chile, Brazil, Cuba, Peru, Indonesia, Iran and Afghanistan) have reflected Rockefeller interests is noteworthy. Gore Vidal may well have been pondering this congruence between presidential decisions and Rockefeller interests when he wrote in 1980 of "that loyal retainer of the Chase Manhattan Bank, the American president".[50]

Instrumentalities of Intervention

Washington's willingness to intervene in the affairs of other countries to protect Rockefeller and Corporate USA interests elucidates a basic principle of US foreign policy. It is, as historian Gabriel Kolko has noted, that "the final intended result of the whole course of United States foreign policy after the Civil War was to optimize the power and profit of American capitalism in the global economy, striving for the political and military preconditions essential to the attainment of that end".[51]

Optimizing "the power and profit of American capitalism in the global economy" meant supporting the foreign operations of US multinationals, the most important component of the US economy.

The health of the American economy and the welfare of its citizens are inextricably tied to the profitability of US corporations, which, in turn, is dependent on gaining access to the markets and to the resources (mineral wealth, oil supplies, commodities, raw materials) of foreign countries.

For a long time, military force was the instrumentality of choice for expanding the domain of American corporations, facilitating the US, its corporations and investors in gaining control over the resources and markets, and even over the governments, of target states. However, the use of force had one major drawback. Control over the affairs of foreign nations, having been attained through the use of force, could usually only be sustained through the continuing use of force. Despite America's vast military superiority at the end of the Second World War, it was inconceivable that this dominance would suffice to guarantee international obeisance to the exploitative demands of Corporate USA. Other instrumentalities of intervention or coercion were required.

In exercising their control over America's corporate/trade-driven foreign policies, Washington's corporate and Rockefeller-linked elites created such instrumentalities. These took the form of new global institutional structures, whose institutions included the World Bank, the International Monetary Fund, the General Agreement on Tariffs and Trade and the United Nations. All had close ties to Corporate USA and the Rockefellers and pursued pro-corporate agendas that ultimately culminated in the birth of globalization.

Notes

1. Laurence H. Shoup and William Minter, *Imperial Brain Trust: The Council on Foreign Relations and United States Foreign Policy* (New York: Monthly Review Press, 1977), p. 119.

2. Peter Grose, *Continuing the Inquiry: The Council on Foreign Relations 1921 to 1996* (New York: CFR, 2001).

3. *Policy Planning Study 23*, 24 February 1948. Reprinted in the State Department's Foreign Relations of the United States, 1948, vol. 1.

4. The quotations are from NSC–68. See William H. Chafe and Harvard Sitkoff, eds., *A History of Our Time: Readings on Postwar America* (New York: Oxford University Press, 1999), pp. 36–40.

5. The $13 trillion figure is cited by US Deputy Secretary of State Strobe Talbott in "After the Madrid Summit", *Time*, 14 July 1997.

6. See Grose, *Continuing the Inquiry*.

7. Peter Grose, *Gentleman Spy: The Life of Allen Dulles* (London: Andre Deutsch, 1995), p. 293; Gregory Mitrovich, *Undermining the Kremlin: America's Strategy to Subvert the Soviet Bloc, 1947–1956* (Ithaca, New York Cornell University Press, 2000), pp. 18–21.

8. Victor Marchetti and John D. Marks, *The CIA and the Cult of Intelligence* (London: Coronet, 1976), p. 309.

9. *Final Report of the Church Committee*, 1976, as quoted in Frances Stonor Saunders, *Who Paid the Piper?: The CIA and the Cultural Cold War* (London: Granta, 1999), p. 135. The author details the roles of the Chase bank and the Rockefeller, Ford and other foundations in CIA covert operations. The role of the Ford Foundation is also referred to in Kai Bird, *The Chairman: John J. McCloy – The Making of the American Establishment* (New York: Simon & Schuster, 1992), pp. 426–29. See also Seymour M. Hersh, *The Price of Power: Kissinger in the Nixon White House* (New York: Summit Books, 1983), p. 290.

10. For the names of Chase bank directors 1970–82, see Gerard Colby with Charlotte Dennett, *Thy Will Be Done: The Conquest of the Amazon – Nelson Rockefeller and Evangelism in the Age of Oil* (New York: HarperCollins, 1995), pp. 789–90.

11. Alexander Cockburn and Ken Silverstein, *Washington Babylon* (London: Verso, 1996), pp. 24–25.

12. C. D. Jackson, later a founder of the American wing of the Bilderberg Group, became Eisenhower's special assistant for psychological warfare. John Foster Dulles was chairman of the Rockefeller Foundation (1950–52) and a trustee from 1935–50, and a CFR member. Allen Dulles was president of the CFR (1946–50), vice president (1944–46), secretary (1933–44) and a director (1927–69). Appointees recruited from the corporate sector filled many of the most important posts in Eisenhower's "Cadillac Cabinet". Charles E. Wilson, president of General Motors, became secretary of defense. George M. Humphrey, president of the M. A. Hanna Company, was appointed secretary of the treasury. Wilson was succeeded as defense secretary by Neil H. McElroy, president of Procter and Gamble. Mc Elroy was succeeded by Thomas S. Gates, a partner in investment bankers Drexel and Co. In 1957 Eisenhower replaced Humphrey with Robert B. Anderson, who had been general manager of the W. T. Waggoner oil estate in Texas.

13. Quoted in Stanley Karnow, *Vietnam: A History* (London: Pimlico, 1994), p. 184.

14. *Ibid.*, p. 192; William Blum, *The CIA: A Forgotten History* (London: Zed Books, 1986), p. 134.

15. Dorothy Buckton James, *Outside, Looking In: Critiques of American Policies and Institutions, Left and Right* (New York: Harper and Row, 1972), p. 89, citing *New York Times* of 3 August 1953.

16. Other CFR members appointed by President Kennedy included his national security adviser, McGeorge Bundy; CIA Directors Allen Dulles and John A. McCone; the CIA's deputy director for plans, Richard Helms; Under Secretaries of State W. Averell Harriman, Chester Bowles and George W. Ball; Chairman of the State Department's Policy Planning Council Walt W. Rostow; Assistant Secretaries of Defense Paul H. Nitze and William Bundy; Deputy Secretary of Defense Roswell Gilpatric; and Presidential Adviser John J. McCloy, chairman of the CFR.

17. See Shoup and Minter, *Imperial Brain Trust*, p. 64.

18. Michael Schwartz, ed., *The Structure of Power in America: The Corporate Elite as a Ruling Class* (New York: Holmes & Meier, 1987), p. 113.

19. See Shoup and Minter, *Imperial Brain Trust*, p. 240; Philip H. Burch, Jr,

Elites in American History (New York: Holmes & Meier, 1980), vol. 3, pp. 208–09.

20. George Brown Tindall and David E. Shi, *America: A Narrative History* (New York: W. W. Norton, 1996), p. 1441.

21. John Stockwell, *In Search of Enemies: A CIA Story* (London: Andre Deutsch, 1978), pp. 43, 217.

22. Henry Kissinger, *The White House Years* (London: Weidenfeld & Nicolson/Michael Joseph, 1979), pp. 4, 1475.

23. For details of the programme's funding, see Walter Isaacson, *Kissinger: A Biography* (London: Faber and Faber, 1992), pp. 70–71; Marvin Kalb and Bernard Kalb, *Kissinger* (London: Hutchison, 1974), pp. 48–49.

24. See Isaacson, *Kissinger*, p. 289; Hersh, *The Price of Power*, p. 273; Kissinger, *The White House Years*, p. 673.

25. See Kate Clark, *Chile: Reality and Prospects of Popular Unity* (London: Lawrence and Wishart, 1972), p. 102.

26. For details of the Rockefeller-Anaconda links, see David M. Kotz, *Bank Control of Large Corporations in the United States* (Berkeley, California: University of California Press, 1979), pp. 37, 120; Peter Collier and David Horowitz, *The Rockefellers: An American Dynasty* (New York: Signet, 1977), p. 43; Ron Chernow, *Titan: The Life of John D. Rockefeller, Sr.* (London: Warner, 1999), pp. 378–79; Colby with Dennett, *Thy Will Be Done*, p. 821.

27. *Report of the Senate Select Committee to Study Governmental Operations With Respect to Intelligence Activities*, 94th Congress, 1st Session.

28. See Hersh, *The Price of Power*, p. 260; Colby with Dennett, *Thy Will Be Done*, p. 474; Collier and Horowitz, *The Rockefellers*, pp. 413–14.

29. See Hersh, *The Price of Power*, p. 266; Colby with Dennett, *Thy Will Be Done*, p. 664; John Ranelagh, *The Agency: The Rise and Decline of the CIA* (London: Sceptre, 1988), p. 515; Anthony Sampson, *The Sovereign State: The Secret History of ITT* (London: Coronet, 1985), p. 239.

30. See Colby with Dennett, *Thy Will Be Done*, p. 442.

31. Philip Agee, *Inside the Company: CIA Diary* (Middlesex: Penguin, 1978), p. 321.

32. *Ibid.*, p. 362.

33. Quoted in Vernon A. Walters, *Silent Missions* (Garden City, New York: Doubleday, 1978), p. 376.

34. Eduardo Galeano, *Open Veins of Latin America: Five Centuries of the Pillage of a Continent* (New York: Monthly Review Press, 1997), p. 217.

35. Che Guevara, television broadcast, 20 March 1960. Published in *Hoy*, 23 March 1960.

36. For details of Rockefeller support for the Eisenhower campaign, see Collier and Horowitz, *The Rockefellers*, p. 269.

37. The roles of Standard Oil and the Chase bank in Peru are analysed in Richard R. Fagen, ed., *Capitalism and the State in US-Latin American Relations* (Stanford, California: Stanford University Press, 1979), pp. 217–253.

38. For an account of how the US government compelled Sukarno to bow to its pressures, see Roger Hilsman, *To Move A Nation: The Politics of Foreign Policy in the Administration of John F. Kennedy* (Garden City, New York: Doubleday, 1967), pp. 387–90. Apart from obtaining favourable tax

and profit concessions, Hilsman wrote of how "most important of all, the companies got, not only the right to market Indonesian oil under profitable arrangements, but the right to conduct exploration for new deposits subject to the same arrangements for a period of twenty-five years. The oil companies were delighted – not only with the agreement, but with the active co-operation of the United States Government."

39.   The role of the CIA, CFR members and American oil companies in influencing political and economic affairs in Indonesia is examined by Peter Dale Scott in Malcolm Caldwell, ed., *Ten Years Military Terror in Indonesia* (Nottingham: Spokesman Books, 1975).

40.   For details of the Rockefeller family's role in Iran's affairs, see William Shawcross, *The Shah's Last Ride* (London: Pan Books, 1989).

41.   Jimmy Carter, *Keeping Faith* (London: Collins, 1982), p. 454.

42.   Thomas Plate and Andrea Darvi, *Secret Police* (London: Abacus, 1983), p. 165; Shawcross, *The Shah's Last Ride*, p. 169.

43.   See Shawcross, *The Shah's Last Ride*, p. 356.

44.   *Ibid.*, p. 105; Daniel Yergin, *The Prize: The Epic Quest for Oil, Money and Power* (New York: Touchstone, 1993), pp. 672–73.

45.   Interview in *Le Nouvel Observateur* (France), 15–21 January 1998, translated by William Blum. See also William Blum, *Rogue State: A Guide to the World's Only Superpower* (London: Zed Books, 2001), pp. 4–5.

46.   Ahmed Rashid, *Taliban: The Story of the Afghan Warlords* (London: Pan, 2001), p. 130.

47.   Rand Corporation analyst Laurent Murawiec at briefing for Defense Policy Board, 10 July 2002.

48.   Penny Lernoux, *In Banks We Trust* (Garden City, New York: Anchor Press, 1984), p. 6.

49.   See Fagen, *Capitalism and the State in US-Latin American Relations*, p. 184.

50.   Gore Vidal, *Esquire*, August 1980. Reprinted in Gore Vidal, *United States: Essays 1952–1992* (London: Abacus, 1994), p. 938.

51.   Gabriel Kolko, *Main Currents in Modern American History* (New York: Harper and Row, 1976), pp. 49–50.

Chapter 6

The United Nations

Policing the Cold War World

The Cold War provided the United States with a pretext for intervening in, and dominating, the affairs of other countries. However, on its own the Cold War could not procure the degree of global economic and political dominance that Washington wanted. It needed to create structures through which US superintendence of the post-Second World War global order could be facilitated.

In a 1960 discussion document, Cold War architect Paul H. Nitze analysed "the main elements of the structure we have been trying to erect since 1946" to sustain a new global order compatible with US interests. The new structure, he observed, "had to have its political, its economic, and its military parts. It had to provide for certain world-wide functions. It had to foster closer regional institutions within the worldwide system." Nitze summarized the principal steps taken to foster this Washington-conceived institutional structure. They included the creation of the United Nations, the World Bank, the International Monetary Fund, GATT (General Agreement on Tariffs and Trade) and regional military alliances – the North Atlantic Treaty Organization (NATO), the Organization of American States (OAS) and the Southeast Asia Treaty Organization (SEATO). These were reinforced by regional and bilateral programmes and other initiatives such as the Marshall Plan and the Organization for European Economic Cooperation.[1] Through these the United States intended to ride herd on the Cold War world.

This process of constructing a post-Second World War international order compatible with US interests began in earnest in August 1941 when President Franklin D. Roosevelt met secretly at sea off the coast of Newfoundland with the British prime minister, Winston Churchill. The fruit of their deliberations was an agreement, the Atlantic Charter, which sketched goals for the post-bellum world. The agreement, Churchill remarked later, "was a plain and bold intimation that... the United States would join with us in policing the world until the establishment of a better order".[2]

However, joint Anglo-American policing of the world was unrealistic without the collaboration of other powers. Seven months before the meeting with Churchill, Roosevelt had promised "a world-wide reduction of armaments to such a point and in such a thorough fashion that no nation will be in a position to commit an act of physical aggression against any neighbour – anywhere in the world".[3] To accomplish this, he proposed that there should be "four policemen" in the world, comprising the United States, the United Kingdom, Russia and pre-communist China. The rest of the world would be compelled to disarm by the four globocops. Nations caught arming would first be threatened with quarantine, and if quarantine did not halt the arming process, they would be bombed.[4]

The proposal was startling in its implications. With other nations compelled to disarm, military dominance in the post-bellum world envisaged by the American president would become the preserve of the "four policemen". It was a formula for big power hegemony.

The Roosevelt administration proposed a means through which a measure of global dominance by the "four policemen" could be achieved. In October of that year, Roosevelt's secretary of state, Cordell Hull, at a meeting in Moscow with his Soviet and British counterparts, discussed a proposal for the formation of an international organization for "the maintenance of international peace and security".[5] The following year, at meetings at the Dumbarton Oaks estate in Washington, DC, proposals for its establishment were endorsed by the "four policemen".

On 25 April 1945, representatives of fifty governments gathered in San Francisco to discuss the proposed body. Before the end of the year, a charter for the organization had been ratified by a majority of the participating nations. The US-mooted United Nations had become a reality.

The United Nations and the CFR

Describing the CFR's central role in shaping the post-war world, G. William Domhoff wrote of how "monopoly capitalists in the Council on Foreign Relations carefully and secretively planned the policies of modern-day imperialism and then introduced them into government".[6] A CFR book, *Continuing the Inquiry: The Council on Foreign Relations from 1921 to 1996*, commenting on the matter in more muted language, noted how during the Second World War council members proposed a programme "that would guide American foreign policy in the coming years of war and the challenging new world that would emerge after".[7] This discreet venture "is strictly confidential", wrote

CFR director Isaiah Bowman, "because the whole plan would be 'ditched' if it became generally known that the State Department is working in collaboration with any outside group".[8] The CFR's collaborative role included the creation of an organization to police that world, the United Nations.

This role began following a 12 September 1939 meeting between three CFR members – Assistant Secretary of State George S. Messersmith, CFR executive director Walter H. Mallory and CFR director Hamilton Fish Armstrong. At the meeting Mallory and Armstrong outlined a council proposal for CFR War and Peace Studies groups to draw up plans for shaping a post-war global order over which Pax Americana could reign supreme. Their reports were to be submitted to the State Department and President Franklin D. Roosevelt for consideration.[9]

The council's offer was accepted by Secretary of State Cordell Hull. Shortly afterwards a new research division was set up within the State Department to study post-war issues. To head it, Hull chose his special assistant, Leo Pasvolsky, making him one of the department's principal formulators of plans for shaping the post-war world. He was a CFR member.[10]

In January 1940, the State Department established an Advisory Committee on Problems of Foreign Relations to "survey the basic principles which should underlie a desirable world order to be evolved after the termination of the present hostilities". It was chaired by Under Secretary of State Sumner Welles, a CFR member, and also included CFR President Norman H. Davis.[11]

In January 1943, the State Department formed a new policy planning body, the Informal Agenda Group. Apart from its founder, Secretary Hull, all of its other original members were CFR members – the CFR president Norman H. Davis; CFR directors Isaiah Bowman and Myron C. Taylor; Hull's special assistant for post-war planning, Leo Pasvolsky; and Under Secretary of State Sumner Welles. The Informal Agenda Group became one of the State Department's principal forums for coordinating plans for the post-war world.[12]

The same five CFR members – Davis, Bowman, Pasvolsky, Welles and Taylor – were also members of another State Department-created body, the Advisory Committee on Postwar Foreign Policy. Altogether, eight of the committee's original fourteen members were drawn from the CFR and its War and Peace Studies groups.[13]

By 1942, the CFR War and Peace Studies groups had, effectively, been merged into the State Department's post-war planning structure, with the groups' research secretaries becoming consultants to the State Department.[14]

The task of devising strategies to ensure US global supremacy after the war had thus become the responsibility of a small number of groups, most of which were dominated or heavily influenced by CFR members. A key objective was the establishment of a US-manipulable international forum through which US supremacy could be imposed, the United Nations.

At a May 1942 CFR meeting, Isaiah Bowman, a director of the CFR since its inception in 1921, suggested that US hegemonic power could be accomplished in the post-war era through creating a United Nations body. Such a scheme, he opined, would avoid the taint of "conventional forms of imperialism", since Washington could exercise its power globally under the aegis of the proposed multilateral United Nations organization, rather than exercising its power unilaterally.[15] The scheme would give US interventions a façade of legitimacy and acceptability.

To ensure that the proposed UN would be susceptible to manipulative influences by Washington would require a US-friendly UN charter. Proposals conceived by CFR-dominated planning groups formed the basis for the US-sponsored charter draft presented at Dumbarton Oaks and later, in modified form, at the founding conference of the UN in San Francisco.[16]

CFR members were present in considerable numbers at the founding conference to lobby for acceptance of the charter draft. These included long-time Rockefeller Foundation trustee John Foster Dulles, John J. McCloy, later the head of the Rockefellers' Chase bank, and Assistant Secretary of State for Latin American Affairs Nelson Rockefeller. Rockefeller arrived in San Francisco accompanying Latin American diplomats, who constituted the largest and most important voting bloc at the meeting. His assignment was to liaise with delegates from the region to secure their support for US proposals.[17]

Articles 51 and 52 of the UN Charter owe their existence to Nelson Rockefeller. In his "diary file", former Assistant Secretary of State Adolf A. Berle noted how Rockefeller "was able to compel the inclusion in the charter of the United Nations" of the two articles and "as a result the present structure of American foreign policy has taken form". Article 51, he observed, was "Nelson Rockefeller's personal achievement".[18]

Availing of the articles, which endorsed the right of "individual or collective self-defense" and "regional arrangements or agencies" to respond to threats to peace and security, the United States would subsequently be able to intervene militarily in the affairs of other countries, under the pretext of regional defence exigencies.

The Rockefellers made one other significant contribution to the United Nations. In late 1946, Nelson's father presented a large site in New York as a headquarters site for the infant United Nations, thereby ensuring that the United States would be the permanent home of the international body's principal organs.

The Security Council: Serving US Interests

Although the charter agreed at the San Francisco conference espoused the principle of "the equal rights. . . of nations large and small", its American framers disingenuously created an organization in which nations had neither equal influence nor equal power. The UN was created to serve US foreign policy interests, not to promote a more equitable and democratic international order.

As the principal framer of the charter, the United States was afforded the opportunity of creating a body that would function as an extension of the US foreign policy apparatus, to consolidate and expand American hegemony. Such functions could not be performed in an organization where democratic procedures prevailed, since democracy entailed being subject to majority rule and to the interests and caprices of other countries. To circumvent this problem, the charter's American framers created a framework for the organization that conveyed an impression of democratic collegiality, yet shaped a UN in which real power was vested in a few member states, particularly the United States.

To provide the UN with a veneer of democracy, the charter's US drafters opted for an organization with two main discussion forums, the General Assembly and the Security Council. The assembly, although comprising all UN member states, was little more than a toothless talking shop. Resolutions passed in the assembly lack the power of international law, are unenforceable by the UN and are often ignored or flagrantly violated.

Responsibility for pursuing the UN's foremost objective, "to maintain international peace and security", rests almost exclusively with the Security Council, the organization's pre-eminent organ and also its most undemocratic. The council comprises just fifteen of the UN's 190 or so member states. Of these, five – the United States, Russia, the United Kingdom and China (the "Four Policemen") and France – are permanent members of the council, and the other ten are non-permanent. Permanent members (the "Perm Five") cannot lose their places in the council. Non-permanent members are elected to the council by the General Assembly for a two-year term and on completion of their term are ineligible for immediate re-election.

Although each member state of the Security Council has one vote, the votes are not all equal. Those of the "Perm Five" each has the power of veto. A clear denial of the most basic democratic principles, this privilege met with huge opposition at the founding conference in San Francisco. Later, Harry S. Truman, president of the United States at the time of the San Francisco conference, admitted that this power of veto was "the thorniest" issue at the conference, "coming under attack from practically all the smaller countries".[19] Nevertheless, Washington's will prevailed. It got its power of veto and through the veto the ability to dominate the affairs of the United Nations.

The veto gave each of the "Perm Five" the power to brush aside the opinions and wishes of all other UN member states. This disparity was further aggravated by the exclusory nature of the "Perm Five", whereby Third World regions such as Latin America and Africa were not allowed to have even one permanent member in the Security Council. India is barred from permanent membership although its population comprises one-sixth of the earth's total population, larger than the combined populations of four of the "Perm Five".

For over twenty years, until 1971, Washington ensured that communist China could not become a member of the United Nations, although its population exceeded the aggregate populations of all the "Perm Five". Instead, a US ally, the Republic of China, was not only granted UN membership, it was also granted "Perm Five" membership although, absurdly, it administered little more than Taiwan (Formosa), an island with a land area less than half the size of Maine.

In forming the United Nations, Washington created a body that was deliberately undemocratic (the word "democracy" is not used in the UN Charter), disempowering Third World countries whose citizens constitute the great majority of mankind. This disempowerment and the privileged and powerful position which the US demanded, and obtained, within the UN enabled Washington to use the organization as a vehicle for expanding US hegemonic control over the world's nations. It helped the US, with less than 5 per cent of the world's population, to impose its will on nations representing more than 95 per cent of the human race.

The US power of veto gave Washington the capability to defeat all Security Council resolutions which it chose to nullify, even though the consensus within the fifteen-nation council and within the General Assembly, with its 190 or so member nations, might be overwhelmingly in favour of the resolutions.

The power which attaches to Washington's "Perm Five" status in the Security Council is enormous, as the Council is the sole United Nations body with the power to declare war and to impose peace on nations. In 1991, the world witnessed the grisly consequences of Washington's abuse of its self-conferred power within the Security Council.

The Gulf Wars

On 2 August 1990, the armed forces of Iraqi leader Saddam Hussein swept into neighbouring Kuwait, overran the token resistance and annexed the territory. Five months later, UN-mandated forces led by the United States launched a counter-offensive. When it ended six weeks later, the Iraqi forces had been routed, Kuwait had been freed, and peace had been restored to the region. To all appearances the United Nations response was an outstanding success. A regional tyrant's ambitions to annex a smaller and weaker country and to subjugate its people had been foiled by UN member states acting in concert.

In the eleven-year period prior to the invasion, since his seizure of power in Iraq in 1979, the psychopathic leader had routinely resorted to torture and terror against his own people. The forms of torture used by his security forces included hacking off breasts, limbs, noses, ears and penises, electric shocks, mock executions, nails hammered into victims' bodies, sexual abuse, the extraction of finger and toe nails, burning with cigarettes and being hung from metal hooks by handcuffed wrists.[20] His persona is accurately reflected in the soubriquet "The Butcher of Baghdad" with which he was dubbed by some critics.[21] In the weeks following his successful putsch, dozens, perhaps hundreds, of the most senior members of his party, government ministers and political opponents were executed. In March 1988, his forces attacked the Kurdish town of Halabje with chemical weapons, killing up to 5,000 men, women and children.

His propensity for violence was first witnessed by the world in September 1980 when, barely a year after installing himself as president, his forces invaded neighbouring Iran, thereby starting an eight-year war between the two countries. In August 1990, his forces invaded another neighbour, Kuwait.

The two invasions exposed a bewildering aptitude on the part of Washington for moral somersaulting and Damascan about-turns. When Saddam's forces invaded and annexed Kuwait, the US response was potent and effective. Under the aegis of the United Nations, it coordinated and led the most destructive military operation since the Vietnam War, driving the Iraqi forces of occupation out of Kuwait, devastating Iraq and killing up to 200,000 Iraqis.

In contrast with Iraq's invasion of Kuwait, which cost few lives prior to the US-led counter-offensive, Iraq's invasion of Iran began a war which claimed, possibly, over 500,000 lives. On this occasion, the United States chose not to muster a UN-mandated force to remove the invaders. Instead, it aided the Iraqi tyrant, removing Iraq from its list of terrorist countries, re-establishing diplomatic relations with Baghdad, covertly providing the Iraqi military with invaluable satellite intelligence on Iranian defences and troop deployments and supplying guarantees for credits and loans for Iraqi purchases, including American exports with potential military uses. The US aid helped to transform the vulnerable Iraqi leader into a lethal regional tyrant.[22]

Condemning Washington's wooing of the Iraqi dictator, Rep. Charles E. Schumer (D-New York) opined that "Saddam Hussein is President Bush's Frankenstein – a run-of-the-mill dictator the president fed with billions of US tax-payer dollars and turned into a monster".[23]

Rep. Henry Gonzalez (D-Texas) argued that in aiding the despot both President Bush and President Reagan bore huge responsibility for the invasion of Kuwait and the carnage of the Gulf War. "Behind closed doors, and out of sight of the people and the Congress, they courted Saddam Hussein with a reckless abandon that ended in war and the deaths of dozens of our brave soldiers and over 200,000 Muslims, Iraqis and others."[24]

Hijacking the United Nations

The Gulf War was only the second occasion that the United Nations authorized a war to be waged under its aegis. The first was the Korean War, which followed a June 1950 invasion of US-dominated South Korea by troops from communist North Korea. A series of UN Security Council sittings followed, which the North Koreans were not allowed to address. Ultimately, a resolution was passed requesting UN member states to provide military forces for service in Korea under US leadership, thereby legitimating US military aggression in the country under the UN banner. The forces were commanded by an American general, Douglas MacArthur, who received his orders from Washington, not from the Security Council.

Directing the war were Secretary of State Dean Acheson, a CFR member, and Defense Secretary Robert Lovett, a trustee of the Rockefeller Foundation (1949–53). The director of the CIA at the time was Walter Bedell Smith, later a co-chairman of the US branch of the Bilderberg Group. In July 1953, the war ended and the country was repartitioned.

The conflict was a heinous chapter in the history of warfare. Atrocities were committed by both sides. An estimated two million-plus were killed, many of them civilians slaughtered during US air attacks on cities, towns and villages. Throughout the Korean peninsula, almost everything of significant economic importance was destroyed. America's awesome air superiority enabled its forces to napalm-bomb populated areas, incinerating the inhabitants, to destroy agricultural irrigation dams, bridges, factories and homes and to burn crops. Some civilians were summarily executed. Shortly after the war began, US soldiers shot over 200 refugees at No Gun Ri. The atrocities were carried out under the banner of the United Nations.

Afghanistan was another country in which the US waged a war with UN approval. On the day after the 11 September 2001 attacks on the World Trade Center and the Pentagon, the Security Council unanimously approved the largely US-drafted Resolution 1368, which implicitly sanctioned the use of force by the United States in self-defence, in accordance with Nelson Rockefeller's Article 51 of the UN Charter. On 7 October, the United States and Britain launched a massive joint aerial blitz of targets in Afghanistan, thus beginning the first war of the twenty-first century.

Resolution 1368 placed no restrictions on how the United States should conduct its war against the al-Qaeda terrorists and Afghanistan's tyrannical Taliban regime, thereby enabling Washington to wage its war with the approval of the UN but unencumbered by any UN supervision. It was a license to kill.

The Korean War, Iraq's invasion of Kuwait and the US-led war in Afghanistan reveal a strange anomaly in the conduct of UN-approved military campaigns. Whereas territorial violations by North Korea and Iraq against two US allies, and the attacks on the World Trade Center and the Pentagon, were met by colossal military retaliation from the United States in the name, or with the approval, of the international community of nations that comprise the United Nations, the US and the military forces of US-supported regimes could engage in similar aggression, territorial occupation and terrorism without fear of retaliation from UN-mandated forces. The UN had become what its CFR-influenced US creators had intended it should be – an instrumentality of Pax Americana.

The Korean and Gulf wars, especially, present case studies of how the United States can "hijack" the United Nations for its own ends. Both wars, although under the auspices of the UN, were not UN wars. They were US wars. Like the Korean War, at every stage of the Gulf War's development after the invasion of Kuwait, the crisis was stage-managed by Washington. The Bush administration was the prime mover behind the series of Security Council resolutions that steered the UN towards a military counter-offensive, was the principal contributor to the 700,000-strong UN-mandated force, determined the military strategies to be used, directed the onslaught by the UN forces and acted unilaterally in rejecting peace overtures and in declaring a cease-fire. The White House determined when the war began, how it was waged and when it would end.

Bullying and Bribing

Washington's superintendence of the Gulf crisis began in the Security Council, where resolution after resolution was drafted by the US delegation and then pressure was applied on other delegations to support them. Finally, on 29 November 1990, Resolution 678 was formally proposed. If passed, it would have the effect of giving the United States unrestrained power to secure an end to Iraq's occupation of Kuwait, by "all necessary means" deemed expedient by Washington. To create an illusion of international solidarity and unanimity for a US-waged war, Washington needed to have the resolution overwhelmingly endorsed by all fifteen Security Council member states. The UN's imprimatur was an essential fig leaf to conceal the real rationale for the coming war – to reimpose US control over the oil-rich region.

To discourage opposition to the resolution, Washington embarked on a campaign to bully and bribe UN member states, particularly those in the Security Council. Pliant nations were rewarded. Egypt had much of its foreign debt either written off or deferred. Ethiopia was granted a new investment package. The Soviet Union received $4 billion in aid from Saudi Arabia and other Gulf states in a deal arranged by Washington. Syria and Turkey received military aid. Zaire was promised economic aid and had part of its foreign debt written off. The United States dropped its opposition to Iran and China receiving World Bank loans. Other countries were also rewarded.[25]

Despite Washington's efforts to fabricate a sham consensus, Resolution 678 did not receive unanimous endorsement. Twelve Security Council members voted in favour, two (Cuba and Yemen) voted against and China abstained. US retaliation against Yemen was immediate. An agreed multi-million dollar US aid package was cancelled and hundreds of thousands of Yemeni workers were expelled from Saudi Arabia. All because, as former US Attorney General Ramsey Clark observed, "little Yemen. . . had the courage to stand up and vote No to Resolution 678".[26]

Resolution 678 was not an explicit licence to wage war against Iraq. The word "war" was not in the resolution. What it sanctioned was the use of "all necessary means", thereby stipulating that options other than war could be explored. Many interpreted the phrase as authorizing force only as a final resort. However, all moves which held out any prospect of a peaceful settlement of the crisis were thwarted by the United States.

Denis Halliday, a former UN assistant secretary-general and former head of the UN's humanitarian programme in Iraq, has commented publicly on Washington's eagerness to wage a war against Iraq, remarking how "the UN Security Council was in fact discussing a peaceful withdrawal" of Saddam Hussein's forces from Kuwait when the US launched its war. "The Arab League and King Hussein [of Jordan] had been given 48 hours by President Bush to find a peaceful solution! As the Secretary-General of the Arab League informed me. . . James Baker [then secretary of state] panicked at the possibility that peaceful withdrawal might succeed at the last moment. He was delighted when a peaceful solution failed and the US could go to war."[27]

When Washington launched its war, the Security Council was in session, uninformed of the timing and the nature of the offensive. The Security Council, the General Assembly and the UN secretary-general had been excluded by the Bush administration from the decision-making loop.

Extraordinarily, Resolution 678, achieved through US bribery and arm-twisting, did not require that the United States, in acting against Saddam Hussein, should act under UN direction or even that it should consult with any UN organ. The most extreme motion to be approved by the council in forty years, it gave Washington carte blanche to deal as it wished with the aberrant Saddam and Iraq. President Bush chose war.

Bush's War

The US-led offensive became a massacre, with retreating Iraqi forces, some flying white flags of surrender, mown down for over thirty-six hours by wave after wave of American jets and helicopters. Non-military targets were prioritized. Among the civilian and non-military installations hit were municipal water processing plants, reservoirs and pumping stations, hospitals, churches, mosques and schools.

The conflict left Iraq in ruins, transforming it from one of the richest Arab nations into a pitiable Third World country. Iraq, a UN observer mission concluded, had been "relegated to the pre-industrial age".[28] The country's immiseration was further exacerbated by the imposition of a US-sponsored and UN-approved embargo that restricted the sale of Iraq's oil. The punitive sanctions had devastating effects, with up to 1.5 million Iraqis dying in the first ten years, including around 500,000 children who died from malnutrition.

In 1998, appalled by the consequences of the sanctions, Denis Halliday resigned from his post as UN humanitarian coordinator, saying that he was not prepared to oversee "the destruction of an entire nation".[29] In November 1999, the Clinton administration sought the removal of Halliday's successor, Hans von Sponeck, whom it accused of not being forceful enough with Iraq's leaders. He resigned, as did the head of the UN's World Food Program in Iraq, Jutta Burghardt, because of the devastating effects of the UN sanctions on Iraq's population. Later, von Sponeck argued that Washington's hostility towards Saddam Hussein had led to "the conversion of the UN from an instrument of conflict resolution to an instrument of conflict promotion".[30]

Although President Bush unilaterally announced a ceasefire on 28 February 1991, US military aggression against Iraq continued for the rest of his term in office and throughout President Clinton's eight years in the White House. In mid-2001, the Iraqi authorities claimed that since the ending of the war American and British forces had fired over 65,000 bombs or missiles at Iraq.

Washington held that its post-ceasefire assaults against Iraq complied with the terms of earlier Security Council resolutions, a view not shared by many UN member states. UN Secretary-General Boutros Boutros-Ghali held that Washington "would have faced insuperable obstacles if it had tried to get the Security Council to bless its use of force against Iraq" in the post-war years.[31]

The deaths and destruction were the price an entire population had to pay to ensure the security of US oil supplies in the region. Washington's support for Saddam's invasion of Iran (where the bitterly anti-American Khomeini regime held power) and its war against Saddam's forces following his invasion of Kuwait (where a US client-regime had held power) were motivated by one overriding factor – oil. Iraq, Iran and Kuwait are located around the oil-pumping Persian Gulf, the world's most strategically important region. "Of course it's about petroleum," admitted Commerce Secretary Robert Mossbacher, who, like President Bush, had been an oilman.[32] Bush's war against Saddam Hussein and the people of Iraq, conducted in the name of the United Nations, was waged to maintain Washington's, and Corporate USA's, control over the Persian Gulf's vast oil resources.

The Gulf War and the Korean War are just two instances of the capacity of Washington's ruling Rockefellerian and corporate-linked elites for using the United Nations as an instrumentality of US foreign policy, especially when US corporate interests are at risk in strategically important areas. Indonesia provides us with another example of US power and influence in the UN.

Indonesia and East Timor

On 7 December 1975, Indonesian forces invaded and annexed East Timor, a former Portuguese island colony north of Australia. Since then, according to Amnesty International, "at least 200,000 East Timorese, one-third of the population, have been killed or died of starvation".[33]

Life in Indonesian-ruled East Timor was marked by the destruction of villages, the torture of civilians, the castration, decapitation or detention of suspected opponents in concentration camps, the raping of women and butchery on a massive scale.

Resolutions approved in the UN General Assembly and Security Council calling for the withdrawal of the Indonesian forces of occupation were ignored by the United States. US support for Indonesia's president, General Raden Suharto, one of the worst mass-murderers of the twentieth century, ensured that no UN sanctions were applied and no UN-mandated forces were dispatched to oust his forces from East Timor.

The US ambassador to the United Nations, Daniel P. Moynihan, boasted of his success in ensuring that UN resolutions on the illegal annexation of East Timor would be ineffective: "The United States wished things to turn out [in East Timor] as they did, and worked to bring this about. The Department of State desired that the United Nations prove utterly ineffective in whatever measures it undertook.

This task was given to me, and I carried it forward with no inconsiderable success."[34]

A 1994 Amnesty International report explained Washington's alliance with Suharto. "Sitting astride critical sea-lanes of Southeast Asia which link the Pacific and Indian Oceans, Indonesia was then, and remains today, of considerable strategic importance. As a result, from 1965 and throughout the Cold War, the United States of America and many other western countries provided abundant economic, military and political support, and found it expedient to ignore clear evidence of systematic human rights violations."[35]

Suharto's utter ruthlessness was condemned by Amnesty, which reported that the "savage massacre in East Timor is only a tiny part of the terror that has gripped Indonesia itself since 1965, when the military, led by General Suharto, seized power. Inside a year, between 500,000 and 1 million people had been murdered by, or with the compliance of, the military. . . Amnesty has been tracking the Indonesian Government for nearly thirty years. We have found every form of human rights abuse – and on a staggering scale – imprisonment without trial, political murder, killing of petty criminals, execution of the old and sick, torture, rape, 'disappearance' and mass murder. . . human rights abuse has become part of the system of government. Over and over, year after year, Amnesty has warned the world's leaders. Again and again, they have turned a deaf ear." This "cynicism of realpolitik" extended to the United Nations, even to the UN Commission on Human Rights, according to Amnesty International.[36]

Suharto had admirers in the United States and in the United Nations. He earned plaudits from President Reagan, who praised his "most responsible influence in world affairs".[37] In 1989, it was announced that he was being awarded the UN Fund for Population Activities Prize for his government's record in the sphere of population control/family planning, a truly bizarre award for a person responsible for the enforced sterilization of Timorese women and for the massacre of up to one million Indonesians and around 200,000 East Timorese, the ultimate form of population control.

(Years earlier, the UN honoured another controversial figure, Princess Ashraf Pahlavi. The twin sister and close confidante of the shah of Iran – whose reign was marked by terror and torture, including the torture of women – she was, ironically, chosen to chair meetings of the United Nations Commission on Human Rights and the United Nations Commission on the Status of Women.)

Passive Witnesses

Indonesia and East Timor, Iraq and Kuwait – two annexations, two contrasting UN and US responses. Iraq subjected to massive air and ground attacks by US-led forces operating under the banner of the United Nations, Indonesia's murderous leader lauded by the president of the United States, provided with US weapons and chosen as the recipient of a UN award.

The dissimilar United Nations actions speak volumes about the organization and about its record as a manipulable tool of US foreign policy. No one seriously expects the United Nations to take meaningful action against US-supported despots such as Indonesia's Suharto or Angola's Jonas Savimbi. Two of history's monsters, the former was responsible for the killing of up to one million Indonesians and 200,000 East Timorese and the latter for a war which cost over one million people their lives and which displaced perhaps five million.

Washington's manipulative influence over the UN was commented on in 1952, seven years after the organization's establishment, by Professor Leland M. Goodrich of Columbia University. A CFR member, Goodrich observed that because the United States was the wealthiest and most powerful UN member state, "no important action can be undertaken by the United Nations with any reasonable prospect of success in the face of United States opposition".[38]

As a rule, the UN can only mount meaningful humanitarian, peacekeeping and military operations when Washington wishes it to do so. When operations are mooted at the Security Council or the General Assembly that might imperil or seriously discommode US-backed regimes or might otherwise be injurious to US interests, the proposed operations will invariably be aborted. No major security or peace-related operation can be undertaken by the UN without Washington's approval.

At the end of the 1990s, around twenty African countries were at war with one another or racked by internal conflicts. Millions died. The butchery was marked by lack of interest or an inadequate response from the US hyperpower and by UN impotence. In Rwanda, three months of genocide beginning in April 1994 left an estimated 800,000 dead and forced over two million to flee to neighbouring countries for refuge. In Burundi, Sierra Leone and the Democratic Republic of Congo, a total of perhaps two and a half million civilians lost their lives during armed hostilities, many as a consequence of hunger. An internal war in Sudan cost an estimated two million lives. As the catastrophes unfolded, Washington issued vacuous condemnations of the slaughter and did little else. The UN dithered.

In Liberia, a civil war left at least 150,000 dead and forced around a half of the country's 2.5 million population to flee from their homes. In April 1996, a US commando unit entered Liberia's capital to evacuate Americans and other foreigners trapped by the fighting. The Liberian people were left to fend for themselves.

In December 1992, American troops were deployed in another

African country, Somalia, under the auspices of the United Nations, during a period of anarchy, clan warfare and massacres. Eighteen US Rangers were killed in a gunfight with militia members. In early 1995, the UN-mandated forces were withdrawn with little accomplished, leaving Somalis to face a perilous future amid continuing inter-clan fighting.

In the 1990s, Europe experienced its most savage conflict since the Second World War. The breakup of Yugoslavia resulted in years of ethnic conflict, slaughter and destruction, during which, probably, over 150,000 were killed and over four million were compelled to leave their homes. For the United Nations, the conflict was a public relations disaster and a military and humanitarian debacle. Capitulating to the savagery of the warring factions, the UN forces watched helplessly as civilians were massacred in front of them, as UN-proclaimed "safe areas" were bombed and overrun by faction forces, as UN food relief convoys were intercepted and plundered and as its soldiers were captured and held hostage by Bosnian Serbs.

Unable to fulfil its mandate, the credibility of the United Nations as a peacekeeping and peace-enforcing organization was in tatters. The use of American ground forces had been ruled out by the Clinton administration, except as a last resort to help in the evacuation of UN-mandated forces.

Formed to protect people "from the scourge of war" and "acts of aggression", the United Nations almost totally abdicated its responsibilities during the 1990s, especially in war-torn African countries. It did so because Washington wished it to do so. Unlike the oil-rich Gulf region, in a post-Cold War world impoverished African countries were of little strategic or economic value to the United States.

US Unilateralism

As a signatory to the United Nations Charter, the United States pledged to resolve tensions and quarrels with other countries "by peaceful means", to refrain from "the threat or use of force against the territorial integrity or political independence of any state", to promote "respect for human rights and for fundamental freedoms for all" and to "live together in peace with one another as good neighbours". If honoured, Washington's pledge would represent an about-turn in the conduct of US foreign policy, ending the country's "gunboat diplomacy", unilateral interventionism and support for repressive and undemocratic regimes.

In practice, Washington honours its pledge to uphold the lofty ideals of the charter only when it suits it to do so. When these ideals and US foreign policy interests are irreconcilable, as they often are, the hegemon is wont to ignore the charter and to override the wishes of other member states.

On 20 August 1998, without any warning or ultimata and without UN approval, US cruise missiles hit a "terrorist" camp in Afghanistan and destroyed the El Shifa pharmaceutical plant in Sudan's capital city, in retaliation for the recent bombing of US embassies in Kenya and Tanzania. The El Shifa plant was vital to the health and welfare of the Sudanese people, since it produced most of the country's human and veterinary drugs.

The attack in Afghanistan was an attempt to kill Osama bin Laden, leader of the al-Qaeda terrorist movement, who Washington alleged was responsible for the embassy bombings. The El Shifa plant in Sudan, the US further alleged, was owned by bin Laden and produced a chemical used in the manufacture of VX nerve gas, a claim later proven to be false.[39] The bombings were an assertion of Washington's self-conferred right to unilaterally attack, without UN approval and regardless of international laws, any nation in which terrorists were based or allegedly had business interests.

In November 1999, US and UN premises in Pakistan's capital city were attacked with rockets. The attacks were in retaliation for the imposition by the UN Security Council, at Washington's behest, of economic sanctions against Afghanistan for its refusal to hand over Osama bin Laden for trial in the United States or in a third country. Once again, Washington had secured UN support for US foreign policy objectives.

Between 1993 and 1996, around thirty-five countries were subjected to US-imposed sanctions. The UN collaborated in some of these. Sanctions can be considered as a form of warfare – a "less expensive alternative to military intervention", according to a Council on Foreign Relations book.[40] Among the UN-sanctioned countries was Libya.

In April 1986, a bomb exploded in the La Belle discotheque in West Berlin, killing an American serviceman and a young Turkish woman. Washington blamed Libya for the attack. Using the La Belle outrage as justification, US bombers attacked the Libyan capital of Tripoli, seeking to kill the country's leader Muammar Gaddafi. A reported one hundred Libyans died in the attack, including Gaddafi's fifteen-month-old adopted daughter. A Security Council resolution condemning the US bombing was vetoed by the United States. A similar resolution was approved by the General Assembly.

In early 1992, on the initiative of the United States and Britain, the Security Council imposed sanctions on Libya because of its refusal to hand over for trial abroad two Libyan nationals accused of responsibility for the December 1988 bombing of a passenger plane over Lockerbie in Scotland, which killed 270 people. In early 2001, one of the accused was found guilty of the bombing after a trial in Holland.

Washington's ruling Rockefellerian and corporate-linked elites had long harboured a deep aversion towards Gaddafi. After seizing power in 1969, he nationalized the Libyan holdings of the Bunker Hunt oil company, crowing that this was an overdue blow to America's "cold insolent face".[41] Later, Gaddafi announced that he intended to expropriate 51 per cent of each oil company with interests in Libya, including subsidiaries of offshoots of the Rockefellers' Standard Oil company.

Washington's attacks against Libya, Sudan and Afghanistan and also its support for anti-government UNITA terrorists in Angola had one thing in common – oil. The three African nations have considerable oil resources, while Afghanistan is located close to what is being hailed as the world's largest untapped oil fields.

Libya is unquestionably a terrorist state, its erratic leader dabbling with terrorism in pursuit of vague revolutionary objectives. In February 1980, there was an official call for the "physical liquidation of enemies" within Libya and abroad.[42] In that same year, Libyan forces invaded neighbouring Chad. In 1984, a policewoman was killed when shots were fired from the Libyan embassy in London during a demonstration outside the building. Weapons and explosives were supplied to foreign rebel and terrorist groups, including the Irish Republican Army (IRA). A number of Gaddafi's opponents died in custody, reportedly while being tortured.

However, Gaddafi is a comparatively small-scale terrorist. His activities pale into insignificance when compared to those of some Washington-backed despots who receive a dispensation, even military and financial support, from the US for their terrorist activities and are not subjected to sanctions or any other restraining mechanism by the United Nations. His terrorist activities are mere misdemeanours when compared to the atrocious records of US-supported mass murderers such as General Suharto in Indonesia and Jonas Savimbi in Angola and of a patron of such terrorism, the Rockefeller-created "statesman" Henry Kissinger.

Latin America and the Caribbean

In Latin America and in Caribbean countries, Washington has intervened virtually as it wished, often in defiance of UN resolutions and in contravention of the UN Charter.

In Cuba, it imposed an economic and trade blockade, engaged in economic sabotage, attempted to assassinate political leaders and invaded the island at the Bay of Pigs in April 1961. All these actions were violations of the UN Charter, as also is, probably, the continuing US occupation of Cuban territory at Guantanamo Bay. Beginning in 1992, each year the UN General Assembly voted in favour of resolutions asking Washington to lift its embargo. Although the United States was almost totally alone on this issue – in 1998 the vote was

157–2 (US, Israel) – Washington continued its illegal extra-territorial economic warfare against its neighbour.

In October 1983, President Reagan ordered a US invasion of another Caribbean island, the 100,000 population midget state of Grenada. The purported purpose of the invasion was to protect the lives of American students on the island. Its real objective was to halt the island's brief flirtation with socialism.

Six years later, US forces invaded Panama in a bid to capture the country's military dictator and former US ally General Manuel Noriega. The operation, in which 1,000 to 3,000 Panamanians were killed, was a travesty of international law. It culminated in Noriega's arrest, his removal to the United States to stand trial for drug trafficking, his subsequent imprisonment in the United States and the installation of the Washington-endorsed Guillermo Endara as president.

In 1973, the United States directed a military coup to overthrow the democratically elected Salvador Allende in Chile. In Nicaragua, it financed, armed and trained Contra terrorists in a successful effort to topple the democratically elected Sandinista-led government.

Following almost all major post-1970 US interventions in the continent, UN General Assembly resolutions condemned the aggression. Washington ignored them. Security Council resolutions condemning the interventions were often vetoed by the United States.

Massacre at Qana

In April 1996, over 100 refugees sheltering at a United Nations compound at Qana in southern Lebanon were killed by Israeli shells during a sixteen-day bombing offensive which forced around 400,000 people to flee from their homes. The offensive was a response to a Muslim Hizbollah rocket attack on areas of northern Israel, which caused no loss of life. Successfully opposing a Security Council resolution on the crisis, Washington ensured that the council was powerless to intervene.

In his autobiography, former UN Secretary-General Boutros Boutros-Ghali commented on the Qana shelling. The attack, he claimed, "was unprecedented. The armed forces of a UN member state had launched an attack on a UN peacekeeping post."[43] Following the shelling, he submitted a report on the incident to the Security Council. His failure to water down the critical tone of the report drew sharp criticism from Washington, which condemned the report for its "unjustified conclusions".[44] Washington's anger at Boutros-Ghali led to speculation that the US would oppose a second term for the Egyptian. In November of that year, the Security Council voted 14–1 (the US) in favour of supporting him for a second term in office. Nevertheless, through using its veto, Washington's will prevailed. Boutros-Ghali was discarded through the unilateral diktat of the hegemon.

Theo van Boven

In 1982, another senior UN official fell foul of the United States. As director of the UN Division of Human Rights, Dr Theo van Boven constantly focused attention on those who had "disappeared", been tortured or murdered in UN member states by government forces. In January 1982, journalists received an advance copy of a speech that he intended to deliver at the opening session of the UN Commission on Human Rights. His speech drew attention to gross abuses of human rights in two US client states, El Salvador and Guatemala, and observed that if the commission failed to take appropriate action, then it would hardly be worthy of its name.

UN Secretary-General Javier Perez de Cuellar requested that the text be altered. Van Boven declined to comply. A few days later he was dismissed. According to the UN, his contract was not being renewed.

A US Dependency

In September 2002, Mary Robinson was replaced as UN high commissioner for human rights. In voicing condemnation of aspects of America's war on terrorism, she had alienated Washington's powerful foreign affairs overlords. The departures of Robinson, van Boven, Boutros-Ghali, Denis Halliday, Hans von Sponeck and Jutta Burghardt are indicative of Washington's grip over the UN and its operations.

In early 1994, John Bolton, who had served as assistant secretary of state for international organization affairs during the presidency of George H. Bush, made an astonishingly frank admission regarding Washington's ability to dominate the organization: "There is no United Nations. There is an international community that occasionally can be led by the only real power left in the world, and that is the United States. When the United States leads, the United Nations will follow. When it suits our interest to do so, we will do so. When it does not suit our interests, we will not."[45] At the Democratic National Convention in August 1996, James Rubin, director of foreign policy and spokesman for the Clinton/Gore '96 Campaign, was equally blunt: "The UN can only do what the US lets it do."[46]

Washington's domination of the UN is pervasive, extending to all the body's principal organs, its agencies and its programmes. Using its power of veto, the US can block each and every unwelcome resolution in the Security Council. It can ignore resolutions passed by the 190 or so member nations of the General Assembly. It can attack, invade and blockade other nations in violation of international law and of the UN Charter, which requires that "All Members shall settle their international disputes by peaceful means."

It can show its utter contempt for the fundamental principles of the UN, without fear of penalty. To take one example, in the course of the US-directed, decade-long Contra war in Nicaragua, the CIA mined the country's seaports. Subsequently, in June 1986, the International Court of Justice (usually called the World Court), the judicial organ of the United Nations, condemned the mining of the ports and other forms of US aggression against Nicaragua, ruling that the US, "by training, arming, equipping, financing and supplying the Contra forces or otherwise encouraging, supporting and aiding military and paramilitary activities in and against Nicaragua, has acted against the Republic of Nicaragua, in breach of its obligations under customary international law".[47]

The Reagan administration refused to accept that the court had legal jurisdiction over US interventions in Central America. This stance was a clear signal to the international community of nations that the country's foreign policy, with its reliance on state-directed terrorism and interventionism, would not be hindered or bound by the norms of international law and of civilized behaviour or by the charter of the UN, which requires that "Each member of the United Nations undertakes to comply with the decision" of the court in any case to which it is a party.

Washington's ability to snub the international community, to disregard and transgress the norms of international law and behaviour and to dominate and manipulate the United Nations in pursuit of US foreign policy objectives underlines an alarming fact. It is that no nation or group of nations can rein in the world's only superpower, the United States.

Policing the post-Second World War world was, purportedly, to be the responsibility of the United Nations. However, the organization has become so eviscerated and so dominated by Washington that it can only perform this role when Washington allows it to do so. U Thant, later secretary-general of the UN, observed in 1952 how US power was so great that the General Assembly functioned "like a one-party system".[48]

Former Irish diplomat Conor Cruise O'Brien, the UN secretary-general's representative in war-torn Katanga in 1961, has commented on the asphyxiating power of the US within the United Nations. In the General Assembly, he stated, "any delegate soon learns that the most important thing to know in relation to any proposition is how the United States stands on it. Where the United States has been flatly opposed, the proposition has had no chance of being carried. . . resolutions not actively supported by the United States have remained unheeded 'recommendations'."[49]

According to former UN Secretary-General Boutros-Ghali, the "first priority of a secretary-general. . . has to be the relationship between the United States and the United Nations". To curry favour with Washington, he had appointed numerous Americans "to UN jobs at Washington's request over the objections of other UN member states. I had done so. . . because I wanted American support to succeed in my job."[50] Among those appointed was Carol Bellamy, director of the US Peace Corps and a member of the CFR, whom he chose over a hotly favoured European to head the UN Children's Fund (UNICEF). The post has always been held by an American.

Hernane Tavares de Sá, the UN's under secretary for public information from 1960–65, candidly summarized Washington's power within and over the United Nations: "If Washington does not want something to be done either by the General Assembly or by the Security Council (and without having to use its veto power) it will simply not be done. . . Any initiative of genuine scope by the UN must satisfy political needs and interests of American foreign policy. . . The United Nations is not an international body but rather a dependency of the United States."[51]

Increasingly, the United Nations is also becoming a dependency and an ally of the corporate sector.

The UN and the Ford Foundation

Money is a major factor in the UN's susceptibility to US pressures. Through withholding its assessed annual dues from the financially strapped organization, Washington can hold the UN hostage to its dictates. By the end of 1999, US arrears to the UN totalled around $1.6 billion. By drip-feeding its arrears to the UN at tactically advantageous times, the United States can frustrate or facilitate the organization in carrying out its operations. The impoverishment of the UN, through delaying the payment of dues, increases the body's dependence on its major funding source, the United States, and thus renders the UN more vulnerable to pressures from Washington.

Article 17 of the UN Charter states that the "expenses of the Organization shall be borne by the Members as apportioned by the General Assembly". However, a number of UN agencies and programmes, particularly ones involved in humanitarian work and economic and technical assistance to Third World countries, are largely funded by voluntary, not mandatory, contributions. The levels of financial support, and hence the viability of the agencies and their programmes, are thus contingent on the goodwill and generosity of the wealthiest member states, particularly the United States. Voluntary funding makes it difficult for such UN organs to make commitments for the future, due to the uncertainty of future income levels. It also enables Washington to set its own priorities and agendas by endowing particular UN agencies and programmes generously while restricting funding to others.

The withholding of the United States' mandatory dues and the principle of voluntary contributions creates a financial vacuum within the United Nations. It is a vacuum that the US corporate sector, under the stewardship of CFR members and other Rockefeller-linked figures, has moved to fill.

Corporate-linked support for the UN began with the Rockefellers' gift of a site for the UN headquarters. Starting in 1951, a corporate-connected philanthropic body, the Ford Foundation, provided about $80 million in direct support of UN agencies and programmes over a forty-five year period.[52] Presumably as a result of its largesse, the foundation attained a remarkable degree of influence within the United Nations. In response to concerns about the UN's financial difficulties and in close cooperation with Secretary-General Boutros-Ghali, in 1992 the foundation established an Independent Advisory Group on UN Financing. The "independent" nature of the group may be assessed from its leadership. The co-chairmen were one of the Rockefellers' closest associates, Paul A. Volcker (at the time of the formation of the Advisory Group he was chairman of the North American branch of the Trilateral Commission and a director of the CFR and was former-ly a trustee of the Rockefeller Foundation and a senior banker at the Chase Manhattan) and Japanese banker Shijuro Ogata (shortly to become deputy chairman of the Trilateral Commission in Japan, he was an adviser to the Rockefellers' Chase Manhattan Bank). The Advi-sory Group's report was submitted to UN Secretary-General Boutros-Ghali and then to the General Assembly.[53]

In late 1993, at the request of Boutros-Ghali, the Ford Foundation embarked on an even more prestigious project, the formation of an Independent Working Group on the Future of the United Nations. Its purpose was to suggest specific reform proposals to enable the orga-nization to successfully confront the challenges and opportunities of the next half-century.

Invited to co-chair the Working Group was Mary Robinson, pres-ident of Ireland, who was an executive member of the Trilateral Com-mission immediately after its formation. The group's meetings were held at the Pocantico Conference Center in New York, made available by the Rockefeller Brothers Fund. The only American in the Working Group's small core committee was investment banker Felix Rohatyn, a CFR member and Trilateral commissioner. (The invitation to Presi-dent Robinson to co-chair the Working Group was declined by her, fol-lowing opposition from the Irish government to her accepting the post.)

The Ford Foundation is closely connected with Rockefeller foreign policy forums. For decades it has been a major financial sponsor of the CFR, contributing $1.5 million in 1954,[54] and, with David Rockefeller, largely funded the establishment of the Trilateral Commission.

The foundation has relied considerably on Rockefeller and corporate-linked figures for its leaders. In 1971, seven of the foundation's sixteen trustees were CFR members. In 1997, the foundation's officers and trustees included:

- Susan V. Berresford, president of the foundation, who was a member of the CFR and of the Trilateral Commission
- Henry B. Schacht, chairman of the foundation's board of trustees and a director of Lucent Technologies (CFR and Trilateral Commission and a trustee of the Rockefeller Foundation in the 1970s)
- Paul A. Allaire, chairman and CEO of the Xerox Corporation, (CFR, Trilateral Commission and Bilderberg Group)
- Robert D. Haas, chairman and CEO of Levi Strauss (CFR and the Trilateral Commission)
- Vernon E. Jordan, Jr, (CFR, Trilateral Commission and Bilderberg Group)
- David T. Kearns, former chairman and CEO of Xerox (CFR).

The UNA-USA

One of the Ford Foundation's principal partners in its UN activities is the United Nations Association of the United States of America (UNA-USA), which in 1997 was approved for a $2.5 million grant from the foundation, by far the largest pledge or contribution the UNA-USA received in that year.[55]

According to a UNA-USA publication, with "a growing membership of 20,000, and with more than 100 affiliated national organizations representing a collective membership in the tens of millions, UNA-USA is uniquely positioned to mobilize the American people in support of a strong UN system, and strong US leadership within that system".[56]

In September 1997, the UNA-USA hosted a function in New York at which US media billionaire Ted Turner announced that he planned to donate $1 billion to the United Nations over a ten-year period, the single largest philanthropic pledge ever made anywhere in the world. UN Secretary-General Kofi Annan, whose college education in the US from 1959 to 1961 was sponsored by the Ford Foundation, expressed his hope that the gift marked the start of a "new and promising relationship" between the United Nations and the private sector.[57]

The UNA-USA is an elitist body. Like its major sponsor, the Ford Foundation, the UNA-USA has ties to Corporate USA and is dominated by Rockefeller-linked figures. Its 1997 leadership included:

- its chairman, banker John C. Whitehead (CFR, Trilateral Commission and Bilderberg Group and director of Rockefeller University)
- William J. van den Heuvel, chairman of the association's board of governors (CFR)

- Elliot L. Richardson, co-chairman of the association's national council (Trilateral Commission and a director of the CFR, 1974–75)
- former Secretary of State Cyrus Vance, co-chairman of the UNA-USA's national council (Trilateral Commission, former vice chairman of the CFR and a former trustee and chairman of the Rockefeller Foundation)
- business tycoon Maurice R. Greenberg, one of America's richest citizens (Trilateral Commission, Bilderberg Group and a director of the CFR).

In November 1998, John C. Whitehead was succeeded as chairman of the UNA-USA by William H. Luers. An active member of the CFR, Luers was on the board of the Rockefeller Brothers Fund at the time of his appointment.

Rockefeller funding and David Rockefeller's circle of corporate associates and friends have played a significant role in the success of the UNA-USA, an organization that might be described as part of the Rockefeller/Corporate USA political power nexus. Among the UNA-USA's National Council members in 1998 was Steven C. Rockefeller, chairman of the Rockefeller Brothers Fund. In that same year, the organization received contributions from David and Laurance S. Rockefeller (each of whom donated $100,000–$250,000) and the Chase Manhattan Bank N.A. Listed in that year's UNA-USA annual report as recent recipients of the organization's Global Leadership Award were six members of the Rockefeller family.[58]

Following the Ford Foundation's formation of its Independent Advisory Group on UN Financing, the UNA-USA prepared its own report, *Crisis and Reform in United Nations Financing*. Among the committee members responsible for the report were long-time Rockefeller associates Paul Volcker and Clifton Wharton, Jr. Beginning in the late 1940s, Wharton spent twenty-two years promoting Rockefeller philanthropic interests in Latin America and south-east Asia. In 1969 he was a member of Nelson Rockefeller's presidential mission to Latin America, which provoked almost continent-wide riots. From 1970 to 1987, he was a trustee of the Rockefeller Foundation and its chairman from 1982 to 1987. A trustee of the Rockefeller Institute of Government, a director of the CFR and a Trilateral commissioner, he was appointed, as Rockefeller-linked figures are wont to be, to political offices by Presidents Ford, Carter, Reagan, George H. Bush and Clinton, the latter appointing him deputy secretary of state.

The Rockefeller/corporate-dominated Ford Foundation and UNA-USA have sought, and acquired, a huge degree of influence within the United Nations. This Rockefeller/corporate-guided influence is of immense importance, since the United Nations System – which encompasses the General Assembly, the Security Council, the

Economic and Social Council, the World Court, the World Health Organization, numerous other agencies and bodies and, in theory, the World Bank and International Monetary Fund – has the potential to effect colossal economic, political and social changes throughout the world, for better or for worse.

An analysis of the proposals drawn up by the foundation and the UNA-USA for UN reform is very instructive. Proposals drawn up by the foundation's Independent Working Group on the Future of the United Nations advocated closer ties between the UN and the corporate sector. "It is particularly important", the group's report stressed, "to involve the private sector much more than previously in addressing global issues. . . the United Nations itself needs to work with the private sector if it is to play a significant role in improving the common good."[59] For private sector read corporate sector.

President Clinton was also an advocate of closer United Nations-corporate ties, enthusing about "the potential for partnership between the UN and the private sector".[60] Kofi Annan also advocated closer ties. In a period of just over two years after taking office, the UN secretary-general addressed meetings of the corporate-dominated World Economic Forum on three occasions, advocating "a creative partnership between the United Nations and the private sector".[61] In January 1999, during his third address to the forum, he proposed a global compact between business and the UN which would "give a human face to the global market". He proposed that the corporate sector should "embrace, support and enact a set of core values in the areas of human rights, labour standards, and environmental practices. . . I chose these three areas because they are the ones where I feel that, if we do not act, there may be a threat to the open global market, and especially to the multilateral trade regime."[62]

Critics condemned the UN's proposed engagement with the corporate sector, warning that it threatened the mission and integrity of the United Nations. The compact encourages corporate self-regulation, rather than legally binding regulation, in respect to upholding human rights and environmental standards.

The Ford Foundation and the UNA-USA help to promote Washington's pro-corporate foreign policy, through influencing the direction of the United Nations agenda. However, an analysis of the two organizations' UN roles can only provide us with a hint of the overall influence wielded within the entire United Nations System by corporate and Rockefeller-linked bodies and individuals.

Protecting the Ailing Global Environment?

In 1972, a Canadian, Maurice F. Strong, became the first executive director of the recently established UN Environment Programme, a post he held until 1976. In 1992, the UN Conference on Environment and Development (UNCED), better known as the Earth Summit, was held in Rio de Janeiro. Its secretary-general and chief organizer was Strong. Later, when Kofi Annan needed a coordinator for a programme aimed at radically reforming the United Nations, he opted for Strong. A multimillionaire industrialist whose wealth derived from the oil, gas and energy industries, Strong was a member of David Rockefeller's Trilateral Commission in its early years and a trustee of the Rockefeller Foundation.

UNCED, an Earth Summit on the ailing global environment, was the largest international conference ever held. An estimated 30,000 people travelled to Rio for the event, including well over 100 heads of state and government. As head of UNCED, Strong became, in effect, the guardian of the planet's delicate ecosystem, a guardianship hardly appropriate for a person recruited from the world's greatest polluter, the corporate sector.

The sector had immense influence at the summit's preparatory stage. In mid-1990, two years before the summit began, Strong appointed Stephan Schmidheiny from Switzerland as his principal advisor for business and industry. To assist him in his endeavours Schmidheiny, formed the Business Council for Sustainable Development (BCSD), a lobbying group of forty-eight of the world's top business leaders. Himself one of the world's wealthiest industrialists, his family's businesses are an important component of the Swiss economy.

Rockefeller-linked corporate leaders had a large representation within the BCSD.[63] These included Frank Popoff (CFR), president and CEO of the Dow Chemical Company, USA. The propriety of Popoff's appointment to a body purportedly formed to "play a vital role in the future health of this planet. . . without compromising the welfare of future generations"[64] is questionable, casting doubts over the sincerity of the BCSD's commitment to its stated goal. In 1966, Dow Chemical was the target of one of the largest public protests ever mounted against an American company because of its role in the manufacture of napalm, used to incinerate villagers during the Vietnam War. Dow Chemical also manufactured Agent Orange, a dioxin-containing defoliant used in Vietnam. Dioxin is considered thousands of times more potent than thalidomide as a cause of birth defects in some species. An estimated twelve to nineteen million gallons of the chemical were sprayed in Vietnam, permanently contaminating huge areas of the countryside and leaving a horrific legacy of birth defects.

The World Economic Forum, whose core constituency comprises "the world's 1000 foremost global enterprises",[65] was another corporate-dominated body that had a significant input into UNCED. According to the Forum, its president was "an official adviser to UNCED, and serves now, at the personal invitation of Secretary-General Boutros

Boutros-Ghali, as a member of the High-Level Advisory Board, with the mission to provide advice to the Secretary-General".[66]

Subsequent to the Earth Summit, Maurice Strong's sphere of influence widened even more. He became a director of the World Economic Forum, senior adviser to both UN Secretary-General Kofi Annan and World Bank President James D. Wolfensohn, chairman of the Stockholm Environment Institute and chairman of the Earth Council, a Costa Rican-based non-governmental organization, whose professed mission is "to support and empower people in building a more secure, equitable and sustainable future".[67] At the same time, he continued his business pursuits through his chairmanship of Technology Development Corporation and Strovest Holdings and other business activities.

The Earth Council served as the secretariat of the Earth Charter Commission, whose goal is no less than the drafting of an Earth Charter "with enough constituencies to be adopted by countries at the United Nations as an ethical framework for a covenant on sustainable development by the year 2002".[68] The Earth Council was thus, in some ways, a continuation of Strong's UN Earth Summit. Coordinating the drafting of the charter was the chairman of the Rockefeller Brothers Fund, Steven C. Rockefeller, a member of the UNA-USA's national council.

The selection of the multimillionaire industrialist and Rockefeller associate Maurice Strong to head the Earth Summit was, according to critics, a misjudgement of monumental proportions. To an extraordinary degree, corporate executives and Rockefeller-linked figures determined the summit's agenda, eviscerating proposals aimed at curbing the accelerating destruction of the global environment.

The determination of some of America's largest corporations, among the world's worst polluters, to be a dominant influence in setting the agenda for, and in determining the outcome of, the UN's Earth Summit was reflected in the expenditure of millions of dollars by a group of corporations on the summit and on subsequent conventions on the environment. The purpose of this expenditure was to frustrate positive action on climatic changes and environmental degradation.

Operating under the deceptively eco-friendly title of Global Climate Coalition, the group primarily represented American fossil fuel corporations (such as the Rockefeller-linked Exxon/Esso), chemical manufacturers and motor manufacturers. Through the Global Climate Coalition, the World Economic Forum, the cooperation of President George H. Bush, himself a former oil company owner, and the advisory and lobbying roles of Schmidheiny and his BCSD, the corporate sector ensured that the Earth Summit's deliberations produced little more than aspirational objectives, which largely lacked enforceability, clear-cut targets and firm deadlines, and ceded a central role in UN efforts to preserve the planet's fragile ecosystem to an unregulated or self-regulated international corporate community. The corporate sector, unlike environmentalists, holds the levers of world economic and political power and influence.

Corporate power and influence was also evident in December 1997 at another UN climate change summit, held in Kyoto, Japan. Attended by delegates from over 150 countries, the summit's objective was to ratify a global-warming treaty, including legally binding reductions for "greenhouse" gas emissions. Mobilizing opposition to the proposed accord, the Global Climate Coalition engaged in alarmist propaganda, warning that the agreement would undermine the US economy and result in millions of Americans losing their jobs. A 1997 anti-Kyoto ad campaign cost the GCC an estimated $13 million. In the 1996 election cycle in the United States, GCC members gave millions of dollars in "soft" money to the Democratic and Republican parties and contributed further millions to candidates through political action committees.[69]

A few weeks after entering the White House in January 2001, oilman George W. Bush announced that he did not intend to abide by the terms of the Kyoto Protocol. US oil corporations had contributed generously to oilman Bush's election campaign.

In a poll conducted by Friends of the Earth among government delegates and environmentalists at the Kyoto convention, the Global Climate Coalition was selected as the world's worst climate-wrecking body. In second place was Exxon/Esso. Another Rockefeller-linked oil giant, Mobil, was in ninth place.[70]

In April 2002, the Bush administration blocked the reappointment of Robert Watson as chairman of the Intergovernmental Panel on Climate Change. The panel, which operates under the auspices of the United Nations, was established to assess the causes and impact of global warming. It was later revealed that Dr Watson had been targeted by ExxonMobil, which had sent a memo to the White House asking, "Can Watson be replaced now at the request of the US?"[71]

In September 2002, a second UN Earth Summit was held, this time in Johannesburg, South Africa, to tackle the crises of global poverty, underdevelopment and environmental degradation. However, with the Bush administration and the powerful fossil fuel lobby frustrating efforts to reach agreement on specific targets and timetables on many issues, the summit achieved little. One of the few real successes was the rejection of a controversial proposal which would have ceded the corporate-friendly World Trade Organization primacy over environmental protection.

The Rio and Johannesburg Earth Summits and the Kyoto convention were sequels to an earlier UN environmental initiative, the Brundtland Commission, created by the United Nations General Assembly in 1983. Among the commission's members were the ubiquitous Maurice F. Strong, Saburo Okita and Keichi Oshima from

Japan, and Umberto Colombo from Italy, all Trilateral commissioners, Okita and Oshima being executive members. In 1987 the General Assembly adopted the Brundtland Commission's report as an environmental guide for UN member states.

The Rio, Johannesburg and Kyoto meetings, the Brundtland Commission, the Ford Foundation, the UNA-USA and other bodies have been looked at here to illustrate a disturbing trend – the ease with which corporate leaders and Rockefeller associates can penetrate, influence, become advisers to and even dominate the proceedings of UN organs. In doing so, according to critics, they have transformed the United Nations into an abettor of corporate self-interest rather than defenders of the rights and needs of the world's peoples.

Center on Transnational Corporations

There has long been a conflict of interests between, on the one hand, the developed world and its multinationals and, on the other hand, Third World countries. In 1955, Washington's *bête noire*, Achmed Sukarno, president of Indonesia, hosted a meeting at Bandung which discussed the plight of the Third World. Other conferences followed, at which Third World representatives, perturbed that national resources were the almost private domain of corporations from a handful of Western countries, began to demand a new and more equitable international economic order, which would include regulating the operations of transnational corporations in the Third World. Burgeoning Third World support for these demands led to the establishment in the 1970s of a new body within the UN System, the Centre on Transnational Corporations (CTC), to monitor the dealings of transnationals and their impact on the economies and people of underdeveloped countries. The centre hosted discussions on the regulation of the corporations and on codes of conduct for their operations.

The CTC's formation was a huge blow to the corporations. However, the Third World's victory was short-lived. After taking office in December 1991, the new UN Secretary-General Boutros-Ghali announced a number of organizational changes within the UN System, including the disbandment of the CTC, whose programmes were to become the responsibility of an already debilitated UN organ.

With the CTC's demise, the Business Council for Sustainable Development and its corporate patrons could operate inside and outside the UN system free from the type of monitoring that the CTC was intended to carry out. To Third World leaders, the CTC's disbandment was a clear message that where the interests of developed countries and their transnationals were at odds with Third World needs, the interests of the former would be looked after by the UN and its agencies.

In general, the five agreements signed by most of the governments participating in the Rio Earth Summit were pro-corporate in their orientation, coming closer to the policy of corporate self-regulation favoured by corporate lobbyists rather than the codes of conduct advocated by the Centre on Transnational Corporations before its closure.

The disbandment of the CTC and the diluted Rio, Kyoto and Johannesburg summit agreements were victories for the corporate sector, making a mockery of the UN's professed commitment to promoting "social progress and better standards of life"[72] for all the earth's people. Instead of the UN serving the interests of mankind, it was being used to serve the interests of the US and big business.

The same is true, to an even greater extent, of other US-conceived multilateral institutions such as the World Bank, the International Monetary Fund and GATT. Like the United Nations, these international institutions became servants of Washington and the corporate sector, helping to shape and superintend a post-Second World War global order compatible with the interests of the United States and of Corporate USA.

Notes

1. Paul H. Nitze in Don K. Price, ed., *The Secretary of State* (Englewood Cliffs, New Jersey: Spectrum, 1960), p. 8.
2. Quoted by Lloyd C. Gardner in Warren F. Kimball, ed., *Franklin D. Roosevelt and the World Crisis, 1937–1945* (Lexington, Massachusetts: D. C. Heath, 1973), p. 144.
3. Roosevelt address to Congress, 6 January 1941. Quoted in Hugh Brogan, *The Penguin History of the United States of America* (London: Penguin, 1990), p. 595.
4. Channel 4 (United Kingdom) television documentary, *Proud Arabs and Texas Oilmen*. See also Kimball, *Franklin D. Roosevelt*, p. 250; Townsend Hoopes and Douglas Brinkley, *FDR and the Creation of the UN* (New Haven: Yale University Press, 1997), p. 100; Brogan, *The Penguin History*, pp. 593–95; Thomas G. Paterson and Dennis Merrill, eds., *Major Problems in American Foreign Relations* (Lexington, Massachusetts: D. C. Heath, 1995), vol. 2, pp. 193–95.
5. Charles Patterson, *The Oxford 50th Anniversary Book of the United Nations* (New York: Oxford University Press, 1995), p. 16; Amos Yoder, *The Evolution of the United Nations System* (Washington, DC: Taylor & Francis, 1993), p. 27.
6. Laurence H. Shoup and William Minter, *Imperial Brain Trust: The Council on Foreign Relations and United States Foreign Policy* (New York: Monthly Review Press, 1977), p. vii.
7. Peter Grose, *Continuing the Inquiry: The Council on Foreign Relations from 1921 to 1996* (New York: CFR, 2001). See http://www.cfr.org/public/pubs/grose/grose04.html
8. *Ibid.*

9. See Shoup and Minter, *Imperial Brain Trust*, pp. 119–20.
10. *Ibid.*, p. 150. See also Hoopes and Brinkley, *FDR and the Creation of the UN*, p. 44.
11. See Hoopes and Brinkley, *FDR and the Creation of the UN*, p. 44.
12. See Shoup and Minter, *Imperial Brain Trust*, p. 170.
13. *Ibid.*, pp. 148–53.
14. *Ibid.*, p. 156.
15. *Ibid.*, pp. 169–70, citing Memorandum T-A25, 20 May 1942, CFR, War-Peace Studies, Hoover Library on War, Revolution and Peace, Stanford, California.
16. See Shoup and Minter, *Imperial Brain Trust*, p. 153.
17. Washington's representatives at the UN's founding conference in San Francisco are listed in the UN publication, *United Nations Conference On International Organization* (vol. 1, document 639, entitled "Delegates and Officials, United Nations Conference on International Organization"), pp. 65–75. See Emanuel M. Josephson, *Rockefeller "Internationalist"* (New York: Chedney Press, 1952), pp. 400–01. Among the American delegates, advisers and technical experts present at the conference were CFR members Alger Hiss (assistant secretary of state), Leo Pasvolsky, Isaiah Bowman, Ralph Bunche, Commander Harold E. Stassen, Lt Bernard Brodie, Joseph E. Johnson, Admiral Arthur J. Hepburn, Hamilton Fish Armstrong, John E. Lockwood, Edward G. Miller, Jr, Charles Noyes, Wilder Foote and Arthur Sweetser. The head of the delegation was Secretary of State Edward R. Stettinius, a CFR member since 1938.
18. Beatrice Bishop Berle and Travis Beal Jacobs, eds., *Navigating the Rapids 1918–1971: From the Papers of Adolf A. Berle* (New York: Harcourt Brace Jovanovich, 1973), pp. 475, 775.
19. Harry S. Truman, *Memoirs: Year of Decisions* (New York: Signet, 1965), vol. 1, pp. 317, 319.
20. Judith Miller and Laurie Mylroie, *Saddam Hussein and the Crisis in the Gulf* (New York: Times Books, 1990), pp. 252–53; John Sweeney, *Trading with the Enemy* (London: Pan, 1993), pp. 22–24.
21. See Miller and Mylroie, *Saddam Hussein and the Crisis in the Gulf*, p. xiv.
22. J. F. O. McAllister, 'The Lessons of Iraq', *Time*, 2 November 1992; Jack Colhoun, 'Trading with the Enemy', *CovertAction Information Bulletin* no. 37 (Washington, DC), Summer 1991, pp. 20–24.
23. Geoff Simons, *Iraq: From Sumer to Saddam* (London: Macmillan, 1994), p. 290.
24. *Ibid.*, p. 49, citing *The Guardian* (London), 2–3 May 1992.
25. See Channel 4 documentary, *Proud Arabs and Texas Oilmen*; Phyllis Bennis, *Calling the Shots: How Washington Dominates Today's UN* (New York: Olive Branch Press, 1996), pp. 31–32, 37.
26. See Channel 4 documentary, *Proud Arabs and Texas Oilmen*.
27. Denis Halliday, 'Continuing UN Sanctions Against Iraq only Serve US Ambition to Control Middle East', *The Irish Times*, 11 August 2000.
28. Roger Normand, 'Sanctions Against Iraq: New Weapon of Mass Destruction', *CovertAction Quarterly*, no. 64, Spring 1998, p. 6, citing 'Report to the Secretary-General on the Humanitarian Needs in Kuwait

and Iraq in the Immediate Post-Crisis Environment', UN Doc. S/22366 (March 1991), p. 5.

29.   Michael Jansen, 'Saddam's Eldest Son Tipped as New Speaker after His Election Success', *The Irish Times*, 30 March 2000.

30.   Hans von Sponeck, 'UK Envoy Fails to Justify Iraq Sanctions', *The Irish Times*, 28 July 2001.

31.   Boutros Boutros-Ghali, *Unvanquished: A US-UN Saga* (London: I. B. Tauris, 1999), pp.296–97.

32.   Quoted in Miller and Mylroie, *Saddam Hussein and the Crisis in the Gulf*, p. 217.

33.   Amnesty International statement, headed 'How Embarrassing', *The Irish Times*, 2 April 1994.

34.   Daniel P. Moynihan, *A Dangerous Place* (New York: Little, Brown, 1978), p. 247.

35.   *Indonesia and East Timor: Power and Impunity – Human Rights under the New Order* (London: Amnesty International, 1994), p. 9.

36.   See Amnesty International statement, *The Irish Times*, 2 April 1994.

37.   *Washington Post*, 27 April 1986. Cited in John G. Taylor, *Indonesia's Forgotten War: The Hidden History of East Timor* (London: Zed Books/Australia: Pluto Press, 1994), p. 170.

38.   Arnold Beichman, *The "Other" State Department: The United States Mission to the United Nations – Its Role in the Making of Foreign Policy* (New York: Basic Books, 1968), p. 30.

39.   Richard Becker et al, 'Sudan: Diversionary Bombing', *CovertAction Quarterly*, no. 66, Winter 1999, pp. 12–19.

40.   Richard N. Haass, ed., *Economic Sanctions and American Diplomacy* (New York: Council on Foreign Relations, 1998), p. 2.

41.   Quoted in Daniel Yergin, *The Prize: The Epic Quest for Oil, Money and Power* (New York: Touchstone, 1993), p. 585; Anthony Sampson, *The Seven Sisters* (London: Coronet, 1976), p. 259.

42.   *Torture in the Eighties* (London: Amnesty International, 1984), p. 236.

43.   See Boutros-Ghali, *Unvanquished*, p. 262.

44.   *Ibid.*, p. 263.

45.   See Bennis, *Calling the Shots*, p. xv, citing John Bolton address at Global Structures Convocation, Washington, DC, February 1994.

46.   See Boutros-Ghali, *Unvanquished*, p. 321.

47.   Quoted in Holly Sklar, *Washington's War on Nicaragua* (Boston: South End Press, 1988), p. 314.

48.   Quoted in Ian Williams, *The UN for Beginners* (New York: Writers and Readers Publishing, 1995), p. 58.

49.   Conor Cruise O'Brien and Feliks Topolski, *The United Nations: Sacred Drama* (London: Hutchinson, 1968), pp. 23–24.

50.   See Boutros-Ghali, *Unvanquished*, p. 6.

51.   See O'Brien and Topolski, *The United Nations*, p. 21.

52.   *The Ford Foundation and The United Nations* (New York: Ford Foundation, 1996), p. 3.

53.   *Financing an Effective United Nations: A Report of the Independent Advisory Group on UN Financing* (New York: Ford Foundation, 1993).

54.   See Grose, *Continuing the Inquiry.*

55. *United Nations Association of the United States of America, 1998 Annual Report*, p. 26.
56. *Ibid.*, p. 1.
57. 'Clinton Urges UN to Set Up Court for Rights Abuse', *The Irish Times*, 23 September 1997.
58. See *UNA-USA 1998 Annual Report*, pp. 4, 11, 28.
59. *The United Nations in Its Second Half-Century* (New York: Ford Foundation), p. 34.
60. 'Clinton Urges UN to Set Up Court for Rights Abuse', *The Irish Times*, 23 September 1997.
61. UN press release on Mr Annan's speech at the WEF, Davos, Switzerland, 31 January 1999.
62. *Ibid.*
63. Rockefeller-linked corporate leaders within the BCSD included Maurice R. Greenberg, one of the world's wealthiest businessmen and a governor of the UNA-USA (Trilateral Commission, CFR and Bilderberg Group); Alex Krauer (Bilderberg), head of Ciba-Geigy AG, Switzerland; Samuel C. Johnson (Trilateral Commission), chairman of S. C. Johnson and Son Inc., USA; and William D. Ruckelshaus (CFR, Trilateral Commission), chairman and CEO of Browning-Ferris Industries, USA.
64. Stephan Schmidheiny, *Changing Course: A Global Business Perspective on Development and the Environment* (Cambridge, Massachusetts: MIT Press, 1992), p. xi.
65. *World Economic Forum, 1993–94 Annual Report*, p. 3.
66. *Ibid.*, p. 17.
67. See Earth Council website – http://www.ecouncil.ac.cr/about/backgrnd.htm
68. See http://www.ecouncil.ac.cr/eccharter.htm
69. *Los Angeles Times*, 7 December 1997, cited by Environmental Working Group, Washington, DC. See http://www.ewg.org/dirtymoney/gcc.html. See also statement by Earth Policy Institute (Washington, DC), 'The Rise and Fall of the Global Climate Coalition', 25 July 2000.
70. Friends of the Earth International (Amsterdam), press release, 4 December 1997.
71. This memo was obtained by the Natural Resources Defense Council (New York) through the Freedom of Information Act and released by the council on 5 April 2002.
72. Preamble to Charter of the United Nations.

Chapter 7
The World Bank and IMF

US Agendas

In siring the United Nations and midwifing at its birth, Washington's intention was to create a body through which the US could further its ambition of becoming the principal moulder and custodian of the post-war global order. Almost a year prior to the holding of the UN's founding conference, a three-week conference had already been held at the New Hampshire resort of Bretton Woods. Attended by representatives from forty-four countries at the invitation of President Franklin D. Roosevelt, it provided Washington with two other US-parented bodies, the International Monetary Fund (IMF) and the International Bank for Reconstruction and Development, better known as the World Bank.

As the World Bank later noted, the objective of the meeting was no less than "to shape the institutional structure of the postwar international economy".[1] The twin institutions founded at Bretton Woods became instruments of global financial governance, the two most powerful supranational financial institutions in the post-bellum world.[2]

The two institutions would substantially follow US-guided agendas. US mastery over the affairs of both bodies was accomplished, like Washington's domination of the UN Security Council, through a transparently undemocratic voting system. Within both the World Bank and IMF, a nation's voting strength was to be proportionate to its shareholding or "quota" in the bodies. The size of each nation's shareholding, and hence its voting strength, was determined by the relative size of its economy.

This voting system gave the world's seven leading industrial powers, headed by the United States, enormous control over the World Bank's decision-making process. In the 1990s, the seven countries controlled around 45 per cent of the total votes, the US alone controlling around 17 per cent. The world's two most populous countries, China and India, which together comprised around 40 per cent of the earth's total population, held an aggregate of only 6 per cent of the bank's votes.[3] The voting strength of the US compared to the combined voting strength of China and India was over 20 times greater per million of population.

Its voting strength effectively gives the US alone the power of veto within both the bank and the fund. In the bank, its 17 per cent voting strength gives America the sole power, among the 180 or so member states, to unilaterally veto any proposals to alter the bank's Articles of Agreement and the institution's capital base, since such adjustments require the combined support of nations controlling 85 per cent of the shares. Within the IMF a similar pattern of domination exists, with the US controlling around the same percentage of the total votes.

The voting strength of the United States within the World Bank and IMF is approximately the same as the combined voting strength of all the 80 or so member states in Africa, Latin America and the Caribbean. The two institutions created by the United States at Bretton Woods were not intended to be democratic. Third World countries, regardless of the size of their populations, would be virtually powerless within both bodies.

Like the United Nations Charter, the World Bank's Articles of Agreement facilitate US domination of the organization. Its general operations are managed by a board of twenty-four executive directors. As in the UN Security Council, where "Perm Five" membership confers privileged powers on five UN member states, the bank's Articles of Agreement confer similar privileges through stipulating that only the five member states with the largest shareholdings (the United States, Japan, Germany, France and the United Kingdom) can *appoint* their own choice of executive directors to the bank's board. The other nineteen executive directors are *elected* to the board to represent the interests of the remaining 175 or so member states. The same five countries enjoy a similar privileged position within the IMF.

US dominance within the bank and IMF is further simplified by the location of the headquarters of both institutions in Washington, the hub of US political power. According to the World Bank book *Bankers with a Mission*, the bank's placement in Washington made clear that US officials "expected to exercise decisive influence over the activities of the new institution". The United States, it continued, "insisted that the bank be located in Washington, D.C., close to officials of the Treasury and State departments. . . It was to be an institution that served the interests of US foreign policy."[4]

The bank and fund would serve the interests of the US, and of Corporate USA, with heartless efficiency.

The CFR, World Bank and IMF

Proposals for the establishment of US-dominated multilateral organizations, the World Bank and IMF, to manage and enforce a new global economic order in the post-war era had their origins within the CFR War and Peace Studies groups, which by 1942 had, effectively, been absorbed into the State Department as planners of the post-war world.

The concept of an IMF and World Bank partnership was mooted by one of the five CFR studies groups. Headed by Alvin Hansen and Jacob Viner, by late 1940 the group had as one of its goals to set forth "the economic requirements of the United States in its potential leadership of the non-German world area".[5] In February 1942, Viner advocated the creation of "two financial institutions: one an international exchange stabilization board and one an international bank to handle short-term transactions not directly concerned with stabilization".[6] It was the first tentative blueprint for the establishment of twin organizations that would later find expression as the IMF and World Bank

A similar concept was being explored by the Department of the Treasury. In April 1942, the department released a document entitled *Proposal for a United Nations Stabilization Fund and a Bank for Reconstruction and Development of the United and Associated Nations*, which further advanced the idea of a fund and bank. The document was a sequel to an earlier, December 1941, memorandum prepared by Harry Dexter White, who had been instructed by Treasury Secretary Henry Morgenthau, Jr, to draft proposals for the formation of bodies to oversee the post-war international economic order.[7]

The proposals were considered and expanded by two committees established by the Roosevelt administration. The structures of the fund and the bank largely followed along the lines recommended by the two committees, whose members included Harry Dexter White (who was not in the CFR), Alvin Hansen, a head of one of the CFR's study groups, CFR member Leo Pasvolsky and Assistant Secretary of State Dean Acheson and Adolf Berle (who would both become CFR members).[8]

The purpose of the International Monetary Fund was to stabilize currencies and to promote international free trade, while the World Bank's task was to provide loans to war-ravaged countries for reconstruction and development.

Within the international economic and financial structures agreed by conference participants at Bretton Woods, the United States enjoyed a uniquely privileged position. The agreement created a world monetary system in which national currencies were to be "pegged" to (had a fixed value against) the US dollar, which became the principal reserve currency held by the world's central banks to meet their foreign debts and to provide finance for imported goods.

The stability of the international monetary system was thus dependent on the stability of the US dollar and on the health of the US economy. The international monetary system ordained at Bretton Woods was a formula for post-war US hegemony in the monetary-financial sphere, virtually guaranteeing US dominance over the international economy.

Officially the IMF and World Bank were to be UN "specialized agencies", operating under the guidance of the General Assembly. In practice, the United Nations was unable to exercise any control over the two bodies and their operations, the levers of power within both institutions being held by their most powerful member nations, particularly by the United States.

The World Bank's American Presidents

Americans have always dominated the affairs of the World Bank. Of its principal officers in mid-1973, around 45 per cent were American citizens.[9] Since its inception the bank has had nine presidents. All were US citizens. All had ties to the Rockefeller family and/or Corporate USA.[10]

In the short period between the creation of the World Bank and the appointment of its first president, the institution's affairs were directed by its American executive director, Emilio G. Collado. A member of the Council on Foreign Relations, Collado later occupied one of the highest offices in the Rockefeller-linked Standard Oil of New Jersey (Exxon/Esso).

The bank's first president was Eugene Meyer, the multimillionaire owner of a Wall Street brokerage firm and of the *Washington Post* and a CFR member in the 1940s.

Meyer was succeeded by John J. McCloy. A CFR member and later its chairman, McCloy was a confidant of the Rockefellers, a trustee of the Rockefeller Foundation (1946–49) and, later, chairman of the Rockefellers' Chase bank. Prior to his appointment to the World Bank, he had been offered the presidency of Standard Oil of California by the Rockefellers. For months after his appointment to the World Bank, he resided at the Washington home of Nelson Rockefeller.

McCloy chose as his successor Eugene Black, a vice president of the Rockefellers' Chase National Bank for over a decade, after McCloy's first choice, Robert Lovett, a trustee of the Rockefeller Foundation and a CFR member, had seemingly declined to accept the post.

A World Bank book identified "the people Black was thinking of as his successors – Douglas Dillon or David Rockefeller".[11] Dillon was a former trustee and later chairman of the Rockefeller Foundation. The person actually appointed president of the bank was George D. Woods, a director of a Chase Manhattan Bank investment affiliate and a trustee of the Rockefeller Foundation.

Five other appointees subsequently filled the post, up to the end of the century:

- President Johnson's Secretary of Defense Robert McNamara, a former president of the Ford Motor Co. Among his coterie of outside advisers during his tenure of office was David Rockefeller. Subsequent to holding this office, McNamara joined Rockefeller as a Trilateral Commission lifetime trustee.
- Trilateral commissioner Alden W. Clausen, head of the bank of America.
- Former Republican Congressman Barber B. Conable, a Trilateralist, who succeeded Clausen after US Labor Secretary William E. Brock and Paul Volcker, chairman of the Federal Reserve, had declined to accept the post. Volcker was also a Trilateralist, a long-time executive of the Chase Manhattan Bank and a trustee of the Rockefeller Foundation. Brock was both a Trilateralist and a CFR member.
- Banker Lewis Preston, who had been a director of the CFR (1981–88) and also its treasurer (1987–88).
- James D. Wolfensohn, a founder of a New York investment banking firm, who took over the helm at the World Bank in June 1995. He was a member of the CFR and of the Bilderberg Group's steering committee and a trustee of the Rockefeller Foundation, thus continuing the tradition of appointing Rockefeller-linked figures to the presidency of the bank. In 1997, he was the first recipient of the David Rockefeller Award, an honour bestowed on him by the Museum of Modern Art, which David Rockefeller's mother had helped to create and where David was chairman emeritus.

Theoretically, World Bank presidents are elected by the bank's executive directors. In practice, they are nominated by the US president of the day and ratified by the bank's executive directors. Perhaps predictably, all nine presidents of the bank have been American citizens associated with the Rockefellers and Corporate USA.

Dominating the World Bank and IMF

While insisting that the bank's most powerful office be the exclusive preserve of Americans, Washington has waived its entitlement to nominate a US citizen as a candidate to head the IMF. As a consequence, all managing directors of the fund have been Europeans. Third World aspirants for the top posts in both the bank and fund are unceremoniously brushed aside. Washington contents itself with the office of first deputy managing director of the fund, the second most powerful post. Despite this, the United States exercises an overwhelming dominance over the IMF.

Like the World Bank, ties to the Rockefellers and/or the corporate sector are commonplace within the IMF's upper echelons. In early 2000, Trilateralists Horst Köhler and Stanley Fischer held the two most powerful posts within the organization, managing director and first deputy managing director, respectively. In mid-2001, Fischer was succeeded by Anne O. Krueger, like Fischer a US citizen and CFR member.

American dominance within the twin institutions derives from its superpower status, from the bodies' dependence on US funding, from the weighted and undemocratic voting system whereby a member state's voting power is related to the size of its economy, from its privileged entitlement to elect its own executive directors to both the bank and fund and from Washington's success in having the headquarters of both organizations located in the United States.

Although the heads of the bank and fund are supposed to take decisions on the basis of merit, they cannot easily ignore the demands of the bodies' largest shareholder, the United States, which has dominated the proceedings of both bodies since their inception.

Rescuing US Banks

On the surface, both the World Bank and IMF have admirable goals. In his speech to the inaugural meeting of the bank and fund, Britain's John Maynard Keynes, who chaired the commission responsible for the creation of the bank at the Bretton Woods conference, spoke of how the two institutions "belong to the whole world and their sole allegiance is to the general good, without fear or favour to any particular interest".[12] According to the bank, its "mission is to help developing countries reduce poverty and promote sustainable development".[13] The self-professed goals of the IMF include contributing "to the promotion and maintenance of high levels of employment and real income and the development of the productive resources of all members".[14] These purported objectives should be borne in mind when considering the policies pursued by the twin institutions in the course of the debt crisis that erupted in 1982.

During the crisis the institutions showed little allegiance "to the general good". Instead, they functioned as pliant servants of the United States and the West's largest banks. The debt crisis, the most critical financial imbroglio since the Wall Street crash, was precipitated by a four-fold increase in oil prices in late 1973, which poured billions of additional dollars into the coffers of oil-producing countries. Much of this revenue was then deposited in the West's commercial banks. These decided that it would be prudent, and profitable, to lend the petro-dollars to Third World countries, which had earlier been beating a path to the bankers' doors seeking funds, usually with little success. As loans flooded into non-oil producing Third World countries, their aggregate foreign debt soared from $130 billion in 1973 to around $2,000 billion in 1997.[15] As their indebtedness spiralled upwards, cash-strapped debtor countries found it increasingly difficult or impossible to pay even the interest due on the debts. Progressively larger volumes of new borrowings were procured to repay existing debts. The new borrowings increased the countries' indebtedness, and the amount of interest payable, which in turn necessitated recourse to further loans, entailing still higher repayments.

Such spiralling debts and repayments could not continue ad infinitum. Soon debt-mired countries began to fall behind in their interest payments. In August 1982, Mexico threw the world's financial sector into a state of turmoil when it announced that it was on the verge of bankruptcy, crippled by a foreign debt of $80 billion. In 1972, its debt had been less than $8 billion.[16]

The seriousness of the situation was commented on by *Latinamerica Press* in March 1984. In Latin America, it reported, "most countries are experiencing the worst economic storms since the Depression. Unable to obtain new loans or repay old ones, they are slipping down what *The Economist* calls a 'black hole' of foreign debt. Growth rates have stagnated, thousands of industries have collapsed, and in many countries up to half the labor force is unemployed or underemployed. So severe is the debt crunch that it has wiped out two decades of industrial development in Argentina, Brazil and Chile. Signs of rising social tensions abound – almost daily protest demonstrations in Chile, mob sackings of supermarkets throughout Brazil, riots in Bolivia and the election of a Marxist mayor in Lima, the politically tense capital of Peru. . . Thanks to the heavy exposure of US banks, which hold the lion's share of Latin America's $350 billion debt, the United States has been drawn into a financial cauldron. . . Many Latin American countries are behind on interest payments; some, such as Venezuela and Argentina, are in effective moratorium, having paid neither interest nor principal. And they are in no position to do so. Interest payments on Argentina's $43 billion debt equal 60 per cent of the country's exports and 70 per cent of its net savings. . . If any of the major debtors officially declares a moratorium, the survival of the biggest US banks will be on the line. Citibank, for example, has more on loan to Brazil than its entire shareholders' capital. . . The possibility of moratorium is under serious discussion in Argentina, Brazil, Venezuela and lesser debtor nations like Bolivia and Ecuador. . . Defaults in two or three countries – perhaps even one – might lead to the collapse of the Bank of America, Citibank, even Chase Manhattan, and the entire international financial edifice would then be in danger of tumbling like a house of cards."[17]

America's largest banks were in an extremely precarious position. By 1983, the nine largest, including Citicorp, Chase Manhattan, New

York's Chemical Bank, Bank of America and Manufacturers Hanover, had loaned out around 130 per cent of their stockholders' equity to three Latin American countries.[18]

As repayment arrears mounted and creditor banks teetered on the brink of insolvency, the bankers and political leaders in the creditor nations, but particularly in the United States, fearful that the debts might prove to be unpayable and uncollectable, turned to the IMF and World Bank for help. The Bretton Woods institutions took centre stage in the crisis. With a primary goal of securing repayments of the debts to the banks, they wrestled with dozens of Third World countries for control of national economies. In this unequal struggle, the institutions always prevailed. By the late 1980s, over seventy countries had succumbed to the power of the institutions.[19]

The bank and fund became debt collectors for the private banks. The modus operandi adopted by the IMF and World Bank for resolving the deepening crisis was to make access to further loans contingent upon debtor countries implementing IMF-tailored economic programmes to facilitate debt repayment. These draconian IMF-imposed austerity measures, euphemistically called Structural Adjustment Programs (SAPs), were, according to the two sister organizations, an indispensable process for ameliorating the economic crises of debtor countries and for stimulating economic growth and social progress.

What the programmes actually achieved was to extricate the creditor banks from their self-inflicted financial nightmare. For people in debtor countries, the creditor-friendly programmes brought suffering and death on a vast scale. For the United States and Corporate USA, the programmes functioned as a new form of intervention in, and mastery over, the affairs of Third World countries, helping to open up their markets and economies to foreign trade, investment and control. The programmes represented a giant step on the road to globalization.

Structural Adjustment Programs

In theory, member nations govern the IMF and World Bank. However, as the debt crisis deteriorated, a reversal of roles occurred, with the two institutions becoming, under Washington's guidance, the de facto rulers of around half the world's nations, the most debt-laden Third World countries.

The principal tool employed by the IMF and World Bank to gain mastery over the affairs of Third World debtor countries were structural adjustment programmes, whose terms debtor nations had to abide by in order to gain access to further loans. Without such loans, debtor countries would be unable to obtain oil and other imports vital for development, industry and agriculture. Economic chaos and collapse would inevitably ensue. However, SAPs compelled ruling regimes to drain enormous financial resources from enfeebled minnow economies to defray debts to creditor banks in developed countries, rather than alleviating the suffering and the underdevelopment in their own countries.

Christian Aid, a British Third World development and aid agency, outlined the vast new power of the two Bretton Woods institutions. "To people in Third World countries it seems that the World Bank and the IMF now run the world. Certainly their world," the agency remarked.[20]

Instead of aiding Third World debtor countries, SAPs decapitalized them. The enormous haemorrhaging of capital from Latin America to service the region's debts was reported in *Latinamerica Press*. "From 1980 to 1992 Latin America had a net negative transfer of capital of US $220 billion, meaning that $220 billion more left the region than entered. Despite this enormous drain, the foreign debt did not decrease, but increased from $250 billion in 1980. . . to $450 billion in 1992."[21] By 2001 Brazil owed close to $250 billion to foreign creditors.[22] The result was predictable. Before the end of 1990, another edition of *Latinamerica Press* noted, 50 million Latin Americans were living in "extreme poverty" and an estimated 750,000 children had died in Brazil from malnutrition.[23]

In famine and disease-racked Africa, the IMF's structural adjustment programmes siphoned money from health, education, development and social programmes. In Uganda, one of the world's poorest countries, the government was forced by the IMF and World Bank to spend more than four times as much on debt repayments as on its woefully inadequate health services.[24] By the end of the millennium, around a half-million Ethiopian children were dying each year as a consequence of diarrhoea and other easily preventable illnesses. Yet the country was expending approximately six times more on debt repayments than on primary health clinics and on low-cost life-saving measures.[25] Mozambique's annual budget for primary health care and primary education was around $52 million, at a time that $68 million was flowing out of the country in foreign debt repayments.[26]

According to a United Nations report, in the early 1990s debt repayments of sub-Saharan African countries amounted to over $13 billion per year, while the total additional annual cost of meeting basic human needs in the region for health, education, nutrition and reproductive health for everyone would be only around $9 billion.[27]

The terms of IMF-enforced SAPs had enormous negative repercussions in debtor countries, including increased immiseration of the masses, a loss of human dignity, rising unemployment, repression, malnutrition and the undermining of the most basic human rights. To finance debt repayments, agricultural produce was exported, sometimes creating food shortages and hunger in the exporting countries.

Food subsidies were removed or reduced, thereby raising purchase prices. State employees were dismissed. Instead of increasing lending to the poorest countries, it was reduced. By the mid-1990s, the poorest countries, with about 20 per cent of the world's people, were receiving a meagre 0.2 per cent of the world's commercial lending, plunging their populations deeper into poverty.[28]

The IMF-imposed SAPs constituted an institutionalized structural poverty, fashioned to ensure the repayments of debts by Third World countries to Western creditor banks. Hundreds of thousands of lives, probably millions, were sacrificed to ensure that IMF and World Bank repayment targets were met. The deaths occurred because of hunger, "diseases of poverty" (diarrhoea, enteritis, dehydration, tuberculosis and respiratory ailments) and vaccine-preventable illnesses (whooping cough, measles, polio and tetanus).

For many, the phonic similarity of debt and death had a very real significance.

The Backlash

A 1996 United Nations report provided an insight into the sorry plight of Third World countries in the years after Mexico's near-bankruptcy in August 1982, years during which the IMF and World Bank performed the dual roles of regulators of Third World economies and debt collectors for creditor banks. "If present trends continue," the report stated, "economic disparities between the industrial and developing nations will move from inequitable to inhuman." These widening economic disparities were "creating two worlds – ever more polarized. . . Of the $23 trillion global GDP in 1993, $18 trillion is in the industrial countries – only $5 trillion in the developing countries, even though they have nearly 80% of the world's people."[29]

The SAP and debt-induced worsening of the economic and social conditions in the Third World sparked an enormous backlash. A *Latinamerica Press* report told of how in Venezuela "in the three years since IMF agreements were signed. . . there have been more than 5,000 public protests. . . with over 2,000 ending in violence".[30] In February 1989, during anti-IMF riots in the capital city, up to one thousand were shot dead. Venezuela's President Carlos Andres Perez accused the IMF of applying a strategy of "economic totalitarianism which kills not with bullets but with famine".[31]

Anti-austerity explosions of discontent occurred throughout the Third World, most notably in Latin America.[32] In the Bolivian city of Cochabamba, six people were killed in March 1982 while protesting against the effects of an IMF austerity programme. In May 1984, labour unrest and a hunger strike by 4,500 Bolivian trade unionists against the severity of IMF-imposed measures forced the government to temporarily suspend repayments to foreign banks and multilateral lending agencies. In September of the following year, thousands of Bolivians were arrested after a state of siege was declared by the government in a bid to break an anti-austerity general strike.

By 1984, dozens of anti-IMF protestors had been killed in Peru by the security forces. A smaller number were killed in neighbouring Ecuador. Acceptance of IMF loan conditions by the government of the Dominican Republic led to widespread riots in April 1984, which left dozens dead and an estimated 150 injured. Further protests followed in February 1985. In Peru, President Fujimori's closure of Congress and his suspension of the judiciary in 1992 was, to a considerable extent, motivated by his determination to overcome opposition to SAPs and to suppress the social unrest that ensued after their imposition. Riots in Jamaica against IMF-enforced economic policies at the beginning of both 1984 and 1985 claimed around a dozen lives. The hardship brought on by neoliberal economic policies in Argentina in 1993 provoked demonstrations in the northern town of Santiago de Estero, which were brutally crushed by troops and police. The attacks left nine dead and dozens injured. In December 2001, anti-government riots left at least twenty-five Argentines dead and more than 150 wounded. Saddled with debts of $132 billion, and with the IMF refusing to honour an agreed loan package because of government overspending, the country descended into a state of near-anarchy.

An August 1995 general strike in Panama against an economic reform package left five workers dead, nineteen people missing and hundreds of people injured or detained. In Costa Rica in the same month, 100,000 workers took to the streets to protest against strict economic measures. In Brazil, employees of the state-owned Petrobras oil giant carried out a prolonged strike to protest against the planned privatization of the company, in accordance with IMF/World Bank neoliberal policies. Privatization plans also sparked protests in Paraguay, where two days of civil unrest in July 2002 left two dead and dozens injured. The protests forced the government to cancel its planned privatization of water and telecommunications networks. In early 2001, indigenous Indians clashed with police in the highlands around Ecuador's capital city following the implementation of IMF-stipulated economic measures.

Protests also occurred in Africa. A decade of protests in Morocco, beginning in 1981, against IMF-dictated economic policies left at least 200 dead. In January 1984, around 100 Tunisians were killed while protesting against IMF-initiated price rises. Nigeria's armed forces closed universities in 1989 during anti-SAP student demonstrations. In October 1997, President Chiluba of Zambia survived an attempted military coup during a period of mounting unemployment and suffering caused by an IMF/World Bank restructuring programme. The

Third World protests were largely unseen and unheard in developed countries.

Watchdog of US Imperialism

World Bank loans, IMF structural adjustment programmes and other policies pursued by the twin institutions have been inhuman in their conception and implementation. Ostensibly aimed at alleviating poverty and hunger and at promoting economic and social development in the Third World, they have been responsible for impoverishing hundreds of millions of people, for the enforced displacement and dispossession of further millions and for widespread environmental degradation. World Bank loans have also helped to prop up illegal and brutal regimes.

A 1981 report issued by the Permanent Peoples' Tribunal, an international group of jurists, intellectuals and political, labour and church leaders,[33] detailed how in the Philippines up to 100,000 people faced being forced at gunpoint to abandon their ancestral lands and rice terraces to enable the World Bank-funded Chico River Basin Development Projects to go ahead. In the cities "hundreds of thousands of slum dwellers" were being evicted from their homes to make way for World Bank and Asian Development Bank-funded projects, which the tribunal held would "benefit transnational corporations and local commercial interests".[34]

When the people resisted their worsening immiseration and repression, members of the US-aided armed forces of the Marcos regime brutally crushed the opposition. In south Philippines, faced with armed resistance from the Moro people, government forces conducted "a war of extermination including the use of napalm and chemical warfare", according to the tribunal. US troops from the US military bases in the Philippines were "increasingly participating in direct military operations against the Filipino people", the report alleged.[35]

The World Bank, the IMF and foreign creditor banks were denounced by the tribunal for backing the Marcos regime. The twin institutions, the tribunal reported, were "playing a crucial role in sustaining, supporting and encouraging the Marcos regime, despite its commission of systematic state crimes". The IMF was perceived to be an instrument used by the United States "to impose its will on the Philippines". It was becoming, the tribunal's report claimed, "the watchdog of US imperialism".[36]

According to the tribunal, the "increasing impoverishment of the Filipino people in the last eight years of martial law rule is the direct result of the economic policies of the Marcos dictatorship. But where do these policies come from? They are, in the first instance, the result of direct and indirect pressure from the United States and US-controlled multilateral lending institutions such as the World Bank and IMF."[37]

IMF/World Bank activities elsewhere also had devastating effects on people's lives. World Bank-funded dams in Pakistan, Ghana and on the Zambezi River between Zimbabwe and Zambia displaced over 200,000 local residents, many being reduced to a state of near-absolute poverty. In India, the bank agreed to part-fund the construction of over 3,000 dams along the Narmada River and its tributaries, entailing the resettlement of at least 300,000 people and the submersion of hundreds of villages. Local opposition to the project transformed the region into a zone of conflict, forcing the bank to reconsider its financial support. Ultimately, the Indian government released the bank from its loan undertakings.

A dam construction project between Argentina and Paraguay – promoted by the Stroessner dictatorship in Paraguay and military juntas in Argentina and part-funded by the World Bank – was criticized in 1990 by Argentina's President Carlos Saul Menem as "a monument to corruption".[38]

An agreement signed in 1981 between the World Bank and Brazil's military rulers, for an "integrated regional development" mega-project in Rondonia in the Amazon region, sank the bank's reputation to a new low. Over $500 million was provided by the bank for the programme, which involved the construction of a massive highway and the colonization of the region. The programme caused one of the planet's worst ever ecological calamities. Within a few years of the programme's launch, the colonizers had burned and cleared rainforest covering an area the size of the state of Arkansas. The rainforest is regarded as the earth's lungs, functioning as a cleanser of the planet's polluted air. Thousands of Indians living in the project area were killed, either in clashes with the colonizers or from imported illnesses.

Supporting Despots

The World Bank's loan agreement for the colonization in Rondonia was signed with Brazil's military rulers, who ruled the country for two decades after the 1964 overthrow of President João Goulart. Brazil's military regime was just one of a host of dictatorships and military-run administrations which had taken the reins of political power, many of them with the help of the CIA, in Third World countries. By the mid-1970s, most of Latin America's population was under military control. It was to such US-supported regimes that much of the early petro-dollar loans were channelled by American creditor banks.

Most of Brazil's foreign debt, up to the debt crisis of 1982, was incurred by military regimes and the private sector. In Nicaragua, US bank loans provided a lifeline for the ailing dictatorship of General Anastasio Somoza Debayle, before he fled the country in 1979 after looting the national treasury. Other beneficiaries of US bank loans in Latin America included Uruguay's military rulers, who held power for eleven years after a 1973 *coup d'état*; Paraguay's dictator General Alfredo Stroessner, who governed his country from 1954 to 1989; Argentina's military juntas, which held power from 1976 to 1983; General Augusto Pinochet, Chile's dictator from 1973 to 1989; General Hugo Banzer, who ruled Bolivia from 1971 to 1978; and other Latin American military regimes, including ones in El Salvador, Guatemala and Honduras.

The kleptocratic dictatorships of "Papa Doc" and "Baby Doc" Duvalier in Haiti, Ferdinand Marcos in the Philippines, General Suharto in Indonesia and General Mobutu in Zaire, among the world's most corrupt rulers, were also recipients of loans furnished by American banks. Mobutu, who seized power through a coup, was subsequently covertly aided by the CIA. His personal wealth has been estimated at $5 billion, which he plundered from the nation's coffers and from the bank loans and used to purchase French chateaux and to construct lavish palaces. This in a country which in 1979 had a per capita GNP of $260, an adult literacy rate of around 15 per cent and a life expectancy at birth of just forty-seven years.[39] Suharto may have looted up to $40 billion from his subjects and Marcos around $5 billion.[40] The World Bank and IMF were also actively involved in lending to such repressive governments.

Such loans are indicative of a general trend. A disproportionately large percentage of World Bank and US bank loans to Third World regions were directed to countries ruled by undemocratic and unelected regimes that retained power through repressing, torturing and killing their own citizens. Summarizing the role of the Bretton Woods institutions, one commentator wrote of how they lined "the pockets of dictators and western corporations while threatening local democracies and forcing cuts to social programs".[41]

Reinstating Colonial Patterns of Control

Loans given to Third World regimes between 1974 and the debt crisis of 1982 were, for the most part, financially irrational. Discarding traditional conservative lending criteria, the bankers permitted despotic loanees to borrow vast sums, while disregarding the nations' capacity to repay the loans and the enormous burden they placed on the populations of those countries.

In assessing loan applications, the creditor banks were rarely very discriminating about the merits of loan-funded projects, many of which were obscenely expensive, superfluous or impracticable. President Marcos' nuclear plant in Bataan is a particularly transparent example of the financial negligence of the creditor bankers. Constructed in an earthquake zone, safety considerations ensured that there was never any realistic possibility of the plant being operated.

Squandered on ill-advised ventures or appropriated for the rulers' personal enrichment, the loans were often of little or no benefit to the general public. Some loans were consumed by the countries' armed forces to augment their military and repressive capability. Hundreds of thousands of civilians were killed by these forces, including 50,000 Nicaraguans killed by the Somoza dictatorship prior to the triumph of the Sandinistas in 1979; 30,000 murdered by Argentina's military rulers; and 200,000 East Timorese killed following the invasion of their country by the forces of Indonesian despot General Suharto.

Loans granted to repressive, corrupt and ruinous ruling cliques that had no legitimacy and no electoral mandate to borrow money in the name of the people were morally reprehensible. Such foolhardiness, immorality and illegality deserved to be punished. If a bank provides a known criminal with loans to finance nefarious activities, it is hardly reasonable to expect the criminal's victims to repay the loans. However, this is almost precisely what occurred in the case of bankers' loans to murderous Third World rulers, where the banks demanded that the people who had suffered under the regimes should repay debts illegally incurred, and often stolen, by the tyrants. When the loan repayments became difficult to collect, the creditor banks turned to the IMF and World Bank for help.

Far from rebuking or penalizing the creditor banks for such foolishness and moral blindness, the Bretton Woods institutions became the creditor banks' debt collectors, helping the banks to recover ethically unjustifiable loans from totally innocent parties – impoverished Third World populations that had neither sought nor been consulted about the loans, had not chosen the governments that acquired the loans, had not benefited to any great degree, if at all, from the loans and in many instances had greatly suffered under the loan-funded regimes.

In their efforts to recoup the debts, the IMF and World Bank had the assistance of a powerful patron, the United States government. To protect US banks against default in the wake of the 1982 debt debacle, Washington transformed the country's foreign policy virtually into a private foreign policy run in the interests of the banks. The US-sired World Bank and International Monetary Fund were co-opted by Washington to collaborate in the implementation of a foreign policy designed to rescue the endangered banks.

US governments, one commentator pointed out succinctly, had "discovered a way of combining unregulated international banking and financial markets with minimal risk of the US banking and financial systems suffering a resulting collapse. Using its control over the IMF/WB and largely with the support of its European partners,

Washington discovered that when its international financial operators reached the point of insolvency through their international activities, they could be bailed out by the populations of the borrower countries at almost no significant cost to the US economy."[42]

President Alan Garcia of Peru, one of the regimes to be blacklisted by the IMF, denounced the fund as "an agent of exploitation and domination".[43] American civil rights leader Jesse Jackson spoke of how those seeking to intervene in the affairs of Third World countries "no longer use bullets and ropes. They use the World Bank and IMF."[44] The IMF's structural adjustment programmes amounted to economic *coups d'êtats*, giving the West's richest nations and mega-corporations economic control over the Third World.

Supranational Colossi

As the US/IMF/World Bank-orchestrated bleeding process continued, with huge financial resources being drained from the Third World by creditor banks, Church leaders began to openly question the morality of the process. In Brazil, a Catholic prelate, Cardinal Paulo Arns of Sao Paulo, condemned the outflow of debt repayments which was starving and killing Brazilians. The loans, he stated, "were contracted by the military, mostly for military ends – $40 billion were swallowed by six nuclear plants, none of which is working today. The people are now expected to pay off these debts in low salaries and hunger. But we have already reimbursed the debt, once or twice over, considering the interest paid. We must stop giving the blood and the misery of our people to pay the First World."[45]

Coerced by the fund and bank, Brazil's government continued its debt repayments. By 1987, around 40 per cent of Brazil's 160 million people had been reduced to a state of absolute poverty.[46] The country's economy was being run by the two Bretton Woods institutions to rescue and maintain the profits of US banks that had precipitated the crisis with foolhardy loans.

Third World indebtedness caused by the loans became synonymous with political and economic powerlessness; that is, an inability on the part of the debtor nations to make crucial political and economic decisions without first obtaining the imprimatur of the fund and the World Bank. The debt crisis transformed the twin institutions into supranational colossi that imperiously dictated the economic policies to be followed by debtor countries. The immense power wielded by both bodies was such that they could alter the balance of political power within countries and could reshape national economies, or paralyze them.

The IMF's structural adjustment programmes constituted a new model of debt slavery, responsible for the greatest ever transfer of wealth from the Third World to the developed world, specifically to Western banks such as the Chase Manhattan. Hostages of the IMF and the World Bank, Third World populations watched helplessly as immense wealth was bled from their countries to repay the banks, as safety nets for the poor were abolished, legislative safeguards were discarded, citizens were deprived of basic necessities and subjected to repressive measures, countless millions were immiserated or reduced to a state of beggary and state-run enterprises were privatized, often sold off to foreign multinationals.

Colonial patterns of control by foreign powers were restored, with the twin Washington-based institutions aiding in the takeover of Third World wealth and resources. In Ethiopia, the IMF demanded that the country's banking system be opened to outside competitors and that its largest bank be split up. If acceded to, the demands would enable the West's megabanks to swamp local competitors. When the government resisted the demands, the IMF temporarily suspended its lending programme to the country.[47] In another poverty-racked African country, Chad, the World Bank agreed to provide a $300 million loan to the country to facilitate the extraction of oil from a vast deposit in the south of the country. However, control over the project would rest with a consortium led by the Rockefeller-linked ExxonMobil giant, not by Chad's government, and the expenditure of the country's oil revenues would largely be determined by the bank. Chad had ceded part of its sovereignty to the corporate-friendly institution.[48]

Even member states of the once-feared Soviet superpower succumbed to IMF/World Bank economic mastery and implemented IMF-demanded austerity measures after the collapse of communism. The measures often failed. In 1998, the IMF had to coordinate a rescue package for Russia, thereby bailing out Western creditor banks that stood to lose billions of dollars. Russia's economic collapse, a former World Bank senior vice president admitted, had been inadvertently accelerated by the IMF, which, through its "insistence on Russia maintaining an overvalued currency and its supporting that with billions of dollars of loans ultimately crushed the economy".[49]

A corporate-friendly neoliberal (or "free-market") economic model was being forced upon Third World and post-communist nations by the sister organizations. Democracy was sabotaged and sovereignty undermined. National economies were reshaped and opened to foreign goods and investors. The capacity of debtor nations to determine their own future and maintain control over national resources was curtailed. The IMF and World Bank had become the institutional drivers of a new and inequitable model of global economic governance that was being imposed on the world's peoples – globalization.

The US Defeats Vietnam

In February 1994, the US lifted its longstanding economic blockade of Vietnam. Complying with IMF demands for economic restructuring, Vietnam was finally approved by the fund and the World Bank as a suitable loan recipient. However, the embargo was lifted and the loans were provided only after Hanoi had agreed to honour the debts of the former US-financed government of South Vietnam. Instead of receiving war reparation payments from the United States, Vietnam, which had suffered so much and had lost perhaps three million of its citizens during the course of the US-waged Vietnam War, was expected to refund part of the aggressor's expenditure. It was a nauseating demand, similar to a rapist insisting on being paid by a victim for the sexual violation and for the physical, psychological and emotional scarring.

Full agreement on the repayment of the debts to the United States was reached in April 1997. A US Treasury Department press release provided the details: "Treasury Secretary Robert E. Rubin and Vietnamese Finance Minister Nguyen Sinh Hung agreed today that Vietnam will repay the United States approximately $145 million in economic debts owed by the former Republic of Vietnam. . . Vietnam acknowledged its responsibility for the economic and social debts of the Republic of Vietnam – the government in the south prior to April 30, 1975. . . The bilateral agreement between Vietnam and the United States covers the entire amount of economic debt outstanding to the United States."[50]

Subsequently, under IMF and World Bank supervision, US-approved "free-market" economic policies were implemented in Vietnam, entailing the closure or privatization of state-owned enterprises, the dismissal of hundreds of thousands of employees, the introduction of tax and other incentives for foreign investors and the removal of tariff barriers. Many of the country's most valuable industrial and mineral assets were to be converted to "joint ventures" with foreign partners. Vietnam's socialist economy was being dismantled.

American and Japanese corporations and investors vied for control of the country's resources, its principal industries, its markets and its exports. Corporate USA investments and consumer goods flooded into the country. Meanwhile, Vietnam's Central Bank operated under IMF supervision.

The Vietnamese people, who had fought so bravely, so long and at enormous human cost, had been recolonized. Their new imperial masters were the US government, Corporate USA and the corporations of other capitalist nations, the IMF and the World Bank. The United States had finally won its war against the Vietnamese people.

The Bretton Woods Committee and Corporate USA

The role of multilateral development banks (MDBs), such as the World Bank, as instruments of US foreign policy, especially as promoters of free market economic policies around the world and as allies of Corporate USA, was noted in a 1997 document, *The Multilateral Development Banks and the United States*. Published by the Washington-headquartered Bretton Woods Committee, the document noted how the "MDBs serve key US interests. MDBs are an effective policy tool. America increasingly relies on the MDBs to promote critical US interests around the world. . . the MDBs provide vital support for US global objectives on a scale that cannot be replicated by our bilateral programmes. . . Multilateral support for major trade and investment liberalization clears the way for new market entry and competition by US firms. Such work by the World Bank and the Asian Development Bank in India, for example, has helped US firms become this huge economy's single largest foreign investor. . . In one especially important task – encouraging developing countries to undertake the economic policy reforms necessary to become free market-oriented democracies – the MDBs are America's most effective aid instrument. This is because developing countries are more likely to respond to the MDBs, with their international clout and prestige, than [to] the United States or any other single donor."[51]

The Bretton Woods Committee is Corporate USA's principal private channel for lobbying the IMF and the World Bank. Located close to the sister institutions, the BWC "includes over five hundred leaders from industry and finance throughout the US as well as former government officials".[52] Funding for the organization derives from US corporations and from predominantly corporate-linked members and foundations.

The committee is a Rockefeller-linked corporate forum and pressure group. An undated document furnished to the author by the committee in mid-1997 listed 107 BWC committee members and officers,[53] around seventy-four of which, or 69 per cent, were members or alumni of one or more of the Rockefeller and corporate-dominated foreign policy forums: the CFR, the Trilateral Commission and the Bilderberg Group.

The Bretton Woods Committee draws its membership from leading American establishment figures, but especially from the Rockefeller forums and from the corporate sector. In 1997, it had two co-chairmen, Rockefeller intimate Paul A. Volcker and Henry Owen, a member of the Trilateral Commission's executive committee in the 1970s and a CFR member. Its members in the late 1990s included David Rockefeller, Henry Kissinger and heads of many of America's largest financial and non-financial corporations. Its membership also included all nine living former treasury secretaries. These outlined the importance of the fund and bank to Washington. "The international financial institutions are a cost effective way to meet our foreign policy goals," they stated.[54]

With its super-elite membership of many of America's most powerful corporate chiefs, Rockefeller associates and former US cabinet members, the BWC is a powerful corporate lobbying organization. Its claim that it "provides a forum which ensures that the voice and interests of the business community are considered by Congress, the Administration and the management of the international financial institutions",[55] specifically the management of the World Bank and IMF, is not an idle boast. Its function is to ensure that US foreign policy is corporate-friendly and that the World Bank and IMF act as instrumentalities of this foreign policy.

Tearing Down Trade Barriers

A World Bank publication has acknowledged that Washington intended that the bank should "be an institution that served the interests of US foreign policy".[56] The IMF was intended to serve a similar function. In furthering US interests, the twin institutions showed little accountability or loyalty to those comprising the vast majority of mankind, the peoples of the Third World.

In the wake of the 1982 debt crisis, the policies pursued by the sister institutions were purportedly intended to help in the development of the world's poorer regions. However, according to Doug Hellinger, a former consultant to the bank, the post-1982 economic order being forced upon Third World countries by the fund and bank "isn't a development strategy, it's a corporate strategy".[57] The bank and fund – together with GATT and its successor, the World Trade Organization, both of which will be discussed later – comprise the vanguard of US economic and corporate imperialism.

Today, overt US military aggression and covert CIA operations are rarely necessary to achieve US hegemonic political and economic objectives in non-Islamic Third World countries. The IMF and the World Bank, through structural adjustment programmes and other measures imposed by the bank and fund on debtor countries, are far more cost-effective and PR-compatible instruments of intervention and of US foreign policy.

SAPs constitute one of the most successful interventionist strategies ever employed by Washington. In the space of a few years, they achieved a US objective that four decades of Cold War era gunboat and B-52 diplomacy, CIA covert operations and low-intensity conflict failed to accomplish – gaining control over Third World markets and economies.

Since the Second World War, America's corporate-dominated ruling elite has had as one of its fundamental foreign policy objectives, the creation of a free-market global capitalist economy, dominated by the United States and its multinational corporations, where goods and capital could flow with little governmental regulation or interference. However, protectionist trade and economic policies made it difficult for US corporations and investors to penetrate the markets of Third World countries where more than four-fifths of the world's people live.

Structural adjustment programmes imposed by the IMF forced debtor governments to dismantle obstacles to foreign imports and investments and to remove subsidies to local manufacturers. SAP stipulations left governments virtually powerless to control their countries' economic policies, created huge breaches in the economic borders of the Third World, opened up countries to foreign capital, promoted the entry of multinational corporations and facilitated the repatriation of corporate profits.

Countries which had previously relied on defensive economic measures to shield their underdeveloped industrial, financial, agricultural and service sectors from competition from foreign behemoths were forced by the IMF and World Bank to jettison these mechanisms. Unable to compete with the multinationals, many Third World enterprises closed or were taken over by foreign competitors, throwing countless workers on the unemployment scrap heap. Other workers were made redundant by IMF/World Bank policies which prevailed upon governments to withdraw from public enterprise through privatizing state-run concerns of any significant value, much of the proceeds often being used to pay back foreign debts. Many of these privatized enterprises were purchased, sometimes at giveaway prices, by multinationals, thereby further increasing the hold of foreign corporations over wealth-creating enterprises in the Third World.

The United States, the IMF and the World Bank were the principal catalysts in this process of economic and political debilitation and of the concurrent corporate "colonization". Elections in debtor Third World countries became an almost meaningless exercise. What was the point of electing a government when it would be unable to perform its democratic mandate to represent the interests of its electorate and, instead, under the supervision of Washington's twin institutional surrogates, would have to adapt the national economy and amend legislation to accommodate the interests of creditor banks and of predatory multinational corporations and foreign investors? The institutions were doing more to undermine democracy than to promote it.

A new US and corporate-dominated international economic order was being enforced in most of the Third World. Called globalization, the new economic realignment was one of the most pivotal occurrences in the post-Second World War half-century and one of the most far-reaching accomplishments of American Rockefellerian and corporate-linked foreign policy strategists.

Notes

1. *World Bank Group: Learning from the Past, Embracing the Future* (Washington, DC: World Bank Group, 1995), p. 8.
2. Supranational institutions are ones which can dominate or override the decision-making authority of individual member states, generally on a limited range of issues.
3. *World Bank Annual Report 1996* (Washington, DC: World Bank), pp. 178–81, 225.
4. Jochen Kraske et al, *Bankers with a Mission: The Presidents of the World Bank, 1946–91* (New York: published for the World Bank by Oxford University Press, 1996), pp. 8–9.
5. Laurence H. Shoup and William Minter, *Imperial Brain Trust: The Council on Foreign Relations and United States Foreign Policy* (New York: Monthly Review Press, 1977), p. 128, citing Memorandum E-A10, 19 October 1940, CFR, War-Peace Studies, Baldwin Papers, Box 117, Yale University Library, New Haven, Connecticut.
6. *Ibid.*, p. 168, citing Memorandum E-A26, 7 February 1942, CFR, War-Peace Studies, Baldwin Papers, Yale University Library.
7. See Kraske et al, *Bankers with a Mission*, pp. 14–15.
8. See Shoup and Minter, *Imperial Brain Trust*, pp. 168–69.
9. Miriam Camps, *The Management of Interdependence: A Preliminary View* (New York: Council on Foreign Relations, 1974), pp. 73–74.
10. For information on the careers and connections of the bank's first seven presidents, see Kraske et al, *Bankers with a Mission*.
11. *Ibid.*, p. 115.
12. Manuel Guitian, "The IMF as a Monetary Institution: The Challenge Ahead", *Finance and Development* quarterly (Washington, DC: IMF and World Bank), September 1994, p. 38.
13. World Bank brochure, *Questions about the World Bank*.
14. Quoted in *The Poverty Brokers: The IMF and Latin America* (London: Latin America Bureau, 1983), p. 17.
15. See Harold Lever and Christopher Huhne, *Debt and Danger: The World Financial Crisis* (Middlesex: Penguin, 1985), p. 39; Michel Chossudovsky, *The Globalisation of Poverty: Impacts of IMF and World Bank Reforms* (London: Zed Books/Malaysia: Third World Network, 1997), p. 15.
16. See *The Poverty Brokers*, p. 3; Elmar Altvater et al, eds., *The Poverty of Nations* (London: Zed Books, 1991), p. 172.
17. *Latinamerica Press* (Lima, Peru), 29 March 1984 – special Issue: *The Debt Crisis*.
18. "The Debt-Bomb Threat", *Time*, 10 January 1983.
19. Kevin Danaher, *10 Reasons to Abolish the IMF and World Bank* (New York: Seven Stories Press, 2001), p. 11.
20. John Madeley et al, *Who Runs the World?* (London: Christian Aid, 1994), p. 10.

21. Humberto Campodonico, "Neoliberalism and Poverty in Latin America", *Latinamerica Press*, 23 December 1993.
22. *Newsweek*, 9 July 2001.
23. Samuel Blixen, 'Latin Americans Live with Economic Shock', *Latinamerica Press*, 8 November 1990.
24. Colm Keena, "IMF policy is linked to poverty in Africa", *Irish Press*, 27 June 1994.
25. Kevin Watkins, "G7 Summit Has Chance to End Debt and Close Obscene Rich, Poor Gap", *The Irish Times*, 19 June 1999.
26. Statement by Justin Kilcullen, director of Trócaire (Irish Catholic Agency for Development), *The Irish Times*, 6 March 2000.
27. *Human Development Report 1996* (New York: published by Oxford University Press for the UN Development Programme, 1996), p. 73.
28. *Ibid.*, p. 9.
29. *Ibid.*, pp. iii, 2.
30. West Cosgrove, 'Coup Attempt Highlights Venezuelan Troubles', *Latinamerica Press*, 6 February 1992.
31. Quoted in Chossudovsky, *The Globalisation of Poverty*, p. 36.
32. Details on anti-IMF protests and deaths were compiled from Chossudovsky, *The Globalisation of Poverty*, p. 36; Peter Körner et al, *The IMF and the Debt Crisis: A Guide to the Third World's Dilemmas* (London: Zed Books, 1992), pp. 138–40, 159; *Latinamerica Press*, 7 June 1984, 11 April 1985, 7 June 1990, 6 February 1992, 13 October 1994, 24 August 1995; *The Irish Times*, 27 April 1984, 20 September 1985, 4 March 1989, 29 October 1997, 8 January 2000, 5 February 2001, 20/21/22 December 2001, 17 December 2002; *Irish Press*, 31 May 1984; *Granma International* (Cuba), 6 May 1984.
33. Tribunal jurors who documented the situation in the Philippines included Mexican Catholic Archbishop Sergio Mendez Arceo; Harvey Cox, professor of theology at Harvard; Richard Falk, professor of international law at Princeton University; Andrea Giardina, professor of international law at the University of Naples; and Irish lawyer Muireann O'Briain.
34. *Philippines: Repression and Resistance* (Philippines: KSP, 1981), p. 11.
35. *Ibid.*, p. 13.
36. *Ibid.*, pp. 80–81, 277–78.
37. *Ibid.*, p. 77.
38. Catherine Caufield, *Masters of Illusion: The World Bank and the Poverty of Nations* (London: Macmillan, 1997), p. 247.
39. *World Development Report 1981* (Washington, DC: published for the World Bank by Oxford University Press, 1981), p. 134.
40. For figures on personal wealth, see 'Where Did All the Money Go?' *Newsweek*, 13 March 2000.
41. See Danaher, *10 Reasons to Abolish the IMF and World Bank*, p. 16.
42. Peter Gowan, *The Global Gamble: Washington's Faustian Bid for World Dominance* (London: Verso, 1999), p. 29.
43. Peadar Kirby, "Peru Will Pay – but not Through IMF", *The Irish Times*, 22 August 1985.
44. Kevin Danaher, ed., *50 Years Is Enough: The Case Against the World Bank and the International Monetary Fund* (Boston: South End Press, 1994), p. 6.

45. Susan George, "Dealers in Debt and Death", *The Word* (Ireland), March 1989.
46. Sue Branford and Bernardo Kucinski, *The Debt Squads: The US, the Banks and Latin America* (London: Zed Books, 1990), p. 28.
47. Joseph Stiglitz, *Globalization and Its Discontents* (London: Allen Lane, 2002), pp. 25–34.
48. David Hecht, "Africa's New Deal", *Newsweek*, 22–29 July 2002.
49. See Stiglitz, *Globalization and Its Discontents*, p. 135.
50. Treasury Department press release, 7 April 1997.
51. *The Multilateral Development Banks and the United States* (Washington, DC: Bretton Woods Committee, 1997), pp. 3–4.
52. *Ibid.*, p. 12.
53. BWC leaflet, *What Is the Bretton Woods Committee?*
54. Undated BWC brochure, *The Bretton Woods Committee*, p. 9.
55. *Ibid.*, p. 5.
56. See Kraske et al, *Bankers with a Mission*, p. 9.
57. See Caufield, *Masters of Illusion*, p. 159.

Chapter 8
Towards Global Corporate Hegemony

Corporate Gigantism

The immense IMF and World Bank-imposed changes that convulsed and scarred Third World countries in the wake of the 1982 debt crisis forced debtor countries to involuntarily integrate into a new international economic order dominated by the US and corporate giants. This global power realignment was reinforced in the 1990s through a further concentration of economic power in the boardrooms of corporate colossi and in the hands of a super-moneyed class. The GATT Uruguay Round was the most crucial catalyst in this power-realigning process, or globalization.

Globalization is a form of global governance. Global governance should not be equated with world government, which implies a system of government through which the powers of nation states are vested in a central ruling body. Global governance is a concept of structures and regulatory mechanisms for the management of international relations, including trade. Although globalization functions without any formal central global government, nevertheless the global economic (and hence social) order is strictly regulated or governed. This is done by, essentially, a few multilateral institutions, most notably the IMF, World Bank and World Trade Organization, under the leadership of the United States.

The most remarkable feature of globalization is the degree of power and influence achieved by corporate giants within the new structures and within the institutions and the nexus of Washington elites that shaped and maintain the structures. Economic globalization may be considered as a form of global capitalism that concentrates economic power around megacorporations. This "corporatization" of the world order accelerated after January 1995, when GATT was replaced by the World Trade Organization. Around eight months after the start-up of the WTO, details were announced of the largest merger in US banking history, between the Rockefeller-linked Chase Manhattan and the Chemical Bank, creating the biggest bank in the United States and also one of the world's largest. In December 2000, the Chase Manhattan took over JP Morgan, once the most powerful financial institution in the world. The Chase/Chemical union launched a wave of merger mania in the global financial sector, culminating in dozens of mergers, takeovers and alliances among the world's largest banks and other financial institutions. An era of corporate gigantism and monopolism had begun. To the fore in this process were numerous Rockefeller-linked corporations and figures.

In August 1998, shock waves reverberated throughout the international oil industry with the announcement by British Petroleum (BP) that it had reached an agreement on a $48 billion takeover of American oil giant Amoco, billed as the world's biggest ever industrial merger. Co-chairman of the new firm, BP Amoco, was Peter Sutherland, the broker of the Uruguay Round accord.

Less than eight months after the announcement, BP Amoco agreed a $26.8 billion takeover of Atlantic Richfield (ARCO). In late 1998, Exxon and Mobil announced that they intended to merge, creating the world's largest transnational behemoth, with a presence in 200 countries on six continents by 2001. A subsequent merger between Chevron and Texaco created another oil giant, with operations in 175 countries.

Six of these seven pre-merger oil giants had Rockefeller links. Exxon (Standard Oil of New Jersey), Mobil (Standard Oil of New York), Amoco (Standard Oil of Indiana) and Chevron (Standard Oil of California) were all offshoots of John D. Rockefeller's Standard Oil company. Sohio (Standard Oil of Ohio) had been acquired by BP as its American arm. Atlantic Richfield was formed by a merger between Richfield and Atlantic Refining, yet another Standard Oil company spin-off.

Megamergers also occurred worldwide in other sectors around this time, most notably in the pharmaceutical, telecommunications, motor, aerospace and defence sectors. In 1998, the value of mergers and acquisitions worldwide totalled $685 billion in the computer, biotechnology and telecommunications sectors alone. In 1988, the figure was just $37 billion.[1]

In July 1997, Boeing shareholders approved the company's pending marriage with McDonnell Douglas. The nuptials gave Boeing a clear lead over competitors as the world's largest aerospace and defence corporation. When members of the European Commission launched an anti-trust probe into the proposed union, seventy-five US senators sent a letter to President Clinton insisting on a trade war with European Union countries should the commission persist in opposing the merger. The letter was authored by Senator John (Jay) Rockefeller

IV (D-W.Virginia). Between 1991 and July 1997, Boeing and McDonnell Douglas along with employees and their relations had contributed
around $3 million to congressional election campaigns and to nation-
al party committees.[2]

The concept of antitrust enforcement was being undermined by
corporate-friendly US elites, many with Rockefeller links, over a hundred years after the United States had invented antimonopoly legislation. The Sherman Antitrust Act of 1890 forbade contracts and
conspiracies conducive to "the restraint of trade or commerce".
Megamergers and corporate acquisitions centralize control over production, distribution, patents and research, thereby fostering monopolization, the most extreme form of restraint on fair trade and
commerce and the converse of the free-trade model purportedly being
promoted by globalization's Rockefellerian and corporate overlords.

Megamergers were usually followed by the purging of "surplus"
employees. Among these were a projected 12,000 job losses in the case
of the Rockefellers' Chase/Chemical bank merger, 9,000 in the merged
Exxon and Mobil and 6,000 in BP Amoco.

New International Economic Order

In the 1970s, concerns about the power of multinational corporations and injustices being perpetrated by them led UN member states to
create the Centre on Transnational Corporations (CTC), an autonomous
body within the UN Secretariat. A "Code of Conduct for Transnational
Corporations" was scheduled to be completed for the seventh session of
the CTC in May 1981 "to assist fulfillment of the aims of the New International Economic Order",[3] a concept originated by Third World countries within the Non-Aligned Movement. The New International
Economic Order (NIEO) was intended to be a form of "international
redistributive economic justice", where existing economic mechanisms
of imperialist control would be weakened, national sovereignty would
be a right of all states, countries could adopt the economic and social
models most appropriate to their needs and the operations of transnational corporations would be regulated. Third World countries also
demanded sweeping reforms of the terms of trade and of the operations
of the major multilateral institutions such as the IMF and World Bank.[4]

At that time, most member countries of the Non-Aligned Movement were "experimenting with non-capitalist paths of development" and demanding "a greater share of the world's resources"
through the proposed NIEO, as one commentator noted, actions that
threatened the capitalist hegemonic ambitions of Washington and
Corporate USA.[5]

The CTC's Code of Conduct and the NIEO never came to fruition.
In December 1980, the United States was the only country to vote

against a UN General Assembly resolution seeking the establishment of the NIEO. The vote was 134–1. Following intense pressure from Washington, the Centre on Transnational Corporations was closed. Its work was taken over by an already weakened body, the UN Conference on Trade and Development (UNCTAD).

Democratic Deficit

With the NIEO strangled at birth, globalization's masters – Washington, the IMF and World Bank – set about subordinating the rights of people and governments worldwide to the greed of the world's largest corporations and of the most influential owners and managers of capital. Using debt as a tool, they compelled Third World countries to open their markets to foreign goods and capital, thereby exposing small local firms and farmers to competition from multinational manufacturers and US agribusiness, to sell state-owned enterprises to foreign multinationals and to expend loan funds to provide infrastructure, grants and other incentives to corporate investors. They imposed corporate-friendly economic and trade policies worldwide, fostering the emergence of big business as a collective global power.

Opposition to this process was widespread, even coming from within the institutions shaping and supervising the new order. In late 1999, the World Bank's chief economist and senior vice president, Joseph Stiglitz, quit his job, allegedly following pressure from the bank's largest shareholder, the US Treasury. Stiglitz argued that the debate over the new global order must become more open and democratic, holding that policies being promoted by Washington, the bank and the IMF were plunging crisis-stricken Third World countries into deeper recession. The following year, Professor Ravi Kanbur of Cornell University resigned from his post as the lead author of a World Bank report on global poverty, following pressure to tone down his critical analysis of the downside of globalization.

Subsequently, Stiglitz voiced his concern at the revolving-door syndrome within the bank and fund, whereby their most senior office-holders were often recruited from the corporate sector and returned to the sector after leaving the sister institutions. Stiglitz instanced the case of Stanley Fischer, a vice president at the World Bank from 1988–90 and first deputy managing director of the IMF from September 1994 to May 2001, when he resigned to become vice chairman of the giant Rockefeller-linked Citigroup financial firm and president of Citigroup International. "Was Fischer", Stiglitz asked, "being richly rewarded for having faithfully executed what he was told to do?"[6] Denying that he sought to besmirch Fischer's good name, he argued that he was merely voicing his misgivings at the apparent conflict of interest. A director and member of Citigroup's management committee at the time was

Robert Rubin, who, as secretary of the treasury, had played a lead role in formulating IMF policies. Rubin's career in finance began in the Goldman Sachs investment bank in 1966, from where he was recruited to become treasury secretary, which he left to become, like Fischer, a Citigroup head.

Stiglitz – who was elected to membership of the CFR in 1997 – held that the IMF and World Bank were dominated by the wealthiest industrial countries and by the commercial and financial interests in those countries, which determined the institutions' policies. The IMF had a hidden agenda, promoting "the interests of the financial community". Although almost all of the activities of the fund and bank are in the Third World, it had never been a prerequisite that their heads "should have any experience in the developing world", he wrote. "The institutions are not representative of the nations they serve."[7]

The resignations of Stiglitz and Kanbur raise questions about who are the real decision-makers within the bank and fund and about their intolerance towards, and suppression of, information and views that contradict or challenge the rationale for the institutions' promotion of globalization and other inequitable agendas that promote corporate interests. Heading the bank at the time was a Rockefellerian and corporate elite figure, James D. Wolfensohn, a former investment banker, CFR member, Bilderberg Group steering committee member and trustee of the Rockefeller Foundation.

Globalization is not a democratic process. It represents an imposed global order. Decisions are made in secret, with little or no public input, supervision or control or informed public debate. Electorates acquiesce to vital decisions about their future, taken by bureaucrats, corporate leaders and especially by political leaders who rarely seek a mandate from their citizens for the decisions taken.

In theory, representative democracy is a system where governments rule as representatives of their citizens and guardians of their rights, obeying no other authority than that of their peoples. In practice, since the advent of globalization, governments pay little heed to their electorates, especially on matters relating to economic and international affairs.

Averse to tolerating a culture of consent by the governed, globalization's political and corporate patrons, while revelling in the rhetoric of democracy, exercise power without authority whenever corporate interests are threatened. Electorates are sidelined, even in regions regarded as bulwarks of democracy. Influential opponents such as Stiglitz and Kanbur are often pushed to the margins, silenced, sacked or forced to resign, highlighting the vulnerability of the institutions, and hence of their member-governments and electorates, to corporate pressures and demands.[8]

In today's era of globalization, governmental policies and programmes can no longer be equated with the wishes and needs of electorates. As the process of globalization accelerates, it is not being paralleled by public debate on the nature and impact of the changes involved or by any consultation with, or approval from, electorates for the changes. With rare exceptions, the changes are presented to the public as a fait accompli after being agreed in secret behind closed doors in the new interlinked hubs of global power, namely the IMF, the World Bank, the World Trade Organization, the boardrooms of megacorporations and in the corridors of hegemonic power in the United States and the European Union, and also in corporate consensus-seeking forums such as the Trilateral Commission and the Council on Foreign Relations. Recent developments in the European Union provide us with an example of the alarmingly undemocratic nature of the new world order.

In February 2001, a treaty was signed by the foreign ministers of the fifteen member states of the European Union. Called the Nice Treaty, its purpose was to prepare for the expansion of the European Union from fifteen to twenty-seven or more member states. Most of the applicant countries were former communist states in central and eastern Europe. The proposed enlargement was depicted by its patrons as a victory for democracy and an expression of friendship and solidarity towards the peoples of the candidate states.

The treaty was a scheme of breathtaking ambition, seeking to create a new federation or "superstate" of around 500 million people, accounting for around 25 per cent of global gross domestic product (GDP).[9] It could only come into effect if ratified by all existing member states. In June 2001, the Republic of Ireland's electorate rejected the treaty 54 per cent to 46 per cent, with thirty-nine of the country's forty-one parliamentary constituencies voting against it. Irish Prime Minister Bertie Ahern admitted that the vote underscored "a widespread sense of disconnection between the institutions of the [European] Union and its citizens".[10]

Less than 35 per cent of the country's electorate bothered to vote. Voter apathy, one Irish newspaper columnist wrote, was "a direct consequence of feeling that your vote does not matter, that forces outside your control shape your destiny".[11] The fundamental problem, she wrote, was that the EU "is effectively a system which allows government by elites, and requires passive populations in order to function".[12]

A former Irish attorney-general, John Rogers, wrote of his belief that the anti-Nice Treaty vote in Ireland "was dictated by the people's concerns at our ongoing loss of sovereignty to the institutions of the Union which, it was planned, should be given much more centralized powers". The Irish government's approach, he stated, should be based on the premise that "an enlarged superstate-like union is not achievable if the citizens' democratic rights are diminished to a point where the people become cynical and alienated".[13]

Public cynicism and alienation was hardly surprising. Incredibly, the Irish electorate was the only one given an opportunity to vote on the treaty. In other EU member countries, it was ratified by the governments or parliaments rather than by their electorates, who had given no mandate to their elected representatives to accept the treaty. Self-determination, long held to be a cornerstone of democracy, was being denied to citizens of the EU.

Following the Irish rejection, media reaction within the EU suggested that if electorates in other member states were allowed to vote on the treaty, the referenda in some countries were likely to produce a similar result. Thus, in a sense, the Irish vote was a victory for democracy – a protest vote on behalf of the 99 per cent of the EU's total electorate who were being denied the right to vote. (The Irish referendum was a legal requirement, not an altruistic act by a benign government.)

The reluctance of the EU's political leaders to seek a mandate from their electorates was, almost certainly, motivated by the probability that the treaty would be spurned. The EU's ruling elites were determined to circumvent the Irish rejection of the treaty and to ignore demands for referenda to be held in other member states. After Ireland's No vote, intensive private negotiations began to ensure a reversal of the vote, thus permitting the proposed enlargement of the EU to take place. Later, the EU's commissioner for external relations, Chris Patten, warned that another No vote in a second Irish referendum would have serious political consequences for the country, though denying that the European Commission was "trying to bully the Irish people into voting in a certain way".[14]

The Irish No was an answer that the EU establishment was unwilling to accept. Critics of the EU and of globalization condemned what they perceived as jackboot-style bullying, which lacked only the stiff right-armed salutes and the "we have ways of making you vote Yes" threats that one associates with an earlier era of European history. To vote No was unacceptable. Why bother voting at all, critics asked.

In October 2002, in a second referendum on the treaty, just under half of the Irish electorate bothered to vote. However, on this occasion the Yes voters swamped No voters by a massive 63–37 per cent. The result, anti-Nice campaigners complained, was a consequence not only of the litany of thinly veiled threats by EU and Irish political leaders about the economic consequences for Irish people of a second No vote, but was also a consequence of a massive infusion of corporate money into the Yes campaign. Some estimates suggested that the Yes campaign had around twenty times as much funds as the anti-treaty campaign.

The determination to overturn the perfectly valid first Irish vote through a constitutionally suspect second referendum on the rejected and unrevised treaty bred a perception that democracy was regarded by the EU's ruling elites as a good thing only when it was likely to produce the result desired by the elites. This denial of democracy highlighted a worrying reality – the resolve of an EU pro-globalization elite to create a superstate without the consent of its peoples. Whose interests benefit from such changes?

Significantly, while electorates were deprived of the right to determine the direction that the EU should follow, powerful corporate lobby groups, representing many of the world's largest multinationals, were exercising enormous influence behind the scenes. An enlarged 500 million population EU would be especially beneficial to the corporate sector, since a condition of entry for all applicant states was their espousal of free-market economies and their acceptance of EU laws and regulations which would curb the power of sovereign governments and their electorates while consolidating and expanding the economic power of corporate giants. Barriers to corporate penetration and control of the industrial and financial sectors of candidate countries would be removed, under the terms of their entry into the EU.

Among the most influential of the pro-treaty corporate lobby organizations was the EU Committee of the American Chamber of Commerce which, in its own words, "supports European integration and aims to provide positive input into the development of EU policy. . . We communicate our message through direct and regular dialogue with officials from the European institutions." The organization's members include 140 of the largest US multinationals, including the Rockefeller-linked ExxonMobil. The organization coordinates EU affairs for the European Council of American Chambers of Commerce, whose 16,000 member companies represent over $225 billion of US investment in Europe.[15]

Another influential pro-treaty corporate lobby group is the European Round Table of Industrialists (ERT). Of its forty-six members in 2001, thirteen were listed in the Trilateral Commission's 1998 membership roster, including Peter Sutherland, who brokered the Uruguay Round accord, the most important border-opening trade agreement in history. Closeted behind closed doors with the EU's decision-makers, ERT representatives had a major influence on the EU's post-1992 agenda of deregulation, privatization and monetary union between member states.[16]

The Nice Treaty, critics argue, was shaped to perform a similar function in Europe as NAFTA and the Free Trade Agreement of the Americas were intended to perform in the Americas – to promote capitalist globalization, deregulation and privatization of the public sector. According to Article 133 of the treaty, the EU's "common commercial policy shall be based on uniform principles, particularly in regard to changes in tariff rates, the conclusion of tariff and trade

agreements, the achievement of uniformity in measures of liberalization, export policy and measures to protect trade". This means that
whatever applies in one country must apply in all countries. "Uniformity in measures of liberalization" means conforming with the
corporate-driven agenda of privatization and deregulation that opens
up huge swathes of the public sector (including essential services such
as water and electricity supplies) to corporate control and profit-making. Such issues were not raised by treaty proponents during Ireland's
two referenda campaigns.

A week after the June 2001 Irish rejection of the Nice Treaty, a
meeting of EU leaders was held in Gothenburg, Sweden. Up to 20,000
demonstrators gathered to protest against the new capitalist order –
including corporate influence within the EU, the militarization of the
EU and the determination of its ruling elites to continue the process of
EU enlargement without a mandate from electorates. During clashes
between police and demonstrators, three protestors were shot with
live bullets.

Nine days after the Irish electorate voted for the Nice Treaty, an
EU convention released a draft of a proposed constitution for the
enlarged Union. To implement such a proposal requires a constitutional treaty. Although such a treaty will involve enormous changes to
EU member states – the objectives of the draft treaty include the formulation of common foreign, defence and security policies – it is likely that the changes will be agreed without the approval of the states'
electorates.

Elites and the New World Order

The creation, and subsequent incremental expansion, of the EU
have been important factors in the growth of "free trade" and globalization. What is remarkable about the evolution of the interconnected
globalization/trade-liberalization process is the ever-present role of
corporate and Rockefeller-linked figures. Like other instrumentalities
of post-war US political, economic and military dominance – the
World Bank, the IMF, GATT, the Marshall Plan, the United Nations,
NATO, the Organization of American States, the Southeast Asia Treaty
Organization and the Cold War – the European Union (previously
known as the European Economic Community or EEC) was a creation
of Washington's ruling elites. It was created as a consequence of US
initiatives for expanding US trade opportunites in Europe. (See
Appendices for the role of US elites in the formation of the EEC,
NATO, the Marshall Plan and GATT.)

Elites associated with the Rockefellers and Corporate USA became
the driving force behind moves for trade liberalization in the post-
Second World War era. In 1953, two CFR members, corporate lawyer

George W. Ball and an executive of Macy's department store, Ralph Straus, were largely responsible for the formation of the Committee for a National Trade Policy, an organization representing export trade businesses. It became the corporate sector's principal lobbying organ for reciprocal trade and tariff liberalization. In the early 1960s, it coordinated corporate support for President Kennedy's Trade Expansion Act of 1962, which aimed to reduce trade tariff barriers. The legislation was prepared by George W. Ball, who had become under secretary of state for economic affairs.[17]

Trade liberalization, and the advance towards globalization, was given a fresh impetus in the 1980s through the debt crisis and the consequent IMF-imposed structural adjustment programmes, which forced debtor countries to open their markets to foreign corporations, investors and speculators. The Uruguay Round and NAFTA accords accelerated this process in the 1990s.

The first steps towards a North American Free Trade Agreement were undertaken by President Reagan's trade representative, William E. Brock. Before Reagan's departure from the White House, a bilateral trade agreement had been concluded with Canada and restrictions on trade between the US and Mexico had been eased.

When George H. Bush replaced Ronald Reagan in the White House, the pro-NAFTA campaign in the United States was intensified. It was directed by Bush himself and his trade representative, Carla A. Hills, aided by National Security Adviser Brent Scowcroft, Secretary of Commerce Barbara Hackman Franklin and a host of other figures. The agreement was brought to completion by President Clinton, his trade representative, Mickey Kantor, and others including Secretary of Commerce Ronald H. Brown and the US ambassador to Mexico, James R. Jones.

All of these NAFTA creators had Rockefeller and/or corporate links. President Bush and his successor Bill Clinton were members of David Rockefeller's Trilateral Commission, as also were Brock, Hills, Scowcroft and Jones and Hills' Canadian counterpart, Roy MacLaren, Canada's minister for international trade.

Bush (1977–79) and Scowcroft (1983–89) had both been directors of the Council on Foreign Relations. Barbara Hackman Franklin was appointed commerce secretary in 1992, the same year that she became a member of the CFR. Ron Brown, her successor as commerce secretary, was a corporate lawyer and lobbyist. Bush's trade representative, Carla Hills, had been a partner in a corporate law firm and a director of a number of corporations. Clinton's trade representative, Mickey Kantor, had been a corporate lawyer and lobbyist. Ronald Reagan's rise to political power had been financed by corporate sponsors, initially by oil millionaires Cy Rubel and Henry Salvatori; Leonard Firestone, president of the Firestone Tire and Rubber Company; Justin

Dart, president of Rexall Drugs; and wealthy Los Angeles business-man Holmes Tuttle.[18]

To secure the passage of NAFTA through Congress, President Clinton had to contend with widespread disaffection in the Democratic party and among the electorate, especially in large segments of the organized labour movement, traditionally a supporter of the party. Many labour leaders, senators and representatives depicted the proposed accord as a betrayal of American workers, who were at risk of losing their jobs through a relocation of manufacturing plants to industrial zones south of the Rio Grande. In return for votes supporting NAFTA, President Clinton promised to reward wavering legislators with a multi-billion dollar expenditure of taxpayers' money in their constituencies.

Corporate lobbyists thronged the corridors of the two houses of Congress. USA*NAFTA, a business coalition representing the interests of Fortune 500 companies, mounted a media and PR campaign to sway congressional and public opinion. Its estimated cost was $30 million. Legislators were warned by corporate lobbyists that campaign contributions would be withheld if they voted against the accord.

USA*NAFTA's campaign to manipulate public opinion and congressional votes, together with President Clinton's taxpayer-funded bribing of Congress, secured passage of the accord, thereby overriding the concerns of a large mass of the general public. The American electorate was not consulted about NAFTA.

In Canada, an irate electorate exacted its revenge on the pro-NAFTA Progressive Conservative party in October 1993, when the party suffered the most stunning landslide defeat ever in national elections, winning just two of the 295 seats in the House of Commons. (In the 1988 elections, it had won 169 of the 295 seats.) Even party leader Kim Campbell lost her seat, the first time a sitting Canadian prime minister had done so.

Mexico's ruling PRI party, which organized Mexico's participation in NAFTA, was ousted in July 2000 after seventy-one years in power. Remarkably, Mexico's three top NAFTA negotiators, Dr Herminio Blanco, Dr Jaime Zabludovsky and Aslan Cohen, had each been a recipient of US taxpayers' dollars as Fulbright programme grantees.[19] The grants were sponsored by a US government agency, the United States Information Agency, whose public diplomacy responsibilities included "disarming Mexico's greatest potential opposition to NAFTA".[20] The head of the USIA was CFR member Joseph Duffey, the husband of USA*NAFTA lobbyist and CFR member Anne Wexler, probably the most prominent female corporate influence peddler in Washington.

Some of USA*NAFTA's corporate patrons were accorded special access to Washington's NAFTA negotiators through their representation on official committees advising the US trade representatives.

Peter Sutherland and Globalization

Rockefellerian and corporate elite figures were also the driving force behind the Uruguay Round agreement. These included US Presidents George H. Bush and Bill Clinton and their trade representatives, Carla Hills and Mickey Kantor. The elites also held the key posts within GATT – under whose auspices the Uruguay Round agreement was formulated – and within the WTO, which would enforce the agreement.

The Uruguay Round accord was based on a 1991 draft prepared by GATT's director general, Arthur Dunkel, a Bilderberger. In 1993 he was succeeded by Peter Sutherland, who guided the negotiations to a successful conclusion the following year. The appointment of Sutherland, Washington's nominee, was an event of immense importance, since he would have responsibility for reshaping the global economic order. Interestingly, he had never held an elective national or international political office. In 1973, he sought a seat in the Irish parliament, but was rejected by the electorate.

Peter Sutherland can be considered as Mr Uruguay Round and Mr WTO. More than any other individual, he was responsible for coordinating the advance of economic globalization, through removing barriers to trade and investment and supervising the institutionalization of rules and regulations governing international trade and investment. His appointment, at Washington's instigation, as director general of GATT was unprecedented in the annals of the Republic of Ireland. Never before had a citizen of the small republic (it has a land area smaller than the state of Maine and a population of around 3.8 million) been the holder of an office with such immense control over world affairs.

In 1997, another Irish citizen, Mary Robinson, was chosen, with Washington's approval, to head another important international body, the UN High Commission on Human Rights, thereby becoming the holder of the second most powerful office ever held by an Irish citizen. Sutherland and Robinson were both members of the Trilateral Commission, Robinson being an executive member in the commission's early years and the person instrumental in launching its Irish branch.

The appointment of two Irish Trilateralists to such powerful offices was remarkable. Between its formation in 1973 and Mary Robinson's UN appointment in 1997, there had been a mere fifteen Irish members of the Trilateral Commission.

Described by an Irish newspaper as a person with "impeccable pro-American credentials",[21] Sutherland was an important figure within the global Rockefeller/corporate network at the time of his GATT appointment, being a member of the Trilateral Commission, a Bilderberg Group alumnus and a member of the Eminent Persons Group on

World Trade, two of whose members were a chairman of the European branch and a deputy chairman of the Japanese branch of the Trilateral Commission.

In January 1995, the GATT organization was superseded by the World Trade Organization. Its first director-general was Sutherland. A few months later he was succeeded by former Italian Minister of Foreign Trade Renato Ruggiero, a member of the Trilateral Commission and a Bilderberg Group alumnus. Ruggiero's successor was a former prime minister of New Zealand, Michael Moore, a member of the Eminent Persons Group on World Trade.

Nobody, it would seem, could attain the highest offices in GATT or the WTO unless they had ties to the Rockefellers.

After stepping down as WTO director-general in 1995, Peter Sutherland's ties to the Rockefellers and to the corporate sector became even closer. In 1995, he was appointed to the international advisory board of the Council on Foreign Relations. In 2001 he became European chairman of the Trilateral Commission. He became chairman and managing director of investment bankers Goldman Sachs International, a member of the foundation board of the corporate-dominated World Economic Forum and, following the merger between BP and Amoco, co-chairman of the new corporation. By the beginning of the new millennium, these ties had made him one of the wealthiest people in Ireland.

In 1997, he became chairman of the Washington-based Overseas Development Council (ODC), a think-tank on trade and development. Largely funded by Corporate America, the ODC's establishment was made possible by grants from the Ford and Rockefeller Foundations. The membership of its first board of directors was largely determined by David Rockefeller and Eugene Black (former president of the World Bank and former vice president of the Chase National Bank).[22] The ODC's chairmen emeriti and directors under Sutherland's chairmanship were a *Who's Who* of Rockefeller and corporate-linked figures, including Theodore M. Hesburgh (chairman, Rockefeller Foundation 1977–82), Clifton R. Wharton, Jr, (chairman, Rockefeller Foundation 1982–87), Robert B. Zoellick (Trilateral Commissioner and a director of the CFR), and banker Pascal Lamy.

After George W. Bush's inauguration as US president in January 2001, Zoellick became his trade representative. In the European Union, Lamy was the commissioner for trade. Michael Moore, like Sutherland a member of the Eminent Persons Group on World Trade, was the head of the WTO. Thus, in early 2001, three Rockefeller-linked figures were the world's most powerful trade negotiators and the most influential determiners of the course of economic globalization.

An Economic Elixir?

As the third millennium began, the process of globalization had taken root almost everywhere. Its compass had become so all-embracing that, since the collapse of communism in the Soviet Union, a feasible alternative no longer apparently existed for countries to remain outside the new order, particularly the near-global "free-trade" system which is presided over by the WTO and dominated by the United States and multinationals.

Depicting globalization as a virtual economic elixir that offers the world's peoples the prospect of a more prosperous future, devotees trot out statistics to show globalization's "successes" – South Korea with its 8.3 per cent GNP annual growth rate between 1975–95; Thailand with a rate of 7.8 per cent for the same period; Indonesia and Malaysia 7.1 per cent.[23] However, the greatest benefits from such growth usually accrued to the top 10 per cent of society. The prosperity of many of these star performers within the new order of globalization was transitory, their economies later experiencing a near meltdown. Post-Allende Chile was one of just a few Third World countries to experience growth during and after this period. In the years 1975–95, which coincided with the years of Pinochet dictatorship and the subsequent return of democratic rule, Chile had a 5.5 per cent GNP annual growth rate. By 1997, it had achieved a per capita GNP of $4,820.[24] Others were not so fortunate. In 1999, over eighty countries had per capita incomes lower than they had a decade or more earlier,[25] a statistic that highlights the worsening income distribution between developed and underdeveloped regions in the new era of globalization. An analysis of world income distribution between countries shows that the ratio between the richest and poorest country was about 3 to 1 in 1820, 11 to 1 in 1913, 44 to 1 in 1973 and 72 to 1 in 1992.[26]

As the profits and power of megacorporations and their super-moneyed shareholders rose, institutionalized injustices and inequalities worsened under globalization, with the severest effects of the collateral damage being endured by disempowered Third World populations. For most Third World countries, globalization proved to be a disaster. A flight of foreign capital precipitated economic slumps in many countries, depressing trade. Left at the mercy of corporate-manipulable market forces that they could not control, country after country in Africa, many already weakened by IMF-imposed structural adjustment programmes, imploded economically, with horrific human consequences. By 1997, several Asian countries were nearly bankrupt. By 1999, Latin Americans were experiencing the highest levels of unemployment in recent decades. In August 2001, amidst fears of an imminent debt default, Argentina's near-bankrupt economy was temporarily shored up by a multibillion dollar IMF loan. In

June 2002, Peru's president authorized the suspension of constitutional rights and the use of military force to restore order after days of anti-government riots against the government's sale of state-owned enterprises. The following month Uruguay's Central Bank was forced to suspend almost all the country's banking operations to halt the country's deepening currency crisis. Weeks later, the IMF agreed a $30 billion rescue package for Brazil in an attempt to prevent the country defaulting on its $250 billion debt. The losers were not the creditor banks, whose rash loans were being salvaged by the IMF, but taxpayers around the world whose taxes fund the IMF and the people of Brazil who were being burdened with even more debts.

After almost two decades of IMF-imposed belt-tightening, market-opening reforms and huge debt repayments, populations were still being crushed by debts, pushed to the brink of economic collapse. IMF policies had betrayed the Third World.

Third World countries are almost powerless to extricate themselves from their indebtedness and underdevelopment. To obtain hard currencies to repay their foreign debts, they need to greatly increase their income from exports, which often largely comprise foods grown for foreign markets. However, the prices they obtain for some exports are, in real terms, lower than what they got during the 1930s depression years. In the early 1990s, the total annual turnover worldwide in the sugar industry was around $30 billion, of which farmers received around $10 billion. A decade later turnover had doubled to around $60 billion, but farmers, many in the Third World, received a mere $5.5 billion. The real winners were the handful of corporations that monopolize the sugar trade.[27]

Globalization's agendas had globalized corporate power and exploitation but had eschewed parallel agendas to globalize justice, human rights and democracy. Driven by market expansion, more progress was being made in this new world order "in norms, standards, policies and institutions for open global markets than for people and their rights", a UN report noted.[28]

Another UN report highlighted the stark inequality of this world order. "It is estimated that the additional cost of achieving and maintaining universal access to basic education for all [the world's people], basic health care for all, reproductive health care for all women, adequate food for all and safe water and sanitation for all is roughly $40 billion a year. This is less than 4% of the combined wealth of the 225 richest people in the world," the report noted.[29]

Globalization v. Communism

For post-communist Russia, the transition, under IMF supervision, from a centrally planned and regulated economy to a largely open-market economy was ruinous. Prior to the collapse of communism, approximately 2 per cent of Russians lived in poverty. After a decade of more liberalized trade, almost a half of the population had been snared by the poverty trap. The life expectancy of men fell, national productivity nosedived (Russia's GDP halved between 1989 and 1999) and the country's new-style democracy was as illusive and corrupt as during the communist era. Violent crime, prostitution and drug addiction soared. The number of people with HIV and AIDS rose, as did the incidence of tuberculosis and other almost forgotten diseases.[30] A carpetbagging oligarchy gained power, subsequently stealing the country's corporate assets and the savings of Russian workers and pensioners. Communist-era cradle-to-grave social security for its citizens was discarded. Hardest hit were the old and the sick. Many Russians yearned for a return to the security, predictability and rigidity of communist rule and a revival of Soviet-era power and pride, instead of being governed in the interests of a new economic ideology that placed corporate rights above human rights.

Other communist and post-communist countries also came under the superintendence of globalization's Rockefellerian and corporate-linked governors. The elites headed the European Bank for Reconstruction and Development (EBRD), which dominates, often with the IMF, the economic affairs of numerous former communist countries in eastern and central Europe and in the Commonwealth of Independent States, formed after the disbandment of the Soviet Union. At the start of the new century, the bank was operating in twenty-seven such countries.

Detailing the bank's operations in one of these countries, Bosnia, Michel Chossudovsky, professor of economics at the University of Ottawa, wrote of how "the EBRD headed the Commission on Public Corporations which supervises operations of all public-sector enterprises including energy, water, postal services, roads, railways, etc. The president of the EBRD appoints the chairman of the commission which also oversees public-sector restructuring, meaning primarily the sell-off of state and socially-owned assets and the procurement of long-term investment funds."[31]

The small state became a virtual colony of the United States and the European Union, power being handed over to an administration which stripped the Bosnian people of almost all political and economic sovereignty. The EBRD and the IMF supervised the country's economic affairs, functioning for all practical purposes as receivers of the Bosnian economy and unelected rulers of the Bosnian people, the IMF being responsible for appointing the first governor of Bosnia's central bank. The state, a British columnist wrote, had become "the world capital of interventionism".[32]

Washington's explicit foreign policy goal as regards Yugoslavia, of which Bosnia had been a part, had long been to integrate the country into a US-dominated free-market system. According to a secret 1984 National Security Decision Directive, American policy towards Yugoslavia sought "to promote the trend toward an effective, market-oriented Yugoslav economic structure. . . to expand US economic relations with Yugoslavia in ways which benefit both countries and which strengthen Yugoslavia's ties with the industrialized democracies".[33]

The EBRD "exists to foster the transition towards open market-oriented economies", according to its website,[34] operating as a regional facilitator/enforcer of economic globalization. It funds private sector activities, economic restructuring and privatization and opens up countries to foreign investment, and exploitation, helping multinationals to swallow up local companies and increase their market share in post-communist countries. Governments in such countries that baulked at the efforts to plunder their states' best assets quickly found themselves under siege from multilateral financial institutions, which wage a form of financial warfare against non-compliant nations. In Romania, where the EBRD is active, IMF and World Bank loans were suspended when the government restricted the participation of outside investors in the country's privatization scheme.[35] The EBRD is also active in the oil and gas-rich former Soviet republics such as Kazakhstan – "probably the largest unexplored oil-bearing region in the world"[36] – whose resources are so much sought after by US oil corporations, several with Rockefeller links.

Even in developed Western nations, electorates can only watch as state-run enterprises such as airlines, telecommunications systems, national broadcasting networks, railways, banks and electricity providers are fattened with taxpayers' money before passing into the control of the private sector. It is a practice comparable to selling off the family silver. The state sector, long regarded as the guardian of national wealth in the interests of citizens, is being compelled to relinquish its control over wealth-creating enterprises to the corporate sector

Even Communist China, with over one-fifth of the earth's total population, could not ignore the reality of the new near-global order and risk being isolated outside it. In November 1999, prolonged negotiations between the United States and China opened the way for the latter's admission to the WTO and for making China's vast markets accessible to American exporters. In mid-2000, the US House of Representatives voted to grant China permanent normal trade relations (PNTR) status, which guaranteed that the country would be accorded normal US tariff rates. The vote was preceded by intense lobbying by American corporate groups and by threats of a cut off of corporate campaign contributions to dissenting congressmen. In a repeat of its pro-NAFTA campaign, Corporate USA spent millions lobbying for China's admission. Leading the campaign was Anne Wexler's lobbying group, which set up a "PNTR War Room" in Washington prior to the House vote.

Coordinating the PNTR push was a coalition of hundreds of the largest companies within Corporate USA, cooperating under the umbrellas of the Business Coalition for US-China Trade, the US-China Business Council, the Business Roundtable, the Emergency Committee for American Trade and the US Chamber of Commerce. In October 1997, a luncheon was hosted for the visiting Chinese President Jiang Zemin by the America China Society, the National Committee on US-China Relations, the US-China Policy Foundation, the Council on Foreign Relations, the Asia Society and the Committee of 100.[37] What is striking about this broad alliance is the number of Rockefeller-linked figures involved in leadership positions in these bodies around this time.

Heading the America China Society were Henry Kissinger and Cyrus Vance (former chairman of the Rockefeller Foundation and former director of the CFR). The Asia Society was founded in 1956 by John D. Rockefeller III. It provides "access to policy makers and business leaders who play key roles in US-Asia relations".[38] The president of the US-China Business Council was Robert A. Kapp, a CFR member. Among the US-China Policy Foundation's small group of honorary advisors were Alexander Haig (former Chase bank director, a member of the Trilateral Commission from 1982–89 and a CFR member), Dianne Feinstein (Trilateral Commission) and Barbara Hackman Franklin (CFR) who, as commerce secretary, played a pivotal role in developing US-China trade relations.

The assimilation of China and Russia, previously America's arch enemies, into a US-led and corporate-dominated global order were events of momentous significance, leaving both of these once-powerful communist nations at the mercy of capitalist forces they could not control.

A New Dictatorship

The new post-Cold War world order, whose rules and agreements even China, Russia and other communist and post-communist countries have to abide by, is one in which mega-mergers between transnationals facilitate the attainment of corporate monopolization of the global economy. As the relentless succession of giant mergers continues, global economic power is being concentrated in the boardrooms of fewer and fewer corporations.

If this trend continues, a few corporate giants will come to control virtually every economic and industrial sector, giving them full discretionary power to do and charge whatever they may wish and to determine which countries will be fostered with, or deprived of, investment capital. This growth of megacorporations is supplanting democratic capitalism with monopoly capitalism. Multinational corporations are becoming more powerful than governments – a new power elite whose domain is the entire world.

Ironically, in giving birth to this new global order, the United States may have dug its own economic grave. The new order has vested a vast amount of unaccountable economic power in megacorporations. This unaccountability was referred to in a UN report, which noted how multinationals "influence the lives and welfare of billions of people, yet their accountability is limited to their shareholders, with their influence on national and international policy-making kept behind the scenes".[39] Since the corporations owe loyalty to no country, only to the maximization of profits to their shareholders, they locate their operations wherever they will be best rewarded, generally in countries where labour is inexpensive, disorganized and compliant, where environmental standards are lax, workplace health and safety regulations are toothless, poorly enforced or easily circumvented, and where tax codes are conducive to increased corporate profits.

Operating through the WTO, the IMF and World Bank and through trade accords such as the Uruguay Round and NAFTA, Washington's elite rulers have made it easier for corporations to move their plants from one country to another and to outsource production by contracting foreign companies and "sweatshops" to manufacture goods. Low-wage Third World and post-communist countries have become obvious attractions. Hence the haemorrhaging of transnational-owned plants, and also the outsourcing of production, from the US and other developed countries to low-wage regions.

The mobility of corporate plants and investment capital under globalization creates a pressure for a downward equalization of employees' wage scales between developed regions, such as North America and the European Union, and underdeveloped countries. As long as workers in the most developed nations continue to demand higher wages, better job security and safer and healthier working environments than their Third World counterparts are willing to accept, the seepage of plants and jobs from developed nations to poorer ones will continue. The seepage may become a torrent.

Globalization is a journey into the unknown, along uncharted roads. As more and more economic power percolates into corporate boardrooms, governments are divested of authority, and national economic models become expendable pawns of megacorporations, which collectively are becoming a global power capable of steamrolling almost all smaller business enterprises. If corporate giants such as the Wal-Mart retailing chain can annihilate local competition in the United States, leaving in its wake shuttered shops and shattered dreams, it is frightening to contemplate the dominance corporate giants could quickly attain and the havoc they could wreak in the world's poorest and weakest countries.

Who will, or can, rein in these megabanks and non-financial mega-corporations in this new century? Not the UN Centre on Transnational Corporations, set up to strengthen the negotiating capacity of national governments in their dealings with transnationals but abolished following pressure from the United States and Corporate USA. Not the IMF, World Bank and the World Trade Organization which, in collusion with Washington, have constructed a global framework to serve corporate interests. Hardly Third World countries whose economies are dwarfed by corporate resources. Not America's legislative branch of government with its bought senators and congressmen. And certainly not the nation's executive branch with its Rockefeller and corporate-linked elites, whose post-Second World War agenda placed the interests of the country's corporate sector at the very heart of US foreign policy.

In facilitating the transfer of so much power to the corporate sector and in placing the activities of transnationals outside the control of national governments, Washington's elites may be begetting an uncontrollable corporate hyperpower that may ultimately rival the global US hegemon. If this is so, the world may witness a waning of Pax Americana and the birth of a corporate colossus capable of determining what kind of society will exist globally in the twenty-first century.

Notes

1. *Human Development Report 1999* (New York: published for the UN Development Programme by Oxford University Press, 1999), p. 67.
2. Charles Lewis and the Center for Public Integity, *The Buying of the Congress* (New York: Avon Books, 1998), pp. 290–94.
3. *Handbook of World Development: The Guide to the Brandt Report* (Harlow, Essex: Longman, 1981), p. 64.
4. Hilbourne A. Watson in A. W. Singham, ed., *The Nonaligned Movement in World Politics* (Westport, Connecticut: Lawrence Hill, 1978), p. 137.
5. See Singham, *The Nonaligned Movement in World Politics*, p. xi.
6. Joseph Stiglitz, *Globalization and Its Discontents* (London: Allen Lane, 2002), pp. 207–08.
7. *Ibid.*, pp. 19, 206.
8. The departure of Stiglitz, a CFR member, from the World Bank highlights an important aspect of the control exercised by corporate and Rockefeller-linked individuals over US foreign and domestic policy and over international institutions, disproving accusations that all such elite appointees are pliant and willing accomplices of corporate paymasters. In general, it is fair to say that members of the CFR, Trilateral Commission etc. are initially chosen as members of the organizations, and subsequently appointed to key positions of political and economic power, not only because of their abilities but also because of their *perceived* support for corporate-

friendly policies, such as open markets and globalization and also US foreign policy. It is also probably fair to say that the vast majority of these individuals, where they support such policies, do so because they genuinely believe in the righteousness and efficacy of the policies. However, some appointees such as Stiglitz fail to fulfil their anticipated roles. Disillusioned with the consequences of the policies that they have responsibility for implementing or supporting, some resign. Others are sacked or fail to be reappointed. Thus, Mary Robinson, an executive member of the Trilateral Commission in its early years, failed to have her term as UN Human Rights Commissioner extended after she criticized aspects of the globalization process and of Washington's "war on terrorism".

9.   These statistics are from an address by Pat Cox, an Irish member of the European Parliament, at University College Cork, 11 May 2001.

10.   Statement by Mr Ahern at EU Summit, Gothenburg, Sweden, 15 June 2001.

11.   Breda O'Brien, "Another 'No' to Nice Would Be Welcome", *The Irish Times*, 16 June 2001.

12.   Breda O'Brien, "EU's Democratic Deficit Is Causing Resentment". *The Irish Times*, 14 September 2002.

13.   John Rogers, "Nice Vote Was a Fundamental Statement by the Irish People", *The Irish Times*, 16 June 2001.

14.   Denis Staunton, "Patten Warns of the Effects of a Second Rejection of Nice", *The Irish Times*, 18 February 2002.

15.   See http://www.eucommittee.be/Pages/profhome/htm

16.   Ankie Hoogvelt, *Globalization and the Postcolonial World: The New Political Economy of Development* (Basingstoke, Hampshire: Palgrave, 2001), p. 149.

17.   Morton Berkowitz et al, *The Politics of American Foreign Policy: The Social Context of Decisions* (Englewood Cliffs, New Jersey: Prentice Hall, 1977), pp. 112–33.

18.   See Ronald Reagan, *An American Life* (New York: Simon & Schuster, 1990), p. 156.

19.   Nancy Snow, *Propaganda, Inc.: Selling America's Culture to the World* (New York: Seven Stories Press, 1998), pp. 48, 78. Dr Snow worked in the USIA on Fulbright programmes.

20.   *Ibid.*, p. 48, citing an internal 1994 USIA report.

21.   Jim Dunne, "A Man with All the Right Credentials", *The Irish Times*, 30 April 1993.

22.   See http://www.odc.org/about/history.html

23.   See *Human Development Report 1999*, pp. 181–82.

24.   *Ibid.*, p. 180.

25.   *Ibid.*, p. 2.

26.   *Ibid.*, p. 38.

27.   John Humphrys, "The Earth Summit is just News from Another Planet", *The Sunday Times* (UK), 11 August 2002.

28.   See *Human Development Report 1999*, p. 2.

29.   *Human Development Report 1998*, p. 30.

30.   See Stiglitz, *Globalization and Its Discontents*, pp. 143, 153; Peter Gowan, *The Global Gamble: Washington's Faustian Bid for World Dominance*

(London: Verso, 1999), p. 205; Joseph Stiglitz, "For Economists, No Time to Party", *Newsweek*, Special Issue, December 1999-February 2000; Fareed Zakaria, "Lousy Advice Has Its Price", *Newsweek*, 27 September 1999.

31. Michel Chossudovsky, *The Globalisation of Poverty: Impacts of IMF and World Bank Reforms* (London: Zed Books/Malaysia: Third World Network, 1997), p. 257.

32. Simon Jenkins, "Ulster of the Balkans: British Troops Have Been Sent on a Mission Impossible in Bosnia", *The Times* (UK), 17 December 1997.

33. National Security Decision Directive 133 (White House, 14 March 1984), cited in Sean Gervasi, "Germany, US and the Yugoslav Crisis", *CovertAction Quarterly* no. 43 (Washington, DC), Winter 1992–93, p. 42.

34. See http://www.ebrd.com/english/main.htm

35. See Peter Gowan, *The Global Gamble*, p. 216.

36. Ahmed Rashid, *Jihad: The Rise of Militant Islam in Central Asia* (New Haven: Yale University Press, 2002), p. 61.

37. See http://www.asiasociety.org/politics-society/jiang-speech.html

38. See http://www.asiasociety.org/membership/corp_membership.html

39. See *Human Development Report 1999*, p. 12.

Chapter 9

The Future

Directing the Twenty-first Century World Order

By the start of the new century the United States had attained an unimaginable level of global economic and military pre-eminence. Globalization had been synonymous with the Americanization of the international economic order, while militarily there had not been, for several hundred years, a greater gap between the capabilities of the world's leading power and other nations. At the apex of its power and prosperity, unrestrained by any equivalent military rival and dominating the three principal institutions of global economic planning and enforcement – the World Trade Organization, the IMF and the World Bank – the US had become master of the world, capable of imposing Pax Americana as never before.

The potential for American dominance in the twenty-first century was speculated on by President Clinton's secretary of state, Warren Christopher, who opined that although the world was nearing the end of the American Century, if "we. . . continue to lead", then "the end of this millennium can mark the start of a second American century".[1] In January 2000, President Clinton himself alluded to Washington's proposed leadership role in the new century, referring to "the fundamental challenges I believe America must meet to shape the 21st century world".[2] Henry Kissinger prognosticated that the US "will be the dominant power in the 21st century. No groups of states will be able to prevent this."[3] In 2001, Vice President Cheney was equally blunt. The "arrangement [for] the twenty-first century is most assuredly being shaped right now. . . the United States will continue to be the dominant political, economic and military power in the world."[4]

In 1999, Trilateral Commission analyst Samuel Huntington wrote, in a CFR publication, of how "in the eyes of many countries it [the US] is becoming the rogue superpower. . . the single greatest external threat to their societies".[5] America's ambition is to be a rogue global superbully that can use its power to further expand its economic and military dominance, becoming the ultimate arbiter of the direction of the international economy and the enforcer of international peace and security in the twenty-first century. Within this new world, order the interests of the United States, and especially those of Corporate USA, are to be paramount, overriding the interests and needs of other nations.

Presiding over this world order are elite champions of globalization recruited from Rockefeller and corporate-linked political leadership incubation centres such as the CFR, Trilateral Commission, the Bilderberg Group and Rockefeller foundations, and directly from Corporate USA. At the start of the new century, these elites headed the international and regional institutions that were setting the economic agenda for the twenty-first century – the World Trade Organization, the World Bank, IMF, the OECD and the European Bank for Reconstruction and Development. They directed NATO. They headed organs of the United Nations. They were at the helm of the world's leading hegemon, dominating foreign policy posts in the Bush administration. They held some of the highest offices in many other Western and post-communist countries, especially in the principal institutions of the world's second most powerful hegemon, the European Union – in the European Commission, the European Central Bank, the Council of Ministers and the European Parliament.

Almost all the key offices around the world that had responsibility for economic globalization, especially free trade, towards the start of the new century were filled by Rockefellerian elites. As President Bush's trade representative, Robert Zoellick became trade negotiator for the world's sole hyperpower, effectively making him the world's key helmsman of economic globalization, with the wherewithal to apply the vast political and economic muscle power of the United States in imposing economic globalization and "free trade" even more on the world's peoples. He was a board member of the Rockefeller and corporate-dominated Overseas Development Council, a director of the Council on Foreign Relations, an executive member of the Trilateral Commission and a Bilderberg alumnus. In the European Union, the commissioner for trade was Pascal Lamy, a Bilderberger and, like Zoellick, a director of the Overseas Development Council. In the third locus of "Trilateral" global power, Japan, the finance minister was Kiichi Miyazawa, a founder member of the Trilateral Commission and former chairman of the commission's Japanese branch (1993–97). Such elites were in a position to formulate and to impose the trade and economic agendas for the world.

Threats to US Hegemony

With so many Rockefeller and corporate-linked figures controlling the key centres of political, military and economic power around the world, the security of the corporate-friendly and US-protected world order of globalization would seem to be unchallengeable. If change within this new order can only come from these powerful ruling elites, then it is probably futile for the vast numbers of people worldwide who are marginalized within this elite-shaped order to hold any real hope for a better, more moral and more equitable future.

In this sole-hyperpower world, it is almost impossible for weak and impoverished countries to resist Washington's imposed world order and US jugular diplomacy. The US economy, the US dollar and the Pentagon are the dominant forces on the global stage. The hegemon's military superiority is so great that the US, and only the US, can wage war anywhere around the globe without assistance from other nations. Washington's intention to employ this superiority to impose its will on other nations and to punish dissenting nations was made clear in its new "Full-Spectrum Dominance" doctrine, a Pentagon blueprint for its military.[6] This requires that US forces, operating alone or with allies, have the capability to defeat any adversary and control any situation across the entire spectrum of military operations, including conflicts involving employment of strategic forces and weapons of mass destruction, major theatre wars, regional conflicts and peace-keeping and peace-enforcement operations. However, US military superiority cannot provide a universal solution for suppressing all forms of resistance to US rule and to the US-directed new global order.

By the start of the new century, the United States was facing challenges and threats to its global leadership in most parts of the world. In late 1998, American hegemony suffered an enormous setback in Latin America with the election of Hugo Chavez as president of Venezuela, one of America's biggest suppliers of oil. A friend of Cuban President Fidel Castro, Chavez was opposed to globalization, the worst excesses of which had already economically devastated the continent. Globalization was an ugly word in Venezuela, where up to 1,000 anti-IMF protesters had been killed by an earlier administration.

Chavez planned to use the country's oil wealth and radical social reforms to improve the lives of the poorest sectors of society. His "Bolivarian" doctrine had widespread appeal throughout Latin America, since it advocated unity among the continent's poor majority in pursuit of an equitable redistribution of wealth and also state control over many wealth-creating resources. Such a transformation would curb US control, slash the profits of Corporate USA in the region and hinder the globalization process.

Inauspiciously, by late 2001, Washington's policy makers, aided by sections of the US media (*Newsweek* carried an article headed "Is Hugo Chavez Insane?"),[7] were hinting at a more confrontational stance with the independent-minded reformist leader. In April 2002, he was overthrown by a military coup, which had eerie similarities to the CIA-aided 1973 coup in Chile against another democratically elected leader, Salvador Allende. Appointed by the military to head a transitional government was Pedro Carmona, the head of Venezuela's largest business association, which had been active in fomenting opposition to Chavez. Congress was closed, the country's constitution was revoked and political opponents were detained. The coup leaders, *Newsweek* noted, "had extensive ties to the US political and economic establishment".[8] Shortly after the coup its leaders were overthrown through a civil insurrection, and Chavez was returned to power.

Washington's top Latin American policy maker at the time was Assistant Secretary of State Otto Reich, a former lobbyist for corporate clients including Lockheed Martin and British American Tobacco. Numerous anti-Chavez politicians and business leaders had held talks with Reich in the weeks prior to the coup, prompting speculation that Washington had coordinated the plot.[9]

Shortly after Chavez' return to power, the country's political crisis deteriorated as the US-backed political opposition, Venezuela's upper class and the country's corporate and media sectors renewed their efforts to oust him from office, culminating in a general strike that paralyzed the country. Opposed by President Bush and his Oil Cabinet, who were intent on installing a more corporate-friendly government in the oil-rich country, Chavez appeared to be a president living very much on borrowed time.

In October 2002, another left-wing figure became the president of a Latin American country through the ballot box, when the leader of the Workers Party, Luiz Inacio Lula da Silva, won 61 per cent of the vote in an election run-off in Brazil, the region's largest and most populous country.

Elsewhere in the continent, Washington and Corporate USA were experiencing problems of a different nature, with left-wing insurgents resisting US-backed regimes. To justify armed interventions against these rebels, the United States found a new crusading cause for the era of globalization, drug trafficking. The US coupled its aid to some countries in the region to counter-insurgency operations against rebel groups, with the local regular forces functioning as proxy armed units of the United States.

In January 2000, President Clinton unveiled a $1.3 billion aid package for Colombia to train and arm anti-drug forces. The package included helicopter gunships and American military advisers, inevitably raising questions about the possibility of Colombia becoming America's next Vietnam. The aid sucked Washington further into the country's civil war, underpinning government forces that had an atrocious record of murder, torture and terrorism against peasant communities. By then an estimated 1.5 million Colombians had already been forced by guerrilla warfare and, especially, by state-directed ter-rorism to flee from their homes. The killing of peasants was conve-niently blamed on left-wing guerrillas, particularly the FARC rebel group which controlled around 40 per cent of the national territory and which used taxes levied on drug traffickers to finance its insur-gency campaign.

In Mexico, left-wing Zapatista guerrillas enjoyed enormous sup-port among the country's poorest peasants.

Fuelled by repression, poverty and hunger throughout the conti-nent, Latin America may be facing a contagion of rebellion and social upheaval. A growth in resistance to US-supported pro-globalization regimes is likely, an occurrence that Washington has already taken steps to counter. In 2001, the US government provided $6.15 million, through USAID, to prevent the Sandinistas regaining power in nation-al elections in Nicaragua.[10] The following year, Otto Reich warned that Washington could halt its aid to Bolivia if the electorate chose as pres-ident the socialist candidate Evo Morales, a staunch opponent of globalization.[11]

Other problems also faced Washington and Corporate USA in Latin America. In October 2000, five American oil workers were kid-napped in Ecuador. One hostage was later murdered. The following year, nineteen US citizens were kidnapped in the continent, including five each in Colombia and Haiti and four in Mexico. In April 2001, two McDonald's restaurants were firebombed in Ecuador and another in Brazil in October.

In April 2001, almost 100 employees of the American Occidental oil corporation were kidnapped in Colombia by the left-wing Nation-al Liberation Army.[12] Rebels also bombed Occidental's Cano Limon pipeline, halting the flow of oil for almost a year. By early 2002, it had become clear that Washington's military aid to the country was for more than its alleged war against drugs. In February of that year, the Bush administration announced that it was giving $98 million in aid to Colombia to pay for Colombian soldiers to protect the oil pipeline, increasing suspicions that the administration's wars against terrorism in Latin America and Central Asia were, in reality, motivated by its close ties to America's energy sector. Suspicions that US policy towards Colombia had little to do with combating the flow of drugs were reinforced by Washington's support for President Alvaro Uribe. The manager of his presidential election campaign and his closest adviser was businessman Pedro Juan Moreno, whose chemical prod-ucts company was the largest importer of potassium permanganate, a chemical used in the production of cocaine.[13]

Attacks on the foreign operations and personnel of US corpora-tions also occurred elsewhere. In November 2001, Maoist rebels in Nepal attacked one of the most universal symbols of US corporate hegemony, a Coca-Cola plant in the country's capital. Subsequently, the Bush administration asked Congress for $20 million in military aid for the country.

In May 2001, the United States failed to be re-elected to the UN Human Rights Commission. Outraged at the rebuffal, the US House of Representatives voted to make the payment of over $200 million in US arrears to the United Nations conditional on America's re-election. For the first time since the body's formation over fifty years earlier, the US had failed to win a seat in the influential body. Was this failure yet another indication of growing resistance to Washington's imperial rule?

People Power

The events in Venezuela, Colombia, Ecuador, Brazil, Haiti, Mexico and Nepal and the rebuffal in the UN commission represented setbacks for the joint hegemony of Washington and Corporate USA. They were containable problems. However, if challenges and threats also arose elsewhere, Washington's capacity to contain them would become more tenuous. Such challenges and threats did arise.

As resentment at Washington's inequitable and increasingly brutal stewardship of the new world order of globalization intensified, it engendered acts of public resistance throughout the world, even in the United States and other leading Western countries. In December 1999, ministers and heads of government from around the world met in Seattle at a conference convened by the World Trade Organization to launch the first post-Uruguay Round international trade negotiations. If successfully completed, the talks would copper-fasten the supremacy of economic globalization and the privileges of megacorporations. However, the negotiations were held against a backdrop of street demonstrations by over 40,000 protesters from dozens of countries, pitched battles between rioters and police, overnight curfews, the arrest of hundreds of demonstrators and a shutdown of part of the city. The protest marked the first major expression of anger by diverse groups from nations around the world at the steamrolling advance of global corporate capitalism and at the powerlessness of Third World governments and of the electorates of all nations to halt or influence this process.

What occurred at Seattle was of immense importance. Frustrated at their inability to make any meaningful contribution, Third World representatives, barred from the private negotiations of the big powers, blocked the proposed trade negotiations, thus temporarily derailing the process of economic globalization. Outside the negotiation chambers, areas of the city were transformed into battle zones by anti-globalization protesters. The size of the protests, which encompassed students, human rights and environmental activists, priests, nuns, labour groups and Third World solidarity organizations, and the protesters' willingness to confront police, National Guardsmen and armoured personnel carriers and to risk arrest, tear gassing, pepper spraying and injury or death reflected the concern of people worldwide at the exploitative and inequitable nature of the corporate-driven conference agenda. People Power, which had not been witnessed in the United States since the Vietnam War, had made a dramatic reappearance.

The anti-WTO protests at Seattle marked the start of a global backlash against the new world order and against its principal institutional, corporate and political patrons. For the first time, the little known, almost surreptitious, agenda of globalization's masters had been brought to the attention of the world's peoples. The protests were followed by other mass anti-globalization demonstrations, including protests against the WTO, the European Union, the World Economic Forum, the IMF and World Bank. Tens of thousands often participated in the protests, which were usually circled by thousands of riot police. Violence was common. In March 2002, a remarkable 200,000 to 300,000 participated in protests during an EU meeting in Barcelona, Spain.

In April 2001, political leaders from thirty-four countries attended a Summit of the Americas in Quebec. Its goal was to achieve agreement on the creation of a free-trade area of 800 million people stretching from Alaska to Cape Horn by 2005, encompassing North, Central and South America and the Caribbean, with Cuba being excluded. High fences, tear gas and water cannons were employed against an estimated 30,000 protesters besieging the summit. Numerous intending protesters were refused entry to Canada at crossing points from the United States.

Three months later, a protester was killed in Genoa, Italy, during a meeting of leaders of G8 countries, comprising the world's seven most industrialized countries plus Russia. The protest, which had around 100,000 participants, was the most violent anti-globalization demonstration ever held. Over 500 were injured and an estimated $40 million worth of damage was caused. Around 18,000 police and military personnel, many equipped with automatic weapons, sidearms, tear-gas grenades and riot shields and backed by army sharpshooters and helicopters, turned part of the city into a fortress.

Public Impotence and Disaffection

Fears about the earth's environment were a key factor in the growth of People Power, uniting movements and groups that had seldom interconnected in the past and serving as an emotive issue for rallying resistance to those shaping and directing the new order of globalization. Without a reduction in greenhouse gas emissions, many scientists forecast that the world faces cataclysmic changes that could make the planet uninhabitable. Rising rates of greenhouse gas emissions, ozone depletion, accelerating global warming and predictions of crop failures, food shortages and famines, malaria plagues and the spread of other tropical diseases, increases in cancer and heat-related deaths, desertification, melting glaciers, dying coral reefs, landslides, rising sea levels, massive displacement of people and more extreme weather conditions (droughts, cyclones, heatwaves and floods) may mean an imminent slow-motion global environmental apocalypse and the extinction of species.

As the world's population grows from today's 6.1 billion to a projected 9.3 billion in 2050, with all this growth taking place in the Third World, and as the pollution of water, air and soil worsens, living conditions will deteriorate rapidly in most poor countries. Within fifty years, at current rates of deforestation, the world's principal tropical forests will have almost disappeared, accelerating global warming.[14] Low-lying land, such as parts of the Netherlands and the United States, the east-southern African coast and small island states, may be submerged by rising sea-water levels. Many believe that the very survival of a life-sustaining planet and of mankind is now at stake.

However, the dismaying reality is that, no matter how great the consensus may be among the world's peoples – and given the opposition of Corporate USA and the passivity of Americans on the issue – any impetus for meaningful action is likely to be opposed by America's money-grabbing legislators, presidents and vice presidents, many of whose election campaigns have been part-financed by morally invertebrate corporate polluters. The implications are frightening.

In the new world of globalization, with its police-ringed IMF, World Bank, World Trade Organization, United Nations, European Union, World Economic Forum, G8 summits, Summits of the Americas and other meetings, the votes of the world's electorates are proving to be almost totally ineffective in achieving any significant beneficial changes in the new world order or any improvement in the planet's environment, while street protests are merely a mild irritant to Washington and Corporate USA, the sires and pace-setters of globalization and the leading opponents of positive action on climate change.

To minimize the potential for disorder at subsequent meetings, inaccessible or isolated venues were chosen. In the wake of the "Battle of Seattle", the WTO opted to hold its next important meeting, to launch the first post-Uruguay Round trade negotiations, in remote Qatar, an oil-rich Gulf mini-state with no parliament or political parties. Protesters were barred from entering the country by the Qatari authorities. Following the Genoa violence, the next G8 meeting was held in the isolated ski resort village of Kananaskis in the Canadian Rockies, which was protected by around 1,000 police, 5,000 troops, surface-to-air missiles and jet fighters.

Such repressive and sometimes vicious measures are signs that the anti-globalization movement is seen as a very serious threat. Nevertheless, positive, human-oriented changes to the new world order and also to the global environment will be difficult to achieve through People Power. Lacking a coherent ideology, the disparate movement cannot offer a feasible political and economic alternative. Peaceful protests, unless the number of participants increases enormously, are unlikely to achieve anything worthwhile, while violent demonstrations tend to alienate potential and even existing supporters. Under Washington's stewardship, the WTO/IMF/World Bank triple alliance will continue to foster globalization behind closed doors and, if necessary, behind lines of riot police, away from public scrutiny and beyond public control.

This culture of secrecy and impenetrability in the bodies most responsible for shaping the new world order leaves electorates ignorant of the issues and options discussed and of the positions adopted by their governments. Electorates are expected to blindly accept decisions taken within these forums, without any informed public debate on the issues. They are rarely made aware of the stances taken by their governments or of the full repercussions of decisions agreed at meetings hosted by the institutions fostering globalization. On the occasions when governments issue statements following such meetings, they generally put a "spin" on the issues involved, conveying information in the best positive light for domestic consumption. The public is told what governments want them to hear, not what they need to hear in order to make well-informed judgements on the issues. In such a climate of politically manipulated information, knowledge can be equated with power and lack of knowledge with impotence. Something becomes "true" if people can be convinced that it is true.

The manipulation of the popular sentiment and the use of repressive measures (live bullets, rubber bullets, tear gas, pepper sprays, stun grenades, batons, water cannon, riot police, National Guardsmen, armed commandos, security fences, curfews, police dogs, armoured personnel carriers, arrests and restrictions on entry to countries, deportations and declaring protests illegal) are actions that one associates more with despotism than with democratic rule. Increasingly, such tactics are being resorted to by globalization's patrons to impose their fiat in the new world order and to curtail opposition from the People Power movement and other disaffected segments of the world's electorates. Repression is becoming an instrumentality of globalization.

As repression increases within a system that shields globalization's governing institutions and national leaders from popular influence and as governments are forced, more and more, to respond to the new realities of the global market place rather than to their electorates' wishes and needs, the public's sense of alienation increases, as does public anger. The indifference of globalization's masters to the earth's deteriorating environment and their failure to address issues of social and economic justice around the world may be sowing the seeds of more anger and resistance, including terrorism.

11 September

The threats facing the US hyperpower in the post-Cold War world were referred to in 1993 by the incoming head of the CIA, CFR member R. James Woolsey, who remarked that although the West had slain the Soviet "dragon", the world was still "a jungle filled with a bewildering variety of poisonous snakes".[15] In policing the new world order, the task of Washington's national security community would be to crush the "snakes" that threatened America's global supremacy. However, the imposition of Washington's diktat and the projection of raw US military power abroad have limitations, and also potentially serious repercussions for the United States and its citizens. As a 1997 report by members of the Defense Science Board noted, historical data "show a strong correlation between US involvement in international situations and an increase in terrorist attacks against the United States".[16]

Commenting on the potential for armed resistance to the new global order, US Marine Corps Commandant General A. M. Gray argued that the Third World's "growing dissatisfaction over the gap between rich and poor nations will create a fertile breeding ground for insurgencies. These insurgencies have the potential to jeopardize regional stability and our access to vital economic and military resources. . . we must maintain within our active force structure a credible military power projection capability with the flexibility to respond to conflict across the spectrum of violence throughout the globe."[17]

In October 2000, *Newsweek* speculated on the form that armed resistance to the US might take, opining that terrorism "might represent the new price of hegemony – one that is likely to grow over time". Terrorist attacks, the report argued, could expose the vulnerability of the United States in an increasingly hostile and unpredictable post-Cold War world. The United States, *Newsweek* added, "may well be the Goliath of the world. But don't forget it's David, not the giant, who wins in that story."[18]

The Goliath's hegemonic ambitions for the new century suffered a setback of enormous proportions on the morning of Tuesday, 11 September 2001, when three planes were crashed into two imposing symbols of US economic and military might, the World Trade Center and the Pentagon, killing around 3,000 people. The apocalyptic event numbed Americans. Never before in modern history had a terrorist organization attacked their country with such gruesome success. The world's sole superpower had been successfully attacked by low-tech terrorists armed only with knives, who used hijacked passenger aircraft as missiles. It was the first serious challenge to Washington's hegemonic ambitions for the new century.

Washington's response to the challenge was swift, and brutal. To the ruling Taliban regime in Afghanistan, the refuge of the attacks' sponsor, Osama bin Laden, leader of the Islamic al-Qaeda movement, President George W. Bush directed a chilling message: "The Taliban must act and act immediately. They will hand over the [al-Qaeda] terrorists, or they will share in their fate."[19]

The coming war, President Bush warned, would be global and prolonged. The United States intended to respond to the terrorism of al-Qaeda with a potentially unlimited conflict, arrogating to itself the right to wage war not only in Afghanistan but also to extend the conflict into other countries. It was an ironic scenario. A country that had itself so often resorted to the use of terrorism, on a massive scale and with impunity, was about to wage war against others for doing likewise. A flaunting of unreined hyperpower bellicosity, it signalled the resolve of the new administration to pursue a go-it-alone agenda of war and coercion around the globe against US-designated "rogue" nations and other challenges to US dominance, regardless of international opinion and, if necessary, without a UN mandate.

Opposition to the administration's foreign policy agenda was temporarily smothered in the United States and countered abroad. Dissention was seen as unpatriotic. In the days after 11 September, numerous political prisoners in the United States, including peace activists, were placed in solitary confinement, denied visits from their families and attorneys. After UN Human Rights Commissioner Mary Robinson criticised aspects of the US war on terrorism (including the proposed use of US military tribunals to try alleged accomplices in the 11 September suicide plane attacks and Washington's treatment of al-Qaeda and Taliban internees at the US naval base at Guantanamo Bay, Cuba), the United States opposed an extension of her period in office. In September 2002, she was replaced by Brazilian Sergio Vieira de Mello.

The goal of the war was hinted at by the US president. Regardless of coming struggles and dangers, the hyperpowerful United States, he insisted, "will define our times, not be defined by them".[20] The first war of the twenty-first century was to be an assertion of America's global hegemony, thus continuing the US tradition of employing war to accomplish foreign policy goals.

Anti-Americanism in the Muslim World

Within the vast Muslim and Arab diaspora and in Third World countries, the prospect of pending US interventions and wars fostered a perception that the US was virulently anti-Islamic and anti-Arab, further polarizing attitudes towards the United States and raising the possibility of a retributive cycle of tit-for-tat butchery and destruction. It was an inauspicious start to the hoped-for Second American Century, with a terrorism-disordered future dangling over the American people like a Damoclesian sword.

Anti-American acts of terrorism by Islamic extremists should not have been unexpected. Comprising around one-fifth of the planet's population and controlling well over a half of the world's oil resources, Muslims have long perceived themselves to be under a state of siege from Pax Americana. Anti-US hatred, and terrorism, were predictable repercussions.

Washington's attempts to overthrow political leaders in Islamic nations (Gaddafi in Libya, Mossadegh and later the Ayatollah Khomeini in Iran, Saddam Hussein in Iraq, the Taliban regime in Afghanistan and Sukarno in Indonesia); its imposition of repressive pro-Western regimes on Muslim societies (Suharto in Indonesia and Mohammed Reza Pahlavi as the shah or monarch of Iran); its targeting of Islamic nations through economic sanctions (Iran, Iraq, Libya, Pakistan and Afghanistan); its direct military aggression against Libya, Afghanistan, Sudan, Iraq and Lebanon; its training of counter-insurgency units to fight Muslim rebels in the Philippines; the July 1988 shooting down by a US warship of an Iranian passenger plane, with the loss of almost 300 lives; Washington's indifference to the appalling crimes perpetrated by Russian forces against Muslims in Chechnya; and, especially, US military aid to Israel, which was used to kill and repress Palestinians – all caused outrage in Islamic countries.

During the war in Yugoslavia, thousands of Bosnian Muslims were slaughtered by superior Serb forces, including over 7,000 men and boys captured and then killed in the UN "safe area" of Srebrnica, Europe's worst civilian massacre since the Second World War. In the eyes of many Muslims, the United States was responsible for the killing of their co-religionists, through its support for a UN arms embargo which made it difficult for the Muslims to arm and defend themselves.

In January 1992, members of the Algerian armed forces cancelled national elections, which the fundamentalist Islamic Salvation Front was certain to win. The coup plunged the country into a bloodbath that claimed the lives of over 150,000 Muslims. As the killing escalated, Washington averted its gaze.

Anti-Americanism in the Muslim world was also fuelled by the

Gulf War, in which the most lethal military force in the world engaged in a needless orgy of killing against retreating Iraqi forces and against civilians. Up to 1.7 million Iraqi Muslims died in the war and through subsequent US-proposed sanctions.

Hostility towards the United States was also kindled by US control over the destinies of Islamic nations. Washington's penchant for dictatorships and vassal states has been, and is still, responsible for the imposition of vile autocracies in numerous Muslim states, facilitating the plundering of national resources, especially oil, by Corporate USA. Most of America's closest allies in the Muslim world, especially in the oil-rich Gulf states and central Asian republics, are execrable tyrannies or sham democracies whose gross human rights violations Washington ignores.

US interventions and acts of terror in Islamic countries precipitated acts of revenge and counter-terrorism against American targets, including the 1983 attacks on the US embassy and the US Marine headquarters in Beirut; the 1993 bombing of the World Trade Center in New York; the 1996 bombing at a US military complex in Saudi Arabia; the 1998 bombing of US embassies in Kenya and Tanzania; the 2000 attack on an American warship in Yemen. These created a groundswell of Islamophobia in the United States, facilitating Washington in justifying further interventions in Islamic nations. Most Americans believed that it was acceptable for the US to engage in state-directed terrorism, butchery, economic sanctions, exploitation and covert interventions against Islamic nations, yet unacceptable for the targeted nations and their allies to retaliate. And retaliate they did, and on a huge scale, on 11 September.

In the aftermath of the September attacks, Afghanistan was transformed into a US theatre of war. Like the Gulf War against Iraq, this war would never have taken place if Afghanistan was in a region that produced potatoes rather than oil. The war provided the US with an opportunity to establish military bases in central Asia. Within a few months of the 11 September bombing, it had around a dozen bases ringing Afghanistan and in the Persian Gulf region, helping to guarantee access to the huge oil and gas reserves in central Asia and in the Gulf states and to discourage the reimposition of communist control in central Asia. Terrified by the prospect of future disruptions to, or hostile takeovers of, the two regions' oil supplies, Washington's ruling elites were content to befriend and support any dictator who could guarantee stability and peace in the regions and US access to the oil supplies. Conversely, the elites were determined to topple regimes that were inimical to US interests.

If Osama bin Laden did not exist, it would have been necessary for the US to invent a bin Laden clone or other enemy to serve as a justification for US military aggression, and a semi-permanent military presence, in oil-rich central Asia, as Saddam Hussein had done in the Gulf region during the presidencies of George Bush Senior and Bill Clinton.

Axis of Evil

President Bush Junior's war in Afghanistan was just one element of a proactive and interventionist foreign policy fashioned to defend US hegemony and interests in a volatile post-Soviet world. Throughout history, empires have been constructed through wars and interventions and subsequently required military bases in their subject nations to enforce their rule. By the early years of the new century, the imperial eagle[21] had expanded its military hegemony to record levels, with military bases established in almost sixty countries and separate territories and US forces deployed in over a half the world's nations to protect US interests.[22]

Imperial power is about control. To impose their will globally, Washington's rulers are willing to resort to extraordinary measures. In March 2002, a leaked Pentagon report revealed contingency plans to use nuclear weapons against Russia, China, North Korea and four Muslim-populated countries: Iraq, Iran, Libya and Syria.[23] Huge sections of the world had become potential US nuclear battlegrounds. Throughout the world, countries deemed to be a threat to US interests were at risk of being attacked by a hyperpower with unmatched access to weapons of mass destruction, including nuclear warheads and biological and chemical weapons and also cruise missiles, depleted uranium munitions, colossal "daisy cutter" bombs and, perhaps in the near future, a "common aerospace vehicle" being developed by the Pentagon that could be positioned over selected countries, ready to aim precision missiles at targets below. Many view the United States as the greatest danger to mankind in today's world.

In June 2002, President Bush explained the thinking behind his administration's new interventionist strategic doctrine. The United States, he insisted, needed "to be ready for pre-emptive action"[24] against nations and terrorist groups possessing or developing weapons of mass destruction. Eschewing the Cold War doctrine of deterrence and containment, which argued that other countries were unlikely to attack the US since it would inevitably be followed by devastating retaliatory attacks, President Bush was intent on confronting perceived threats before they emerged through attacking nations that might possibly, at some future date, choose to use their weapons against Americans. The US would be free to possess and use such weapons, but not potentially hostile nations. Ominously, communist North Korea and the Islamic nations of Iran and Iraq had previously been denounced by Mr Bush as a terrorist-sponsoring "axis of evil" that posed a threat to the US and its allies with weapons of mass destruction.[25] Subsequently, socialist Cuba was added to the list of "axis of evil" countries, accused of developing biological weapons and providing dual-use biotechnology to alleged "rogue states", accusations denied by Havana.

Yemen – a country with which the United States was not at war – soon experienced the consequences of Washington's new "pre-emptive action" doctrine. In November 2002, an unmanned CIA Predator drone aircraft attacked a vehicle carrying alleged al-Qaeda members in the country, incinerating all the passengers.

President Bush's war on terrorism was a godsend for America's military-industrial complex, the immensely powerful and influential partnership of military and corporate elites that profit so much from wars. The murder of around 3,000 Americans was facilitating this partnership and its bankrolled political servitors in justifying possible future armed aggression against nations which had played no role in the September attacks, notably Saddam Hussein's Iraq, which had already greatly suffered at the hands of the United States. After the Gulf War, Iraq had a 11 September every few weeks, as around 5,000 Iraqi children died each month from hunger and illnesses caused by a US-inspired trade embargo. The overthrow of Saddam Hussein had been a priority of several of the president's most powerful appointees, long before they took office. The attack on the World Trade Center now offered them a pretext to accomplish this.

In January 1998, a letter had been sent to George W.'s predecessor, President Clinton, urging him to adopt a policy towards Iraq aimed at "the removal of Saddam Hussein's regime from power". The eighteen signatories disingenuously argued that "the US has the authority under existing UN resolutions to take the necessary steps, including military steps, to protect our vital interests in the Gulf. In any case, American policy cannot continue to be crippled by a misguided insistence on unanimity in the UN Security Council."[26] It was a demand for a policy of unilateralist interventionism and of bypassing the Security Council to protect US oil interests in the region.

Twelve of the eighteen signatories were listed in the CFR's 1997 membership roster. Among the eighteen were Donald Rumsfeld, Paul Wolfowitz, John Bolton and Robert Zoellick, who would be appointed, respectively, defense secretary, deputy defense secretary, under secretary of state for arms control and international security affairs and US trade representative by President George W. Bush. The letter was sent by an organization, Project for the New American Century, whose goals were outlined in a June 1997 "Statement of Principles", which was signed by twenty-five people, including seventeen whose names appear on the CFR's 1997 membership roster. The signatories included

Rumsfeld, Wolfowitz, Dick Cheney (who became vice president under George W. Bush) and George W.'s brother Jeb Bush.[27]

Ironically, Bush's own defense secretary – one Donald Rumsfeld – had been a catalyst in Saddam Hussein's emergence as a regional tyrant. In 1983, as a special envoy of President Reagan, Rumsfeld travelled to Iraq to offer Washington's help to the Iraqi leader. His visit marked the start of a seven-year alliance between the two countries, during which the US backed Saddam Hussein in his war against Iran and helped to consolidate his power, while ignoring his gross violations of human rights.

The Project for the New American Century letter was sent to President Clinton almost four years before the 11 September attacks. These attacks created the required psychological climate in the US to facilitate President Bush's Oil Cabinet in waging war not only in the strategically important Afghanistan against the Taliban and bin Laden's al-Qaeda but also against Saddam Hussein in another oil-rich region. In July 2002, President Bush vowed to topple the Iraqi leader, admitting that it was "a stated policy of this government to have a regime change. . . And we'll use all tools at our disposal to do so."[28] Washington was determined to pursue a virtually unilateralist policy of aggression against Iraq, despite the initial opposition of almost all of its closest allies, until the overwhelming power of the US had prevailed. War, which should be a political instrument of final resort, had become the Bush administration's first option. This assertion of Washington's unilateral right to attack other countries and to topple governments around the world arrogates to the country's ruling elites a prerogative that has no historical precedent. When Corporate USA interests are at risk, the end always justifies the means.

As Washington's hawkish elites made their preparations for wars in Iraq and elsewhere, they were initially paralleled by a perplexing non-debate and absence of anti-war ferment in the United States. The country's media fostered a climate of fervent, bellicose, flag-waving patriotism. Strangling critical and rational debate on the issues, such as the inevitable bombing and killing of probably thousands of non-combatant civilians in targeted countries, the coming wars and destruction were depicted by the media as not only acceptable but also a moral imperative. Washington's absolute right to intervene brutally and unilaterally in the affairs of other countries was increasingly being taken for granted, too obvious to merit discussion or analysis. Americans were being prepared for endless war around the world.

America's pseudo-moralist "war on terrorism", its contingency plans to nuke up to seven countries, its demonization – often a prelude to US military intervention – of hostile ruling regimes and President Bush's bellicose post-11 September speeches clearly indicated that, under Washington's stewardship of the world order, the country's corporate-driven imperial presidency intended to continue America's tradition of jugular diplomacy in the new century, regardless of the consequences for targeted populations or the opinions of the world's peoples.

In October 2002, an estimated 400,000 to 500,000 protestors gathered in the Italian city of Florence for an anti-globalization demonstration, which turned into a giant rally against Washington's expected war against Iraq. A few weeks later, following intense behind the scenes pressures from Washington, the UN Security Council overwhelmingly approved a resolution facilitating US aggression against Iraq.

The destructive power being unleashed in the name of all the people of the United States was, according to Noam Chomsky, being used by the Bush administration "to organize the world to satisfy the demands of the narrow sector of domestic power and privilege that it represents. In service of the same interests, Bush and company are quite openly conducting an assault against the domestic population. They are seeking to impose obedience by undermining civil liberties and fostering a distorted brand of patriotism that aims at suppressing democratic debate. The Bush Administration is also breaking new ground in the brazenness of its contempt for international law and treaty obligations. The language and processes of multilateralism, international rule of law, treaties, and international cooperation have been thrown into the trash heap of history: the Kyoto protocol, International Criminal Court, arms control treaties, human rights conditionality on US military aid – indeed any impediment to unconstrained US force and coercion. Emboldened by their historically unprecedented and rapidly escalating military hegemony, leading Bush planners make no secret of their intention to validate the four-word definition that George Bush Sr. gave to his new world order – 'What we say goes.'"[29]

The implications of Bush Junior's jugular diplomacy were spelled out in a Council on Foreign Relations article. The sweeping new ideas circulating in Washington amounted to an American "nascent neoimperial grand strategy" that sanctioned the unilateral and preemptive use of America's unrivalled military power to manage the global order, "unconstrained by the rules and norms of the international community". This "neoimperial vision" removed constraints on Washington's response to perceived threats, permitting the US to arrogate to itself "the global role of setting standards, determining threats, using force, and meting out justice". Such radical strategic ideas and impulses, the author opined, "could transform today's world order in a way that the end of the Cold War, strangely enough, did not".[30]

However, this grand strategy, the author cautioned, could "rend the fabric of the international community and political partnerships precisely at a time when that community and those partnerships are urgently needed. It is an approach fraught with peril and likely to fail. It is not only politically unsustainable but diplomatically harmful. And if history is a guide, it will trigger antagonism and resistance that will leave America in a more hostile and divided world."

The Poverty Time Bomb

Anti-American terrorists rarely hate Americans. They hate American foreign policy and its consequences, especially the denial of freedom, democracy and human rights in Third World countries, the slaughter and destruction inflicted on peasant societies, the US-imposed authoritarian regimes, the exploitation of resources and the impoverishment of billions of people in a US-shaped and US-dominated world order. In this world order, the poor and exploited have virtually no control over the levers of global power. They can only use whatever other mechanisms are available to them to effect change. Often a desperate revolt against injustice, terrorism is one of the few instrumentalities available to the powerless billions of people around the world.

Hours before he left office, President Clinton acknowledged that global poverty, which left billions living "on the knife's edge of survival. . . is a powder keg that could be ignited by our indifference".[31] With their plight worsening under globalization and under Washington's near-global hegemonic rule, it is conceivable that the world's most marginalized and oppressed people may increasingly turn to terrorism out of desperation or spurred by anti-American hatred. This is a concept that Americans have difficulty in comprehending. A thirst for revenge for the 11 September outrage blurred the collective objectivity of Americans, who failed to understand the depth of anti-American hatred in other countries created by far worse US-initiated or US-supported acts of terrorism, which had claimed millions of lives. Think Vietnam, Cambodia and Laos. Think Indonesia, Angola, Nicaragua, Palestinians. Americans are quick to cast light on the brutal activities of anti-American terrorists but unwilling to recognize their own country's even more grotesque reflected image.

The 11 September low-tech attacks may give encouragement to others to follow suit. They amounted to a menacing act of defiance against the US, exposing the vulnerability of the hegemon and the intrinsic fragility of the economically interdependent international order. 11 September marked the turning of America's economic tide, ending an era of prosperity and confidence. The attacks buffeted stock markets around the world, plunged national economies into recession, reduced international travel and trade, precipitated huge job cuts worldwide, dampened consumer expenditure, increased commercial insurance premiums and compelled governments to introduce new restrictions on the transborder movement of people, vehicles and goods, thereby undermining multinationals' earnings and temporarily curtailing the integrative economic process of globalization.

Warmongers and Peacekeepers

Since stability and peace around the world are prerequisites for economic globalization, wars, terrorism and social disorder represent threats to the new world order. Agreements on the removal of barriers to global trade and the movement of capital become somewhat futile exercises if transborder flows of trade and capital are prevented or hindered by national or regional armed conflicts, terrorism and political and social upheavals. The preservation of stability and peace in the post-Cold War world is essential if globalization is to become the all-pervasive economic force aspired to by Washington's rulers.

The collapse of communism in the Soviet Union and its satellite countries was followed by years of instability in all the countries and also by war in Yugoslavia and Chechnya. Washington's goal was to achieve peace and stability, followed by the imposition of open-market economies compatible with the process of globalization. Rockefellerian elites would play central roles in achieving this goal. As Yugoslavia disintegrated after the collapse of communism, war engulfed Bosnia. Following the outbreak of this war, both the European Union and the United Nations appointed peace mediators. The European Union's appointees were, in turn, Lord Carrington, another member of Britain's titled class Lord Owen and former Swedish Prime Minister Carl Bildt. The successive UN appointees were former US Secretary of State Cyrus Vance and Thorvald Stoltenberg from Norway. All five were Rockefellerian elites.

Lord Carrington was chairman of the Bilderberg Group and a Trilateral commissioner. Lord Owen was a member of the Trilateral Commission. Bildt was a Bilderberger and later a Trilateral commissioner. Vance had been a CFR vice chairman (1973–76, 1985–87), a member of the Trilateral Commission in its earliest years, a Bilderberger and chairman of the Rockefeller Foundation (1975–77). Stoltenberg was a Trilateral commissioner.

In December 1994, former US President Jimmy Carter travelled to Bosnia as an "independent" peace negotiator. Ultimately, the principal architect of the Dayton peace accord was President Clinton's envoy Richard Holbrooke. Carter and Holbrooke were both Trilateral commissioners. Holbrooke was a CFR director.

As in Bosnia, wherever serious discord arose in other countries in the post-Soviet era or already existed, it was usually Rockefellerian and corporate-linked elites that exercised the most power in attaining and maintaining peace and waging war to ensure regional and global stability and US hegemonic pre-eminence.[32]

Globalization's Vulnerabilities

Some of the threats to the hyperpowerful joint dominance of the United States and Corporate USA, and to globalization, have already been outlined: Islamic terrorism, People Power protests, the emergence of independent-minded and reformist leaders such as Hugo Chavez, left-wing guerrilla movements and attacks against the personnel and property of US multinational corporations. However, possibly the most serious threat to this dominance and to globalization in the new century may not come from such sources but rather from the inherent instability of economic globalization. The structures and mechanisms that safeguard the global capitalist economic system are alarmingly weak and vulnerable. The towering edifice of globalization may have been constructed on quicksand-supported foundations.

Cracks appeared in the world order's structure throughout the 1990s and into the new century when several countries teetered on the brink of economic meltdown, among them Brazil, Argentina, Uruguay and Mexico in Latin America. In 1997, the economies of Thailand, Malaysia, Indonesia, South Korea and the Philippines went into a tailspin when foreign gypsy capital poured out of Asia. Japan's economy fell into deep recession. In the Soviet Union and its satellite countries, a Washington-moulded formula of trade liberalization, privatization and democratization was supposed to invigorate their economies. Instead, most experienced huge declines. In Moldova and Ukraine, ten years of free-market reforms saw their GDPs collapse to around a third of their pre-liberalization levels.[33]

Even the United States experienced its own economic roller coaster ride. In the 1990s, investor hyperirrationality sent high-tech and other share prices soaring. When prices crashed, millions of Americans lost heavily, some all their savings or their homes.

Share prices were further undermined in December 2001 when the giant energy trader Enron became the biggest corporate bankrupt in US history, having employed complex accounting procedures to conceal massive losses. In mid-2002, a $7 billion accounting fraud was disclosed at one of America's largest telecoms companies, WorldCom. The frauds were on an almost unimaginable and certainly unprecedented scale. Improper practices were also revealed in some of the country's other foremost companies, including the world's largest investment firm, Merrill Lynch, and industrial giant Xerox.

In July 2002, attention was focused on two banks, JP Morgan Chase (formed in December 2000 through a merger between Chase Manhattan and JP Morgan) and Citigroup, the financial cornerstones of the Rockefeller business empire, following reports that the Securities and Exchange Commission was investigating the companies' alleged links to the Enron fraud. One of America's most respected auditors, Arthur Andersen, was convicted of shredding evidence of fraud within Enron. The exposure of extensive corporate fraud sent share prices crashing as many of America's estimated 80 million stock market investors rushed to sell, plunging prices to even lower levels than those recorded after bin Laden's attack on the hub of American capitalism.

The revelations hinted at a cancer gnawing at the very heart of the United States, corporate kleptocracy. Obsessed with maximizing reported earnings, and hence their own profit-related bonuses and stock options, profits were artificially inflated by top-tier corporate leaders who discarded integrity in pursuit of wealth. The ensuing cynicism and anger left stock market indices fluctuating wildly, mostly downwards. During the first five months of 2002, around 44,000 employees lost their jobs on Wall Street. The events exposed the frailty of the US-led global economy, whose well-being was seen to be predicated on alarmingly capricious and uncontrollable factors, such as the integrity or corruptibility of Corporate USA leaders, the confidence of American investors and also on the possibility of further acts of terror.

In his January 1999 State of the Union Address, President Clinton had hailed America's economic miracle, the country's "longest peacetime economic expansion in our history, with nearly 18 million new jobs, wages rising at more than twice the rate of inflation, the highest home ownership in history, the smallest welfare roles in 30 years and the lowest peacetime unemployment since 1957".[34] Three and a half years later, the economic bubble had burst. As hyperinflated high-tech share prices plunged and as evidence of massive corporate corruption was exposed, investors panicked. US markets fell. By August 2002, the markets had lost over $7 trillion.[35] Subsequently, business investment and consumer spending, key pillars of economic expansion, were slashed.

Investor confidence in the corporate sector and its leaders is vital for economic stability and growth in the new corporate-led era of globalization. But how can investors have confidence when leaders of Corporate USA, the engine of the global economy, have already betrayed the trust of investors? While crooked CEOs walked away with millions of dollars from their collapsed corporations, millions of Americans and workers worldwide, who had money invested in stocks either directly or through their pension schemes, faced huge losses on their purchased stocks and the prospect of deferring their retirement as trillions of dollars were wiped off the world's markets. Directors of twenty-five corporations reportedly cashed in $23 billion worth of stock as the value of their companies fell by 75 per cent or more.[36] Enron bosses disposed of millions of dollars worth of company stock, while employees were barred from selling their pension-linked stock as prices fell. Public anger at the chicanery of corporate millionaire thieves and fraudsters was further fuelled by revelations that hundreds of US corporations were availing of US laws that allowed them to use offshore tax havens to avoid paying billions of dollars in taxes to the US government.

Responsibility for reforming America's corporate governance rests with the Bush administration, a CEOcracy of corporate CEOs, executives and lobbyists. Heading the administration are a president and vice president whose own corporate records undermine their credibility as serious corporate reformers and regulators. Years earlier, George W. Bush was investigated for alleged insider trading in Harken Energy after he sold shares in the company for $850,000 shortly before it reported huge losses. A few months later, the shares would have been worth less than $250,000. His most generous patron during election campaigns had been one of the most vilified of the alleged corporate fraudsters, Kenneth Lay, chairman and CEO of Enron. In mid-2002, Vice President Cheney was sued for his alleged role in fraudulent accounting practices while chairman and CEO of Halliburton, the giant energy services company. Halliburton stock options and sales made him a multimillionaire. When Thomas White left his post as vice chairman of Enron Energy Services to become Bush's army secretary, he sold Enron stock worth millions, not long before the company collapsed. Even Bush's top securities and options watchdog, Harvey Pitt, chairman of the Securities and Exchange Commission, appeared to be too compromised to be credible following revelations that he had met companies under investigation by the SEC – companies which had been his clients during his years as a corporate lawyer.

In November 2002, Pitt resigned, after offering the chairmanship of the new Public Company Accounting Oversight Board – created by Congress to monitor corporate financial reports – to the former head of the audit committee of a company which had been sued for fraud.

Shortly after Pitt's resignation, President Bush's treasury secretary, Paul O'Neill, and his economic policy coordinator, Lawrence Lindsey, were forced to resign, highlighting their failure to boost the ailing economy. To replace Pitt, O'Neill and Lindsey, President Bush turned to Corporate USA. The three vacancies were filled, respectively, by William Donaldson (co founder of an investment bank and former head of the New York Stock Exchange), multimillionaire businessman John Snow (chairman of a railway company) and banker Stephen Friedman (former co chairman of Goldman Sachs and a Trilateral commissioner).

In the wake of the revelations of massaged corporate earnings and other corporate wrongdoing, America's superdollar, a crucial determinant of the country's economic health and global dominance, began to wane. Although it has for long reigned supreme globally (by 1995 it comprised 61.5 per cent of all central bank foreign exchange reserves and 76.8 per cent of all international bank loans were denominated in dollars),[37] the US currency is far from secure in the volatile world order of globalization. As revelations of corporate malpractices continued, some of the foreign investors who held US stocks and government and corporate bonds valued at just under $5 trillion[38] sought safer havens elsewhere for their investment capital.

The precarious nature of the US economy was seen in June 2002, when the national currency slumped to a sixteen-month low as a consequence of fading, post-Enron, investor confidence. The economy was becoming dangerously unstable, undermined by the corporate scandals, falling equity markets, an outflow of foreign investment, an expanding trade imbalance, a continuing federal government budget deficit, excessive tax cuts and increased military expenditure to fund the Bush administration's "war on terrorism".

The history of capitalism is one of perpetual instability – periods of prosperity, followed by periods of recession or depression. One thinks of the "Black Tuesday" stock market collapse on Wall Street in October 1929, which almost brought capitalism down. One also thinks of the New York Stock Exchange's "Black Monday" of October 1987, when America's financial system came close to a meltdown. Without improved regulatory mechanisms in the United States and elsewhere, a stable global financial and economic environment is impossible and economic disasters are almost inevitable. Worryingly, those most in a position to protect capitalism from corporate and superrich capitalists through imposing such regulatory mechanisms are members of the Bush administration CEOcracy.

The interests of Corporate USA and America's superrich are generally better served by a minimum of government regulatory mechanisms. Consequently, any reform by the CEOcracy of the regulatory system in order to prevent further Wall Street share debacles is unlikely to address the fundamentals. This is in keeping with a basic principle of globalization – that states should not interfere with the prerogatives of big business and the superwealthy, which take virtually universal precedence over the rights and the needs of citizens, particularly the world's poorest.

The pro-corporate and pro-wealth bias of America's ruling elites is evident in the foreign and domestic policies of every Washington administration. It was especially evident in September 1998, during the presidency of Trilateralist Bill Clinton, when the New York Federal Reserve Bank organized a $3.65 billion rescue of the flagship US hedge fund, Long-Term Capital Management, thereby helping the fund's superwealthy speculators and creditor banks. Hedge funds are notoriously high-risk ventures, with potentially enormous profit returns, or losses. In the years prior to the debacle, LTCM's speculators had sometimes earned returns of about 40 per cent per year on their investments. When their speculative gambles eventually flopped, the New York FRB helped to reduce their losses.[39] The rescue recalled the bailout of American banks whose unwise and often ethically unjustifiable loans in the pursuit of increased profits caused the 1980s debt crisis, which brought numerous Third World countries to their knees. Through such acts of "crony capitalism", the financial recklessness and greed of the country's foremost bankers and investors were being rewarded by Washington and its IMF and World Bank surrogates, though often at considerable cost to American taxpayers and to people worldwide.

A lesson of the LTCM debacle, one commentator pointed out, was that the "welfare of literally billions of people" had been jeopardized by fund managers engaging "in an orgy of reckless speculation".[40] The loosening of financial regulations during the past two decades has left the global economy highly vulnerable to the whims and greed of such money-capitalists.

In today's world, globalization's masters ensure that the privileges of capital ownership and stewardship are virtually sacrosanct. Ignoring the lessons provided by past debacles – the Great Depression, the debt crisis, the LTCM scandal and recent corporate collapses and frauds, all of which were precipitated by the greed of superwealthy and corporate-linked elites – globalization's masters have chosen to grant even more privileges to such malefactors of great wealth. In promoting monopoly capitalism, they are risking even worse economic catastrophes. Merger mania in the late 1990s, amounting to around $9 trillion in the US and Europe, created corporate giants. However, in the year 2000 alone, corporate giants valued at around $2 trillion failed or were in deep trouble.[41] The solvency of numerous other financial and non-financial giants is now in doubt, leaving the world's peoples facing an uncertain future. The financial resources of monopolist megabanks and hedge funds have become so enormous that if some of these experience severe financial difficulties it may prove impossible for Washington's elite rulers to successfully coordinate a rescue, as they did during the 1980s debt crisis for some of the megabanks' premerger constituent banks. In such circumstances, an economic depression of unprecedented proportions could follow, precipitating violence, instability and a surge of opposition to US hegemony and globalization.

There is another danger. As the exodus of corporate plants to underdeveloped countries continues, high-earning consumers are being replaced by low-waged ones. Paying workers less than enough to purchase the goods they produce constricts trade and enfeebles the market-driven global economy. Nevertheless, corporations are persisting with their closures of manufacturing plants in developed countries and transferring production to poorer countries, such as China.

China's entry into the World Trade Organization at the end of 2001 opened the country's huge workforce and its vast market of over a fifth of the world's consumers to foreign corporations and investors. China's entry was fraught with dangers. Some commentators outlined a scenario in which China, with its enormous pool of labour and poverty-level wages of around 50 cents an hour, would blossom into a regional economic giant, swamping other nations with low-cost exports, thus sowing the seeds of economic depression in Asia, and perhaps worldwide. Other commentators outlined a converse scenario, in which tens of millions of Chinese workers faced the prospect of unemployment as their government streamlined and privatized state enterprises to cope with the harsh realities of the new economic order and in line with China's WTO commitments. By early 2002, perhaps 40 million jobs had been lost. The incomes of Chinese farmers fell, leading to violent protests. Millions of farmers, perhaps hundreds of millions, may ultimately lose their jobs. A large increase in the number of Chinese living in poverty and on the verge of poverty could lead to an explosion of mass discontent in the world's most populous country and precipitate international economic instability.

Economic instability in almost all areas of the world has been a feature of the past two decades. During these decades, which coincided with the growth of economic globalization through the breaking down of barriers to trade and financial flows, around two-thirds of IMF member states endured financial crises, some on more than one occasion.[42] These two decades were also marked by a mushrooming of political instability and social disorder. In its first forty years, the United Nations fielded just thirteen peacekeeping operations. By the early 1990s, the need for such operations had become so widespread that at the start of 1993 thirteen peacekeeping forces had been deployed around the world.[43]

Falling Empires

Today, the stability of the international economy, the security of the imposed order of globalization and the US hyperpower's near-global authority all face challenges. World poverty, human degradation, repression and exploitation are creating undercurrents of resistance. The 11 September terrorist attacks represent the most extreme form of opposition to date.

Instead of seeking to assuage the grievances that fuelled the terrorists' hatred, Washington's ruling elites chose to pursue an unapologetically unilateralist and interventionist foreign policy that eschews any restraints limiting its freedom of action. However, the death and destruction rained on Afghanistan embittered countless millions around the world, probably spawning a new generation of anti-American Islamic terrorists. US attacks on other countries in the next stage of President Bush's war are likely to breed even more terrorists. Far from increasing the security of the United States and its people, Bush's war may be begetting a new era of international terrorism in which the United States will become an even more hated target.

As long as military force is used to impose Washington's will on other nations and as long as globalization remains a process driven by US imperial ambitions and by a corporate agenda of unfettered profiteering rather than a people-centred agenda, anti-American terrorism and other challenges to US imperial power and to globalization are likely to grow. In persisting with the imposition of such a grossly inequitable and unpopular global order, Washington's ruling elites – Eugene V. Debs' "master class" – appear to have learned nothing from the lessons of history.

History teaches us that empires are transitory. The hegemonic, military and economic supremacy of a nation relative to that of other nations is volatile and impermanent. The history of the world is littered with the remnants of once powerful empires – the Inca and Aztec empires in Latin America, China's Ming empire, the Mogul empire of Kubla Khan, the Persian empire, the Ottoman empire of Muslim states that once threatened Christendom, the Soviet empire, and the Roman, Habsburg, British, Napoleonic and other European-ruled empires. Whither the American "empire"?

Today, the United States is the world's leading imperial power. However, it is a lonely hegemon. It has allies but few friends. It is feared, but rarely respected. In some countries, notably Islamic and Arab ones, it is loathed. The prestige of a nation and the admiration for its leaders and people in the international community does not rest on national prosperity, a cloying foreign policy moralism or on a nation's ability to enforce its fiat globally through military might, economic sanctions or other coercive measures. It rests on its humanity, its moral integrity, its idealism, its pursuit of justice, its defence of freedom and on the richness of its cultural heritage. Third World populations may look enviously at America's standard of living, but the envy often mirrors feelings of resentment rather than respect.

Around the world, phrases such as a "compassionate United States", "American democracy", and a "benign US foreign policy" have become oxymorons. Time after time, the people of Islamic, communist and socialist countries and other underdeveloped regions have witnessed the ability of the United States to operate above international law and outside the norms of international behaviour: refusing to approve a treaty setting up an International Criminal

Court, because it could be used against America's own military personnel; repudiating an international protocol to curb the spread of germ warfare capabilities; rejecting a treaty banning landmines, which kill and maim thousands of civilians each year; pursuing policies that accelerate the destruction of the global environment; and refusing to abide by World Court rulings. And, time after time, the people of such countries have experienced the devastation of US-waged wars, the consequences of other forms of US interventions, the imposition of US-supported regimes and US corporate exploitation of their resources. To behave in such a manner is the prerogative of an imperial power.

US and corporate imperial power is not a natural order. By its nature, imperialism is oppressive and unpopular. Oppression breeds resistance. Resistance occasions even more oppression. Thus, the greater the opposition to the new order of US and corporate imperialism, the greater the resolve of Rockefeller and corporate-linked ruling elites is likely to be in Washington, the imperial capital. The greater the terrorism employed by anti-American, anti-globalization and anti-corporate movements, the more brutal Washington's counter-terrorism is likely to be. The larger the People Power protest movements become and the more insistent their agenda-setting demands, the more repressive the measures employed in countering them are likely to be.

Within the United States, People Power and other forms of popular opposition threaten to hinder the new world order being fashioned and imposed by the country's ruling elites. Can this threat be transformed by the elites into a violation of acceptable public behaviour punishable by law? Probably. If, as many critics of the new order allege, globalization results in a flight of American industrial plants and jobs to poorer countries and in decreased wages, more job insecurity, unemployment, poverty and inequality in America, then it is likely that public unrest will rise in the United States. The potential for a public backlash is already evident. A 1999 survey in the US found that 52 per cent of respondents were sympathetic towards the anti-World Trade Organization protesters at the Seattle summit, 75 per cent felt that the benefits of the "New Economy" were unevenly distributed and 52 per cent thought that America's business sector had too much power and influence.[44]

As Washington intensifies its efforts to impose its inequitable order of globalization and as it widens its war against "terrorism", anti-Americanism will grow. An intensified struggle between the world's haves and have-nots seems inevitable. In the recent past, the have-nots have always lost out. If they lose out again, the prospects for the three-quarters of mankind living in underdeveloped countries are grim. If they win, and undermine globalization and US imperial power, the prospects may also be grim. The collapse of empires has usually entailed enormous cost not only to the imperial power but also to the subject nations.

The lessons of history offer little reassurance for America's ruling elites. No great empire has ever been able to withstand the internal strains that imperialism engenders. All have collapsed. Although America's "empire" has no formal territorial boundaries, the country's imperial reach is unprecedented in the annals of history. Not even the Roman empire exercised such vast, almost unchallengeable, power. Never before has one nation been able to impose its will so universally as the US has done since the advent of globalization, enabling it with less than 5 per cent of the world's population to, effectively, rule over and determine the future of the remaining 95 per cent.

This imbalance in global power in an increasingly rancorous world cannot be sustained. The US will be unable to impose its brutal fiat and its grossly inequitable economic ideology indefinitely. To curb opposition to Pax Americana and globalization, the hyperpower's foreign policy needs to undergo a metamorphosis – deviating from its imperial course, using diplomacy as an alternative to military force, abating the worst excesses of globalization that serve to impoverish and plunder the Third World and addressing the grievances that motivate Islamic and Arab extremism. Such a metamorphosis is unlikely, since the interests of America's ruling Rockefellerian and corporate-linked elites are perceived to require a continuation, even intensification, of America's global directorate. But what if further acts of terrorism occur in the US, creating a groundswell of opposition among Americans to President Bush's anti-terrorism "crusade"? Chalmers Johnson, professor emeritus at the University of California, San Diego, has opined that in the long run "the people of the United States are neither militaristic enough nor rich enough to engage in the perpetual police actions, wars, and bailouts their government's hegemonic policies will require".[45] The need for such US interventions and bailouts is likely to increase.

The United States faces another challenge to its global hegemony. In December 2002, European Union leaders, in accordance with the terms of the Nice Treaty, opened the way for the admission of ten new member states in 2004, which would create a superstate of around 500 million people with a GDP amounting to around a quarter of the world's total. The enlarged EU would be in a position to challenge America's economic supremacy. A mid-2002 poll by the corporate-dominated World Economic Forum of its "Global Leaders of Tomorrow" found that 58.5 per cent of them believed that there was a medium likelihood of Europe emerging as the dominant economic power of the next decade.[46]

The United States is now at a crucial watershed in its history, facing enemies, threats and challenges in all parts of the globe. The clear demarcation lines and certitudes of the Cold War, when Washington could focus on one enemy, no longer exist. Washington's ultimate dilemma in this dangerously volatile world is that the more it relies on its unilateralist diplomacy of brutal diktat – of war and military and economic interventions – to impose its will globally, the greater the resistance is likely to be. The greater the resistance, the more vulnerable US hegemony and globalization may become.

In a world order of enormous injustices, inequality and inhumanity, peace can never be imposed. International affairs become less predictable. Realizing Washington's bombastic prediction of a "Second American Century" and maintaining its world order of globalization in its current inequitable form will be immense challenges for the lone, and increasingly lonely, hyperpower and its ruling Rockefellerian and Corporate USA elites.

Notes

1. Quoted in Walter LaFeber, *America, Russia and the Cold War, 1945–1996* (New York: McGraw-Hill, 1997), p. 361.
2. President Clinton, State of the Union Address, 27 January 2000.
3. Quoted in Fareed Zakaria, "America's New Balancing Act", *Newsweek*, 6 August 2001.
4. John Maguire, *Defending Peace: Ireland's Role in a Changing Europe* (Cork: Cork University Press, 2002), p. ix.
5. Samuel P. Huntington, "The Lonely Superpower", *Foreign Affairs* magazine (New York: Council on Foreign Relations), March/April 1999. See http://www.foreignpolicy2000.org/library/issuebriefs/reading-notes/fa_huntington.html
6. "Full-Spectrum Dominance" is the key term in *Joint Vision 2020*, America's military blueprint for the future. Released on 30 May 2000, it is available on the Web at www.dtic.mil/jv2020
7. Phil Gunson, "Is Hugo Chavez Insane?", *Newsweek*, 12 November 2001.
8. Joseph Contreras and Michael Isikoff, "Hugo's Close Call", *Newsweek*, 29 April 2002.
9. *Ibid.* See also *Newsweek*, 8 July 2002.
10. USAID press release, 16 November 2001.
11. "US Warns Bolivia over Choice of President", *The Irish Times*, 15 July 2002.
12. Occidental was a major financial backer of the political career of the father of former US Vice President Al Gore and provided his father with a lucrative job when he stood down as a senator in the 1970s. Regardless of whether Al Gore, Jr, or George Bush, Jr, won the 2000 presidential election, an oil-connected figure would sit in the White House.
13. Michael McCaughan, "Clean-up Promises from an Unlikely President", *The Irish Times*, 3 August 2002. See also http://www.narconews.com/uribevsthepress.html
14. *The State of World Population 2001* (New York: UN Population Fund).

15. Quoted in Trond Jacobsen, "Clinton: New Era, Same Old National Security", *CovertAction Quarterly* no. 44 (Washington, DC), Spring 1993, p. 49; Bruce W. Nelan, "A New World for Spies", *Time*, 5 July 1993.

16. Chalmers Johnson, *Blowback: The Costs and Consequences of American Empire* (New York: Metropolitan Books, 2000), p. 9.

17. Commdt Gen. A. M. Gray, *Marine Corps Gazette*, May 1990, as quoted in Noam Chomsky, *Deterring Democracy* (London: Vintage, 1992), pp. 30–31.

18. Fareed Zakaria, "The New Twilight Struggle", *Newsweek*, 23 October 2000.

19. President Bush, address to a joint session of Congress, 20 September 2001.

20. *Ibid.*

21. The hyperpower's use of the bald eagle as its national emblem is particularly appropriate vis-à-vis America's interventionist foreign policies. Eagles are birds of prey. The verb "prey" means to seize by force or violence, to plunder or to exert a harmful or destructive influence for one's own gain.

22. William Blum, *Rogue State: A Guide to the World's Only Superpower* (London: Zed Books, 2001), p. 23; "US Military Bases and Empire", *Monthly Review* (New York), March 2002.

23. Details of the classified report, entitled "Nuclear Posture Review", were published in the *Los Angeles Times*, 9 March 2002.

24. President Bush, address at West Point, 1 June 2002.

25. President Bush, State of the Union Address, 29 January 2002.

26. Project for the New American Century letter to President Clinton, 26 January 1998. See http://www.newamericancentury.org/iraqclinton letter.htm

27. "Statement of Principles", 3 June 1997.

28. President Bush, White House press conference, 8 July 2002.

29. Noam Chomsky circular, Interhemispheric Resource Center (Albuquerque), Fall 2002.

30. G. John Ikenberry, "America's Imperial Ambition", *Foreign Affairs* (New York: CFR), September/October 2002.

31. President Clinton, Farewell Address, 18 January 2001.

32. The war-waging and peace-mediating roles of Rockefellerian elites have been a particularly notable feature of the post-Cold War era of globalization. Peace is a prerequisite for economic globalization, especially for transborder trade. Thus, the outbreak of war in Yugoslavia after the collapse of communism represented a setback for globalization's masters. Among the worst hit areas was Kosovo. After this area was plunged into conflict, a NATO air offensive was ordered by President Clinton in March 1999, after consulting with National Security Adviser Sandy Berger. Europe's largest air war since the Second World War, it was conducted by NATO head Gen. Wesley Clark. Clinton, Berger and Clark were CFR members. When negotiations began to restore peace and stability to the region, the key mediators were US envoys Strobe Talbott and Richard Holbrooke, Russian envoy Viktor Chernomyrdin and Finland's President Martti Ahtisaari. Talbott and

Holbrooke were CFR directors and Trilateral commissioners. Holbrooke was also a Bilderberger. So also was Ahtisaari, who was proposed as an interlocutor in the peace talks by Secretary of State Madeleine Albright, a CFR member. In August 2001, NATO's Secretary-General Lord Robertson and EU foreign policy chief Javier Solana were to the fore at the signing of a peace deal in another part of the former Yugoslavia, between Macedonian and ethnic Albanian political leaders. Both were Bilderbergers. The following year, Solana achieved another diplomatic success, and further stability, in the region with the European Union-inveigled union of Serbia and Montenegro, which consigned Yugoslavia to the dustbin of history.

Wherever serious discord arose elsewhere, it was usually Rockefellerian elites that acted as mediators. In April 1994, during a period of pre-election tension and violence in South Africa, an international mediation team was assembled, led by former US Secretary of State Henry Kissinger and Bilderberg Chairman Lord Carrington. In June 1994, Jimmy Carter helped to ease tensions between the United States and North Korea over the latter's nuclear development programme. In September of the same year, he persuaded a military regime to step down in Haiti. In April 1995, he visited Sudan to negotiate a ceasefire in the country's bloody civil war. In September 1993, President Clinton was a facilitator in a framework peace deal signed by Israeli Prime Minister Yitzhak Rabin and Palestinian leader Yasser Arafat. The following year, his secretary of state, Warren Christopher, travelled to the Middle East in an effort to broker an Israeli-Syrian peace agreement. In mid-2000, Clinton asked his new secretary of state, Madeleine Albright, to act as a peace mediator between Israeli and Palestinian leaders. In November 2001, a European Union delegation, headed by European Commission President Romano Prodi and the EU's foreign policy chief, Javier Solana, attempted to revive the Israeli-Palestinian peace process. In 1995, former US Senator George Mitchell was appointed chairman of the International Commission on Decommissioning of arms in Northern Ireland, an area that had endured terrorism and violence for a quarter century. In 1997 and 1998, Richard Holbrooke, on the instructions of President Clinton, mediated between Turkish and Greek leaders in Cyprus. In 1999, he travelled to Africa on a peace mission to the Democratic Republic of Congo.

All the peace envoys were Rockefellerian elites.

33. Joseph Stiglitz, *Globalization and Its Discontents* (London: Allen Lane, 2002), p. 152.
34. President Clinton, 19 January 1999.
35. Robert J. Samuelson, "The Fear of Falling", *Newsweek*, 5 August 2002.
36. Dominic Rushe, "America's Most Greedy Identified", *The Sunday Times* (UK), 11 August 2002, citing *Fortune* magazine.
37. Ankie Hoogvelt, *Globalization and the Postcolonial World: The New Political Economy of Development* (Basingstoke, Hampshire: Palgrave, 2001), p. 157.
38. Robert J. Samuelson, "Superdollar: Friend or Foe?", *Newsweek*, 3 June 2002.

39. For a brief analysis of the effects of capital flows to Asia and Latin America, see Chalmers Johnson, *Blowback*, pp. 204–15.

40. Peter Gowan, *The Global Gamble: Washington's Faustian Bid for World Dominance* (London: Verso, 1999), p. 120.

41. Karen Lowry Miller, "The Giants Stumble", *Newsweek*, 8 July 2002.

42. See Peter Gowan, *The Global Gamble*, p. 49.

43. See William Shawcross review of Marrack Goulding's book *Peacemonger*, in *The Sunday Times* (UK), 23 June 2002; Phyllis Bennis, *Calling the Shots: How Washington Dominates Today's UN* (New York: Olive Branch Press, 1996), pp. 22, 43.

44. "Business Week/Harris Poll: A Survey of Discontent", *Business Week*, 27 December 1999.

45. See Chalmers Johnson, *Blowback*, p. 221.

46. Cited in *Newsweek*, 16–23 September 2002.

APPENDIX A

Rockefellerian and Corporate Elites

In administartion after administration, individuals connected to Corporate USA and the Rockefellers dominated US foreign and domestic policies.

The Kennedy Administration

Among the panellists, advisers and staff members of the Rockefeller Brothers Fund's Special Studies Project appointed to political offices during the Kennedy presidency were Dean Rusk (secretary of state), McGeorge Bundy (national security adviser), Henry Kissinger (consultant to Bundy), Walt W. Rostow (chairman of the Policy Planning Council at the State Department), Chester Bowles (under secretary of state), Harlan Cleveland (assistant secretary of state), Philip Coombs (assistant secretary of state), Richard N. Gardner (deputy assistant secretary of state), Roger Hilsman (director of the Bureau of Intelligence and Research at the State Department and assistant secretary of state), Roswell Gilpatric (deputy secretary of defense), Paul Nitze (assistant secretary of defense), Adolf Berle (chairman, Task Force on Latin America), General Lucius Clay (President Kennedy's personal representative in Berlin during the Berlin Wall crisis of 1961), William Attwood (ambassador to Guinea) and Lincoln Gordon (ambassador to Brazil and a member of the Task Force on Latin America).

The Carter Administration

Among President Carter's appointees were: Walter Mondale (vice president), Zbigniew Brzezinski (national security adviser), Cyrus Vance (secretary of state), Warren Christopher (deputy secretary of state), Richard N. Cooper (under secretary of state), Lucy Wilson Benson (under secretary of state), Richard Holbrooke (assistant secretary of state), W. Michael Blumenthal (secretary of the treasury), Anthony

M. Solomon (under secretary of the treasury), Harold Brown (secretary of defense), Paul A. Volcker (chairman, Federal Reserve Board), Hedley Donovan (special adviser to the president), Robert Bowie (deputy to the director of the CIA), Paul C. Warnke (director of the Arms Control and Disarmament Agency), Andrew Young (ambassador to the United Nations), Leonard Woodcock (ambassador to China), Richard N. Gardner (ambassador to Italy), Henry D. Owen (ambassador at large), Elliot L. Richardson (ambassador at large), Gerard C. Smith (ambassador at large), Lloyd Cutler (counsel to the president), Sol M. Linowitz (Middle East negotiator and co-negotiator of the Panama Canal treaties) and John Sawhill (deputy secretary of energy). All twenty-three appointees, and President Carter himself, were members of the Trilateral Commission.

The Reagan Administration

Trilateral commissioners appointed by President Reagan included: George H. Bush (vice president), Paul A. Volcker (chairman, Federal Reserve Board), Alan Greenspan (who replaced Volcker), Caspar Weinberger (secretary of defense), William E. Brock (secretary of labor and US trade representative), Frank C. Carlucci (national security adviser and later Reagan's secretary of defense), Arthur Burns (ambassador to West Germany), David M. Abshire (ambassador to NATO), William A. Hewitt (ambassador to Jamaica), and Winston Lord (ambassador to China).

Volcker's replacement by Greenspan as chairman of the Fed transferred the post from one Trilateralist to another. The holder of the post is, probably, the second most powerful figure in the United States and in the world, after the president of the United States.

The George H. Bush Administration

Among his fellow Trilateral commissioners appointed by George H. Bush were Brent Scowcroft (national security adviser), Lawrence S. Eagleburger (deputy secretary of state), Donald B. Rice (secretary of the Air Force), Carla A. Hills (US trade representative), Richard Darman (director, Office of Management and Budget), Winston Lord (ambassador to China) and Alan Greenspan (who remained chairman of the Fed).

The Clinton Administration

The presidency of Bill Clinton can be used to gain an insight into the overwhelming control exercised in Washington by political appointees associated with the Rockefellers and Corporate USA.

Clinton's appointees included Warren Christopher (secretary of state), Lynn E. Davis, Peter Tarnoff and Joan Edelman Spero (under secretaries of state), Strobe Talbott and Clifton R. Wharton, Jr (deputy secretaries of state), Winston Lord (assistant secretary of state), Bruce Babbitt (secretary of the interior), William S. Cohen (secretary of defense), Graham Allison (assistant secretary of defense), Donna E. Shalala (secretary of health and human services), Henry Cisneros (secretary of housing and urban development), David Gergen (assistant to the president for communications), John M. Deutch (under secretary of defense and later director of the CIA), Joseph S. Nye, Jr (chairman, National Intelligence Council, CIA), Alice M. Rivlin (deputy director, Office of Management and Budget), Alan Greenspan (who remained as chairman of the Fed), William J. Crowe (ambassador to the United Kingdom), Walter F. Mondale and Thomas Foley (ambassadors to Japan), Richard Holbrooke (ambassador to Germany and later ambassador to the United Nations and assistant secretary of state), Stephen W. Bosworth (ambassador to South Korea), Richard N. Gardner (ambassador to Spain) and James R. Jones (ambassador to Mexico).

All of these twenty-four Trilateral commissioners, and President Clinton himself, were also members of the CFR as of 30 June 1990. Thirteen of the twenty-four were CFR directors.

Within the State Department, the hub of the country's foreign policy-making structure, members of the Trilateral Commission and the CFR exercised an incredible dominance. CFR members in the department included Clinton's Secretaries of State Warren Christopher and Madeleine Albright; Deputy Secretaries of State Clifton R. Wharton, Jr, and Strobe Talbott; Under Secretaries of State Lynn E. Davis, Peter Tarnoff, Joan Edelman Spero, Timothy E. Wirth, J. Brian Atwood and Stuart E. Eizenstat; Assistant Secretaries of State Winston Lord, Tobi Trister Gati, Princeton N. Lyman, George E. Moose, Phyllis E. Oakley, Robert H. Pelletreau, Jr, James P. Rubin, Stephen A. Oxman and Richard Holbrooke; Deputy Assistant Secretary for Public Affairs R. Nicholas Burns; Directors of the Policy Planning Staff James Steinberg and Samuel W. Lewis; coordinator for counterterrorism Christopher W. S. Ross; legal adviser David R. Andrews. At least eighteen US ambassadors were also CFR members.

Other current and former CFR members appointed by President Clinton included his treasury secretaries, Robert E. Rubin and Lawrence H. Summers; national security advisers, W. Anthony Lake and Sandy Berger; Les Aspin (defense secretary); George Stephanopoulos (senior policy adviser and communications director); R. James Woolsey (CIA director); Franklin Raines (director of the Office of Management and Budget); Roger Altman (deputy secretary of the treasury); Laura D'Andrea Tyson (chair, Council of Economic

Advisers); Joseph Duffey (director, US Information Agency); and Carol Bellamy (director, US Peace Corps).

Many of these appointees were also members of the Trilateral Commission and/or the Bilderberg Group. Altogether, well over sixty members of the three bodies were appointed to key posts, and dozens of others to less important ones.

The George W. Bush Administration

When George W. Bush succeeded Clinton in the White House, US foreign policy remained in the hands of members of the three sister bodies, particularly Secretary of State Colin L. Powell (CFR, Bilderberg Group), National Security Adviser Condoleezza Rice (CFR) and Vice President Richard Cheney (CFR director 1987–89, Trilateral Commission). Other appointees included Treasury Secretary Paul H. O'Neill, chairman and CEO of Alcoa; Deputy Treasury Secretary Kenneth W. Dam (CFR director); Trade Representative Robert Zoellick (Trilateral Commission, CFR); Fed chairman Alan Greenspan (Trilateral Commission, CFR); Assistant Secretaries of State Lorne W. Craner and Lincoln P. Bloomfield (CFR); Under Secretary of State Paula J. Dobriansky (Trilateral Commission, vice president and director of the CFR's Washington office); Environmental Protection Agency administrator Christine Todd Whitman (CFR); Richard N. Haass, director of the State Department's Policy Planning Staff (Trilateral Commission, CFR); Secretary of Labor Elaine Chao (CFR); Deputy Secretary of Defense Paul Wolfowitz (Trilateral Commission, CFR); Under Secretary of Defense Douglas J. Feith (CFR); Under Secretary of Defense and Comptroller Dov Zakheim (CFR); Assistant Secretary for International Security Affairs Peter W. Rodman (CFR); Ambassador to the United Nations John Negroponte (CFR); legal adviser to the Secretary of State William Howard Taft IV (CFR); Brent Scowcroft, President's Foreign Intelligence Advisory Board (Trilateral Commission, CFR director); Deputy National Security Adviser Stephen Hadley (CFR); special assistant to the president and senior director at the National Security Council, Jendayi Frazer (CFR); senior director for defense policy and arms control, Franklin C. Miller (CFR); and Secretary of the Air Force James G. Roche (CFR). Roche and the other two service secretaries in the Defense Department were business executives recruited from energy and defence corporations.

Appointees from the energy sector were especially prominent in the George W. Bush administration. Vice President Cheney had headed Halliburton, the world's largest oil industry service company. National Security Adviser Condoleezza Rice was a board member of Chevron, formerly Standard Oil of California, which had been controlled by the Rockefellers. Commerce Secretary Donald Evans was chairman of the board, president and CEO of Tom Brown Inc., a natural gas and crude oil exploration, production and marketing company. Trade Representative Robert Zoellick had been on the payroll of the world's largest energy-trading company, Enron Corp., serving on its advisory council.

Others appointees with ties to the energy sector included Army Secretary Thomas E. White, vice chairman of Enron Energy Services, a branch of Enron Corp; Commerce Under Secretary for Economic Affairs Kathleen Cooper, chief economist at ExxonMobil; Deputy Secretary of Energy Francis S. Blake, senior vice president of corporate business development at General Electric; energy lobbyists Dan Brouillette, who became assistant energy secretary, and Deputy Interior Secretary J. Steven Griles; and assistant attorney general in the Justice Department's Environment Division, Thomas L. Sansonetti, a partner in Holland and Hart, a law firm that advised corporate clients on natural resources and environmental law. Appointed chairman of the Federal Energy Regulatory Commission – which regulates the natural gas and electricity sectors and the transmission of oil by pipeline in the US – was Pat Wood III, a former employee of the ARCO Indonesia oil company and of a law firm which advised clients in the energy sector. Zalmay Khalilzad, an adviser to the US oil multinational Unocal in Afghanistan, became the United States' special envoy to that country. Energy Secretary Spencer Abraham, a former senator, had been the number one recipient of campaign contributions from the automotive industry.

Non-American Trilateral Commissioners

Whereas in the United States political control is exercised by US presidents and by political appointees recruited from the Trilateral Commission, the CFR, directly from Corporate USA and, to a lesser extent, from Bilderberg Group alumni, in other countries where political power is held by Rockefeller or corporate-connected individuals, they are generally members of the Trilateral Commission or Bilderbergers. At the start of the new millennium, such elites held key political offices in several countries. For instance, the Trilateral Commission's membership lists of April 2000 and January 2002 included Kiichi Miyazawa, Japan's finance minister; Yoriko Kawaguchi, Japan's minister of the environment; Viktor Orban, Hungary's prime minister; Marek Belka, Poland's deputy prime minister and minister of finance; Renato Ruggiero, Italy's minister of foreign affairs; French Foreign Minister Hubert Vedrine; France's defence minister, Alain Richard; France's minister of the economy, finances and industry, Laurent Fabius; Norway's minister of foreign affairs, Thorbjorn Jagland; Britain's minister for public health, Yvette Cooper; Peter

Mandelson, Britain's secretary of state to Northern Ireland; Ritt Bjer-regaard, Denmark's minister of agriculture and food; and Karsten Voigt, coordinator for German-American Cooperation in Germany's Federal Ministry of Foreign Affairs.

Also included in the January 2002 membership list were four members of Japan's House of Representatives, two members of Japan's House of Councillors, a member of South Korea's National Assembly, two members of Britain's parliament, three members of Britain's House of Lords, one member of the European Commission, two members of the European Parliament and other parliamentarians, members of councils of state and ambassadors from Canada, Germany, Austria, France, Ireland, Sweden, Hungary, Cyprus, Holland and Estonia. Also listed were two US senators, two US congressmen and five leading Bush appointees, including his vice president.

In Britain the prime minister was Tony Blair, a Bilderberger.

APPENDIX B

The CFR and the Marshall Plan

When the Second World War ended, it elicited a response of relief rather than a burst of euphoria in most countries. There was little to celebrate. The war's legacy was enormous. The task of reconstructing the war-gutted urban areas and of re-sparking the international economy was a daunting one. Only the United States had the necessary resources and will to implement effective post-war economic rescue programmes.

The programmes that Washington chose to pursue were, ostensibly, US efforts to lift the burdens of poverty, hunger and unemployment off the shoulders of European and Third World populations. Humanitarian considerations, however, played only a small part in the genesis of the programmes. Dean Acheson, called "the father" of America's rescue programme in Europe by Arthur M. Schlesinger, Jr,[1] acknowledged that the programmes had been set in train "chiefly as a matter of national self-interest".[2]

Throughout almost all the post-war world there was economic bleakness. The collapse or near-collapse of national economies meant that few countries had reserves of dollars to purchase US goods. Without such purchases the US economy, and US corporations, would also collapse. On the other hand, if the United States could arrange for credits to be extended to the world's countries for the purchase of American goods, it might enable the US, and especially Corporate USA, to dominate the world's markets. Attaining this goal became the priority of the Truman administration, in which an estimated 42 per cent of the top foreign policy decision makers were CFR members.[3]

On 5 June 1947, Secretary of State George Marshall unveiled proposals for a massive US-funded economic aid programme for Europe. The programme, called the Marshall Plan after its patron, began the following year. In January 1949, President Truman launched an aid programme for the Third World, later known as the Point Four programme. Responsibility for designing the framework for this initiative fell on the shoulders of the chairman of the International Development Advisory Board, Nelson Rockefeller.[4]

CFR members were responsible for the conception, creation and implementation of the Marshall Plan. In 1946, the CFR assembled a study group on reconstruction in western Europe under Charles M. Spofford, with David Rockefeller as its secretary. Its deliberations helped to shape the Marshall Plan.[5]

Separately, proposals for Europe's rehabilitation came from, among others, Truman's Under Secretaries of State Dean Acheson, William Clayton and Robert Lovett, Director of the State Department's Policy Planning Staff George F. Kennan, Paul Nitze, Allen Dulles, John J. McCloy, US Ambassador to Great Britain Lewis Douglas, Assistant Secretary of State William Benton and Commerce Secretary W. Averell Harriman.[6]

Clayton, Kennan, Nitze, McCloy, Benton and Harriman were all members of the CFR, where Dulles was president (1946–50) and Douglas a director (1940–64). Acheson joined the CFR by 1948. Lovett was a trustee of the Rockefeller Foundation (1949–53), as were Douglas (1935–47) and McCloy (1946–49).

Under President Truman's direction, discussions on aid for Europe were initiated in early 1947 by Dean Acheson when he asked the inter-departmental State, War and Navy Coordinating Committee to outline proposals for an aid programme. The secretary of war, Robert P. Patterson, was a CFR member. The secretary of the navy, James V. Forrestal, had been a director of a Chase National Bank affiliate. Shortly afterwards, Secretary of State George Marshall instructed George Kennan to begin a similar study within the Policy Planning Staff.[7]

To mobilize support for the Marshall Plan among a cynical and critical public and Congress, a Committee for the Marshall Plan was formed on the initiative of CFR members Alger Hiss and Clark M. Eichelberger. Among its founding members was CFR President Allen Dulles. Headed by CFR members Henry L. Stimson (a Wall Street lawyer and former secretary of state and secretary of war) and Robert

P. Patterson (Truman's secretary of war), sixteen of the committee's executive members were CFR members, including banker Winthrop W. Aldrich, an uncle of David and Nelson Rockefeller.[8]

A Committee on Foreign Aid was set up by President Truman to analyse the proposed programme. Chaired by banker and CFR member W. Averell Harriman, the committee included at least six other CFR members and three trustees of the Rockefeller Foundation.[9]

Managing the aid programme became the almost exclusive preserve of CFR members and corporate elites. The programme was administered by an Economic Cooperation Administration (ECA), headed by Paul G. Hoffman, president of the Studebaker Corporation, and later by former Under Secretary of Commerce William C. Foster and banker W. Averell Harriman. Responsible for the disbursement of much of the ECA aid were John J. McCloy, Thomas K. Finletter and David Bruce. All had CFR ties.[10]

At the time of the ECA's formation, Hoffman, Harriman, Bruce and McCloy were CFR members and Finletter a CFR director (1944–67). Later, Harriman became a director of the council (1950–55), as did Foster (1959–72) and McCloy, who became its chairman (1953–70).

Corporate influence within the ECA was enormous. The three top administrators of the aid programme, Hoffman, Foster and Harriman, were all members of business forums. Hoffman and Foster were trustees of the Committee for Economic Development, as also was James Zellerbach, who directed the aid programme in Italy. Hoffman and Harriman were members of the Business Advisory Council.

Created and implemented by Rockefellerian and corporate elites and financed by US taxpayers' money, the Marshall Plan enriched the US corporate sector. Almost three-quarters of all the monies appropriated for the programme was used by the recipient European countries to purchase US goods, thereby returning the money to the donor nation, greatly boosting US corporate profits and stimulating industrialization, employment and an economic boom in the United States.

The Marshall Plan served another important function. It gained almost open access to European markets for US goods, breaking down barriers to trade and integrating the region into a post-war, US-supervised economic system. The programme was a momentous step on the road to free trade and economic globalization.

Notes

1. Arthur M. Schlesinger, Jr, *A Thousand Days: John F. Kennedy in the White House* (London: Mayflower-Dell, 1967), p. 253.
2. Howard Zinn, *A People's History of the United States* (New York: Harper Perennial, 1990), p. 430.

3.   Laurence H. Shoup and William Minter, *Imperial Brain Trust: The Council on Foreign Relations and United States Foreign Policy* (New York: Monthly Review Press, 1977), p. 62.

4.   Peter Collier and David Horowitz, *The Rockefellers: An American Dynasty* (New York: Signet, 1977), pp. 265–66.

5.   See Shoup and Minter, *Imperial Brain Trust*, p. 35.

6.   The background to the planning of the Marshall Plan is covered in Allen W. Dulles, *The Marshall Plan* (Providence, Rhode Island: Berg, 1993), Michael Wala, ed., and in Morton Berkowitz et al, *The Politics of American Foreign Policy: The Social Context of Decisions* (Englewood Cliffs, New Jersey: Prentice Hall, 1977), pp. 20–38.

7.   James Chace, *Acheson: The Secretary of State Who Created the American World* (New York: Simon & Schuster, 1998), pp. 173–76.

8.   See Dulles, *The Marshall Plan*, pp. xiii-xvi.

9.   *Ibid.*, pp. 55–60. See also Philip H. Burch, Jr, *Elites in American History* (New York: Holmes and Meier, 1980), vol. 3, pp. 98–100.

10.   For details of the ECA programme, see Burch, *Elites in American History*, pp. 100–01.

APPENDIX C

The CFR, Bilderberg and the European Common Market

The Marshall Plan was Washington's economic masterstroke of the early Cold War years. It was motivated by American economic and corporate self-interest and by a crucial strategic goal of creating a sort of United States of Europe, comprising a militarily strong and economically prosperous union of capitalist European nations, tied to US trade and capital and allied militarily with the United States.

Washington linked the aid it provided under the Marshall Plan with progress towards the political, economic and military integration of Europe. Vernon Walters, an assistant to W. Averell Harriman, the administrator of the Marshall Plan programme in Europe, wrote of how "almost all of the assistance we gave was conditioned on steps toward achieving European unity".[1] So eager was Washington to attain this goal that it expended around $13 billion in aid for the region through the Marshall Plan between 1948 and 1952.[2]

A key goal of the US-aided scheme was to promote free trade in the region. Marshall Plan administrator and CFR member Paul G.

Hoffman observed that the consequence of European economic integration would be "the formation of a single large market within which quantitative restrictions on the movement of goods, monetary barriers to the flow of payments, and eventually all tariffs are permanently swept away".[3]

Two significant steps toward European "integration", a euphemism for unification, were the creation in 1948 on Washington's insistence of the Organization for European Economic Cooperation and the establishment in April 1951 of the European Coal and Steel Community (ECSC), a common market for coal and steel in six western European countries. It represented a unique model of limited regional economic integration.

In the summer of 1952, the "High Authority" of the ECSC acquired a headquarters in Europe with a French technocrat, Jean Monnet, as its first president and Max Kohnstamm from the Netherlands as secretary. In 1957, their work was rewarded with the signing of a Treaty of Rome, which established the European Economic Community (EEC). This later became the European Union. It was the world's first modern regional free trade zone.

Its principal European founder was Jean Monnet, "the father of Europe",[4] aided by Kohnstamm, French Foreign Minister Robert Schuman, Dr Joseph Retinger, secretary general of the European Movement, a coalition of bodies committed to European integration, and Walter Hallstein, the head of west Germany's post-war foreign ministry.[5]

The European Economic Community was the product of an unprecedented collaboration between European and American leaders. During this collaborative process, that began with the launch of the Marshall Plan and climaxed with the Treaty of Rome and the establishment of the EEC, members of two organizations had an almost constant presence and influential input, the CFR and the Bilderberg Group.

After the Bilderberg Group's formation in 1954 on the initiative of Polish *éminence grise* Dr Joseph Retinger and Prince Bernhard of the Netherlands, members of this CFR-linked body (in its early years all Americans on Bilderberg's steering committee were CFR members or CFR officers) were key participants in the collaborative process, notably Retinger and Hallstein, an early alumnus of the Bilderberg Group.

George McGhee, a Bilderberger and an assistant secretary of state in the Truman administration, credited Bilderberg as a procreator of the EEC, expressing the belief that "you could say the Treaty of Rome, which brought the Common Market into being, was nurtured at these [Bilderberg] meetings".[6] In the years between the Bilderberg Group's formation in 1954 and the signing of the Treaty of Rome three years later, the group provided a forum for European integrationists. Its American alumni during this period included Paul G. Hoffman, administrator of the Marshall Plan (1948–50) and James Zellerbach, the Marshall Plan's chief in Italy.[7]

Apart from Marshall Plan funding, the United States covertly funnelled money to pro-unification groups. Bilderberg's co-founder, Dr Retinger, was secretary general of the European Movement, a CIA-funded body. Finance was channelled to the movement via the CIA-created American Committee for a United Europe (ACUE), whose members included its chairman, US spymaster William Donovan, the head of the wartime OSS, the precursor of the CIA; its vice-chairman, Allen Dulles, head of the CIA (1953–61) and a director (1927–69) and president (1946–50) of the CFR; and ACUE's executive director, Tom Braden, head of the CIA's International Organizations Division (1950–54).[8]

Retinger's proposals for European unity and for closer Euro-American ties received the seal of approval from corporate and CFR leaders whom he consulted in the United States, including CFR Chairman Russell C. Leffingwell, David Rockefeller and his brother Nelson, Rockefeller in-law and CFR executive director George S. Franklin, John Foster Dulles and Adolf Berle.[9]

The ties between the Rockefellers and the European creators of Europe's Common Market were very close. When Retinger and Prince Bernhard convened the first Bilderberg meeting, among the attendees was David Rockefeller, who became a member of the steering committee. Dean Rusk, president of the Rockefeller Foundation since 1952, became Bilderberg's US co-chairman (1955–57).

When David Rockefeller hosted a meeting in July 1972 at the family's estate in Tarrytown, New York, to finalize arrangements for the establishment of the Trilateral Commission, among the small, select group of Rockefeller invitees were Bilderberger Max Kohnstamm and François Duchene, both of whom had worked for European unity under Monnet. Kohnstamm became the first chairman of the Trilateral Commission's European branch and Duchene its deputy chairman. When Kohnstamm relinquished his post as the commission's European chairman, he was replaced by Georges Berthoin, Monnet's private secretary and later international honorary chairman of the European Movement, thereby establishing the precedent that all chairmen of the Trilateral Commission's European branch were drawn from among the leaders of the movement for European economic and political integration.[10]

Jean Monnet had a long association with the Rockefellers, dating back to the 1920s. A French brandy merchant, in 1926 he became vice president and managing partner of the Blair and Company Foreign Corporation, a joint European venture between New York investment bank Blair and Company and the Chase National Bank. During Monnet's six years with Blair, the Chase National was absorbed into the Rockefeller business empire when it merged with the Equitable Trust Company, in which the Rockefellers had a controlling interest.[11]

In 1935, Monnet set up an international financial consultancy firm in New York. On the recommendation of John Foster Dulles, senior partner in the giant Sullivan and Cromwell law firm, the law partnership invested in Monnet's new venture. Described by Allen Dulles' biographer Peter Grose as a "strategic nexus of international finance",[12] Sullivan and Cromwell acted as legal planners and agents for US corporate finance, seeking to mould the global order for the benefit of corporate clients. Its purpose, Grose wrote, was "nothing less than to shape the affairs of all the world for the benefit and well-being of the select, their clients".[13] Monnet, described as "an intimate friend"[14] by J. F. Dulles, would prove to be a valuable ally in Europe in this respect.

During Monnet's years in the United States, he was accepted within the nation's most elite circles, including the CFR. In these and later years, Dean Acheson, the Dulles brothers, W. Averell Harriman and John J. McCloy became friends to the Frenchman and were to the fore in furthering Monnet's objective of a unified west European market, Acheson as the draftsman of the Marshall Plan; Allen Dulles as a founding member of the Committee for the Marshall Plan, as a consultant to the House Select Committee on Foreign Aid and as director of the CIA; John Foster Dulles as secretary of state; McCloy as US high commissioner to Germany; and Harriman as the administrator of the Marshall Plan. All were CFR members, as were others who also worked closely with Monnet towards achieving his goal.[15]

After Monnet's death in 1979, Rockefellerian and corporate elites continued to strive for an even greater degree of coalescence between European nations. In 1983, his former assistant, Max Kohnstamm, a Bilderberg alumnus and former European chairman of the Trilateral Commission, established an Action Committee for Europe. Working in tandem with Jacques Delors, president of the European Commission, Kohnstamm's Action Committee collaborated in one of the most important steps towards unification, the Treaty on European Union which was signed at Maastricht in February 1992.[16] The treaty laid the basis for economic and monetary union in Europe before the end of the century.

Originated and brought to fruition by European and American elites, the European Economic Community and its successor, the European Union, mirrored the interests of its creators. Although their creation brought considerable benefits in the form of increased prosperity and improved standards of living for citizens of member states, this was achieved at some cost. It entailed weakened democratic structures, less democratic accountability, a dilution of the sovereignty of member states and greater centralization of power.

The eviscerated democratic model that today comprises the European Union is, perhaps, a fitting monument for its principal creator, Jean Monnet – a man never mandated to hold any political office by an electorate and thus never a member of a democratically elected government. Monnet's goal has been concisely delineated by his biographer and colleague François Duchene. He was, Duchene wrote, "the champion of a Europe united by free trade".[17]

Throughout the decades in which the European Union moved towards becoming an integrated supranational Europe, Rockefeller-linked figures were to the fore in furthering the process. At the start of the new millennium, these included the president of the European Commission, Romano Prodi, many of his commissioners, national leaders and government ministers in several EU countries, and Wim Duisenberg, the first president of the European Central Bank.

Under Prodi, Duisenberg and other Rockefellerian and corporate-linked figures, the European Union was being converted into a federal superstate, where there would be greater centralization of power, less democratic accountability, less national sovereignty, more porous borders and greater corporate freedom – and a place where the voices of the people would carry little weight.

Notes

1.   Vernon A. Walters, *Silent Missions* (Garden City, New York: Doubleday, 1978), p. 176.

2.   William L. Langer et al, *Western Civilization: The Struggle for Empire to Europe in the Modern World* (New York: Harper and Row, 1968), p. 830; Jack C. Plano and Milton Greenberg, *The American Political Dictionary* (Fort Worth, Texas: Harcourt Brace, 1997), p. 561.

3.   Quoted in Martin Walker, *The Cold War* (London: Vintage, 1994), p. 87.

4.   Holly Sklar, ed., *Trilateralism: The Trilateral Commission and Elite Planning for World Management* (Boston: South End Press, 1980), p. 165.

5.   The early drive towards European unity and the formation of a European Common Market is covered in Sklar, *Trilateralism*, pp. 159–189 and François Duchene, *Jean Monnet: The First Statesman of Interdependence* (New York: W. W. Norton, 1994).

6.   See Sklar, *Trilateralism*, p. 170; Kai Bird, *The Chairman: John J. McCloy – The Making of the American Establishment* (New York: Simon & Schuster, 1992), p. 472.

7.   *Spotlight on the Bilderbergers: Irresponsible Power* (Washington, DC: Liberty Lobby), pp. 22, 24.

8.   Philip Agee and Louis Wolf, eds., *Dirty Work: The CIA in Western Europe* (London: Zed Press, 1978), pp. 194, 201–03; Bird, *The Chairman*, p. 471; Sklar, *Trilateralism*, pp. 162, 184–85.

9. See Sklar, *Trilateralism*, pp. 162–63.
10. *Ibid.*, pp. 78–79; Stephen Gill, *American hegemony and the Trilateral Commission* (Cambridge: Cambridge University Press, 1991), p. 141.
11. See Duchene, *Jean Monnet*, pp. 44–45.
12. Peter Grose, *Gentleman Spy: The Life of Allen Dulles* (London: Andre Deutsch, 1995), p. 90.
13. *Ibid.*, p. 90.
14. See Duchene, *Jean Monnet*, p. 57.
15. CFR members who worked closely with Monnet included Robert R. Bowie, McCloy's chief legal counsel in Germany and later director of the State Department's Policy Planning Staff; David Bruce, the US ambassador and head of the Marshall Plan mission in France; C. Douglas Dillon, Eisenhower's under secretary of state; William Clayton, Truman's under secretary of state; Felix Frankfurter, the Supreme Court justice; and George W. Ball, later Kennedy's under secretary of state, who worked as Monnet's legal counsel and lobbyist.
16. See Duchene, *Jean Monnet*, p. 340.
17. *Ibid.*, p. 182.

APPENDIX D

NATO, OAS and SEATO

Founded in 1949, the North Atlantic Treaty Organization (NATO) was an important element of Washington's policy to "contain" Soviet power. Its early member states included the United States, Canada, the United Kingdom and all the founding nations of the forerunner of the European Union, the European Coal and Steel Community, which was established two years later in 1951. A forum for protecting US interests, NATO became Washington's primary channel for exerting influence on military and strategic issues over European governments.[1]

A striking aspect of NATO's leadership was the number of top appointees who were members of the CFR, Bilderberg, the Trilateral Commission and the Atlantic Council of the United States, another Rockefeller-linked forum which has considerable overlapping of memberships with the other three Rockefeller foreign policy forums.[2]

Between 1952 and 1961, the United States appointed its first six ambassadors to NATO. Five of them are listed on the CFR's 1949 membership roster. On the same CFR roster are the names of Gen. Dwight D. Eisenhower and Gen. Lyman L. Lemnitzer. In December 1950,

Eisenhower became the first appointee as supreme allied commander Europe (SACEUR), NATO's foremost military post in Europe. Lemnitzer occupied the post from 1963–69. Other Rockefellerian elites later held the office, which centralizes NATO's national forces under US command. In 1969, Lemnitzer was succeeded by Bilderberger Andrew J. Goodpaster.

Rockefellerian elites also filled the post of secretary-general of NATO. In the period 1971–2000, six men held this office – Joseph Luns, Lord Carrington, Manfred Wörner, Willy Claes, Javier Solana and Lord Robertson – all of whose names have appeared on lists of Bilderberg alumni.

NATO was one of a handful of US-forged regional military alliances, created to protect US foreign interests. Throughout the history of the United States, military intervention had been employed for this purpose. However, the unilateral use of military force by the US, or even the threat of force, in the years after the horrors of the Second World War would, almost inevitably, have provoked an anti-US backlash. To diminish or obviate such potential opposition, Washington opted to create regional military alliances through which US hegemonic interests could be protected. The right of nations to join together in alliances such as NATO, the Southeast Asia Treaty Organization (SEATO) and the Organization of American States (OAS) was legitimized by the inclusion of Articles 51 and 52 in the UN Charter. The articles owed their existence to Nelson Rockefeller.

Nelson Rockefeller was a central figure in the formation of the OAS. Appointed assistant secretary of state for Latin America in 1944, he immediately set about organizing an inter-American conference in Mexico City. The result was the Act of Chapultepec, a regional defence pact. It was a precursor of the OAS, which was set up in 1948 by the United States and twenty Latin American nations to provide an institutional structure for joint defence and security. It became a club of Latin American dictators and military rulers, under the direction of the United States.

CFR member Dean Acheson, as secretary of state, was instrumental in the formation and development of NATO.[3]

SEATO was established in 1954 by another CFR member, Secretary of State John Foster Dulles, as a southeast Asian version of NATO and the OAS.[4]

The regional defence pacts, in whose formation Rockefellerian elites played such key roles, provided Washington with new options for imposing Pax Americana.

Before the end of 2002, NATO's role had been redefined and its membership expanded. Seven countries – formerly opponents of NATO until their emergence from communist domination – were accepted as new member states. A new 21,000-strong NATO rapid response force was proposed, capable of intervening far beyond the borders of NATO countries.

NATO's new role was outlined by President George W. Bush when he stated that "because many threats to NATO members come from outside of Europe, NATO forces must be organized to operate outside of Europe".[5] The military alliance was being transformed incrementally into an instrumentality of Bush's "pre emptive action" doctrine, to help perpetuate US hegemony in the twenty-first century world.

Notes

1. For details of NATO's history, see *The North Atlantic Treaty Organization: Facts and Figures* (Brussels: NATO Information Office).
2. The Atlantic Council of the United States has been largely financed by corporations and corporate foundations, including the Rockefeller Foundation and the family-linked Chase bank, Exxon and Mobil. Its officers, directors and honorary directors are a *Who's Who* of Rockefeller and corporate-connected figures. Its objective is to "foster informed public debate; and make recommendations to the Executive and Legislative branches of the US Government and to the appropriate international organizations". (See Atlantic Council Policy Paper, November 1983, "Western Interests and US Policy Options in the Caribbean Basin").
3. James Chace, *Acheson: The Secretary of State Who Created the American World* (New York: Simon & Schuster, 1998), pp. 202, 203; Douglas Brinkley, *Dean Acheson: The Cold War Years, 1953–71* (New Haven: Yale University Press, 1992), pp. 7, 8.
4. John S. Bowman, ed., *The Cambridge Dictionary of American Biography* (Cambridge: Cambridge University Press, 1995), p. 204.
5. President George W. Bush, Prague, 20 November 2002.

APPENDIX E

The CFR and GATT

GATT originated in the July 1944 US-dominated Bretton Woods conference, held to establish the World Bank and IMF. Delegates at the conference agreed on the concept of an International Trade Organization (ITO), which was intended to function as a third pillar of the Bretton Woods system, alongside the bank and fund, in molding a new post-war global economic order.

Before the end of the following year, Washington had drafted recommendations for the proposed ITO. In 1947, a crucial UN-hosted conference was held in Geneva to draft a charter for the ITO, which would reduce barriers to trade. Steering the US delegation at the conference was Under Secretary of State for Economic Affairs William Clayton, a member of the CFR and the Business Advisory Council and a trustee of another corporate body, the Committee for Economic Development. The secretary of commerce at the time was W. Averell Harriman, who was also a member of the CFR and BAC.

The Truman administration, in which an estimated 42 per cent of the top foreign policy posts were filled by CFR members, was the driving force behind the ITO. However, concerns about the effects of a new trade agreement on sectors of the US economy and fears that the agreement would entail a surrender of US sovereignty to a multilateral institution stoked opposition in Congress.

The proposed ITO was never born. Instead, a set of rules for trade liberalization, a General Agreement on Tariffs and Trade, which had been formulated as part of the ITO's projected agenda, became the focus of attention, resulting in the subsequent establishment of a GATT organization to implement the rules.

The eight GATT trade negotiating rounds, culminating in the Uruguay Round and the establishment of the World Trade Organization, were central to the success of Washington's schemes for open markets and economic globalization.

APPENDIX F

Presidential Commissions

The perpetuation of elite rule in the United States, as a Trilateral Commission report, *The Crisis of Democracy*, has pointed out, requires a degree of apathy and submissiveness on the part of segments of American society. It also requires incomprehension on the part of the broad mass of the American people regarding the existence and nature of elite rule, whose fundamental objective is to formulate and implement foreign and domestic policies and strategies that serve the interests of Corporate USA, which supplies so many of the elite rulers.

Occasionally, these policies and strategies give rise to public disquiet or generate undercurrents of public opposition, which, if allowed to grow, could create a backlash against the policies and strategies and against the ruling elites that conceived them. What is vitally necessary to the elites is that public disquiet be allayed and that public opposition be contained and smothered. Usually, this can be achieved through the collaboration of America's largely pro-establishment national news media and through making minor concessions to allay the fears and to diminish the opposition.

At times, such as during the 1970s when the CIA was accused of conducting illegal operations in the United States against American citizens, it may be difficult to cool down public anger and assuage public distrust. In such instances, the elites may resort to an effective artifice devised by the elites themselves – presidential commissions.

Presidential commissions can serve numerous functions. They can be used to allay fears and to undermine opposition to government policy proposals. They can also be used to fashion and to promote new policy initiatives. However, almost all have one thing in common. They are dominated by corporate and Rockefeller-linked figures.

This domination of presidential commissions was referred to by G. William Domhoff in his book *The Powers That Be: Processes of Ruling Class Domination in America.* "Fifteen commissions dealing with aspects of foreign and military policy were established between 1945 and 1972. Twelve were headed by a member of the Council on Foreign Relations; two others were headed by trustees of the Committee for Economic Development," he wrote.[1] The CED is an organization of the heads of the country's largest corporations.

The same pattern of domination of presidential commissions continued after 1972. In 1975, following the allegations of illegal CIA spying operations in the United States, President Ford appointed a commission to investigate the allegations. It was headed by Nelson Rockefeller. Rockefeller family interests had been major beneficiaries of CIA coups in several countries, including the 1964 coup in Brazil in which the Nelson Rockefeller-founded IBEC had funnelled funds into a coup-linked CIA front organization.

Five of the eight members of the Rockefeller Commission were CFR members – Nelson Rockefeller, C. Douglas Dillon, Lane Kirkland, John T. Connor and Lyman L. Lemnitzer. Lemnitzer (as President Kennedy's chairman of the Joint Chiefs of Staff) and Dillon (Kennedy's treasury secretary) had participated in the planning of the CIA-directed Bay of Pigs invasion in Cuba. Dillon was chairman of the Rockefeller Foundation (1971–75) and a director of the Chase Manhattan Bank. Lane Kirkland was a head of the American Institute for Free Labor Development, described by former CIA official Philip Agee as a "CIA-controlled labour centre".[2] He was also a trustee of the Rockefeller Foundation, a member of the Trilateral Commission since its formation and a member, and future director (1976–86), of the CFR. Connor was a director of the Chase Manhattan Bank.

A week after the 22 November 1963 assassination of President John F. Kennedy, his successor, Lyndon B. Johnson, created the Warren Commission to investigate the murder. Two men were chosen from "private" life to serve on the seven-member commission, CFR Chairman John J. McCloy and Allen Dulles, a director and former president of the CFR.[3] McCloy had served as chairman of the Rockefellers' Chase Manhattan Bank and as a trustee of the Rockefeller Foundation.

On 19 July 1983, President Reagan established a National Bipartisan Commission on Central America to "study the nature of United States interests in the Central American region and the threats now posed to those interests".[4] Created at a time of mounting public and congressional opposition to the president's covert and overt counter-insurgency and destabilization operations in the isthmus, the unstated purpose of the commission was to provide justification for escalating US-directed, low-intensity warfare there, particularly in Nicaragua.

Called the Kissinger Commission, it was chaired by Rockefeller protégé and CFR and Trilateral Commission member Henry Kissinger. The other eleven members of the commission included CFR director and Trilateralist Lane Kirkland and CFR members Henry G. Cisneros, mayor of San Antonio, Texas; banker Nicholas F. Brady; Robert S. Strauss, President Carter's special trade representative; and Dr Carlos F. Diaz-Alejandro, a professor in Ivy League Yale, who was described in newspaper reports as a consultant to the Rockefeller Foundation. CFR President Winston Lord was a senior counsellor to the commission.

The commission's report focused on Sandinista-ruled Nicaragua, providing a flawed vindication for President Reagan's Central American policies. By portraying Nicaragua as a Soviet and Cuban base and a threat to the region, it justified Reagan's interventionism in the isthmus, especially against Nicaragua. Overall, the commission's Rockefeller and corporate-linked members provided the findings that President Reagan's ruling Rockefellerian and corporate elites intended it to provide.

In the months after 11 September, families of victims as well as congressional Democrats called for an independent inquiry into Washington's intelligence failures, that enabled the attacks to be carried out. In November 2002, President Bush finally acceded to the demands, appointing Henry Kissinger as chairman of an "independent" commission to investigate the intelligence lapses. Former Senate majority leader George Mitchell, a CFR member, was chosen by the Democratic party as the commission's vice chairman.

Critics claimed that Kissinger's chairmanship would make an open and objective investigation impossible, arguing that he would ensure that no embarrassing revelations emerged that might jeopardize President Bush's re election campaign in 2004. Suspicions were raised that neither the administration nor Kissinger himself would want a serious investigation of Saudi links to the hijackers and al-Qaeda, especially the alleged funding of an al-Qaeda 11 September-connected suspect by the wife of the Saudi ambassador to Washington – a friend of Kissinger and of the Bush family,

Shortly after his appointment, Kissinger resigned following further denunciations of his insider links with many of the governments and institutions he was due to investigate. Mitchell also resigned. Both had ties to oil companies with interests in the regions that should be the focus of the commission's attention – Central Asia and the Gulf. Kissinger had been a consultant to Unocal – and probably to other energy companies – with interests in Central Asia. Mitchell had been a partner in a consortium that had planned to invest in the privatized state oil giant Socar in the post Soviet republic of Azerbaijan.

Notes

1. G. William Domhoff, *The Powers That Be: Processes of Ruling Class Domination in America* (New York: Vintage Books, 1979), p. 89.
2. Philip Agee, *Inside the Company: CIA Diary* (Middlesex: Penguin, 1978), p. 600.
3. *Report of the Warren Commission on the Assassination of President Kennedy* (New York: Bantam Books, 1964), pp. 2, 4, 5.
4. Executive Order 12433 of 19 July 1983, as cited in *The Report of the President's National Bipartisan Commission on Central America* (New York: Macmillan, 1984).

APPENDIX G

US Elites and the News Media

The Cold War era was a period of irrational anti-communism and of naked national self-interest; of illegal domestic CIA propaganda campaigns that served to define the nation's political debate; of covert CIA operations that overthrew Third World governments and replaced them with puppet regimes; of CIA psychological warfare operations against Third World governments; of US support for right-wing death squads and terrorist organizations in Latin America; of US-waged or US-aided wars in Vietnam, Laos, Cambodia, Angola, Nicaragua and elsewhere; and of CIA funding of political candidates and political parties abroad, including Chile in the 1960s and 1970s, the Philippines, Nicaragua, Brazil and Italy. In Italy, US covert election funding over a twenty-year period amounted to some $65 million.[1] These anti-democratic and often illegal operations should have spurred the nation's media owners to commission in-depth investigative reports. They rarely did.

While Washington orchestrated its Cold War abroad, the nation's news media, with rare exceptions, generally chose to suppress reports that revealed, or were critical of, the brutality and illegality of America's covert and overt wars and interventions abroad. Instead, information was often falsified or omitted. The use of Orwellian doublespeak became popular. US-perpetrated violence was portrayed as peacemaking. Nicaraguan Contra terrorists became "freedom fighters". Unelected right-wing dictators and military regimes in Central and South America and elsewhere were saluted as defenders of their people against the threat of godless communism. Semi-socialist Nicaragua and the tiny Caribbean island of Grenada were deemed by Washington, and the US news media, to represent threats to the security of the US behemoth. Castro's Cuba was portrayed by Washington administrations and by American newspapers and television and radio networks as the Gulag of the Caribbean, thus justifying decades of US destabilization programmes. The news "spin" or angle was conceived by Washington's policy makers and fostered by the nation's newspapers and television and radio networks.

Increased media monopolization in the last two decades has concentrated news dissemination in the hands of fewer and fewer corporate owners. The preponderance of the country's mass communications sector is now controlled by less than two dozen giant corporations.[2] These owners are the leading opinion shapers in the country. They can decide what the public should know, or shouldn't know. They can manipulate, censor or withhold information. They can support or oppose candidates for elective political offices. They can promote or undermine specific political, economic and social policies and strategies, such as the Cold War, globalization, the Gulf War and US interventions undertaken to protect US corporate interests abroad. Shrouding the country's political system, which is increasingly taking on the appearance of a one-party state, in a mist of lies and deceit, they constantly reserve the moral high ground for Washington's leaders. And while doing all this they maintain a facade of objectivity.

America's national news media can, in general, be regarded as an element of the country's ruling establishment. The San Antonio-based Public Information Research analysed the 1995 membership roster of the CFR. Among the members on the roster were seventy-eight who were "pundits, news anchors, columnists, commentators, reporters, editors, executives, owners and publishers". They included Tom Brokaw, William F. Buckley, Jr, Arnaud de Borchgrave, Elizabeth Drew, Leslie H. Gelb, Georgie Anne Geyer, Meg Greenfield, Jim Hoagland, Marvin Kalb, Joe Klein, Jim Lehrer, Anthony Lewis, Norman Podhoretz and Dan Rather.[3]

The Trilateral Commission's membership has also included several media leaders, such as Gerald Levin, chairman and CEO of Time Warner and Katharine Graham, chairman of the *Washington Post*.[4]

That so many media owners, senior editorial personnel and leading commentators are members of Rockefeller forums should give considerable cause for concern, since these organizations are policy organs of the ruling elite. Journalists' membership of these forums cannot be interpreted as proof that each of them is a member or ally of the ruling elite or a promoter of foreign and domestic policies conceived by the elites. On the other hand, it is true to say that, for the most part, the most powerful media owners are members of the ruling elite and that their media operations function as mouthpieces and opinion moulders for the ruling class.

Writing about corporate control of the media, Robert W. McChesney, associate professor in the School of Journalism and Mass Communication at the University of Wisconsin-Madison, opined that "so long as the media are in corporate hands, the task of social change will be vastly more difficult. . . The biggest problem facing all who challenge the prerogatives of corporate rule is that the overwhelming majority of Americans are never exposed to anything remotely close to a reasoned, coherent, consistent, democratic socialist, pro-labor, or even old-fashioned New Deal Democratic perspective."[5] Such a pervasive politically correct media culture is normally associated with dictatorships.

Throughout the Cold War era, America's news media owners colluded with Washington's ruling elites. Today, most are performing a similar task, promoting the elites' globalization agenda and supporting their post-Cold War interventionist strategies, such as President Bush's war against terrorism. Whereas in the Cold War period Washington and the news media demonized communism and communists, thereby justifying interventions in the name of anti-communism, after the Cold War they demonized Islamic fundamentalists and "pariah" states such as Gaddafi's Libya, Saddam Hussein's Iraq, and Afghanistan.

Since the Vietnam War, it has been deemed expedient to limit the American public's access to the truth in times of US-waged wars. Communications theorist Marshall McLuhan argued persuasively that the Vietnam War was lost in the living rooms of the United States, due to the unparalleled media access to combat zones which exposed the scale of the war's butchery and Washington's lies. Since then, in every US war and military intervention, notably the Gulf War, the war in

Afghanistan, the invasions of Panama and Grenada, journalists' coverage has been rigorously restricted. American's could view the horrors of 11 September time after time, but not atrocities committed in US theatres of war.

Truth is always a casualty in times of war, because lies and propaganda are essential for fostering public support for the initiation and continuation of conflicts. In times of US-waged wars and interventions, America's government and news media fabricate a reality through being persuasive. Shaping public perceptions through substituting reality with illusion and analysis with sound bites, media conglomerates cease to be watchdogs for the public interest. Media censorship and manipulation leave most Americans ignorant of the reality of US foreign policy, simply because they aren't told. Truth in times of war is whatever Washington's ruling elites and allied media conglomerates choose it to be. Once the choreographed propaganda becomes accepted as fact, it is virtually impossible to alter the American public's perception.

Corporate monopolization of the flow of information in the United States is a key element in the governing of so many by so few.

Notes

1.   Finding of House Select Committee on Intelligence, headed by Congressman Otis Pike. See *CIA: The Pike Report* (Nottingham, UK: Spokesman Books, 1977), p. 193.
2.   Robert W. McChesney, *Corporate Media and the Threat to Democracy* (New York: Seven Stories Press, 1997), p. 6.
3.   Daniel Brandt, "Journalism and the CIA: The Mighty Wurlitzer", *NameBase NewsLine* no. 17, April 1997. Issued by Public Information Research, San Antonio, Texas.
4.   Trilateral Commission membership list, 23 March 1994.
5.   See McChesney, *Corporate Media and the Threat to Democracy*, p. 71.

APPENDIX H

Chequebook Diplomacy and US Elites

National Endowment for Democracy

Chequebook diplomacy has long been a widely used instrument of US foreign policy, being customarily conducted covertly, unknown to electorates in targeted countries, to further US foreign policy goals. It constitutes a form of patron-client relationship, in which client governments and other useful foreign collaborators are rewarded for their loyalty in lending support for US goals in their own countries and in international and regional forums.

For the first four decades of the Cold War, chequebook diplomacy was a responsibility of the CIA. In 1983, a new body, the National Endowment for Democracy (NED), was created by the Reagan administration, through an act of Congress, to give a new impetus to this form of diplomacy. It is an innovative interventionist organ of modern US foreign policy, accurately described by *The Washington Times* as "a dynamic, flexible, and cost-effective means of furthering US interests in strategically important parts of the world".[1]

In May 1986, Congressman John Conyers (D-Michigan) testified before the House Foreign Affairs Subcommittee on International Operations on the activities of the endowment. The new organization, he asserted, "has not promoted democracy, but, in my opinion, subverted it by meddling in internal politics of other countries abroad. . . interfering in free elections. . . It interfered in Panama's presidential election, a very close election, supporting there a military-backed candidate, provoking protest from the American Ambassador. . . NED also 'promoted democracy' in France by funding two right-wing organizations. . . One of these had prior affiliation with right-wing terrorist organizations outlawed by the French government. . . Taxpayer money continues to fund through NED conservative political parties in Colombia and in Bolivia. It supports networks of ideologically affiliated organizations throughout the globe. . . US law restricts foreign governments from interfering in our parties and elections the way NED does in theirs."[2]

The endowment interfered in the electoral process in Nicaragua, directing funds to an artificially united anti-Sandinista coalition, helping to destabilize and ultimately to topple the Sandinista government.

In Grenada, NED funds were used prior to the December 1984 general election to mobilize voters and to help the New National Party.

In Guatemala, the endowment funded a voter mobilization project prior to elections in 1984 and 1985.

In Costa Rica, it funded opponents of the incumbent president Oscar Arias, winner of the 1987 Nobel Peace Prize for his efforts to bring peace to Central America – efforts which the Reagan administration sought to undermine.

In Afghanistan, it channelled funds into rebel-held areas after the Soviet invasion, ironically helping to bring the Taliban regime to power.[3]

Within a decade of its formation, the NED had been active in close to one hundred countries, helping to bolster or to establish political parties, groups and alliances and also business, labour, media and other organizations whose interests and ideology broadly coincided with those of Washington's ruling elites. NED funds were used to educate and train officers and volunteers in foreign political parties, to devise and implement party-building and electoral strategies and to secure political power for Washington-approved candidates.

The Endowment and the Rockefellers

The credibility of many of the foreign programmes funded by the endowment is contingent on concealing the original source of the funds, the US government. The labyrinthine nature of its funding conduits has become so successful in this respect that the endowment, which misleadingly promotes itself as "a private organization", has enthused that NED-funded programmes "enjoy a credibility abroad that US government programs may sometimes lack".[4]

Under its authorizing legislation, funds for the National Endowment were to be appropriated annually from Congress and to flow to the endowment via the government's information organ, the United States Information Agency. In turn, the endowment channelled these funds, largely, into four core grantee organizations: the National Democratic Institute for International Affairs (an international wing of the Democratic party); its Republican party counterpart the National Republican Institute for International Affairs; the Free Trade Union Institute (an organ of the AFL-CIO labour federation); and the Center for International Private Enterprise (an organ of the US Chamber of Commerce). The funds are then distributed abroad, sometimes through further intermediaries, to foreign political parties, trade unions, newspapers and other Washington-favoured recipients.

Programmes funded by the endowment and its conduit organizations promote US interests abroad, particularly those of US multinational corporations. Corporate and Rockefeller-linked elites dominate the endowment and its four core grantees. Of the endowment's eighteen officers and directors in 1985, seven were listed in that year's CFR membership roster, including Rockefeller protégé Henry Kissinger. Later, CFR members acquired almost total control over the endowment. In 1999, the NED had five officers. All were listed on the CFR's 1997 membership roster. In 1999, the NED had twenty-three directors and chairmen emeriti. Fifteen of these were on the CFR's 1997 roster of members and a further three on earlier rosters.

The National Democratic Institute has also been dominated by Rockefeller and corporate-linked figures.[5] By the year 2000, the National Democratic Institute had offices in almost fifty countries and had "conducted democratic development programs" in almost one hundred countries.[6] Rockefeller and corporate-linked figures were also prominent within the National Republican Institute.

The two institutes are much more than appendages of the Democratic and Republican parties. Incorporated in April 1983 as conduit organizations for US government funds to foreign political, media and other bodies, neither institute had any operating funds until they received their first grants from the endowment in April of the following year.

The US Chamber of Commerce's Center for International Private Enterprise was also established in 1983 as a funding conduit for NED grants. The centre, according to the General Accounting Office, is "guided by an executive council composed of representatives of leading business organizations". Its purpose is "to encourage the growth of voluntary business organizations and private enterprise systems abroad". According to the GAO, before the centre's establishment, "the business community had no mechanism for coordinating its promotion of overseas business activities".[7]

The Free Trade Union Institute

Established in 1978 as an arm of the AFL-CIO, the Free Trade Union Institute (FTUI) was the endowment's most important funding conduit during the NED's early years. NED grants were funnelled into the FTUI which, in turn, passed them to foreign recipients through regional institutes of the AFL-CIO, namely the American Institute for Free Labor Development, the Asian-American Free Labor Institute and the African-American Labor Center.

In fiscal year 1985, endowment programmes financed through AFL-CIO affiliates were undertaken in around sixty countries in Latin America, Asia, Africa and Europe. Most of the projects funded through these AFL-CIO institutes had obvious political objectives. For instance, within two years of its formation the endowment, through the FTUI, had financed an anti-Sandinista labour federation in Nicaragua.[8]

In fiscal year 1985, the FTUI used $1.1 million of endowment money to assist "the democratic trade union movement of the Philippines".[9] The interference of the NED and FTUI in the internal affairs of his country provoked a former senator in the Philippines, José Diokno, to state that the two US organizations had "opened up an institute here supposedly to teach labor relations. But they teach community organizing and indoctrination, not labor tactics. . . [This is] worse than just a matter of intervening in our internal affairs. It is breeding further discontent."[10]

The AFL-CIO's regional institute for Latin America, the American Institute for Free Labor Development (AIFLD), has engaged in similar interventionist tactics on behalf of its patrons, the National Endowment for Democracy, the US government and the corporate sector.

The Inter-Hemispheric Education Resource Center in Albuquerque, New Mexico, has outlined the usefulness of the AFL-CIO and the AIFLD to Washington and to Corporate USA. "The overriding purpose of AIFLD is not to support efforts by workers and peasants to achieve a better life in their own countries but to serve as an instrument of US foreign policy," a 1987 Resource Center publication opined. "In Central America, operations sponsored by the AFL-CIO form a front line in the ever-expanding US effort to maintain tight political and economic control of the isthmus. . . In the name of democracy and freedom, the AFL-CIO and Washington are stepping up US labor programs throughout Central America. In Nicaragua, this means supporting unions that oppose the Sandinista government and back internal and external counterrevolutionary forces. In Guatemala and El Salvador, it means supporting unions that stand behind repressive governments and undermining the unity of workers and campesinos. . . it aims to obstruct revolutionary and progressive movements and to propagate policies that further US control of the region."

In the name of democracy, it added, "NED and AIFLD support unpopular, military-controlled governments, intervene in the internal politics of much smaller nations and back military campaigns to overthrow other governments. The main thrust of NED and AIFLD is counterrevolutionary, not democratic."[11]

The Labor Research Association in New York expressed similar sentiments: "NED funds, channelled through the AFL-CIO, have been used to finance anti-labor and anti-democratic forces. The AFL-CIO's involvement in NED undermines the interests of workers in the US and abroad."[12]

Formed in 1961, the AIFLD became the main spearhead for US labour policy in Latin America. The vast bulk of the funding for the new AFL-CIO institute was provided by the US government. For the first two decades of its existence, it was part-funded by US multinationals with interests in the continent and had representatives of the multinationals on its board of trustees. The AIFLD's corporate collaborators included ITT, the copper giants Kennecott and Anaconda, and Rockefeller family firms – corporations which had considerable investments in Latin America and had collaborated in Washington's interventions in the continent.[13]

Formed after the start of the Cuban revolution, the AIFLD sought to counter Castroite influence within Latin America's labour movements. In the poverty-racked continent, Cuba's emerging socialist model had considerable appeal. The value of the AIFLD was spelled out by board chairman J. Peter Grace, who lauded the Institute's programmes as "the crucial and significant factor in the steady deterioration of Castro-communism in Latin America".[14] Grace, the multimillionaire head of W. R. Grace, a company with investments throughout Latin America, was one of several business leaders within the AIFLD's leadership in its early years, mirroring the strength of the ties between the US corporate sector and the labour institute at that time.

In Central and South America, the AIFLD allied itself with the most moderate and tame sectors of the labour movement, assisting these to become a bulwark against the more militant left-leaning unions, from which it sought to drain members and support. Company-controlled unions were cultivated, to weaken and replace worker-dominated ones. Averse to criticizing US-supported repressive regimes and social injustices in the region, the AIFLD incurred the wrath and odium of wide sections of the continent's workforce. AIFLD-backed unions were perceived as toothless and pliant pawns of Washington and Corporate USA.

Lane Kirkland provides an example of the AFL-CIO/Corporate USA/National Endowment for Democracy alliance. In 1980, he became president of the AFL-CIO. He was a director of the CFR (1976–86), an executive member of the Trilateral Commission, and a trustee of the Rockefeller Foundation. He was also a director of the National Endowment in its early years.

The creation of the endowment marked the beginning of a new phase in the conduct of US interventionist foreign policy. Under the direction of its Rockefeller and corporate-linked leaders, the endowment would funnel American taxpayers' money abroad, through four core grantee organizations, many of whose leaders also had ties to the Rockefellers and the corporate sector, in furtherance of US foreign policy interests, particularly those of Corporate USA.

Notes

1. James Phillips, "Shortsighted NED-Slayers", *The Washington Times*, 13 July 1993.
2. Congressman John Conyers, Jr, testimony before the House Foreign Affairs Subcommittee on International Operations, 20 May 1986.
3. The NED's activities in Nicaragua, Grenada, Guatemala, Costa Rica and Afghanistan are outlined in its *Annual Report 1985*.
4. *Ibid.*, pp. 4, 58.
5. In 1986, the National Democratic Institute's board of directors included Honorary Chairman Walter F. Mondale, a member of the Trilateral Commission, CFR and the Bilderberg Group; Vice Chairman Madeleine K. Albright, a CFR member; and Directors John T. Joyce, Leon Lynch, Daniel P. Moynihan, Glenn E. Watts, Anne Wexler, Andrew J. Young and Cyrus R. Vance, all CFR members. Vance had been chairman of the Rockefeller Foundation. Corporate lobbyist Anne Wexler would become a leading figure in the drive for global free-market capitalism, particularly through lobbying for the North American Free Trade Agreement. Her husband Joseph Duffey, as director of the United States Information Agency, helped to promote the NAFTA accord and had responsibility

for channelling funding into the National Endowment for Democracy. He was a member of the CFR.

6. National Democratic Institute for International Affairs brochure, *Working to Strengthen and Expand Democracy Worldwide*.
7. US General Accounting Office report to Senator Malcolm Wallop, 6 July 1984, p. 21.
8. *NED Annual Report 1985*.
9. *Ibid.*, p. 36.
10. John Kelly, 'National Endowment for Reagan's Democracies', *The National Reporter* (Washington, DC), Summer 1986, p. 25, citing the San Francisco *Examiner*, 21 August 1985.
11. *AIFLD in Central America: Agents as Organizers* (Albuquerque, NM: Inter-Hemispheric Education Resource Center, 1987), pp. 1–2, 62.
12. Fay Hansen, "The AFL-CIO and the Endowment for Democracy", *LRA Economic Notes* (New York: Labor Research Association), May-June 1985, p. 15.
13. See *AIFLD in Central America*, pp. 7–8; John Ranelagh, *The Agency: The Rise and Decline of the CIA* (London: Sceptre, 1988), p. 249; *Unity Is Strength: Trade Unions in Latin America – A Case for Solidarity* (London: Latin America Bureau, 1980), pp. 51–52.
14. *AIFLD in Central America*, p. 8, citing *AFL-CIO Free Trade Union News*, 27 May 1972.

APPENDIX I

The Military-Industrial Complex and the "War Racket"

In a 1989 book, Edward S. Greenberg of the University of Colorado wrote of Washington's love affair with militarism: "It would be no exaggeration to say that the United States has been on a permanent war footing since 1941. Well over one-half of all federal budget expenditures since that date have been devoted to military activities. Since 1945, the United States has spent over \$2 trillion, or one-tenth of total US economic output; almost one-tenth of the total labor force has been employed by the armed services or in corporations heavily dependent on defense spending."[1] Commenting on America's defence budget, *Time* magazine observed in 1992 that over the past forty years "\$5 trillion that might have been invested in education, public health, housing, highways and other domestic needs instead had to be spent on the armed forces".[2]

America's defence budget normally amounts to around one-third of total world defence spending.[3] The tragedy of this vast military expenditure is that it diverts money and labour away from projects that would benefit the world's people to ones that inflict untold suffering on entire populations, particularly peasant societies. In early 2002, President George W. Bush called for a Pentagon budget for 2003 of almost $400 billion, equivalent to over $60 for every human being on the planet, enough to feed all the world's hungry and to eliminate illiteracy. (Interestingly, in contrast to its huge defence spending, the US devotes less than $10 billion a year to economic aid, a third of the average for Europe. Most of the US aid goes to two countries, Israel and Egypt, or is used to boost US sales abroad or to wage war on drugs abroad, rather than helping the world's poorest peoples.)

President Eisenhower spoke out against the obscenity of defence expenditure: "Every gun that is fired, every warship launched, every rocket fired signifies, in the final sense, a theft from those who hunger and are not fed, those who are cold and are not clothed. The world in arms is not spending money alone. It is spending the sweat of its laborers, the genius of its scientists, the hopes of its children. The cost of one modern heavy bomber is this: a modern brick school in more than thirty cities. It is two electric power plants, each serving a town of sixty thousand population. It is two fine fully equipped hospitals."[4]

The Brandt Commission wrote in a similarly blunt fashion. World military expenditure of only half a day "would suffice to finance the whole malaria eradication programme of the World Health Organization, and less would be needed to conquer river-blindness, which is still the scourge of millions. . . For the price of one jet fighter one could set up about 40,000 village pharmacies [in the Third World]. . . One-half of one per cent of one year's world military expenditure would pay for all the farm equipment needed to increase food production and approach self-sufficiency in food-deficit low-income countries by 1990."[5]

In most Third World countries, money that should have been used to alleviate poverty, hunger, illiteracy, unemployment, underdevelopment and other social and economic problems was instead wasted on instruments of death and destruction, much of it supplied by US corporations which, collectively, are the world's largest arms dealers. By the mid-1990s, the United States accounted for around 70 per cent of the world's weapons market.[6]

Around the world, American embassies became sales organs of American arms manufacturers. Among the clients were regimes which used the weapons against their own people. In other countries, US-supplied weapons fuelled civil wars and terrorist campaigns.

The primary purpose of a nation's armed forces is to defend its territory and its people from external aggression. However, America's armed forces and defence budget serve another important function – to protect and expand US hegemony and to make the world a safer place for American corporations and superrich investors and speculators. The pursuit of this objective led to the emergence of what President Eisenhower called the "military-industrial complex".

In his farewell address to the nation on 17 January 1961, President Eisenhower warned the American people to guard their liberties from a "conjunction of an immense military establishment and a large arms industry", the military-industrial complex. Warning that the "acquisition of unwarranted influence" by the military-industrial complex must be prevented, he said that the "potential for the disastrous rise of misplaced power exists and will persist. We must never let the weight of this combination endanger our liberties or democratic processes."[7]

Since then, the military-industrial partnership has grown so powerful that it has become the single largest factor in America's economy, operates largely outside the boundaries of public accountability and democratic control and corrupts the democratic process. Its influence transformed the Department of Defense into the world's largest single organization and the United States into a warfare state.

Commentators coined the phrase the Iron Triangle for the vastly powerful tripartite partnership between America's defence contractors, military leaders and Congress. The power and influence of this alliance is such that the nation's defence budget has become, in many ways, little more than a means for channelling massive amounts of public funds to private contractors. The profits of these contractors are maximized through non-competitive bidding, the bribing of members of Congress, the toleration of fraud, waste and massive over-charging and through persisting with expensive weapons production programmes long after the programmes can serve any useful purpose.

In the 1980s, Defense Department employee Franklin C. Spinney exposed the cozy relationship between the Pentagon and corporate suppliers, revealing how contractors charged $745 for an $8 pliers and over $7,000 for a $125 coffee maker. Meanwhile, tens of thousands of nuclear bombs were being assembled, even though a small percentage of these would be enough to wipe out all mankind. The cost of the bombs, if diverted instead into health, education and development programmes in the Third World, could have transformed the lives of billions of people.[8]

Public resistance to America's irrational military spending is unlikely to achieve any meaningful changes, since the country's defence contractors buy the loyalty of politicians, contributing heavily through Political Action Committees to the election funds of senators and representatives. During the 1996 election campaign, defence contractors gave over $10 million in political contributions, including over $4 million from three of the largest arms-exporting manufacturers.[9]

In 1997, Washington dismayed the international community when it refused to ratify an international treaty banning anti-personnel landmines, a weapon that Canadian Prime Minister Jean Chretien described as causing "extermination in slow motion".[10] Up to 100 million mines lie buried in countries worldwide, mostly in the Third World, killing or maiming 25,000 civilians each year or one person every twenty minutes. US corporations are among the world's leading manufacturers of landmines. Acceptance of the ban would hit their profits.

For over forty years, the Cold War provided Washington and Corporate USA with a pretext for siphoning vast sums of taxpayers' dollars to defence contractors, thereby creating a form of military welfare state. The success of Pax Americana was predicated on US military supremacy and on Washington's willingness to use this supremacy to defend US foreign policy interests abroad. The consequences were often horrific – countless millions killed to protect the investments of US corporations.

In the post-Cold War era, new enemies were found to replace the moribund communist threat, most notably Islamic fundamentalism and drug trafficking. The September 2001 attacks induced unprecedented levels of patriotic fervour in the United States, fanning flames of revenge and making it easier for Washington's Rockefellerian and corporate ruling elites, and the military-industrial complex, to launch the nation into a new era of interventionist barbarity.

Wars are highly profitable enterprises for Corporate USA, especially for defence contractors. They also perform another function highly advantageous to the nation's corporations – protecting US hegemony and corporate interests abroad.

In the late 1930s, Gen. Smedley Butler recalled spending fifteen years of his Marine Corps career "going about the world guarding Standard Oil tins".[11] The power and influence of the military-industrial complex and Corporate USA, and the post-September 2001 growth among Americans of malice towards Muslims who control so much of the world's oil resources, almost inevitably will ensure that this interventionist practice continues. Washington's cabinet-level corporate and Rockefellerian ruling elites and the bought senators and representatives will continue to funnel vast sums of public funds into the corporate-dominated military-industrial complex to create the world's best-armed military force for use in defending US corporate interests abroad.

Gen. Butler suggested a novel approach for ending this practice – the conscription of business and banking executives to fight in US-waged wars. Echoing Eugene V. Debs' thesis that wars have always been declared by the master class, but always been fought by the subject class, Gen. Butler argued that war "is conducted for the benefit of the very few at the expense of the masses. Out of war a few people make huge fortunes. . . The only way to smash this racket is to conscript capital and industry and labor before the nation's manhood can be conscripted. . . Let the officers and directors and the high-powered executives of our armament factories and our steel companies and our munitions makers and our ship-builders and our airplane builders. . . as well as the bankers and the speculators, be conscripted. . . Give capital and industry and labor thirty days to think it over and you will find, by that time, there will be no war. That will smash the war racket."[12]

Notes

1. Edward S. Greenberg, *The American Political System: A Radical Approach* (Glenview, Illinois: Scott, Foresman), Fifth Edition, p. 306.

2. Bruce W. Nelan, "A Force for The Future", *Time*, 21 September 1992.

3. See *Human Development Report 1998* (New York: published by Oxford University Press for UN Development Programme, 1998), p. 197; Tariq Ali, ed., *Masters of the Universe?: NATO's Balkan Crusade* (London: Verso, 2000), p. 106.

4. As quoted in Leonard Mosley, *Dulles: A Biography of Eleanor, Allen and John Foster Dulles and Their Family Network* (New York: Dial Press/James Wade, 1978), p. 335.

5. *North-South: A Programme for Survival* (London: Pan Books, 1982), p. 14.

6. Mark Thompson, "Gunsmith to the World", *Time*, 19 December 1994.

7. Peter Woll, *American Government: Readings and Cases* (Boston: Little, Brown, 1981), Seventh Edition, pp. 293–94.

8. Norman Cousins, *The Pathology of Power* (New York: W. W. Norton, 1987), pp. 98–106.

9. Douglas Waller, 'How Washington Works. . . Arms Deals', *Time*, 14 April 1997.

10. Randall Palmer, "125 Countries Agree to Sign Mine Ban Treaty", *The Irish Times*, 4 December 1997.

11. Quoted in Jules Archer, *The Plot to Seize the White House* (New York: Hawthorn Books, 1973), p. 235.

12. *Ibid.*, pp. 219–20.

APPENDIX J

Repression in the United States

A few days after the US Congress voted on a crucial component of the globalization process, the NAFTA accord, the Senate "passed 'the finest anti-crime package in history' [Senator Orrin Hatch], calling for 100,000 new police, high-security regional prisons, boot camps for young offenders, extension of the death penalty and harsher sentencing, and other onerous conditions", Noam Chomsky noted. "Law enforcement experts interviewed by the press doubted that the legislation would have much effect on crime because it did not deal with the 'causes of social disintegration that produce violent criminals.' Primary among these are the social and economic policies polarizing American society, carried another step forward by NAFTA."

The globalization process, he added, offered "nothing to the growing sectors of the population that are useless for profit-making, driven to poverty and despair. If they cannot be confined to urban slums, they will have to be controlled in some other way." The coincidence between the NAFTA vote and the new anti-crime legislation, he suggested, "was of more than mere symbolic significance".[1]

Legislative measures have long been instruments of repression in the United States. Since the 1960s, the country has been on a steady upward graph of government repression, especially imprisonment and surveillance. The initial momentum for this increased repression was provided by the political rebellion of the 1960s and 1970s – black militancy, civil rights protests, demands for Native American rights and lands and anti-war activism. Anti-Vietnam War protests and demands by Native Americans and blacks for basic civil and human rights met with a response of harassment, violence and imprisonment from Washington and from state authorities. Imprisonment and other forms of repression were being used to suppress political and social dissent.

In the 1980s and 1990s, America's prison population almost quadrupled, the result of a new law-and-order "justice" regime that impacted most upon the nation's poor and included the use of prison chain gangs, years spent by simple-minded and innocent individuals on death rows and a disproportionately large number of blacks arrested.[2] A 1991 study showed that 70 per cent of black men in Washington, DC, had been arrested by age thirty-five.[3] By the year 2000, US prisons and jails had around 2 million inmates, the largest incarcerated population in any of the world's nations.

Many of these are disenfranchised from voting. In the 2000 elections, an estimated 3.9 million American adults were debarred from voting due to their criminal records. In Florida, where George W. Bush's brother Jeb was governor, thousands of blacks, overwhelmingly Democrats, were removed from the voter rolls, helping George W. to win the state, and the US presidency, by means that were clearly undemocratic. Many of those removed had never committed a crime. In some states, it is possible that up to 40 per cent of blacks will be permanently disenfranchised due to criminal convictions.[4]

Such disenfranchisement serves a very useful political end. It is that the very people – poor blacks, Native Americans and Hispanics – most in need of reform within America's political, social and economic spheres and who are being increasingly marginalized by the globalization process, are the very people least able to effect change because of being denied the right to vote and because of voter apathy.

Post-NAFTA moves to increase the number of police and prisons suggest that America's political establishment is intent on intensifying the nation's fight against crime. However, the definition of crime can be highly selective. As Lawrence M. Friedman, professor of law at Stanford University, has pointed out, "all crimes are acts that society, or at least some dominant elements in society, sees as threats".[5] In the past, America's dominant elites used the nation's criminal justice system and increased repression to crush opposition. Criminal acts were whatever the elites chose them to be. Thus, during the First World War it became illegal to utter or publish "any disloyal, profane, scurrilous or abusive language about the form of government of the United States"[6] or to encourage resistance to the US war effort – from which American industrialists profited so much. During the Vietnam War, thousands of protesters and draft dodgers were arrested, tried and jailed. Activists for black and Native American rights were also imprisoned. Dissention has a low toleration threshold in America's political system when it adversely affects the interests of the country's elites.

Was the introduction of the Senate's anti-crime package so soon after the NAFTA vote, as Noam Chomsky alleged, "of more than mere symbolic significance"? Was it, perhaps, a move towards new repressive measures against those fomenting dissent against NAFTA, the WTO, the IMF, World Bank, Bush's war on terrorism and other elements and institutions of the globalization-driven world order?

The 11 September attacks provided Washington with an opportunity to erode civil liberties in the United States, under the guise of enhancing national security. A secretive Pentagon plan to conduct surveillance on the American people was inaugurated by a new body, the Information Awareness Office. This Orwellian concept entailed sifting through the personal information of millions of Americans, without their knowledge or consent, in a surveillance operation reminiscent of the McCarthy era.

Notes

1. Noam Chomsky, *Profit Over People: Neoliberalism and Global Order* (New York: Seven Stories Press, 1999), pp. 125–26.
2. For an interesting analysis of America's incarceration culture, see Joseph T. Hallinan, *Going Up the River: Travels in a Prison Nation* (New York: Random House).
3. Laurence M Friedman, *Crime and Punishment in American History* (New York: Basic Books, 1993), p. 378, citing *New York Times*, 18 April 1992.
4. Anna Mundow, "The Business of Prison", *The Irish Times*, 12 May 2001.
5. See Friedman, *Crime and Punishment in American History*, p. 8.
6. *Ibid.*, p. 366.

Index

Please note that Mc is treated as Mac.

ALSO PUBLISHED BY BRANDON

KITTY FITZGERALD
Small Acts of Treachery

"A woman of courage defies the power not only of the secret state but of sinister global elites. This is a story you can't stop reading, with an undertow which will give you cause to reflect."
Sheila Rowbotham

"A super book with a fascinating story and great characters. The book is all the more impressive because of the very sinister feeling I was left with that it is all too frighteningly possible." *Books Ireland*

ISBN 0 86322 297 8

 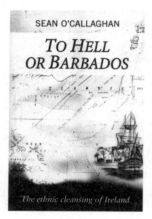

SEAN O'CALLAGHAN

To Hell or Barbados
The ethnic cleansing of Ireland

"An illuminating insight into a neglected episode in Irish history, but its significance is much broader than that. Its main achievement is to situate the story of colonialism in Ireland in the much larger context of world-wide European imperialism." *Irish World*

"A fascinating read." *Sunday Tribune*

"Essential reading." *Irish Examiner*

ISBN 0 86322 287 0

Vist our website at
www.brandonbooks.com

GERRY ADAMS
Before the Dawn

"A definitive history of the Irish struggles of the 1970s, from the nationalist point of view. Adams, a fine writer, presents a straightforward, unapologetic memoir." *Publisher's Weekly*

"One thing about him is certain: Gerry Adams is a gifted writer who, if he were not at the center of the war-and-peace business, could easily make a living as an author, of fiction or fact." *New York Times*

ISBN 0 86322 289 7

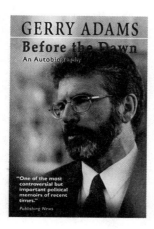 

NIALL O'DOWD
Fire in the Morning

"Captures the humanity, heroism and imperfections that define the millions of decent, hard-working Americans of Irish descent." *Irish Independent*

"A vital testimonial to the lives of working people . . . Its pages are filled with a humanity that transcends Armageddon, ignores the follies of class difference and spending power, and serves to unite the living with their dead." *The Irish Times*

ISBN 0 86322 298 6

Vist our website at
www.brandonbooks.com

HENRY SINNERTON
David Ervine: Uncharted Waters

"There is not a more impressive politician in Northern Ireland than David Ervine." Senator George Mitchell

"Revealing. . . Ervine is an impressive advocate of modern unionism." *Irish Examiner*

"Sinnerton is strong on explaining recent history from a loyalist political perspective." *Fortnight*

ISBN 0 86322 312 5

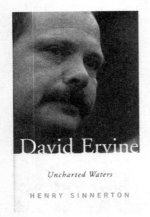

WILSON JOHN HAIRE
The Yard

"This riproaring yarn about a lad plucked from a rural Belfast environment and plonked into the Harland & Wolff shipyard. . . All human life is here." *Books Ireland*

"A true eye-opener. . . a well-crafted, clever and gripping account." *News Letter* (Belfast)

"Gritty realism – writing with no room for sentiment, but which contains a bleak beauty all its own. . . compelling." *Belfast Telegraph*

ISBN 0 86322 296 X

Vist our website at
www.brandonbooks.com